DISROBED

An Inside Look at the Life and Work of a Federal Trial Judge

by Frederic Block

A Thomson Reuters business

For Customer Assistance Call 1-800-328-4880

Mat #41236969

© 2012 Frederic Block

To Betsy

TABLE OF CONTENTS

PREFACE

This collection of reminiscences is enthralling. It will be diverting for lawyers and judges. It will be useful to youngsters trying to decide whether to go to law school. And it will be particularly educational and entertaining to laypersons for whom law is somewhat of a mystery. The author tells it all with an easy humor, flowing style, and a sophistication that makes this volume one of the most enjoyable memoirs of a sitting judge. All—whether professional or not—will share gratitude to Judge Block for revealing himself in this book.

On one wall of our judges' conference room in the federal courthouse in Brooklyn, there is a large copy of the last photograph taken of President Abraham Lincoln. On the facing wall are reproductions of the English Magna Carta of 1215, the Bill of Rights of our own Constitution, enacted as 10 amendments on December 15, 1791, and the Universal Declaration of Human Rights adopted by the United Nations on December 10, 1948. Together they symbolize our continuing struggle for liberty, justice, and equal opportunity for all. Many of the cases Judge Block describes in this book from his private practice and judicial career are protective of those rights.

Lincoln has particular salience to the three dozen judges and magistrate judges of the court on which Judge Block sits, for our Civil War president epitomized the ability of Americans without connections to the mighty or governing elites to rise through entry into the legal profession. They can use their keen intelligence, professional skills, and self-discipline to achieve recognition and to help the nation. Fred Block followed this route to become a federal district judge. Although, like all of us lesser mortals, he scaled heights less daunting than did Lincoln, his accomplishments are significant and admirable.

As a federal judge, the author of this volume was appointed pursuant to Article III of the United States Constitution by the President of the United States and was confirmed by the United States Senate. The term is for life, with removal only by impeachment and conviction, requiring concurrence of the United States House of Representatives and the Senate. Federal judges have independence, power, and responsibility not exceeded by any judiciary in the world.

In his charming and instructive recollections, Judge Block starts with his origins. He attended a first-rate law school—Cornell—graduating in 1959 with honors, having made friends of faculty and fellow students.

Like many future judges, he was employed first as a law clerk to judges. He served in their chambers for a few years and acquired a sense of the mechanics of judging and of the high morale, industry, and ethics of our trial and appellate bench.

Eschewing big firm practice in New York, Fred started his professional life in a small law firm in the then-sparsely populated rural regions of Suffolk County on the east end of Long Island. There he swiftly built his own successful practice. It is amazing that as a neophyte he almost immediately challenged Suffolk County's system of local government as violative of the newly recognized constitutional requirement of "one person, one vote." As a result of the constitutional litigations he prosecuted—all the way to the Supreme Court of the United States—Suffolk County's local governments had to be reorganized to make them more representative and democratic.

He sued on behalf of the badly underpaid New York State Family Court judges, obtaining significant salary increases and back pay for them. That made him a hero to the state judiciary. It also provided him with substantial fees that began to make him financially secure. Other famous cases followed, as the author informs us in his spirited retelling.

He was head of the powerful Suffolk County Bar Association. His voice as a leading representative of the legal profession was heard throughout the state.

Having already developed this distinguished record, Fred became a federal judge on his merits, but with a little nudging on his part of those who had the power to influence his selection. He was nominated by President Clinton on the recommendation of Senator Moynihan and quickly confirmed by the Senate.

Almost immediately, he was recognized as a learned, fair, and adept judge who sped the cases before him to resolution. As the *Wall Street Journal* noted in 2008, in commenting on his handling of a complex securities fraud case, he "views the people who come before him . . . like human beings first." Moreover, the Almanac of the Federal Judiciary reports:

> Lawyers interviewed said Block is a good, experienced judge. "He has excellent legal ability. He is very, very, very good. No question about that."

"He is a good judge." "He is very smart." "He is very shrewd. He gets to the heart of things quickly. He writes beautiful and careful opinions. He was a real trial lawyer. He actually tried cases. He has a wonderful feel for juries." "The thing that he brings to the bench is that he was a practitioner with a diverse practice." "He has a practical approach. He is good at honing in on the central issue." "He is very scholarly. He is very knowledgeable." . . . "He is a wonderful person to try cases before. He understands the dynamics of trial." . . . "He is fair." "He is evenhanded."

The job of being a trial judge in the federal court is to serve as the human face of the law—to see and deal with the real people, in all of their enormous diversity. Presented to the judge is a unique window on the world, particularly in the Eastern District of New York, covering Brooklyn, Queens, Staten Island, and all of Long Island, with its heterogeneous population.

Sentencing in such a court presents particular problems in criminal cases since judges must protect the public without being unnecessarily cruel. Judge Block explains the theory of sentencing, the issues of mandatory minimums, capital punishment, and guideline sentencing in direct and clear prose. He is a strong, but compassionate, judge.

Some of the exotica of federal judgeships are described, such as the role of senior judges, who theoretically retire, but can carry full caseloads (as Judge Block does), and of trial judges sitting on appellate courts throughout the nation (as Judge Block also does).

Particularly interesting is Judge Block's account of how the federal courts train their new judges. One of the great advantages of the federal system is that judges come to the bench after they have made their mark in practice, government, or academia. By then, they are not likely to be intimidated by anyone. Unlike many civil law countries, where law graduates are immediately assigned to the judiciary track without practice outside of the courts, our system sometimes produces judges with little judicial experience except, as in Judge Block's case, through service as a law clerk. Federal judges' schools, seminars, and constant training sessions and discussions with colleagues quickly led to Judge Block's learning of the trade.

There is no need to describe here Judge Block's many 'Big Cases.' The author's description of them is fascinating. Each one presents enough drama for a novel. The tales are related with style and insight.

I would be remiss were I not to point out how engaging Fred is as a companion and colleague. His conversation is captivating; he has the knack for preventing acrimony at conferences; and in tête-à-têtes, he is entrancing. The careful reader of this classic will, I think, come to those conclusions even if he or she has not met the judge face-to-face.

Jack B. Weinstein
Senior United States
District Judge
Eastern District of New York

January 2, 2012

Introduction

Ed Korman, my judicial colleague on the federal district court in Brooklyn for the past 17 years, raised his right eyebrow as I told him about the book I was planning to write. "Alright, if you must really do this," he said, "at least don't put me in it."

Obviously, I did not listen to him. My occasional contrarian nature made me do it—and as long as I was going to, I thought that I might as well go all out and start the book with his name. Knowing me as well as he does, he probably knew that I would do this. We are the best of friends, and he is a wonderful judge.

Judge Korman and I cherish the independence of the judiciary and its judges, and we pride ourselves on not always agreeing with each other. One of the things that we disagree about is to what extent judges should talk publicly about what they do. Judge Korman is of the "judicial lockjaw" school—advocating a form of self-censorship that curtails judges from speaking about the judicial process and from pursuing extrajudicial activities. As one commentator, Leslie Dubeck, has explained in a provocative article that she wrote for the New York University Law Review, *Understanding 'Judicial Lockjaw': The Debate Over Extrajudicial Activity*:

> [a]lthough constitutional and statutory law do not mandate such censorship, factors such as peer pressure and judicial culture, fear of negative public reaction, and the judge's conception of his or her responsibility in a constitutional democracy, contribute to judicial lockjaw.

Most judges, like Judge Korman, believe that judges should only communicate in academic fora, through the formal media of written opinions and official rulings from the bench. I do not subscribe to this. I share the thoughts of those, such as Robert F. Copple, who wrote in his excellent article in the Denver University Law Review, *From the Cloister to the Street: Judicial Ethics and Public Expression,* that:

> [b]ecause of the importance of law in modern society, the public needs reliable and understandable sources of information concerning our legal system. Without such information, the public cannot accurately scrutinize the legal process and correct its abuses. Unfortunately, many citizens possess simplistic insights into the workings of our legal system.

Nowhere is this more apparent than in the lack of understanding by the public of what the federal trial courts actually do—let alone how someone becomes a judge of such a court.

Lesley Lorant is a case in point. Lesley is the brother of my cousin Ray Polen's girlfriend. Over coffee last September when Lesley was visiting his sister, I told him that I was writing a nonacademic book about my life and work as a federal trial judge. He asked me a few questions which reaffirmed my belief that this was a worthwhile project. Lesley had recently retired from a long and distinguished career as an IBM executive and was now the general manager of a real estate investment firm. However, he did not have a clue as to how one becomes a federal district court judge, and he had no sense of the differences between the state and federal courts. He asked me a bunch of questions which made me realize that even well-educated people are basically in the dark about what we federal trial judges actually do. For example, he wondered whether I handle matrimonial cases, whether I try both civil and criminal cases, when I have to retire, and how I got the job.

After I said good-bye to Lesley, I realized how important it would be for me to try my best to write a book that would be read by the general public. While there have been many books written by judges, they have hardly been bestsellers; their readership has invariably been those involved in the legal profession. Yet judges have unique insights to share with the general public about the law and the practical workings of the courts: in my case, our country's federal laws and trial courts. How, though, can a book do this in a

2

way that will not bore the general reader and gather dust on library shelves?

I think that I have done it, but it has not been an easy task. I had to be mindful of the Code of Conduct for United States Judges enacted by the Judicial Conference, a policy-making organ of the federal judiciary headed by the Chief Justice of the United States. There are many provisions in the Code that put limitations on a judge's law-related, financial, fiduciary, fund-raising, civic, and charitable activities.

When it comes to what a judge may write about, the Code recognizes that "[a]s a judicial officer and a person specially learned in the law, a judge is in a unique position to contribute to the law, the legal system, and the administration of justice." However, a judge's writing is subject to a number of limitations. Foremost is that the judge "should not make public comment on the merits of a matter pending or impending in any court." This prohibition does not extend, however, to "public statements made in the course of the judge's official duties, to explanations of court procedures, or to scholarly presentations made for purposes of legal education." The Judicial Conference's Committee on Codes of Conduct—charged with interpreting the Code—has set forth the overarching benchmark: "In every case, the judge should avoid sensationalism and comments that may result in confusion or misunderstanding of the judicial function or detract from the dignity of the office."

I do not think that I've crossed the ethical line, but I wonder why the same constraints do not apply to the Justices of the United States Supreme Court. The Code exempts them. Why the judges of our high court—charged with being the final arbiters of the law—should not be required to comply with the same ethical standards that all of the other federal judges are obliged to honor puzzles me.

* * *

So here's how I've tried to educate and entertain the public at the same time: First, I've told my story—from childhood to the day that I was tapped by the President for the judgeship. The reader will get to know me and how it was that from hanging up a shingle in a semirural community 60 miles from New York City, a small-town practitioner got to be a federal district judge in the Big Apple.

Next, I write about how I broke in as a new judge, tell anecdotes about some of my judicial colleagues, explain how I deal with the juries and lawyers, go about sentencing criminals, deal with death threats, and, in general, run my court.

Finally, I talk about the cases. In chapters titled "Death," "Racketeering," "Guns," "Drugs," "Discrimination," "Race Riots," "Terrorism," and "Foreign Affairs," I meld the law with the major cases that I have handled. The reader will get to know, for example, about the death penalty in the context of the murder trial of Kenneth "Supreme" McGriff, and the Racketeering Act will come to life as I recount the trial of Peter Gotti and his Gambino family buddies—and so on.

I do not know of any book written by a federal trial judge for the general public that is at once informative, provocative, and engaging. Hopefully, this is that book.

PART I
GETTING THERE

Chapter
1

Pathways

The Federal Bar Council is an elite lawyers' association head-quartered in New York City. Many partners from the City's mega white-shoe law firms belong to it, and its leaders are the movers and shakers of the City's legal establishment. The first day that I showed up for work at the federal courthouse in Brooklyn as a new federal district judge, on October 31, 1994, there was, to my surprise, a piece of mail waiting for me. It was the first time that I saw the word "Honorable" in front of my name. Inside the envelope was a letter inviting me to be a guest of the Council at its annual Thanksgiving Day luncheon at the Waldorf-Astoria. I was flattered and immediately faxed my acceptance.

I soon learned, however, that I was not the only judge invited. The Federal Bar Council invites the entire New York City federal bench to this affair and places each judge at one of its big-firm tables to give the lawyers the firms select to attend an opportunity to break bread with a judge. I do not remember the law firm I sat with, but I do remember the young associate sitting next to me,

5

who confessed that he never had heard of me and politely asked, "Judge Block, I assume you were a partner with one of the firms, or perhaps an Assistant United States Attorney, but how exactly did you became a federal judge?"

In between sips of red wine, I told him that I did not come from a big firm, nor was I ever a prosecutor, nor did I ever practice law in New York City. Rather, in 1961, I came to Suffolk County, which then had about as many lawyers as those who were then lunching at the Waldorf. After working for a two-member law firm for nine months, I rented a small house for $120 a month in Port Jefferson Station and also subleased, for $100 a month, a room in a lawyer's office next to the railroad tracks, where I hung up my shingle. I also told that young man that I was so unknown that I did not even have an enemy, let alone a friend. There was a mirror on the wall in front of my metal desk so that, as I was warned, I could sit behind the desk and watch myself slowly starve to death.

When the puzzled young lawyer asked how I got my first client, I explained that I had befriended Charlie McDermott, the owner of the luncheonette I ate at in a small shopping center near the office, and that after I had been looking at the mirror for a few days, he stopped by my office to ask whether there was anything he could do to prevent his landlord from evicting him because he was behind on his rent. At this point in my conversation with the young associate, I paused to mention that in addition to the metal desk and the mirror, there was one other special feature of my one-room office. On the wall to the right of the door as you entered the room was an old attic fan, which I covered with my law school diploma. To my chagrin, when Charlie walked through the door he turned on the attic fan switch, apparently thinking it was a light switch, and blew the diploma off the wall.

By this time the young lawyer was squirming in his chair and probably wishing that he had never spoken to me, so I quickly finished the answer to his initial question by telling him that I had practiced law in Suffolk County for 33 years, during which time I had built up my practice so that I could afford to take on a junior

6

partner and a young associate, as well as hire two secretaries and a file clerk, and that all this obviously impressed Senator Daniel Patrick Moynihan enough to recommend me to the President for the judgeship.

I suspect that when my luncheon companion went home that night he must have told his wife, girlfriend, or significant other that the new judge was a little strange.

* * *

So how did the outsider far removed from the Big Apple break through the big-city establishment barrier and become a federal judge? Obviously, there was more to the story than I told the young, mega-firm lawyer that day at the Waldorf.

I have no profound recollections of the first several years of my life. I was told that I was born in Brooklyn, and I do generally remember living there, going to movies on Saturday afternoons at the Avalon on Kings Highway near Ocean Parkway, listening with my father on the porch of my house on East 4th Street to Red Barber reporting on the radio that Mickey Owen dropped the infamous third strike to Tommy Heinrich, which led to the Dodgers losing the 1941 world series to the hated Yankees, and having a friend named Sherry Shapiro, a dog named Spotty, and a cat named Peggy. I also recall going to elementary school at P.S. 215 on East 3rd Street, where I was an average student.

When I was nine, my parents moved the family—me and my two older brothers, Sheldon and Leonard—to a spacious apartment in Manhattan on 77th Street near the corner of Central Park West, across the street from the Museum of Natural History. My father's mother had died giving birth to him, and he was raised by her sister, who had three sons and a daughter. They lived, like so many other Jewish people at the time, in the Lower East Side. And, true to the principal Jewish means of livelihood in that human cauldron at the turn of the 20th century, the children's father (my father's uncle by marriage) went into the garment business. Eventually, "the boys" manufactured inexpensive men's suits as Sterling Clothing

7

Company. My dad, as a hardworking partner with his male cousins, made a good living.

My new public school was P.S. 87, two blocks down the street, on Amsterdam Avenue, and—for inexplicable reasons—I started to get better grades. Maybe it was because I really liked "the City." I played basketball in Central Park, Chinese handball against the side walls of the New York Historical Society, just next to my apartment, and stoopball against the imposing steps leading to the 77th Street entrance to the museum.

My parents enrolled me in Hebrew school at the Society for the Advancement of Judaism, known as the SAJ. It was the first Reconstructionist Synagogue, a kind of modern reform movement that embraced the world order. It was founded by Rabbi Mordecai Kaplan, one of the renowned theologians of the 20th century, and he had his worldwide office there. I was terrified of him the few times that I saw him. He was then in his 80s but looked to me like 100. He would deliver a sermon to the congregation once a year, on the holy day of Yom Kippur, and when he rose to speak, with his huge white beard resting on his flowing white robe, I thought he was Moses.

I was bar mitzvahed at the SAJ at the appropriate age of 13. Being immature, I would often torment my parents when I did not feel like going to Hebrew school by irreverently referring to this great place of learning as the Society Against Jews or the Society for the Advancement of Jesus.

The same year that I was bar mitzvahed, I took an entrance exam for high school. If your parents did not want to send you to private school or if you did not want to go to the local high school, Commerce High, where the tough guys would surely devour a little Jewish kid, you had better pass that exam. Depending how high you scored—if you passed—you would be sent to one of the three premier boys' public high schools in the City: Bronx Science, Brooklyn Tech, or Stuyvesant. They have since appropriately become coed. I got into Stuyvesant, which to this day is one of the best public high schools in the country. However, I was surprised when my principal at P.S. 87, Mr. Richman, called me into his office, expressed dismay that I had passed the exam for Stuyvesant, and started to counsel me that it might be too tough for me and that an easier private school might be a better choice if my parents could afford it.

I was perplexed, since I had good grades, and asked him why he was talking to me like that. He asked me to sit and told me that he had been looking at the I.Q. scores of those who had passed the exam. He was concerned that since mine was 96—close to idiot—I might not be able to handle Stuyvesant's challenging curriculum or compete with its bright students. Fortunately, I had never known my I.Q. before—I never even remember taking the exam—otherwise I might never have taken the test for Stuyvesant or done so well at P.S. 87.

Notwithstanding my I.Q., I did pretty well at Stuyvesant. I was freshman class president and graduated with a 92 average; however, the student body was so uniformly talented and competitive that this was only good enough to place me 111th out of a graduating class of about 750. I might have gotten better grades if I did not develop a bad habit of cutting classes and coming late to school when I was there. I guess that if Stuyvesant had been coed, I might not have cut so much, but cutting class separated you from the nerdy students, some of whom, of course, would become Nobel laureates and captains of industry. My friends and I would never miss cutting class on the day of a new stage show at the Paramount Theatre on 44th Street and Broadway. We were not alone; thousands of high school students from all over would come to see Frank Sinatra, Johnny Ray, the Four Freshmen, the Ink Spots, the Mills Brothers, Ella, and all the other greats on the first day that they "played the Paramount." This unsanctioned school holiday became known as St. Paramount's Day.

When it came time to choose a college, I thought I would give Harvard a long-shot try, but settled on Cornell as my safe school. To my surprise, I scored poorly on the SATs and was rejected by both schools. I was beginning to think that maybe my I.Q. score was correct, but was reassured by an ophthalmologist that my inability to score well on tests that required focused reading comprehension under time pressure, such as the I.Q. test and the SAT, was probably due to my eyes. Because the muscles did not function the way that they were supposed to, my eyes did not focus properly; the doctor described it as two strong horses pulling in opposite directions. The result was that when I read, my eyes would inadvertently shift focus, and I would skip three or four lines. This made reading tedious and protracted; the doctor was surprised that I did as well as I did in school. I have the same problem today, plus constant eyestrain and tearing.

Being rejected by Harvard was not a shock, but I was so confident that I would get into Cornell that I did not apply to other colleges. Stuyvesant did not then have guidance counselors, so the students were left on their own to decide which colleges to apply to. My rejection by Cornell was the first major disappointment in my life, and I did not know what to do. A call from the principal's secretary put pressure on me to make a fast decision. I quickly applied to Indiana. Why? My counselor in summer camp went there. It was not the most enlightened way to make such an important decision, but it was fortuitous. First, I was accepted. More importantly, it opened my eyes to a new culture and reinforced the lesson that many New Yorkers have to learn—that they have to guard against becoming provincial and parochial in their thinking that New York City is the end-all and be-all of everything worthwhile.

Thus I owe a big debt of gratitude to the Hoosiers for broadening my perspective and understanding that the strength of our country lies in exposing ourselves to, and embracing, the cultural, economic, and political differences that should unite—not divide—us. I owe a special debt of gratitude to a sexy farm gal from the rural heart of the state. She looked like Daisy Mae, but unfortunately I did not look like L'il Abner. In fact, we were the same height. She had never met a Jewish kid from Brooklyn, and I had never met a hillbilly. Somehow we bridged these seemingly insurmountable differences and enjoyed each other's company—in every way. I called her Daisy

Mae, and she could not resist periodically playing it to the hilt, putting on her dumb hick act, chewing straw, and wearing sandals. Lo and behold, though, she graduated Phi Beta Kappa. I often wonder what happened to her—whether she returned to the farm or perhaps became an esteemed professor of philosophy at a major university. Never again would I look upon anyone who happened to come from outside of New York City and spoke differently than I in a lesser light.

At Indiana I had decent, but not great, grades. I got caught up in campus life, joined the Marching Hundred football band, where I played clarinet, was elected treasurer of my sophomore class, and was president of a fraternity, which unwittingly gave me the opportunity to learn another valuable lesson that has served me in good stead.

I had been elected frat prez at the end of my third year. When I returned in the fall, the campus was abuzz to learn that Carolyn Turner, a pretty good-looking Indiana coed, had become Miss Indiana and was runner-up for Miss America at Atlantic City that summer. At the frat house it was decided that the president should call her for a date so that everyone could laugh when she put him in his place and roundly rejected him. To make matters worse, I would have to ask her out for the very night that I called. What choice did I have? I never would have had the guts to call her on my own, but I could not show the guys that I was a coward unworthy of being their leader.

When I called her, after downing a few beers for Dutch courage, I was surprised that she even answered the phone. I sheepishly apologized for calling and confessed that I was put up to it by my fraternity brothers so that I would make a fool of myself. I was taken aback, though, when she thanked me for calling and told me that since she had gotten the runner-up title, no one had asked her out on a date, assuming that there was no chance that she would accept.

You should have seen the look on my fraternity brothers' faces when Miss Runner-up Miss America showed up with me at the

11

fraternity house that night. The message instantly dawned on me that you can get far in life if you can suffer the fear of rejection.

Carolyn Turner was responsible, however, for one of the big disappointments of my adolescent life. While I was back in New York during spring break in my senior year, I got a phone call from a sexy-sounding gal who told me that Carolyn had given her my number. She was a friend of hers from Indiana and had never been to New York City. Carolyn told her that I was a fun guy and would be happy to show her the sights. When I asked her why she was here, she told me that she had a modeling job. When I asked her where she was staying, she told me the Waldorf-Astoria Towers.

Thoughts of Rita Hayworth flashed through my mind as I knocked on the door of her suite 20 minutes later. When it opened, I was face-to-face with the homeliest face I had ever seen. There had to have been a mistake. She could not be a model, let alone one staying at one of the most expensive hotels in the world. Still, she was indeed a model—and a very well paid one at that. She was the Ivory Snow hand model. Being a good sport, I showed her the sights, and we had a lot of fun, but she never let me hold her hands. I think of her to this day to guard against disappointments whenever I have high expectations—like about how successful this book will be.

In my last year at I.U., I took the LSAT. I knew the sciences were not for me. To this day I have a difficult time understanding Archimedes' Principle, and I was happy to pass the physics Regents Exam at Stuyvesant with the minimum grade of 65. Thus law school seemed like a plausible alternative. Once again I had difficulty scoring high on an entrance exam. I did not think my score in about the 80th percentile would get me into a major school, but compared to my past experiences, it was high for me. Seeking revenge for its having rejected me for undergraduate admission, and remembering the lesson that I learned from Miss Runner-up Miss America, I applied to the Cornell Law School. To my surprise, I was accepted. My guess is that coming from Indiana made the difference so that the school could show some Midwestern diversity amongst its East Coast-oriented student body.

On the first day of class at Cornell, Dean Gray Thoron raced through the door to the lectern to welcome the new first-year law students. Everyone stopped talking. He had just been appointed as the new Dean, and he had been the Assistant Solicitor General of the United States, where he argued many cases before the United States Supreme Court. He would be teaching us constitutional law. In his Texas drawl, he immediately challenged us by setting the stage for a discussion of Chief Justice John Marshall's landmark 1803 opinion in *Marbury v. Madison*, establishing the power of the Supreme Court to strike down unconstitutional acts of Congress. He talked about the history of the litigation and then dramatically asked, "Where did the lawyers ultimately hang their hats, Mr. Block?" It was his first question, and why he picked on me will forever remain a mystery. All he wanted was for me to say "the Supreme Court," but I panicked and blurted out, "the cloakroom."

After the laughter subsided, the good Dean entered into a diatribe that made the *Paper Chase* professor, in that classic movie, seem tame by comparison. He told the class that Cornell does occasionally make mistakes by admitting unworthy students who invariably flunk out after their first exams—and that Mr. Block would undoubtedly be one of those.

I was traumatized and stigmatized. When I would be walking with my classmates and the Dean walked by, they would kind of move away from me so that the Dean would not think that they were friends of the class idiot.

Nonetheless, I persevered and buckled down to try to prove to the Dean that he was wrong. I changed all of my bad habits: never missed a class, was always on time, limited my drinking to two beers a week at Johnny's Big Red Grill, did not look for any substitutes for Daisy Mae or Miss Runner-Up Miss America, and studied into the wee hours of the night. In short, I was a perfect student and could not wait for my first spate of exams, especially the Constitutional law test.

Unlike undergraduate school, where there are periodic tests during a course, in law school you only get one test—at the end of the course—and your entire grade rides on it. When I took my first exams, in the middle of the first year, which were all essay questions, I was tight as a tick. I was simply too worried about not doing well, and my written answers were labored and forced. Although I did not flunk out, I scored only in the middle of the class. I rationalized that this was the best I could do and that being an average Cornell Law School student was not the end of the world. Although I thought that I wrote a good exam in Conlaw, and did not hang my hat in the cloakroom, the Dean only gave me a C minus.

The second batch of the first year's exams came in May, four months later, at the end of the second semester. By this time I had reverted to all of my past wayward ways—dating regularly, drinking many more beers, and cutting class. I studied hard, but no longer obsessively. I figured that since I was destined not to be in the top of the class, I should not make myself nuts anymore and enjoy life a little more. The upshot was that when I took my second set of exams, I was relaxed and wrote effortlessly.

I was working in summer camp when my father called to tell me that my grades had arrived at home. He asked me whether he should open them. I said, "What the heck," and girded myself for the bad news—but it was not to be. My dad rattled off a bunch of A minuses and an A in Administrative Law—the highest grade in the class—and told me that overall I had the third highest grades that semester. I slipped a little during the next two years, but did manage to graduate 18th, which was near the top 10%. I might have finished higher if not for the grade that I received from Professor Tucker Dean in my second year final in Trusts and Estates.

The T & E exam was brutal. Professor Dean gave us a complicated factual pattern of a wealthy man's assets, replete with trusts, partnership holdings, off-shore bank accounts, and many potential distributees—some with mental issues—and we had to devise an estate plan. I thought that I was doing a great job, but time ran out and I had not been able to write about what to do with the dog,

Fluffy. So in a state of panic, I smugly, and immaturely, wrote "Gas it."

Little did I know that Professor Dean was a rabid dog lover and that Fluffy was his all-time favorite canine. When he returned our grades, he announced that he was mortified that one of the students had written that Fluffy should be put to death and that he had given that student a D (I guess it stood for "Dog") because of his insensitivity.

My first year I lived in Boldt Hall, a graduate dorm. Other first-year law students, including Tom Fink and Alan Smith, also lived there. We called them Fink and Smitty. They and their parents were good friends from Albany, New York, where Fink and Smitty were raised. Fink was a high-energy, fast-talking, friendly guy. Smitty, by contrast, had an ultra laid-back personality and spoke in a slow, dull, monotone—so much so that he was perceived as not too bright when we all discussed the law.

Concerned that Smitty would do poorly in our first finals, Fink suggested to his parents, a few days before, that they should prepare Smitty's folks that Alan might not do too well. Well, Smitty graduated fourth in the class and was an editor of the law review, while Fink was mired in the middle. Smitty, therefore, joined the ranks of Daisy Mae as another example of why one should always be cautious about prejudging people from the way that they look or speak.

To his credit, Tom Fink turned out to be an exceptional lawyer in Rochester, New York. Smitty, however, did even better. After a successful turn as a tax lawyer at a prominent Philadelphia law firm, he took over his father-in-law's apparel business after he died and built it into a multimillion dollar national enterprise before selling it and retiring at the age of 52.

In my second year I lived in town above Johnny's Big Red Grill with an interesting array of lovable characters. Eddie Weiss was a bookish, nerdy-looking genius-type who had graduated from college when he was 17 and may have been the youngest law student ever admitted to Cornell. Lee Meyers was one of those University of California radicals who you used to read about raising all sorts of hell on its Berkeley campus, where he had reigned as one of the resident gurus.

I remember a number of my classmates who became prominent after they graduated. Actually, one was already prominent. Ed Bloustein was a distinguished professor of philosophy at Cornell, had written a number of highly acclaimed philosophy books, and had just returned from teaching as a distinguished visiting professor at Oxford. He was then in his mid-30s and had decided to get a law degree. He spoke with a British affect and did not suffer fools gladly. Dr. Bloustein was an intimidating, powerful presence, and we were in awe of him. Underneath, he was a very warm, friendly person—if he liked you. It did not surprise us that a year after he graduated he became president of Bennington College and, later, Rutgers University.

Saul Kramer became the country's top labor lawyer; Lee Philips soon was the lawyer to the stars—Barbra Streisand, Linda Ronstadt, and many others; and Bob Douglass would become Nelson Rockefeller's counsel. Many others became successful academics, statesmen, and leaders of the bar, like Manny Gold, who for many years was the minority leader of the New York State Senate.

In addition to Dean Thoron and Professor Dean, we were blessed with other fine faculty members, and I chuckle to this day when I recall two professorial moments. The first was the last day of class in Comparative Law at the end of our final year when the great Professor Rudolph Schlesinger announced that he would be having the pleasure of giving us our very last final exam. As a kind of graduation present, and as a parting gesture of kindness, he told us that he would be giving us the same exam as last year's, and that he had made copies of the exam available at the front desk of the library. However, in his own inimical, impish way, he warned us, in his gravelly voice, that this year he had decided to change the answers. I guess he was trying to tell us that the law does not always have a right or wrong answer and that understanding and analyzing the problem is paramount.

Then there was Professor David Curtis, our criminal law prof, who called upon one of the five females in our class in those prehistoric days (women today generally comprise 50% or more of the law school classes) to explain the criminal definition of rape. The startled woman blurted out, "some amount of penetration," to which Professor Curtis bellowed: "In the law we must be specific. Tell us, how much penetration." She nervously replied, in an almost inaudible voice, "about six inches," to which the good professor responded, "I asked you for the definition of rape, not pleasure." The class laughed, but I thought that this was totally inappropriate behavior and—having been picked on myself by the Dean—I felt sorry for the woman.

My favorite prof was Professor Joseph Sneed. The Dean had conscripted him from the University of Texas Law School after our contracts professor, George Jarvis Thompson, had a sudden, fatal heart attack. Professor Thompson was at the time of his death the country's preeminent contracts scholar as the editor of Williston's great multivolume *Contracts* treatise. Contracts was a full-year course and accounted for a significant portion of our grades. Professor Thompson died halfway through the year, and Professor Sneed had the difficult task of picking up the pieces.

Although Professor Thompson was a luminary, I never understood contracts under his tutelage, and I started to think that the Dean's prediction might come true. However, with Professor Sneed the light bulbs started to flash, and one of the A minuses that I got at the end of my first year was from him.

Professor Sneed was not only my contracts savior, he was in many other ways a very special, wise, and sensitive human being. In particular, I will never forget how he spoke to me after my father died during my third and final year. While he was empathetic and comforting, he also had a sense that I had a little growing up to do and shared with me how he had matured after his father had died.

17

During my last year at Cornell, a few days before Thanksgiving, I got a telephone call from none other than Dean Thoron. To my utter dismay, he invited me to be his guest at the football game between Cornell and Harvard—his alma mater—that Saturday afternoon, and at half-time he put his left arm around my shoulders in a paternal embrace and said, "Mr. Block, I like to think of myself as a big man who is capable of admitting when he made a mistake, and I apologize for being wrong about you." I was flabbergasted. Years later, he asked me to join him as a member of the New York State Bar Association's Ethics Committee, and throughout the years he would invite me to lecture to his classes at Cornell even before I became a judge. I guess that it paid off that I did not let the humiliation that I suffered during that first day in Con Law affect my ability to succeed. To the contrary, whenever I would face rejection in the future, I always remembered the Dean and persevered.

I graduated from Cornell Law School in the spring of 1959, the same day that the class of 1909 was celebrating its 50th reunion. I would return in 2009 for my 50th and wondered how many law students I met that day would be returning to celebrate their 50th in 2059.

* * *

I also thought that day about my father and how much he would have loved to have been at my graduation from law school. When my father died, during my last year at Cornell, he owned and operated Active Telephone Answering Service. The Sterling Clothing Company had faced some hard times after the end of World War II and had gone out of business. My father thought he could make a go out of the telephone answering service business and built Active up from scratch. Its office was in an old, five-story, ramshackle building on Barclay Street which would eventually become part of the site of the World Trade Center.

As I was handed my diploma, I smiled as a recalled the time when I had just turned 16 and asked my dad if I could work for him that summer. He was a good guy and could not say no.

Since there was nothing much for me to do, he had decided to let me try to get new accounts by going door-to-door in the cavernous office buildings in the area. On my first day of work, he sent me to the Woolworth Building in a new suit that he bought for me and told me to knock on each office door, starting at the top, the 57th floor. He would pay me $100 for each new account that I could get.

New York was experiencing a record-breaking heat wave, and the temperature on that day hovered around 100 degrees in the shade. Maybe my father thought that people would feel sorry for me and give me their answering service business, but it was not to be. When I got to an office on the 24th floor, the man who opened the door did indeed feel sorry for me. I was sweating profusely, having walked down 33 floors in a stairwell where the temperature felt like 200 degrees. He asked me to sit, made me loosen my tie, unbutton my shirt, and take off my suit jacket. He brought me a large glass of water, asked me how old I was as I was gulping it down, and demanded that I tell him what beast would send a 16-year-old boy out to canvass the Woolworth Building on such a day. I told him sheepishly that it was my father and gave him a business card with my father's name on it. He either did not believe me or did not care because he called the New York City Labor Department and reported the owner of Active Telephone Answering Service for child abuse.

My father did not tell me the outcome of the subsequent investigation, but he never asked me to solicit new accounts for him again.

My dad was a warm, caring man. His warmth and intelligence made him a great salesman but, paradoxically, he was somewhat of an introspective loner in his personal life. There were only a few occasions that I remember when we had company at our home, and the lack of exposure to the adult world probably contributed to my feeling ill at ease and insecure in the company of older people when I was growing up. When my father came home from work, he would read the newspaper, listen to the news, and try to go to bed early. He had no hobbies—his life was his business—but he could not sleep. I would catch him late at night sitting at the dining room

19

table sketching the rooms of our apartment with pen, paper, and ruler. He was uncannily precise in drawing them to scale. My brothers and I always teased him because he would do the same sketches over and over and was so mechanical and uncreative.

When my older brother Leonard adopted his first child, Patti, he gave my father a Humpty Dumpty paint by the numbers set. He thought that since my dad was so precise he would be able to follow the numbers exactly and paint a great Humpty Dumpty for his new granddaughter. He did. For his next birthday, my brother decided to try to move him beyond his room sketches and Humpty Dumpties. He gave him a set of paints, paintbrushes, a canvass, and a picture of one of the Paris street scenes painted by the famous French painter Utrillo. Within the month, my father—who never took an art lesson and did not have the vaguest clue as to how to mix paints—made a great replica of the Utrillo painting.

My father died seven months later, at the age of 61. The picture hangs in my apartment to this day. It always makes me wonder what untapped potentials lie dormant in all of us and reminds me that new life experiences are always possible at any age—even writing a book for the first time when one is 77 years old.

* * *

In the summer after I graduated law school, America had recently wrapped up the Korean War, and the Vietnam War was on the horizon. The draft was still in place, and I hoped to be an officer in the Judge Advocate General's Corps. However, to become an officer upon graduation from college you had to have taken four years of ROTC. I had taken the basic two-year ROTC course at Indiana and had planned to take the final, advanced two years at Cornell. However, the physical requirements for an officer were more demanding than those for a noncommissioned serviceman, and I flunked the officer physical for the advanced ROTC because of my eyes. Ironically, I was told that although I could not be an officer in the military's legal department, my eye condition would not disqualify me from being drafted as a private. I had a difficult time understanding why if I could not see well enough to be a military lawyer—or to serve as an officer in some other capacity—I could see well enough to shoot a gun.

Nonetheless, I was looking forward to serving my country, even if I would be the only infantryman from the graduating class, and only hoped that I would not shoot someone by mistake. Thus in early July, two days after I had taken the bar exam, I kissed my mother good-bye and reported for induction—but it never happened. I was given a preinduction physical and classified 4F. There was a period of peace in the world at that time, and while the draft had not been disbanded, the military must have been looking for ways to cut back on the number of inductees; my bad eyes now totally disqualified me from service.

Since I expected to go into the armed service, I had not looked for employment. I took advantage of my unexpected, new-found freedom and bummed around Europe for a few months with my law school buddy Sid Devorsetz until my mother called to tell me that I had passed the bar exam. I had mixed feelings. I was having the time of my life, but reality won out, and when I soon returned to New York, I called Dean Thoron to see if he had any thoughts as to how I should start my legal career. He was happy to hear from me and got me my first job as a law clerk in Albany, New York, for the Appellate Division of the New York State Supreme Court. While I certainly would have preferred to be a law clerk for the top court, the Court of Appeals, it was the only clerkship available at that time, and I took it.

Being a law clerk for a state appellate court in Albany for the better part of the next two years was a great way to break into the law. I was part of a pool of five clerks—not nearly enough to handle the court's busy workload—and wrote memoranda or draft opinions for the judges' review. The exposure to reading appellate briefs—both good and bad—would prove to be invaluable since we learned how to research and write effectively. It was tantamount to a postgraduate course in the law and would prove of great value in the future. It also certainly was a good way to see the human side of the bench.

21

In law school, our exposure to judges had been focused on reading their decisions in the casebooks, and we had been somewhat conditioned to viewing them as gods. I was quickly disabused of this perception on my first day at work.

The appellate courthouse in Albany was on the third floor of the old county courthouse, and the judges' private chambers encircled the beautiful library on that floor. I stayed late at night that day working on my first assignment—it might have been about 8:30 p.m.—when I heard a voice calling from the only chamber whose door was open: "Young man, come let me say hello to you." As I timidly entered, there was Judge Francis Bergan in his blue-striped boxer shorts clumsily changing his pants. He asked me what case I was working on. I tried not to notice, but the experience of discussing the law on my first day of work with a judge in his underwear blew my mind.

Judge Bergan was a highly regarded jurist and was elected later that year to the Court of Appeals. He would often work late into the night, as I did, and we had the opportunity for many more chats. He was always concerned about the welfare of the court's law clerks, as was the Chief Judge, Sidney Foster, who was constantly battling the legislature for more money so that he could hire more law clerks for the understaffed law department. Chief Judge Foster, a grand old man, proud of his Republican roots, would not take "no" for an answer and found a clever way of dealing with the problem. The Court was stocked with highly paid, unneeded personnel in basically phantom positions who were the product of the patronage world of Albany's entrenched Democratic political machine under the leadership of Boss O'Connell. When one of them retired, Judge Foster would simply fill the retiree's title with a law clerk. If memory serves me correctly, my official title was Chief Wardrobe Manager, which carried an annual salary of $11,000, a princely sum in those days for a law clerk; the Court of Appeals law clerks, by comparison, were only making $4,000 in their loftier positions. I was easily able to afford the $95 monthly rent for my spacious one-room apartment in a nice garden apartment complex, complete with swimming pool, as well as a brand new Chevy for $2,800.

Shortly after I started my clerkship, I had my first personal encounter with the law. When I was in Europe I traveled around in a little sports car which I bought in London with a small inheritance from my father and brought back with me. It had British license plates, but I was told by the dealer that I could drive it in the United States for 30 days before I needed new plates. I thought I would take it to Albany and register it there. However, as I was driving on the Thruway on my way to my first post-law school job, I was pulled over by a New York State Trooper who asked me whether I knew I was driving in the United States. His exact words: "Hey buddy, I got news for you—you happen to be in New York, not England." He gave me a ticket, and I felt kind of foolish and naive for listening to the British car salesman.

I guess I got caught up in my work and inexplicably forgot about the ticket. Late one afternoon after work I was in my apartment with Sid, who had gotten a job in the New York State Attorney General's Office, when there was a loud knock on the door. As I opened it, I was astonished to see two burly troopers, who told me that they were there to arrest me and transport me to the Village Justice Court in New Paltz, about 70 miles away, for failing to appear on the ticket's return date. Sid followed me in his car and stood by me as I was shaking before Justice Parks Glenn. I apologized for my forgetfulness, told the judge that I now had New York plates, and admitted that given my position as a new law clerk for the appellate court, I was embarrassed for thinking that I could drive with British plates in the United States. He set down a new return date for me to appear, asked me how I liked being a law clerk, and sent me on my way.

A few weeks later, I was taking a shower when my phone rang. I answered it dripping wet. It was Sid. I asked him to call back so I could dry off. Seconds later the phone rang again. I was annoyed because I could not understand why he could not wait a little longer and blurted out: "What do you want, asshole?" I was shocked when the voice on the other end said, "This is Justice Parks Glenn. Is this Mr. Block?" I sheepishly acknowledged my existence, told him that I had thought that he was Sid, and that I might be having a heart attack at the age of 26. He said that he called to tell me that he had dismissed the traffic infraction. Fortunately, he had a sense of humor. He wished me good luck with my clerkship but suggested that I watch my language when speaking with the judges.

The experience has had a lasting impact. To this day, whenever I answer the phone, I say one word: "Hello."

* * *

The beautiful Court of Appeals courthouse was next to the county courthouse. I went there often to listen to appellate arguments before the state's highest court, especially appeals from cases I had worked on. I became friends with a number of its law clerks. Gene Wishod was one of them. Gene went to work for a law firm in Suffolk County on Long Island after he finished his clerkship. I had another year to go. In the middle of my second year, Gene's firm had an appeal which was before my court and he came for oral argument with Herman Schechter, one of the firm's two partners, who argued the case. I listened to the arguments, was impressed with Mr. Schechter's presentation—even though he would lose—and was happy to accept his invitation to join him and Gene for lunch afterwards at Keeler's Steak House.

While munching on one of Keeler's celebrated hamburgers, Herman Schechter extolled the virtues of practicing law in Suffolk County. He and his partner, Irving (his twin brother), had returned from the Second World War to their Suffolk hometown in Smithtown as war heroes, and their small, four-member law firm was bursting with business. Gene would be in on the ground floor. By the time I had to go back to work, I had been sold a bill of goods on the vibrant future of Suffolk County and how the lawyers who shared this vision could become a part of that future.

A few weeks later, Herman called to tell me that he had recommended me to Dranitzke and Lechtrecker, a two-member law firm in Patchogue, a village in the Town of Brookhaven, one of Suffolk County's 10 towns. They were in the market for a young associate. I

24

had yet to look for a post-clerkship job and imagined that I would try to land one with one of Manhattan's big firms. Having nothing to lose, however, I met with Bill Dranitzke and George Lechtrecker, and when I was offered the job, I had to decide whether to venture into this foreign land—where I knew exactly two people, Gene and Herman—or return to my New York City roots.

After some sleepless nights, I realized that I had no contacts with any of the City's mega-firms and did not know where to start. Perhaps of greater importance, I was unsure if I would fit into that world. Bolstered by Gene's positive experiences with the Schechter firm, and Herman's influence as a sort of substitute father figure in the wake of my father's recent passing, I accepted the offer.

I had another father figure at that time: Estelle Kaufman's dad. I had met Estelle at a dance at the Albany Ten Eyck hotel the first week of my judicial clerkship. She had just finished her student teaching preparatory to graduating from SUNY Albany that spring. Her family befriended me, and her father, who was a hardworking news butcher for the Union News Company at the Albany railroad station, took me under his wing. He invited me to join his bowling league and was just a warm-hearted, wonderful person. Cooky, as Estelle had been called by her father ever since she was a little girl, also had a terrific mother and brother. Together, they made me feel part of the family. Cooky Kaufman and I got married at the end of my clerkship and took off months later as 20th-century pioneers for the Suffolk boondocks.

Chapter
2

Practicing
The Sixties

When I showed up for my first day of work at Dranitzke and Lechtrecker's office in Patchogue, in August of 1961, I had no idea what to expect. Patchogue was not New York City. Although it was the largest village in the Town of Brookhaven, it seemed to me like a sleepy little place, and when I was told that it was an Indian name for "turning point," I seriously thought about turning around and getting out of there.

Dranitzke and Lechtrecker had a two-man general practice, and I soon learned how to handle the ABCs of a basic law practice in a semirural community 60 miles east of the "City." I remember how nervous I was at my first real estate closing, wondering whether I was putting the debits and credits in the right columns. I also drafted my first simple will, but I was not being intellectually challenged and dreaded the two days a week that I had to sit in a dingy little one-room branch office which Mr. Dranitzke insisted on keeping on Main Street in Center Moriches, a one-horse outpost 15 miles east of Patchogue. I would sit alone behind a rickety desk with nothing to do but wait for someone to stop by to make an appointment to see my boss. I got my first anxiety attack there, feeling light-headed with tightness in my chest. I had to do something.

One Sunday morning, in the spring of 1962, I drove with my wife and newborn son, Neil, from Patchogue, on the south shore, to the

Town of Brookhaven's north shore hamlet of Port Jefferson and was struck by its charm and beautiful beaches on Long Island Sound. I had been with Dranitzke and Lechtrecker for nine months and decided to give birth to my own law practice. Within weeks I had rented the house and one-room office in Port Jefferson Station. The first day that I walked into the office, I hung my diploma over that attic fan and looked at the mirror on the wall. To this day, I don't know how I had the guts to do it. I knew no one there.

* * *

Until my father passed away, my mother never worked since leaving her job as a bookkeeper at Sterling Clothing Company shortly after the boss took a liking to her and married her. Now she had to make a big decision—whether to learn the answering service business and go back to work or sell it. She was not certain that she could otherwise support herself with just the money that my father left her, which, aside from small sums that he left his children, was his entire, but modest, estate. The thought crossed my mind that maybe I should jettison my incipient legal career and become the new boss of Active Telephone Answering Service. It certainly made economic sense since it would produce an immediate living for me and provide financial stability for my mother.

She would have none of it. My mother told me how proud my father was that I went to law school, even though he never saw me graduate, and that the best gift I could give him was to become a successful lawyer. She would go to work, learn the business, and build it up so that it could be sold at a solid market price. She had great pride—it would not be a distress sale.

I went with my mother to the office a week after my father died. It was the first time that she had been there in a number of years. The answering service business was dependent on operators whose jobs were to sit at switchboards, answer the phones promptly when they rang, take down the messages, and report them to the customers when they called in for them. Such was the technology in those Byzantine, pre-smart phone days. All seven operators were women.

None weighed less than 200 pounds. There was a time when a number of them weighed considerably less, but my mother—who had a jealous streak—prevailed upon my father to fire them.

Within weeks my mother took total control of the business and had it running smoothly. She was a whiz at handling and defusing customer complaints about their service and had a particular knack for collecting delinquent accounts from the mostly male customers. She would shame them into paying by simply telling them that she was not their mother and had no intention of carrying them for nine months.

Shortly after I opened my practice in Port Jefferson Station, my mother had built up the business so that she was able to sell it for a very good price. She was now financially secure, and I was free to try to earn my spurs as a lawyer

* * *

When I worked for Dranitzke and Lechtrecker, I was paid $120 a week and rented a small house in a working-class neighborhood in the hamlet of Brookhaven in the Town of Brookhaven. My next-door neighbor was Ichilio William Bianchi, Jr. He insisted on being called just plain Bill to set him off from his father, who was proud to be called Ichilio. The senior Bianchi was perhaps the country's leading grower of cymbidium orchids. They were world-famous, and a bouquet was delivered each day to Buckingham Palace. The Bianchi hothouses were located in the Town of Brookhaven, not too far from where Bill lived. Old man Bianchi was grooming his son to take over the lucrative family business, but being from the old school, he started him from the bottom and made him live for a short time in a modest house next to mine.

Before Bill moved to his estate in the wealthy part of town, we had a chance to become good friends. We were the same age, 27, and although Bill was not a lawyer, he was well-educated and had a deep interest in government on all levels, as did I. While I was a stranger to Suffolk County, Bill was a native and well-versed in its history.

A few days after March 26, 1962, when the Supreme Court rendered its groundbreaking decision in *Baker v. Carr*, Bill asked me whether I thought it could open the door to challenging the constitutionality of Suffolk County's government. In that case the high court held that "a justiciable federal constitutional cause of action is stated by a claim of arbitrary impairment of votes by means of invidiously discriminatory geographic classification," which soon would evolve into the principle of "one-man, one-vote," as it was then called, as the bedrock principle. The *Baker* decision immediately spawned litigation throughout the states to require their legislative districts to be redrawn to represent equal populations. Still, there had yet to be any lawsuit seeking to apply the one person, one vote principle to local levels of government, like Suffolk County.

Bill explained to me how the County and towns' governments worked. I learned that Suffolk County was divided into 10 towns, each with its own government. The head of the town was called the town supervisor, and there were five councilmen comprising the town council. All were elected at large. Together they tended to the local issues governing the daily lives of the towns' residents, like garbage removal, local road repairs, and zoning.

The 10 town supervisors had additional responsibilities: they also made up the Suffolk County Board of Supervisors, which ran the county government. While the town boards handled local issues within their respective towns, the scope of the county government was much broader, tending to issues that traversed town lines, such as countywide transportation, regional planning, sewer networks, and the building and maintenance of county roads and parks.

Bill laid out the demographics: As of that time, Suffolk County's population was about 600,000. Only about 60,000 came from the five easternmost towns—Southampton, Riverhead, Southold, East Hampton, and Shelter Island—which were largely farmland; the rest came from the five western towns—Islip, Babylon, Huntington, Brookhaven, and Smithtown, which were on the verge of becoming urbanized. It did not take a rocket scientist to realize that the five town supervisors from the eastern towns—with only 10% of the population—could block any legislation favored by the town supervisors from the west, with 90% of the population. The disparity in representation was poignantly reflected by the fact that the supervisor from the smallest town—Shelter Island—with a population of only 1,312, had the same vote as the supervisor of the largest town—Islip—with a population of 172,959.

I was intrigued. If the principle of equal representation were to be extended to all elective levels of government in the country—not just state governments—these facts were as good as you could get to litigate the issue. I was then still working for Dranitzke and Lechtrecker, however, and was preoccupied with thoughts of leaving. I was in no position to do more than think about it.

All of this changed soon after I placed my diploma over the attic fan. While I was in the throes of trying to figure out how I was going to pay my rents and support my family—all I had was a few thousand dollars from my father's estate—I was ready to stretch my legal muscles and dig my teeth into something profound.

* * *

I was able to talk the landlord out of evicting Charlie McDermott, and soon he recommended me to two of his customers who were looking for a collection lawyer. I was in no position to refuse any legal business and was soon collecting past-due fees from former patients of Doctors Ambrose and Gould. They suggested that it might help me meet people, and potential clients, if I joined the synagogue in the neighboring hamlet of Setauket. Its congregation was less than 100, drawn from all of the surrounding communities, and services were conducted in a little building paradoxically located on Christian Avenue. I thought that I could also pray there for my survival.

Soon my prayers started to be answered. Some of the congregants were sympathetic to my plight and gave me a little business—some simple wills, my first house sale, and more collection cases. Herman Schechter referred some small commercial litigation matters to me, and I got my first fender-bender negligence case. I also started to get some court assignments to represent indigents in minor criminal cases in the Suffolk County Court, for which Suffolk County paid me $18.50 an hour. I also joined the Lions Club and Chamber of Commerce, which gave me the chance to network with the local business leaders. With the Chamber, I volunteered to help in its successful effort to get the Long Island Railroad to replace the dilapidated ticket building at the Port Jefferson Station railroad station with a modern passenger waiting room.

The Lions Club reminded me of my fraternity days at Indiana. It was an all-male club that met every Monday for dinner at the Wagon Wheel restaurant. Jokes were told—some of which I would be uncomfortable repeating. The good joke tellers would be elected as a Lion Tamer or Tale Twister, whose jobs would be to use their comedic talents while meting out small fines if you did not have a good excuse for missing a meeting or arriving late. It was all done in good fun, and the monies raised were always spent to support one of the many charitable causes supported by the club. I guess I never was a good joke teller because I was never chosen as a Lion Tamer or Tale Twister. While I thought that my fraternity days were behind me and was not comfortable with some of the childish testosterone antics of my fellow Lions—or that we had no Lionesses—I met some important people who would become clients and enjoyed some of the good-natured bantering. I remember in particular that the town superintendent of highways, Charlie Barraud, would always be called Charlie Badroads.

My first big break came just a few months after I took my first one-third percentage fee for collecting money from one of Dr. Ambrose's deadbeats. I was hanging out at the bar one night at the Elks Hotel and Restaurant—the local watering hole—with the Lion Tamer, who introduced me to Nick Poulos. He had just been elected to the Comsewogue School Board, the Indian name given many moons ago to the Port Jefferson Station School District. We soon became good friends, and Nick paved the way for me to be appointed as the school district's attorney for an annual $10,000 retainer. I do not think that I would have lasted if this had not happened. I remember how excited my wife was. She thought that I was on the verge of becoming a successful lawyer and said that she would be happy if I made $15,000 a year from my practice.

I also joined the Democratic Party, although almost everyone told me I was crazy. At that time, Republicans outnumbered Democrats by about two to one in Suffolk County, and the Republican Party controlled every facet of local government, with one exception. H. Lee Dennison had just been elected as Suffolk County's first county executive. He was a visionary, no-nonsense engineer with an aversion to political perquisites, pomp, and circumstance, and although a Republican, ran as an independent endorsed by the Democratic Party. The public loved him. His election was also fueled by the recent indictment of H. Kingsley Macy, the corrupt Republican county leader, and there were rumors that more indictments against the Suffolk County Republican hegemony were in the pipeline. I did not want to be part of such an organization.

Nonetheless, Dennison's election was considered aberrational, and if you ever had any thoughts about successfully running for public office in Suffolk County, you had to be a Republican, especially in the Town of Brookhaven, where Richard Zeidler ruled as the chairman of the town's Republican Party. Every Suffolk County town board was Republican, and every state legislator from the county was Republican. Thus if you were a lawyer and thought that someday you would like to become a state judge, you would be a fool not to run down to the board of elections and register as a Republican. In Suffolk, all state court judges were elected by popular vote. You simply had no chance of becoming a judge from the county if you were stupid enough to be a Democrat.

The arrogance of the Republican Party was pervasive. Its leaders would boast that it could elect anyone as a judge, even Mickey Mouse. To make matters worse for a lawyer, you would be shut out from representing clients before any local government agency because they had to have a Republican lawyer. At that time Suffolk was on the verge of a building boom, and a principal source of a lawyer's business was representing land developers who needed zoning changes, variances, and building permits. None of this business would ever come my way. I would have a client a few years later who built garden apartments in the Town of Brookhaven, and who told me that he was told by Boss Zeidler that he had to have a particular Republican lawyer represent him before the town board when he needed a zoning change. He could not have me represent him if he wanted to do business with the Town.

It was even worse. New homeowners were told by the local Republican committeeperson that if they registered as a Democrat, their property taxes would be higher. Additionally, if they wanted to become active in their community and become part of the social fabric, they would not be invited to join the local country club or become a member of the hospital board. While all of this did not necessarily come to pass, there was a perception that bad things would happen if you did not join the Republican Party.

Thus lawyer after lawyer who came to Suffolk County did the smart thing and became Republican—and reaped the benefits. John P. Cohalan, who was an active Democrat from Brooklyn, became a prominent Republican when he came to Suffolk in the '50s and became its top judge. A courthouse would even be named after him. In the Town of Brookhaven my lawyer friends made their living as turncoat Republicans and chided me for being so principled. One became the go-to-guy if you needed a zoning change. Another friend become the County Attorney, while others were made counsel to various town agencies or became a Town Attorney or an Assistant Town Attorney. No Democrat had ever been elected as the County's District Attorney, and you had to be a registered Republican if you wanted to be an Assistant D.A.

I became good friends with Morty Weissman. He came to Suffolk County a few years before I did from Queens, one of New York City's five boroughs, and opened a law practice in the middle of the Town of Brookhaven with two other New York City transplants. They each got religion in a hurry and changed their registrations from Democrat to Republican. Morty wanted to become a judge, and he had no chance if he was not tapped by Dick Zeidler. Boss Zeidler had a Lincoln-Mercury car dealership, and when I would attend a meeting of the Brookhaven Town Lawyers Association, my car was one of the few in the parking lot that was not a Lincoln Continental.

Morty's loyalty to the Boss paid off, and he became a local Suffolk County District Court judge, and then a Suffolk County Court judge. Boss Zeidler, the car salesman, would boast about all the judges "he made" at the annual Christmas party he held for all of his political cronies. He would be Santa Claus and would have all of his judges dress up as his reindeer. Morty made a cute Rudolf.

* * *

Being a collection lawyer and handling other mundane legal matters during the start of my law practice was economically necessary but not stimulating. I kept thinking about Bill Bianchi and Suffolk County's unrepresentative government. One spring night, days after I sent out my first dunning letter for Dr. Ambrose, I had a dream that I was arguing the first local reapportionment case in the United States Supreme Court. The next morning I called Bill and met him for dinner that night. Maybe we had too much to drink, but we decided to take a shot at bringing down Suffolk's antiquated form of government by suing the County. He would be the plaintiff. I would be his pro bono lawyer. Coming just months after the Supreme Court opened the door to litigation challenging unrepresentative forms of government, it would be the first local one person, one vote case in the country.

The next day I started to draft my first complaint as a lawyer and titled it *Bianchi v. Board of Supervisors of Suffolk County*. I thought, however, that since Bill and I were both Democrats, we should try to make it bipartisan. Gene Wishod had introduced me to a friend of his from the Town of Huntington—the westernmost and second most populated town in the county—who was practicing law in Huntington with his father. Dick Cahn had recently graduated from Yale Law School and was a Republican. As a brilliant, young, idealistic lawyer, he, too, was smitten by the thought

35

that the one person, one vote principle of representation should apply to Suffolk County, and could not fathom why his town supervisor had the same vote as the town supervisor from tiny Shelter Island on the Suffolk County Board of Supervisors even though Huntington's population was 100 times greater. He agreed to join forces with me as pro bono co-counsel. We still needed a Republican plaintiff to make the lawsuit totally bipartisan. Dick was able to prevail upon Quentin B. Sammis, a prominent Huntington Republican real estate agent, to team up with Bill Bianchi as coplaintiff.

On July 27, 1962, just four months after *Baker v. Carr*, and three months after I hung out my shingle, the complaint Dick and I had prepared was filed with the clerk of the federal court in Brooklyn. It began:

> Plaintiffs, I. William Bianchi Jr., and Quentin B. Sammis, residents of the Town of Brookhaven and Huntington, Suffolk County, State of New York, bring this action in their own behalf and in behalf of all other taxpayers and voters of Suffolk County, against the ten individual defendants, each of whom is an elected Supervisor of his respective town and who collectively constitute the Board of Supervisors of Suffolk County (1) to declare void and invalid as violative of the Fourteenth Amendment of the United States Constitution so much of Section 203 of the Suffolk County Charter, Laws 1958, c. 278 as provides that each Supervisor shall have one vote as a member of the Suffolk County Board of Supervisors, (2) to enjoin the defendants from acting as the Board of Supervisors unless and until a change in their voting strength is made, and (3) to cause to be convened a three-judge court to hear and determine the case.

Thus, for the cost of the $1.50 filing fee, the die was cast.

* * *

Nobody took the case seriously. It got no press coverage. Since the Suffolk County Board of Supervisors was being sued, the Suffolk County Attorney was obliged by law to defend the constitutionality of the county government, and his office filed motion papers to summarily dismiss the lawsuit as frivolous. After all, how could anyone seriously contend that the board of supervisor form of government which Suffolk County had had since its inception in 1683 was illegal?

Dick and I wrote an extensive memorandum of law in opposition, explaining *Baker v. Carr* and the applicability to Suffolk County of the newfound one person, one vote principle of representational government. On the return date of the motion we appeared for oral argument in the grand old federal courthouse in Brooklyn before Federal District Court Judge Walter J. Bruchhausen. He was a crusty old man—if he were alive today, he would be 118 years old. He did not ask us a single question as Dick and I took turns arguing against dismissal of the case. We had the sinking feeling that we were doomed.

Months went by without a word from Judge Bruchhausen. I busied myself with my collection cases and wondered when the axe would fall. It did not happen. On April 8, 1963, a little over eight months after we started the lawsuit, Judge Bruchhausen decided that our case was not frivolous and convened the three-judge court we requested to pass upon the merits. A three-judge court was required to decide all federal constitutional challenges to state statutes, and since the Suffolk County Board of Supervisors was the creature of the state legislature, we thought that that was the route we had to travel. This special court had to be composed of the district judge to whom the case was initially assigned, one additional district judge, and a judge from the circuit court of appeals. In addition to Judge Bruchhausen, the other judges who would now be hearing the case were Circuit Judge Leonard Moore and District Judge John F. Dooling—they were both highly regarded jurists.

The case now started to get some buzz. The Republican Party thought that it was some subversive Democratic plot to undermine the Republican grip on the reigns of county government, believing that Dick and Quentin were really closet Democrats. Dick told me that the Republican county leader, Arthur Cromarty, threatened him with political annihilation. The Republican chairman of the Suffolk County Board of Supervisors, Evans K. Griffing, who happened to be the town supervisor of tiny Shelter Island, had this to say about me, as reported in the press: "I'm sick about this. He (Block) is attempting to upset a tried and proven system of government. No inequities can be shown to prove he's right. This is going to split the county wide open."

The Suffolk County Attorney renewed the motion to dismiss. We updated our opposition papers and our memorandum of law, and the court set the case down for oral argument. This time we did not get an icy reception. Judges Moore and Dooling grilled the County Attorney with telling questions and were receptive to our arguments. Nonetheless, the court reserved decision, and nearly two years would pass before it spoke.

* * *

Wells R. Ritch died shortly after the lawsuit began. He had practiced law in Port Jefferson for over 60 years as a general practitioner and left behind a treasure trove of wills which he had drafted for just about everyone in the community. He was the epitome of the old-school, courtly local lawyer. Everyone called him Lawyer Ritch. He was almost 100 when he died and had been a signatory to the Charter of the Suffolk County Bar Association at its creation in 1908. He left his practice to Robert Burns, a genial solo practitioner, who moved into Lawyer Ritch's old office on Main Street. Bob asked me whether I would like to become his partner. He would handle the estate work, and I could take care of everything else. I jumped at the opportunity. I would bring the few clients I had into the firm.

One of them was Don Weiss, who had just started a local carting company. He named it Nobi Carting, after his Japanese wife, whom he had met while in the service in Korea in the late '50s. I do not remember how I met him, but I do remember that he told me that when he was in Japan, he was friends with a fellow private named Shelly Block. It did not take long to make the connection. Shelly was my brother. Don let me incorporate his fledgling business and prepare a simple carting agreement for his customers.

Margaret West was Burns & Block's one and only secretary. She

38

had been Lawyer Ritch's loyal secretary for over 40 years, and Bob begged her to stay on. She was so classy and proper that I always called her Mrs. West. During the first week that I moved into Wells Ritch's old office, I got my first new client for Burns & Block. Mrs. West told me that there was a gentleman who wanted to see me and ushered a burly-looking man into my little office. He spoke with a thick German accent and asked whether I would handle his house sale. The house was in Yaphank, a German community in the middle of Brookhaven Town. Rumor had it that the first Germans who settled there were deserters from the German U-boats that trolled the shores off Long Island during the Second World War.

I did not know this person, and naturally asked him why he had chosen me as his lawyer. He said that he picked me out of the Yellow Pages as the first German lawyer he came across. It never crossed my mind that my name could be mistaken for German. My ancestral tree dated back to Lithuania, and when the Biabablocksies came to America during the middle of the 19th century, they shortened it to Block. I wondered whether I was morally obligated for the sake of full disclosure to tell him that I was Jewish. I guess that I did not want to risk losing a potential client, so I let him think that I was indeed German. He turned out to be a good client, but he always called me Friedrich.

Buoyed by the prospect of making more money, coupled with the birth of my daughter Nancy, I bought my first house. It was a modest home in a nice, upcoming Port Jeff neighborhood. It cost $26,300. My mother loaned me $3,000, and the Riverhead Savings Bank gave me a $23,000 mortgage. I was able to pay the $300 difference plus the closing costs. I worried whether I was getting in over my head and would be able to make the $325 monthly mortgage payments. The anxiety attacks that I had first experienced when I worked for Dranitzke & Lechtrecker returned, heightened by the additional pressure to bring in new business for my new law firm. When I sat in the office waiting for the phone to ring, I would get so lightheaded that I would have trouble placing my pen into the penholder on my desk.

The worst part was the chest pains. One day they were so severe that I thought I was having a heart attack and went to the emergency room at the local hospital. The doctor assured me that I was fine. I immediately felt better and returned to the office. I realized, however, that I could not sit passively in the office. I needed to find a dynamic way to get out of there and meet lots of people. I decided to run for public office.

* * *

There were just a handful of lawyers in the town who were foolish enough to be Democrats. One was Dominic J. Baranello, who had a small one-man office in Medford, a low-income hamlet just north of Patchogue, where he was raised. Dominic was an incurable Democrat—a true believer in the plight of the little man. He became a committed Democrat while listening with his father, a highway laborer and native of Italy, to President Roosevelt's fireside chats on the radio. He could never betray his father by becoming a Republican.

Dominic was the chairman of the Town of Brookhaven Democratic party. It was a ragtag group of disheveled old-timers who were true believers. Dominic's major problem was to find candidates willing to run for public office against the Republican juggernaut. He was constantly trying to convince party loyalists to allow their names to be placed on the Democratic line so there would at least be a pretense of opposition. They were lambs being led to the slaughter. No one could recall when, if ever, a Democrat from Brookhaven had been elected to the local town board or to the state legislature, as either a senator or assemblyman.

In addition to the Town of Brookhaven, the New York State's First Assembly District embraced Suffolk County's five eastern towns that were the focus of our one person, one vote lawsuit. Thus, it included the towns of Riverhead, Southold, Southampton, East Hampton, and little Shelter Island. I thought that it would be worth my while to get to know them while I was waiting for the three-judge court to decide if they would keep their stranglehold on the

40

county government. The best way to do this would be to run for the New York State Assembly. I thought that this would be a good antidote for my anxiety attacks and would also help me actively cultivate a broad geographic clientele.

Dominic was thrilled that I was willing to be one of his lambs for the 1964 election. There were no other takers, especially since my Republican opponent would be Perry Duryea. The "Silver Fox," as he was called because of his mane of silver hair, was Hollywood handsome. At six foot two, he stood six inches taller than me. He lived in East Hampton and was a millionaire, being the head of the Montauk-based family business that was Long Island's major seafood wholesaler. Mr. Duryea—I called him Mister out of profound respect—was running for reelection for his third two-year term. At 42—I had just turned 30—he was in his political prime and had earned a well-deserved reputation as an outstanding statewide leader. He would later become the speaker of the assembly and a candidate for governor.

I had no money, and all that I could do was go to all of the firehouses and VFW halls that had meet-the-candidates nights. The first time I met Mr. Duryea was right in his back yard at the candidates' night at the East Hampton VFW. We were each given 20 minutes to speak. There may have been about 50 people there. They all seemed to know Mr. Duryea. Nobody knew who I was. Mr. Duryea spoke first. Everyone, including me, was impressed with his smooth delivery and his polished presence. I wished that I were him.

When I stood to speak my knees were shaking. Somehow I managed to make a good speech. I spoke about the need to have a viable two-party system of government in the county and how one-party rule inevitably leads to corruption. I did not mention anything about the lawsuit that I was championing to dilute the voting power of the five eastern towns.

Afterwards a little elderly, grey-haired lady in a Lilly Pulitzer dress told me how much she liked my speech. She also admired my courage and spunk in running against Mr. Duryea. While she was a good friend of his and a lifetime Republican, she said that she was so impressed by me that she was going to do something that she had never done before—not vote for the Republican candidate. However, she quickly told me that she could never bring herself to pull a lever for a Democrat. She would not vote for either of us.

There was one other experience on the campaign trail that I remember after all these years. Otis Pike was a Democrat from Riverhead who had accomplished a miracle two years earlier by being the only Democrat ever elected to Congress from Suffolk County's First Congressional District. He was a local war hero with a strong independent bent and because of his personal popularity was able to get enough Republican votes to just squeeze by.

The First Congressional District covered about the same territory as the First Assembly District, including the Village of Sag Harbor in the Town of East Hampton. The Village was home to many artists and literary figures. It was a Democratic oasis in an otherwise rock-ribbed Republican town. Its most prominent resident was the world-famous author, John Steinbeck, who had recently written his latest memorable book, *Travels with Charley: In Search of America*. In addition to being a committed Democrat, he was a friend of Congressman Pike and hosted a fundraising cocktail party for him. I was invited. When I mentioned this, a relative of mine—a brainy college philosophy professor—told me how disappointed she was that Mr. Steinbeck had never acknowledged the letter she had written to him a few months before critiquing *Travels with Charley*. Indignantly, she said: "Tell Mr. Steinbeck I'm still waiting for his response to my letter."

When we arrived at the affair, my wife and I went to the end of the lengthy receiving line. Cooky was intent on saying something profound, but when she was face-to-face with this literary giant, the best she could muster was, "Hello, my name is Estelle Block. It's so nice to meet you." I was next and was intent on doing better than that. Thoughts of my relative—who shall remain nameless—flashed through my mind, and I told him that one of the reasons I had come was to inquire why he had never answered the letter that she had sent him many months before critiquing *Travels with Charley*. Without missing a beat, he stroked his grey goatee and shot back: "Tell her that I answer all my worthwhile mail." I never told her.

The 1964 election produced a landslide win for Lyndon Johnson over Barry Goldwater for the Presidency. It also swept into office many Democrats on all levels throughout the country, including Robert Kennedy as New York's new United States Senator. I remember when he made a campaign stop in Patchogue and I sat behind him with the other local Democratic candidates while he spoke to a wildly enthusiastic crowd. I was mesmerized by his speech. I was introduced to him as Perry Duryea's opponent. He gave me some perfunctory words of encouragement, shook my hand, and had a picture taken with me. It remains one of my prized possessions.

Johnson's coattails produced upsets galore. In New York, in neighboring Nassau County—also a Republican enclave—the Republican Speaker of the New York State Assembly, Joseph Carlino, was swept out of office. And, shockingly, I almost beat Perry Duryea. However, while he went back to being an assembly-man, I returned to my Burns & Block law practice.

* * *

One day soon after, Don Weiss told me that he had prevailed upon a number of Suffolk County carters to form an association and asked me if I would be willing to do the necessary legal work. These folks were locals who had been picking up Suffolk's garbage for years. They were concerned that they were suddenly losing many of their customers to competitors from New York City. They feared that the mob had decided to take over their businesses.

I incorporated the Suffolk County Cartmen's Association, drafted its certificate of incorporation, prepared its by-laws, and kept the minutes of its meetings. I used a simple dictating machine, and Mrs. West did a nice job typing everything. It was my first incorpo-ration, and I kept the corporate books on a little shelf next to my

desk. I was surprised, however, when within months after the Association's first meeting, Don told me that he had decided to sell
Nobi Carting. When I asked why, since the business seemed to be
thriving, he was evasive. He only told me that he was under a lot of
pressure and had little choice. When he mentioned the sales price,
I thought that it was woefully inadequate. As best as I can remember, it was $80,000—not much higher than the cost of his trucks,
which would be part of the sale.

Although I was his lawyer, there was nothing for me to do. He
just wanted me to be with him at the closing. The paperwork had
been prepared by the purchasers' lawyer. Don would simply turn
over Nobi Carting's name, routes, and trucks to the purchasers. He
would be paid in cash. The closing would take place at the purchasers' home in the Village of Lindenhurst in the Town of Babylon. I
did not know their names.

When we arrived on the scheduled date, we were warmly greeted
by a matronly woman who introduced herself as Mama Limongello.
She escorted us to the basement, where we were greeted by her two
sons. They would be the purchasers. One was called Blind Joe. I do
not remember the other one's name or the name of the person whom
they identified as their lawyer. He was a small, impish-looking man
who was typing on a portable typewriter on a wobbly table. I did,
however, recognize one other person—Salvatore Ribando. He was
the branch manager of Security National Bank in Port Jefferson
Station. I kept my bank account there, and Sal was always nice to
me. I soon learned why he came.

After he finished typing, the purchasers' lawyer presented Don
with the documents that he needed to sign to convey his business to
the Limongello brothers. He also had the Limongellos sign a series
of promissory notes made payable to Security National Bank. When
they finished, Sal Ribando placed the notes into his briefcase and
handed Don a Security National Bank cashier's check for the full
purchase price. Blind Joe gave me a friendly slap on the back and
said that it was time to celebrate. He insisted that I join everyone

upstairs, where Mama Limongello had prepared a feast fit for kings. The pasta was the best I ever ate.

I had a chance to talk to Sal Ribando at lunch since we sat next to each other. He told me that the bank had financed a number of recent carting company purchases in Suffolk County. I naively asked him what kind of security he had for the promissory notes. He told me, "the best." I did not ask any more questions.

Several days later a huge unshaven man easily weighing over 400 pounds wobbled into the offices of Burns & Block and told Mrs. West, who was sitting behind her desk, that he was the new president of the Suffolk County Cartmen's Association. He was there to "pick up da books." Mrs. West was visibly shaking as she came into my office with him. He introduced himself as Fat Angelo Garafolo. Without a word, I gave him all of the Association's papers.

Nobody faintly resembling the looks of this man ever came into Lawyer Ritch's office during the four decades when Mrs. West was his loyal secretary. She was used to a more genteel environment. After Fat Angelo left, she quit.

Soon I also left. Bob had a drinking problem that was getting the best of him, and the clients that he had inherited from Wells Ritch were picking up their files and taking their business elsewhere. I felt badly for him, but I could not stay. I now had enough files to fill the two file drawers on the sides of my desk, I was making more money from the school district, and I had just settled a hit-in-the-rear automobile negligence case for $30,000. I moved into a three-room office in the new post office building across the street and hired my first secretary. A few weeks later a young lawyer, Stuart Namm, asked whether he could share office space with me. I was happy for the company. I was able to throw him a little work, and he became my first associate.

* * *

On February 1, 1965, the three-judge court finally rendered its decision. All hell broke loose. The judges first acknowledged that the case was one of first impression because although the Supreme Court had recently decided that the seats in both houses of a bicameral state legislature must be apportioned on a population basis, the high court had yet to consider whether the equal representation principle "applies as well to the method of electing the officials of hamlets, villages, school, fire, sewerage and water districts, towns, cities or counties." After recounting the population disparities amongst Suffolk's 10 towns, the three judges held that the one person, one vote principle should indeed apply to Suffolk County. As it tersely explained:

> Suffice it to say that the Board of Supervisors is constituted to serve as the legislative body for the County and, upon the present undisputed population disparity, it is not representative of the voters of the County as the Supreme Court has indicated is required of legislative bodies under the Equal Protection Clause.

Thus, the court made it clear that Suffolk's current form of government was unconstitutional. It did not, however, tell the County what new form of government it must create that would satisfy the principle of equal representation. In the exercise of judicial restraint, it left this task to the existing Suffolk County Board of Supervisors. However, it gave the plaintiffs the right to come back to court "in the event that an appropriate governing body has not been created for Suffolk County within the permitted standards for representation." It did not fix a specific time limit for the County to act.

Rather than heed the three-judge court's admonition, the County dug in its heels and sought to appeal to the Supreme Court. In the meantime, the suit was attracting national attention, and our case was being used as a template for challenges throughout the country. In an editorial, the *New York Times* took the Suffolk County Board to task for failing to work out a plan for redistricting and noted that every county throughout the country that followed the New York State pattern of township representation was "now faced with redistricting problems." It specifically named counties in Wisconsin, Illinois, Michigan, New Jersey, and Nebraska. It also noted that in

New York, Westchester County was preparing a plan to reform its Board of Supervisors and that the one person, one vote principle also undoubtedly had application to cities like New York, where the borough president of Staten Island had the same vote as the borough president of Brooklyn on the City's governing body—the Board of Estimates—even though Brooklyn had 10 times as many constituents. In trumpeting the cause for equal representation and admonishing Suffolk County, the editorial ended by stating that "[t]he problem of modernizing antiquated political structures along democratic lines is difficult and sometimes painful, but must be undertaken."

On October 11, 1965, the Supreme Court declined to accept the County's appeal "for want of jurisdiction," and the Suffolk County Board of Supervisors was now faced squarely with the prospect that it had to take some action to form a new government if it did not want the plaintiffs to bring them back to court. Panic set in. Although Supervisor Griffing now begrudgingly appointed 17 members of a proposed 25-member commission to study reapportionment plans, he simultaneously announced that "he would spearhead a campaign to have the thinly populated five eastern towns secede from the rest of the county."

We waited patiently for the better part of the year for something concrete to happen—other than the creation of a study committee—and in December asked the three-judge court to take action. It did. On June 15, 1966, it ruled that since the County had failed to take any corrective steps, immediate action was "imperative." It decreed, therefore, that the vote of each member of the Board of Supervisors would now be weighted as a temporary stop-gap measure until a permanent plan became effective and gave the County until July 11 to propose a plan to the court that would pass constitutional muster. Rather than comply, the County tried once again to get to the Supreme Court. This time the Court noted "probable jurisdiction," stayed the three-judge court's order, and accepted the County's appeal. At the age of 33, I would be arguing before the high court of the land, defending the first complaint I ever drafted just months after I hung up my shingle as a solo practitioner near the antiquated railroad tracks of Port Jefferson Station.

* * *

On April 17, 1967, Dick Cahn and I walked into the awesome building of the United States Supreme Court in our nation's capital. Happily, we were each given permission to orally argue and to decide how to divide our presentation. Thoughts of Dean Thoron flashed across my mind as I hung up my hat in the cloakroom. The majesty of the courtroom was something to behold—flushed with red drapes, chairs, and carpet. We were escorted by meticulously outfitted attendants to the appellees' counsel table and waited nervously for the judges to appear. In the audience were my wife and two children. Neil was then five; Nancy was three and a half. The kids had no clue what was happening and today have no recollection of being there. My brother Leonard and my mother also came, as well as my sister-in-law Naomi, who had helped with some of the research.

The Court grouped our case with three others for argument that day. They each represented a different type of local governments so that the court could consider which, if any, would be required to comply with the reapportionment edict that it had promulgated for the states. They encompassed a city in Virginia, a school district in Michigan, and a tiny county in Alabama. In contrast to that county, Suffolk County was geographically the size of Rhode Island with a population greater than that of nine states. Our case would be the first to be argued.

Although it was only a few minutes, it seemed like an eternity before the judges entered. The most imposing was Chief Justice Earl Warren. He was followed by Justices Black, Douglas, Clark, Harlan, Brennan, Stewart, White, and Fortas. When President Eisenhower appointed Chief Justice Warren in 1953, he thought that as the Republican governor of California he would be a reliable moderate conservative voice. The Chief turned the nation upside down, however, when he authored his famous decision one year later in *Brown v. Board of Education* striking down school segregation. He turned out to be a great believer in the sanctity of the First Amendment and was hailed as a liberal icon. President Eisenhower was dismayed, calling the appointment of Earl Warren as Chief Justice of the Supreme Court the worst mistake he ever made.

The first words out of the Chief's mouth were "Board of Supervisors versus Bianchi," and Suffolk County's lawyer, Stanley Corwin, rose to present the County's argument. I was pleased that the judges grilled him as he argued that the one person, one vote principle should not extend to local governments. After he finished, the Chief bellowed, "Mr. Block." I was trembling as I started to speak, and before I could say two words, Justice Fortas fired a spate of questions at me. I was not sure what he was driving at. It did not seem that he was satisfied with my answers. Eventually he gave up, and I got some friendlier questions from other members of the Court. All in all I thought that I did a pretty good job during my allotted 20 minutes, but when I listened to the tape of my argument the next day, my voice was an octave higher and my delivery was frenetic.

After Dick Cahn handled his end of our oral argument, the Alabama case was next. In contrast to my high-pitched, rapid-fire New Yorker presentation, the attorney for tiny Montgomery County—Truman Hobbs—spoke in a quiet, ever-so-slow Southern drawl. He sounded to me like a dunderhead while telling the court that nothing much happens in that sleepy little county: "The boys just hang around the courthouse in the square talking about goin' huntin' and fishin' cause there's nothing else to do." I could not believe that he was talking like this before the Supreme Court of the United States. However, the judges were strangely deferential and asked him very few questions.

I could not wait to find out who this lawyer was. When I got back to the office, I looked him up and was shocked to learn that he had graduated from Yale Law School and had been a law clerk for Supreme Court Justice Hugo Black. It was then that I realized that he had cleverly portrayed his county as an inconsequential unit of government not worthy of the Court's bother and had brilliantly contrasted this sleepy little place to the big-time county of Suffolk with its fast-talking lawyers. He would be appointed a federal district court judge for the Middle District of Alabama in 1980, and become its chief judge in 1984.

I thought again about Daisy Mae.

* * *

1967 was kind of a watershed year for me. Before I argued the *Bianchi* case in the Supreme Court, I had formed a law partnership with Dominic Baranello. I was soon after appointed counsel for the Education Committee of the New York State Constitutional Convention. A few days later, I was retained by Floyd Sarisohn to handle his appeal to the state's high court—the Court of Appeals—from the decision of the Appellate Division removing him as a local Suffolk County District Court judge. Then on April 20, I had received a decision from Suffolk County Court Judge Stark in the *Clayton* case. He had assigned me to represent Robert Clayton—who was serving a prison term of 30 years to life for killing a fellow migrant laborer on a farm where they were itinerant seasonal potato pickers—to conduct a hearing to determine whether he had voluntarily confessed to the murder.

My decision to become Dominic's partner happened after my Republican friend Bernie Burton called to tell me that Dick Zeidler would like to talk to me. Bernie invited me to have dinner with them as their guest. It was the first time I would meet the Brookhaven Town Republican boss. We ate at a fancy restaurant in the Bellport Hotel on the south shore of the town. We drank good wine, and I remember eating Danish lobster tails as Dick Zeidler spoke to me. The first thing that he spoke about was how he had just been appointed as the chairman of the Suffolk County Water Authority. It was a political plum that would give him a lot of patronage to dispense. He then flattered me with all sorts of accolades but wondered why such a smart young man would not want to get on the Republican gravy train like all of the other smart lawyers. He asked me whether I would be interested in running for public office again and promised that he would arrange for that to happen. All I had to do was switch my registration.

When I came home that night, I woke Cooky and asked her what I should do. She asked me how I would feel if I had to become one of Boss Zeidler's reindeer. The next day I called up Dominic. Within weeks the law firm of Baranello, Block & Namm was formed. I gave up my office in Port Jefferson and moved with Dominic and Stuart Namm into a suite of offices in a new office building in the middle of the town. Dominic had recently become the Suffolk County Democratic leader. We would become the loyal opposition to the powerful Suffolk County Republican Party.

Although our new law firm would have to make its income the hard way, I never regretted not becoming part of what I considered a corrupt political machine. As for Boss Zeidler, in 1969 he would be ousted as the czar of the Water Authority on charges that he had used his public office to make profits in real estate deals.

* * *

In regard to the Constitutional Convention, New York State's Constitution provided that the voters could periodically call for the convening of a convention to see whether significant revisions to the Constitution might be warranted; the last convention had been in 1937. Delegates from each assembly district were elected along party lines. Naturally, no Democrat won in Suffolk County. Since the Democrats elected the majority of the delegates statewide, however, they could shape the agenda, create the committees, select the chairpersons, and appoint the majority of the staff. Anthony Travia, the Speaker of the Democrat-controlled Assembly, was chosen to head the Convention, and Dominic was able to prevail upon him to let me be the Education Committee's counsel. It helped that my position as attorney for the Comsewogue School District gave me the opportunity to master New York State's education law. The PR that I was getting on the reapportionment case also helped.

51

In New York State, judges were prohibited from participating in politics, with one exception. They could be delegates to a constitutional convention. Judge Bergan was elected on the Democratic line from the assembly district covering Albany County. He was made chair of the Education Committee, which gave me the opportunity to work with him again, six years after I had clerked for his court. The hot-button issue that we dealt with was whether the Constitution should mandate tuition-free education for New York State's public colleges. It was an intriguing idea, but in the end it did not carry the day.

Don Mankiewicz was the PR guy for the Convention. He and his brother Frank were the sons of the author Herman Mankiewicz, who wrote *Citizen Kane*. Frank was Senator Kennedy's Chief of Staff. Don was several years older than I, but he befriended me. He loved the horses and invited me once to go with him to the trotters at the charming Green Mountain race track in Vermont, which was only about an hour from Albany. He knew all of the horses that were running and spoke with their drivers before each race. I could not wait to bet on the same horses that he did and wondered what I would do with my winnings. There were 10 races. I bet two dollars to win on each race. I lost $20.

One day Don asked me whether I would come to the library with him to help him with some research he was doing for a speech that he was working on for Senator Kennedy on civil rights. The Senator was an ardent supporter of the great civil rights legislation of the '60s. Although my contribution was inconsequential, I was happy to be a part of the cause.

* * *

As for Judge Sarisohn, the Appellate Division—New York State's intermediate appellate court—was divided into four departments. Each department heard appeals from lower courts within its geographical boundaries. The Third Department, where I had clerked, covered the middle of the state; the Fourth Department took care of the western part; the First Department handled appeals mostly from the Manhattan and Bronx lower courts; and the Second Department heard appeals mostly from the lower courts from Brooklyn, Queens, Staten Island, Nassau County, and Suffolk County. In addition to deciding appeals, each appellate department mostly presided over grievances brought against lawyers from their respective departments and could disbar them for misconduct. At the time of the Sarisohn decision, the appellate departments also were empowered to remove miscreant judges within their respective jurisdictions, subject to their right to appeal to the Court of Appeals.

In 1964 the state legislature created a district court system for both Suffolk and adjoining Nassau County to handle misdemeanors and civil suits up to $10,000. The district courts in Suffolk only covered the populous five western towns. Each town had its own district court and own judge, who had to be elected. Judge Sarisohn was the first elected district court judge from Smithtown. Thus, since he was a Suffolk judge, it was the Second Department of the Appellate Division that defrocked him.

In its decision, the court listed a number of reasons why it thought the judge was not fit to stay on the bench. Foremost were wiretapped telephone conversations that he had had with a client just before he became a judge. She was a prostitute who had been brought up on criminal charges for practicing her profession. Solicitous of her right to make a living without being hassled by the authorities, Sarisohn had advised her how to avoid being caught again. He told her that she should ply her trade in a mobile trailer. The court viewed this advice as obstruction of justice, as well as being incompatible with Judge Sarisohn's general character and fitness to hold his current judicial office. The court also found additional reasons for defrocking the judge based upon his high-handed and oppressive behavior on the bench, such as threatening a lawyer in a case before him that, "I'm going to screw you every way I can short of reversible error."

My mission as the judge's appellate lawyer was clear. I had to at least knock out the obstruction charge because even if the other charges stuck they would only result in his removal from judicial office. He would still be able to practice law. There were papers being prepared to disbar him for the telephone counsel which he had given the hooker.

* * *

As for the *Clayton* case, my clerkship with the appellate division, the notoriety I was getting on the reapportionment case, and a few small criminal matters I had handled got me on the Suffolk County Court's felony criminal assignment list to represent indigent felonious criminal defendants. I had been successful in a case before Judge Stark, and he asked me whether I would do the hearing for Mr. Clayton. At the time of the hearing, Clayton had been in jail for about 12 years after being convicted by a jury for confessing to the murder. Because of a recent Supreme Court decision, Clayton had the right to have a judge determine whether the confession was voluntary.

At the hearing before Judge Stark, I questioned the detectives who had extracted Clayton's confession, and delved into the circumstances surrounding the crime to see whether the confession made sense. I soon was convinced that Clayton was wrongly convicted of murder and that his confession did not square with the facts. Moreover, it was coerced. I believed that Clayton had been in a fight with his fellow migrant laborer late at night which was not of his doing. He hit his attacker in self-defense. There were no guns or knives. The coworker died when he fell and hit his head on a stone. Clayton and another farm worker carried the body into a barn.

Nonetheless, Judge Stark decided against me, as did the majority of the appellate division when I appealed—though it affirmed on other grounds. Judge Christ wrote a dissenting opinion, however, explaining why Clayton's confession was involuntarily extracted from him. As the judge explained, Clayton initially gave an exculpatory account of the events, but he signed the confession, which was written by the police, 60 hours later, after being under constant police pressure. During that time he had had almost no sleep since the police transported him "about the countryside at odd hours of the day and night." Judge Christ concluded, therefore, that this police misconduct made Clayton "so vulnerable to their dominance that . . . his will was overborne by the time he confessed."

Although I had lost, I was buoyed by Judge Christ's dissent and felt confident that the state's high court would agree with him. I was naturally disappointed, however, when the Court of Appeals summarily rejected my appeal and unanimously affirmed the appellate division's decision without comment. It was small comfort that Judge Bergan recused himself. Nonetheless, I gave it one last try and petitioned the Supreme Court. It refused to hear the case. I was disheartened and told Clayton that his last chance—although slim—would be to bring a writ of habeas corpus in the federal district court. I suggested that he attach my appellate briefs to his petition and ask the court to assign a lawyer to handle his federal case. I thought that he might have better luck with a new attorney.

* * *

On May 22, 1967, soon after I had lost the Clayton case in the appellate division, the Supreme Court came down with its decision in *Bianchi*. The three-judge court came back to haunt us. The high court held that it was improper to have the case heard by that special court because it viewed the complaint as only challenging a local county law creating the Suffolk County government rather than a state statute having general, statewide application. In a similar vein, it held that the Alabama case, which also entailed a three-judge court, was also not properly before it because although the challenge there did attack the constitutionality of a state statute, the statute was not of statewide application since it only dealt with "the apportionment and districting for one county's governing board."

Dick Cahn and I thought that the Supreme Court had gone out of its way to duck reaching the issue of whether the one person, one vote principle should apply to local levels of government in both of these cases. We were suspicious because the Court also found reasons for ducking the issue in the other two cases. It noted in the school district case, however, that "we need not decide at the present time whether a State may constitute a local legislative body through the appointment rather than the elective process. We reserve that question for other cases such as [*Board of Supervisors v. Bianchi*], which we have disposed of on jurisdictional grounds."

We were crestfallen. Five years after we began the lawsuit we would have to start all over and go back to Judge Bruchhausen. The next month we appeared before him and asked him to simply render the same decision that he had supported as a member of the three-judge court. We thought that it was a slam dunk.

Judge Bruchhausen sat impassively, without asking any questions, while the lawyers spoke. We thought that we would get a thumbs-up decision within days. The decision did indeed come a few days later. We were shocked. The good judge had a change of heart. He threw out the case. I was so distraught that I went into a deep funk and drowned my sorrows for the next two days at the Elks Hotel and Restaurant's bar.

The only recourse we had was to appeal to the Second Circuit Court of Appeals. We would not be able to get there, however, for many months while we prepared our appellate papers and waited for the court to set the case down for oral argument. It would not happen until the next year. In the meantime, I had to suck it up and write my brief for the Sarisohn appeal.

* * *

On September 25, 1967, I walked into the majestic New York State Court of Appeals building in the state's capital to argue before the state's high court that it should reverse the appellate division's decision removing Judge Sarisohn from the bench. The state's court of last resort is a seven-judge bench. Each of the judges was then elected in a statewide election. This later changed when the New York State Constitution was amended to provide for the Court of Appeals' judges to be appointed by the Governor, subject to confir-

THE SIXTIES

mation by the New York State Senate, from amongst seven qualified candidates recommended by a bipartisan commission. Judge
Bergan was still on the court.

There were five cases scheduled to be argued that day. Sarisohn's
was the first. While I was sitting in the section of the courtroom
reserved for the lawyers who would be arguing, my adversary, Solomon Klein, sat down in the row in front of me. As I anxiously waited
for the judges to enter I thought about the time he had called me
weeks ago to introduce himself. His ulterior motive, I suspected,
was to check out who I was. In a condescending tone he asked me
how long I had been a lawyer and how I managed to make a living
in a place like Suffolk County. He reminded me that he was the attorney whom the appellate division had appointed to prosecute
Judge Sarisohn and made sure that I knew that he was a prominent
New York City lawyer. He added, for good measure, that he had
never lost a case and pompously told me that he had successfully
argued many cases before the Court of Appeals. He asked me how
many I had handled. I told him it was my first.

When the judges filed into the courtroom and the case was called,
Mr. Klein and I took our seats at the designated tables in front of
the bench. As soon as Chief Judge Breitel called the case, Judge
Bergan rose and announced that he would be recusing himself
because of his past professional relationships with Mr. Block. He
said that he thought it best to do so because of the high regard
which he had for Mr. Block. I could have kissed him.

Solomon Klein lost his first case. Judge Breitel, writing for a
unanimous court, agreed with my contention that the wiretaps
were illegally obtained. Thus, Sarisohn's conversations with the
prostitute could not be held against him. The court sent the case
back to the appellate division to decide whether the other charges—
concerning Judge Sarisohn's conduct on the bench—which it upheld, would still warrant his removal. Considering all of the allegations, it was not surprising that the appellate division decided that
even without the obstruction charge, Floyd Sarisohn was not
temperamentally fit to be a judge. However, while his judicial

career was ended, he was allowed to retain his license to practice law. Without the prostitution charge—the only charge relating to his conduct as an attorney—proceedings to disbar him were never brought. The ex-judge returned to the practice of law and became a prominent criminal defense lawyer. I do not know, however, whether he ever represented a hooker again.

* * *

On March 12, 1968, Dick Cahn and I argued the *Bianchi* appeal before the United States Court of Appeals for the Second Circuit in the Manhattan federal courthouse. The Court of Appeals is geographically divided into 12 circuits. The Second Circuit covers appeals from the district courts of New York, Connecticut, and Vermont. Although each circuit has more than three judges, the appeals are heard by randomly selected three-judge panels. At least two of the judges must be circuit court judges; the other could be a designated district court judge. Our panel consisted of District Judge Ryan and Circuit Judges Hays and Kaufman. Judge Kaufman was the notorious judge who, as a district court judge, had sentenced Julius and Ethel Rosenberg to death on espionage charges for passing confidential information to the Russians during the '50s at the height of the Cold War. He had a reputation for being nasty on the bench and lived up to it by mercilessly grilling us. He harped on the fact that there was no Supreme Court decision that had held that the one person, one vote principle applicable to the states should also apply to local governments. He asked very few questions from our adversary, and Dick and I walked out of the courtroom convinced that we were losers. Judge Kaufman would sentence *Bianchi* to death also.

It was not to be. Three weeks later, on April 5, he authored an opinion for a unanimous court reversing Judge Bruchhausen. As luck would have it, on April 1 the Supreme Court came down with its decision in *Avery v. Midland County*, a local county reapportionment case from Texas, answering the question that it had ducked in our case and in the three others that were argued the year before. The high court of the land held foursquare that the one person, one vote principle would apply to all levels of elective government in the nation. Judge Kaufman was constrained to write, therefore, that "[t]he pronouncement by the Supreme Court during the past week makes it apparent that the current organization of [Suffolk County's] Board of Supervisors cannot be justified under the 'one man-one vote' standard." Suffolk County was ordered to reapportion—at once. The *New York Times* commented that the board of supervisors "was considered one of the most blatant exceptions to the one person, one vote decision handed down by the Supreme Court." The following year it reported that Judge Kaufman's decision had "become a precedent for the reapportionment of many other local governments."

While victory had been achieved, I would have preferred that we had won in the Supreme Court. Years later I learned from a reliable source that Chief Justice Warren wanted to use our case and the other three to give full breadth to the extension of the one person, one vote principle. Nevertheless, Justice Clark was still on the high court. The Chief Justice did not think that Justice Clark would support him and that he would only be able to muster a 5-4 vote. He knew that the *Avery* case was in the pipeline and that Justice Clark was planning to retire. It was widely believed that he would be replaced by Thurgood Marshall who, as counsel to the NAACP, was on record as broadly supporting equal representation. The Chief Justice wanted the best vote he could get for extending the one person, one vote principle to all elected legislatures. He had decided it best to wait, therefore, until Justice Clark was off the bench and *Avery* came before the Court. Thus, he found a reason in *Bianchi* and each of the other three cases to expressly reserve deciding the local reapportionment issue for another day. His instinct was correct since only three—rather than four—judges dissented in *Avery*.

Earl Warren was such a passionate believer in the principle of equal representation and that government should be truly the will of the people—each with an equal voice—that when he was interviewed by the press after he retired, he named *Baker v. Carr* and the local reapportionment cases that followed as his crowning

59

achievements during his 16 years as Chief Justice of the Supreme Court.

In the fall of 1968 Suffolk's voters approved a new form of government worked out by the major political parties. The old board of supervisors would be replaced by a new county legislature consisting of 18 elected legislators from equal population districts—officially ending the form of government that had ruled the county for 287 years. As the *New York Times* recounted, "it [was] the most important change in county government since Suffolk was founded in 1683."

The public elected its first county legislators at the general election in November the following year. Although the Republican and Conservative parties worked out a cross-endorsement deal that prevented any Democrat from being elected, many Democrats would be elected in future years. They even would be the majority from time to time. Because the new election districts were composed of smaller, local communities, they were more competitive. Well-known local Democratic candidates could go door-to-door and get elected on the strength of one-to-one contact. A viable two-party system for Suffolk County would come into being.

The creation of the Suffolk County Legislature in 1969 was a fitting end to my first decade as a Suffolk County lawyer. I did not make a penny on the *Bianchi* case. In fact, it cost me money. However, it was obviously, as the saying goes, worth its weight in gold. It was an episodic example of how the law could be employed as a powerful instrument to positively effect social change. It got me in touch with how a handful of individuals—and two local, small-town lawyers—could really make a difference. It dispelled any notion that the legal system was the sole province of the rich and powerful. I could not wait to see what exciting new cases might come my way as 1970 loomed. I was psyched.

Chapter
3

Practicing
The Seventies

It did not take long. On June 6, 1968, I was celebrating my 34th birthday when I learned that Robert Kennedy had been assassinated. It remains the worst birthday of my life. I thought of the time when I was on the campaign trail with him and of the research I had done for the speech that Don Mankiewicz had written for him. I never have come to grips with the senseless loss of this vital life and the fate that had befallen the Kennedys.

Richard Ottinger was nominated as the Democratic candidate for the special election that would be held in the fall of 1970 to fill Senator Kennedy's four-year, unexpired term. He was in the midst of his third term as a highly regarded Congressman from New York's 25th Congressional District in Westchester County. Congressman Ottinger had been a founder of the Peace Corps, was a leading environmentalist, and had impeccable liberal credentials. Nonetheless, for purely selfish political reasons, the Liberal Party decided to support the Republican candidate, Charles Goodell. The Conservative Party picked James Buckley, the brother of the conservative icon William F. Buckley.

Ottinger was in a dogfight. He decided that he needed another line on the ballot to neutralize Goodell's two lines. Capitalizing on his environmental record, he galvanized environmentalists throughout the state to gather thousands of signatures to create an independent line. He named it the Conservation Party. It was a clever name, designed to burnish his liberal credentials and to possibly attract conservatives as well.

However, the Conservative Party was not to sit idly by, and it sued. In the case, *Ottinger v. Lomenzo*, it claimed that the name "Conservation" was too similar to its name and should not be allowed on the ballot. Ottinger needed a lawyer. Dominic Baranello, who as the Suffolk County Democratic leader was getting recognized as a rising player in state Democratic circles, recommended his partner. I never had met Ottinger before, but Dominic told him about the reapportionment case, and the congressman agreed to let me represent him. I was now playing on a bigger stage and was nervous.

I met the congressman only once. I needed his signature on an affidavit that I had prepared as part of the opposition papers I would submit. I traveled to his sprawling estate one night in a remote part of Westchester. I had never been to a home like that or met someone quite like him. He was the son of the founder of U.S. Plywood, the product of a fancy undergraduate private school and Harvard law, and a successful international and corporate lawyer. He was polite but had a patrician air about him. I thought that he would invite me in to chat and offer me a drink, but he simply thanked me for coming and signed the affidavit in the doorway.

The Conservative Party's lawsuit had been brought in the Supreme Court of Albany County. In New York, each of the 62 counties has a supreme court. Its name is deceptive because it is not the highest court in the state. Rather, it is the state's court of general jurisdiction where most civil lawsuits start. Unlike New York State's other judges, the state supreme court judges—as well as the appellate division judges—are called "justices." The supreme court in Albany was housed in the same building as the Third Department of the Appellate Division where I had clerked. As luck would have it, the case was assigned to Justice A. Franklin Mahoney, a good Albany Democrat. On September 16, 1970, Justice Mahoney agreed with my argument that the general public understood that the words "Conservation" and "Conservative" had two distinctive meanings. As he wrote, "each has taken on a special, colloquial meaning that sharply distinguishes one from the other." In his view, therefore, they were "not confusingly similar" and would not "mislead the members of the electorate." I had won, and I was flushed with grandiose thoughts that when Ottinger became the next United States Senator from New York he would reward me by recommending me for a federal judgeship.

The victory was not long-lived. The Conservative Party appealed to my old appellate court. Some of the judges I had clerked for were still there. It was a bitter-sweet homecoming because the court wrote a short memorandum decision reversing the lower court. It ruled that if the Conservation Party were allowed on the ballot, it would violate a provision in New York State's election law barring the adoption by a new party of an important and vital part of the name of an existing political party. Contrary to Justice Mahoney's view, the intermediate appellate court believed that his decision "would defeat the manifest purpose" of the statute "to prevent all possibility of confusion in the minds of the voters in connection with the election machinery."

I immediately appealed. The issue would now be settled by the state's high court. The political stakes were so high that the Conservative Party pulled out all of the stops and retained a former judge of the Court, John Van Voorhis, to argue against me. Three of his former colleagues were still on the bench—Chief Judge Fuld and Judges Burke and Bergan. Presumably because a sufficient period of time had passed since I had worked with Judge Bergan at the Constitutional Convention, he did not disqualify himself as he had when I had argued the Sarisohn appeal.

On October 7, four of the seven members of the court adopted the opinion of the appellate division. Ironically, none of ex-Judge Van Voorhis' three former colleagues voted for him, but I had lost by the barest 4-3 vote. There would be no Conservation Party line on the ballot.

The election the following month was a shocker. Aided by the

Liberal Party line, the Republican candidate pulled enough votes that would normally have gone to Ottinger to allow the Conservative Party candidate to win in a breathtakingly tight race. It would be the only time that New York would have a Conservative United States Senator. The vote was so close that Ottinger undoubtedly would have won if he had had the Conservation Party second line. I never heard from him. I guess he was in no mood to thank me for my failed efforts. My thoughts of being a young federal court judge went out the window.

Ottinger would again become a congressman, in 1975, and was reelected four more times, retiring from Congress in 1985. He then became a professor at Pace Law School, founded an environmental program there, and served as the law school's dean from 1994 to 1999. In the meantime, I returned to the Suffolk outposts.

* * *

On May 13, 1971, Robert Clayton came back into my life. I got a telephone call that morning from a Maurice Brill, who told me that he had been assigned by Judge Bartels of the federal district court in Brooklyn to represent Clayton on his habeas petition. He recounted for me that the judge had decided after reading the appellate briefs which I had written that Clayton should be given a federal habeas hearing. The real reason he called, however, was to tell me that Judge Bartels had just filed a lengthy decision holding that Clayton's confession was indeed involuntary. The judge gave the government 30 days to retry him without the confession—a highly unlikely event 18 years after his conviction—or set him free. Mr. Brill told me that Judge Bartel's decision drew from the testimony that I had elicited from the witnesses who testified at the state hearing before Judge Stark, in addition to his cross-examination of the police in the habeas hearing. I could not wait to read the decision. It undoubtedly would be a great testament to the viability of the great writ of habeas corpus.

The history and origins of the writ trace back to the Magna Carta—over 800 years ago. In 1679 the Brits codified it by enacting the Habeas Corpus Act. Writing at that time, the great British commentator, Blackstone, described the Act as the "stable bulwark of our liberties." It established procedures for issuing the writ and was the model upon which the habeas statutes of the 13 American Colonies were based. The essence of the writ was to ensure that a person in custody had the right to challenge the legality of the loss of his freedom. It stands today as a staple of our Constitution. In its present statutory form it sets forth procedures for anyone in custody to come to federal court to claim that his constitutional rights had been violated, such as being convicted based upon a forced confession. This means that someone who was in state custody, such as Clayton, could have a second bite of the apple. He could lose in the state courts and then bring a habeas proceeding in federal court challenging his conviction on constitutional grounds. The federal judiciary was, therefore, the final arbiter to ensure that the states did not violate the Constitution.

In practice, federal habeas relief was rarely granted. Where the highest state court had passed upon the constitutional claims of a defendant prosecuted in the state system, the federal courts would almost always defer to its decision. The latest statistics show that habeas petitions challenging a state court conviction were denied 99% of the time.

The odds, therefore, that Clayton would be able to get his conviction overturned in the federal court were negligible. To make matters worse, Judge Bartels, to whom the habeas petition was randomly assigned, had the reputation of being one of the toughest judges on the federal bench in criminal cases. He had been a judge for many years. I do not believe that he had ever granted a habeas petition before.

In his decision, Judge Bartels first acknowledged that he did indeed rely in part on the testimony that was adduced at the hearing before Judge Stark. After a review of all of the evidence before him, he concluded that the facts revealed "a clear pattern of police dominance and psychological coercion which rendered the resultant confessions inadmissible." He recounted in detail how Clayton was

65

deprived of sleep and food and was subject to endless hours of interrogation, commenting that "[t]he continual questioning of Clayton
over the course of two and a half days' custody must have had a
substantial effect in eroding his will to resist." He was also critical
of the fact that Judge Stark prevented me from eliciting "whether
Clayton had been advised of his right to counsel and his right to
remain silent." He determined that during the 55 hours that
Clayton was in custody prior to confessing, he was never given these
rights which, "in view of other substantial evidence that actual coercion was exerted to overcome Clayton's will, raised a question as
to the validity of the ultimate determination of voluntariness by
the State Court."

The government was not happy and appealed to the Circuit Court
of Appeals. Maurice Brill was not an appellate lawyer and thought
that I should handle the appeal. I agreed, and was formally assigned to represent Clayton before the intermediate federal appellate court. The court heard oral argument on October 8, 1971, and
reserved decision. I anxiously waited, as the days passed, for the
court to decide whether it would agree with Judge Bartels that
Clayton's confession was coerced.

* * *

In the meantime, my partner, Dominic, decided to challenge the
state Democratic leadership, which had scheduled a special meeting of the New York State Democratic Committee for Tuesday,
December 28, 1971, to select a new state Democratic Party chairman to replace John J. Burns, who had submitted his resignation.
The reigning bosses, led by Meade Esposito, the powerful Brooklyn
Democratic boss, had settled on the Erie County chairman, Joseph
Crangle, as the putative new state leader. Nevertheless, there was
a lot of infighting going on, and a significant number of dissident
committeemen, unhappy with the way that the party had been controlled by the bosses, wanted Dominic to run against Crangle. In
order to mount an effective challenge, they would need some time
to gather their forces and spread the word. Knowing this, the bosses
called the meeting on short notice. Moreover, to keep the opposition

from showing up in significant numbers, they intentionally scheduled it during the last week of the year when many of the disenchanted committeemen might not be able to come because of previously scheduled vacation plans.

Dominic and I hatched a plan to stop the meeting, which was scheduled to be held in Manhattan at 2 p.m. We would try to get a Suffolk County supreme court justice to issue an injunction. Dominic would be the plaintiff; I would be his lawyer. I would argue that the party's rules did not specifically authorize a special meeting for the purpose of selecting a new chairman to fill a vacancy by reason of resignation, and that, in any event, special meetings could only be called by the chairman at the request of at least one-sixth of the committeemen. I would contend that the vacancy would have to be filled under Robert's Rules of Order, which meant that the first vice chairman would fill the void for the unexpired term. This would make Mae Gurevich, who was a Baranello supporter, the interim chairman.

Timing was key. I quickly prepared a set of legal papers and prevailed upon Justice Frank DeLuca to set a court hearing for the day before Christmas to determine whether the special meeting should be held. Justice DeLuca was the only Suffolk Supreme Court judge that I could find—the others were on Christmas vacation. As luck would have it, he was the only Democrat on the Suffolk Supreme Court bench at that time. Dominic had helped engineer a cross-endorsement with the Conservative Party that narrowly enabled DeLuca to beat the Republican candidate.

The hearing would be held at the Suffolk County Courthouse 90 miles from New York City. I was required to serve the legal papers on Chairman Burns two days before the hearing in order to give the party leadership the opportunity to be heard. Meade Esposito sent Monroe Goldwater, a prominent Manhattan lawyer, to represent the party establishment. He was the party's legal beagle and had been the chairman of the New York State Democratic Law Committee since 1957. He was old and crotchety, clearly annoyed that he had to be dragged out to the Suffolk boondocks to deal with this.

At the hearing, Goldwater condescendingly argued that the one-sixth requirement was irrelevant because it was "just to protect minorities, so they can have their say." More remarkable was his chauvinistic dismissal of Mae Gurevich as fit to be the party chairman. He told Justice DeLuca that "from time immemorial the first vice chairman was a lady and was chairman of the women's division;" she was "never selected as a potential leader of the party." Indeed, there had never been a female chairman. Goldwater also ridiculed the venerable Roberts Rules of Order, declaring: "We have no room for Mr. Roberts and his generalities."

Justice DeLuca came down with his decision on Monday, the day before the scheduled meeting. He enjoined it. The judge agreed that the party's rules had no provision for filling a vacancy caused by the resignation of the chairman. As for Roberts Rules of Order, he held that they would control because the party's rules specifically provided that they would apply "in all cases not provided for by law or by the rules." In response to Goldwater's contention that it was never envisioned that a woman as first vice chairman would ascend to the leadership, Justice DeLuca noted that "while this contention may smack of male chauvinism, it is important to note that such a position finds no support in the rules themselves." Because of Justice DeLuca's decision, Mae Gurevich would become the first female leader of the state Democratic Party.

We had won—or so we thought. The appellate division was not sitting that week. The judges were on Christmas break. There was no way that Justice DeLuca's decision could be reversed before the next day. While Dominic and I were celebrating our coup d'état, Goldwater called me late Monday afternoon to tell me that the appellate court would be convening for a special session on Tuesday morning for the sole purpose of hearing his appeal. How he managed to do this flabbergasted us.

I dutifully appeared at the appellate division courthouse in Brooklyn the next day for the hanging. At that time there were 10 judges on the appellate court. It was necessary to have a minimum of four to hear an appeal. The four judges who showed up were led by the acting presiding judge, Vito Martuscello, who had been supported by Meade Esposito for his judgeship.

I gave it the good old college try at oral argument, but the judges sat impassively. They did not ask a single question of either me or Goldwater. Within an hour they handed down a one-paragraph decision reversing Justice DeLuca. It conclusorily stated that the special meeting was legally called because it squared with the "intent and purpose of the Rules of the State Committee."

As I was walking out of the courtroom, I asked Monroe Goldwater how he had managed to pull this off. He smiled smugly and told me that he simply called Meade up, who prevailed upon the judges—three of whom were organization Democrats—to interrupt their vacations so that justice could be done.

Joe Crangle was elected as the new New York State Democratic Party Chairman that afternoon. All was not lost, however. Dominic Baranello was now a principal player on the state Democratic level and would become the chairman a few years later. However, it would be many years before a woman, Judith Hope, cracked the old boys' network and would be elected as the first female to lead the state Democratic Party.

* * *

The following month, on January 17, 1972, the Circuit Court of Appeals unanimously affirmed Judge Bartel's decision. It was a great way to begin the new year. Judge Zampano, writing the opinion for the court, stated that "it is apparent that [Clayton's] lack of education and knowledge of his rights coupled with the circumstances of prolonged custody and repeated periods of questioning by trained interrogators convinced [Clayton] that 'the police wanted answers and were determined to get them.'" He concluded, therefore, that there was

little doubt that [Clayton] was under tremendous psychological strain and physical discomfort. The only way obvious to him to reduce these coercive influences was to do and say what the police demanded of him. Under these circumstances, we conclude that the findings of the District Court that [Clayton's] will was eroded and that the confession was a result of a pattern of police dominance and coercion were not erroneous.

The government was stubbornly not going to give up and petitioned the United States Supreme Court to allow it to appeal. Clayton remained in jail. Six months would go by until the high court decided that it would not hear the case. In the meantime, faced with the realistic probability that the Supreme Court would not intervene, the Suffolk County District Attorney offered me a deal that Clayton presumably could not refuse to take. All he need do to gain his immediate freedom, and avoid a retrial, was to plead to a reduced charge of manslaughter. The time that Clayton had been in jail would satisfy the punishment for that lesser crime.

I immediately arranged to have Clayton brought down to the local Suffolk County jail from his prison in upstate New York to tell him the good news: After going through a brief court formality to change his plea, the murder conviction would be nullified, and he would walk out of the courtroom a free man.

When I came to the jail to tell him this, however, I was astonished by his response. It was the first time that I had seen him since the hearing before Judge Stark five years ago. He was a tall, thin, well-spoken man who was now in his early fifties. He spoke in a respectful, dignified, reflective manner, hardly what I would expect from someone who had been in jail for the last two decades. He was a proud, intelligent man. As best as I can remember, this is what he said: "Mr. Block, I was a troubled man when I came north in the early '50s to try to make some money as a migrant laborer. I had had too much to drink when I got into that fight. I never meant to harm anyone. But I have been in jail a long time and have been institutionalized. I learned to read and write well. I have acclimated myself to life in jail, and I can function well there. I do not think that I can make it in the outside world as a convicted felon for manslaughter."

I could not believe that he was serious, but after talking to him for the next hour, he convinced me that he would absolutely prefer to stay in jail if his murder conviction would not unconditionally be vitiated. I walked over to the county courthouse and reported this to the D.A. and to Suffolk County Court Judge Pierre Lundberg, who was the Judge assigned to now handle the case. We all agreed that we needed some time to decide what to do. I told the judge that in the meantime I would probably ask that Clayton be granted bail. The judge said that he would think about it but wanted me to make a formal application and assure him that Clayton would not be a danger to society if he were set free while everyone was trying to figure things out.

I had heard about the Fortune Society. It was a privately funded organization devoted to rehabilitating ex-cons. It found housing and jobs for them and provided mental health services, such as one-to-one and group counseling sessions. It did not take just anyone under its wing; only those whom it believed would be good rehabilitative prospects. It prided itself on its success; very few of its past criminals ever returned to jail.

I met with the head of the Fortune Society, David Rothenberg, and told him all about Clayton. He was fascinated and agreed to help. Armed with an affidavit from him that the Fortune Society would accept Clayton, I returned to Judge Lundberg with a formal bail application. He set him free. The only condition which the judge imposed was that Clayton had to remain with the Fortune Society and abide by its rules while the D.A. decided whether to retry him or dismiss the case in its entirety.

The next day I picked up Clayton at the local jail to drive him to the Fortune Society in Manhattan. He was dressed to the nines. Somehow he had managed to find a handsome camel-hair overcoat; he had on a freshly pressed pin-striped suit with a starched white shirt and black and white tie; his black shoes were immaculately shined. On the way to the City, I stopped at my home in Port Jefferson; after hearing about the case throughout the years, Cooky wanted to meet him. Our weekly housekeeper, Jane Sadowski, was there on that day. As she saw me walk into the house with this tall, elegantly attired man, she told him that he looked like the lawyer and that Mr. Block looked like he was the one who just got out of jail.

The case got a huge amount of press coverage. It was a compelling human interest story. The newspapers recounted how Clayton had been in jail for all those years because the Suffolk County police coerced him to confess even though he had repeatedly asserted his innocence. They wrote about how Clayton would prefer to live out his life in jail rather than try to make it in the outside world as a convicted felon.

A couple of months later I appeared before Judge Lundberg and asked him to unconditionally dismiss the case because the District Attorney was dragging his heels on deciding whether to retry Clayton. I was disappointed when the D.A. then told Judge Lundberg that he had decided that he did indeed wish to retry him. A heated argument took place between me and the D.A. during which I recounted Clayton's plight as well as the positive nature of his rehabilitation since he had been released on bail; the Fortune Society had gotten him a job and a place to live and was pleased with the way that he was adjusting to his new-found freedom.

Judge Lundberg determined that a retrial was technically timely but, acting on his own initiative, nonetheless dismissed the case in the "interests of justice." In doing so, he found an old statute dating back to 1881 that was still on the books which authorized a court to dismiss a case for that nebulous reason. In doing so, Judge Lundberg simply concluded that the interests of justice would not be served by having a retrial 19 years after Clayton had been convicted.

The District Attorney appealed. He argued that never before in the annals of the law had a murder indictment been dismissed on a court's own motion, and in the absence of the D.A.'s consent, in the so-called interests of justice. The D.A. was correct. My research revealed that there were just a few old cases where a court had dismissed a case for that reason, and they only involved minor crimes and bungled prosecutions. None of them analyzed the precise factors which a court should consider in deciding whether an indictment should be dismissed for reasons of justice.

I was heartened by the oral argument before the appellate division. The judges asked the D.A. a lot of questions which indicated that they were sympathetic to Clayton's plight. On April 2, 1973, it handed down its decision. Justice Hopkins, writing for a unanimous court, first traced the history of the ancient interests of justice statute. He noted that it had been used sparingly, usually to dismiss an indictment "for the insufficiency of evidence before a grand jury," but that it had occasionally also "been employed to reach cases in which the court found for a variety of reasons that the ends of justice would be served by the termination of the prosecution." He concluded, therefore, that "the use of the statute depended only on principles of justice, not on the legal or factual merits of the charge or even on the guilt or innocence of the defendant." Thus, it could be invoked to dismiss even a murder indictment.

Recognizing that no court had previously laid down what factors should be considered in deciding whether a case should be dismissed in the interests of justice, Justice Hopkins then wrote that they should include: "(a) the nature of the crime, (b) the available evidence of guilt, (c) the prior record of the defendant, (d) the punishment already suffered by the defendant, (e) the purpose and effect of further punishment, (f) any prejudice resulting to the defendant by the passage of time and (g) the impact on the public interest of a dismissal of the indictment." Moreover, any judge contemplating such a dismissal would have to conduct a factual hearing, upon notice to the parties, to address these factors. Since Judge Lundberg had not done this, the case would have to be sent back to him to conduct New York State's first "interest of justice" hearing. However, Justice Hopkins noted, in conclusion, that:

> It may well be that the County Court will again conclude that the indictment should be dismissed in the furtherance of justice after giving deliberation to what the parties may offer on the remand. Certainly, we do not say that the court cannot reach such a conclu-

73

sion; and, indeed, the defendant's interest and the public interests may coincide to compel that conclusion. All that we now hold is that full opportunity should be afforded to the People and the defendant to provide the court with such evidence and arguments that they deem relevant to the issue.

At the hearing, I had a number of people testify about how well Clayton was doing since he got out of jail. In particular, David Rothenberg told Judge Lundberg that he was an inspiration to the other ex-cons at the Fortune Society. Perhaps the most compelling testimony came from the manager of the concession stand of the Harris Theatre in Midtown Manhattan; the Fortune Society had gotten Clayton a job there. His testimony tracked a letter he had previously written to me. In it he explained that Clayton was the night-shift man on the concession stand and praised him to the hilt: As he wrote:

> I have been in the concession business for a goodly length of time and I can safely lay claim to more than a mere passing acquaintance with the nature and requirements of the business. I can say, without reservation, that Bob Clayton is, without doubt, the finest all-around man it has ever been my good fortune to employ.
>
> In his capacity as night man he regularly handles and is responsible for considerable sums of money. He also handles and is responsible for a rather considerable inventory of candy, drinks, popcorn, frankfurters and ice cream. In none of this has there been the slightest indication of any but the most conscientious conduct on his part.
>
> Due to the manner in which the monies must be handled on a concession stand such as this, the opportunity, indeed the temptation for petty theft is ever present. Indeed one of the occupational hazards of the concession business is this matter of petty (and sometimes not so petty) theft of cash receipts by those working the stand. Few concessions are free of it and, as a matter of fact, most managers automatically allow for it as matter of course.
>
> Since the manager is, himself, directly responsible for any and all shortages and must make them up out of his own pocket, you can readily see why I lay emphasis on this phase of concession work.

Bob's record is spotless in this as well as all other respects, I am very happy to say.

He concluded his letter by writing that "[i]n the comparatively short time I have known Bob, I, like everyone he comes into contact with, have come to greatly admire and respect this quite remarkable man."

On May 29, 1973, Judge Lundberg once again dismissed the indictment in the interests of justice. The D.A. did not appeal, and Bob Clayton was a free man—with no strings attached.

I wrote an article about the *Clayton* case and, in particular, Justice Hopkins' unprecedented decision. I sent a draft to Judge Bergan, who was now retired from the Court of Appeals. He was a member of the board of editors of the *New York State Bar Journal* and thought that the article should be published in that magazine. He dropped me a note saying that "[t]he case opens up some new possibilities in the criminal law and some aspects of it, especially what is meant by the 'interests of justice,' are important to the whole profession."

In the article, which was published in the October 1973 edition of the *Journal*, I wrote that it took 92 years "before an appellate court chose to enunciate the substantive and procedural standards to be employed before a criminal indictment may be disposed of for reasons of 'justice,' rather than by the traditional standards of the defendant's guilt or innocence." I viewed the court's decision as serving notice "that the judiciary should always be mindful that the law must never lose its human aspect," and concluded:

It is thoroughly refreshing, therefore, to find an occasional reaffirmation, such as manifested by the *Clayton* case, that it is, after all, the principle of 'justice' which is the hallmark of our jurisprudence, and that the letter of the law is not the final word."

I sent a copy of the article to Justice Hopkins. He made me feel like a million bucks when he wrote back:

You were very kind to send me the article which you have written for the New York State Bar Journal on *People v. Clayton*. I enjoyed read-

75

ing your perceptive and thoughtful discussion. I must tell you that it was your argument and brief which prompted me to write as fully as I did in my opinion, and to that degree you are implicated in the opinion.

As assigned counsel for handling the *Clayton* hearing I was paid $515 by Suffolk County, but the feeling of professional and personal satisfaction was priceless. Today, Clayton Hearings are an integral part of the criminal law in New York State.

* * *

While I was in the throes of the last stages of the *Clayton* case, the state legislature had created two new supreme court judgeships for Suffolk County. Suffolk's population was growing rapidly, and more judges were needed. While Suffolk was still heavily Republican—and a Democrat still did not have a chance to be elected to any Suffolk judgeship just running on the Democratic line—the state legislature was split: the Senate was Republican; the Assembly was Democratic. The upshot was that Dominic flexed his political muscles and prevailed upon the Democratic Assembly to insist that before it would vote for the new judgeships the Suffolk Republican Party would have to agree to a cross-endorsement deal to ensure that one would go to a Democrat. The voting public would have no choice, but at least there would now be another Democrat on the Suffolk bench to join Justice DeLuca.

While the public elected most of its judges in New York State, in counties where one of the political parties dominated the political landscape—like the Republican party in Suffolk and the Democratic Party in New York City—the only guaranteed way to get some political balance on the bench was for the New York State Senate and Assembly to engage in this type of political blackmail as the quid pro quo for creating additional judgeships. However, the voters were dupes; the party bosses picked the judges, and the elections were as a practical matter a sham.

Dominic now had the opportunity to pick the first Democrat who would be cross-endorsed by the Republican Party for a Suffolk

County judgeship—and guaranteed election. The party bosses agreed, however, that their candidates would appear before the Suffolk County Bar Association's Judiciary Committee to pass upon their qualifications. While the bosses were not bound by the committee's finding and were free to select a candidate found unqualified by the bar association, Dominic—to his credit—told the association that he would not do that.

Dominic asked me to go before the judiciary committee. I was surprised. I was not yet 40 and would become a judge of the Suffolk County Supreme Court. While a judicial career surely had its appeal, I never thought a judgeship would ever come my way on the state level if I did not become one of Zeidler's reindeer. Moreover, since Ottinger lost, I could not then envision ever being recommended to the President by a United States Senator for a federal judicial appointment, especially since no one from Suffolk County had ever been appointed to the federal bench in the history of the county.

When I appeared before the Suffolk Bar Association's Judiciary Committee, its members all assumed that Dominic had decided that he would give the judgeship to his partner. Although I was found qualified, this was not to be. To my surprise, and embarrassment, he tapped Leon Lazer, an active Democratic lawyer from the Town of Huntington. It was an appropriate political decision since the town had recently elected its first Democratic supervisor and the town's Democratic Party was the most powerful and best organized in the county. It was in Dominic's best interests not to ruffle its feathers.

I told Dominic that I could understand his decision to put Leon on the bench, especially since he was an outstanding and highly respected lawyer, but I could not understand why he did not level with me and made me a political pawn. I started to wonder whether I could remain his partner. I was told by a trusted colleague from Huntington that Dominic would never let me go because I was too valuable to him economically. The promise of our partnership was that Dominic would use his political connections to cultivate a lot of business and I would run the legal shop. Stuart Namm would be the worker bee. However, Dominic got totally preoccupied with his political world. While he was a vibrant and dynamic political leader, he did not generate his fair share of legal business or do any significant amount of the legal work. I brought in more than 50% of the business, and Stuart and I did most all of the legal work. It was foolhardy for me to continue as an equal one-third partner.

The separation was cordial. I think that somewhere in the inner recesses of his mind Dominic realized that I had to leave. Stuart thought that Dominic would somehow reward him if he stayed with him. He was right. Dominic let him run the next year for a local district court judgeship and, miraculously, he won. It was during the Watergate scandal, and some Democrats got elected in Suffolk County. Stuart won by 55 votes.

* * *

I moved into a small office on the top floor of the office building and, once again, was a solo practitioner. In June 1974, after I was done with the *Clayton* case, Dominic came to talk to me. He needed a candidate to run for Suffolk County District Attorney and asked me to do it. He told me that he had been trying to get the Conservative Party to cross-endorse Henry O'Brien, an affable Irish Democrat, but the deal fell through. Henry was not stupid; he would not run without the Conservative Party support. I told Dominic that I was not interested in being the Democratic Party patsy—no Democrat had ever been elected Suffolk D.A.—but said that I would do so if he was able to get the Conservative line for me. The Conservative Party was becoming the balance of power in Suffolk County. It was now the tail that wagged the dog. The Republican Party had to pay dearly to get its support by giving up judgeships, county legislators, and lots of patronage. The Conservative Party's cross-endorsement of Justice DeLuca put him on the bench, and its cross-endorsement of a Democrat for District Attorney would be a nightmare for the Republican Party. If it lost its grip on the D.A.'s job, indictments of its political leaders who were handing out valuable zoning changes in exchange for hefty political contributions were likely to follow.

Dominic did not share with me the reasons why he could not broker a deal with the Conservative Party. He just told me that he doubted if he could get it to support me since it was unlikely that it would support a Jewish candidate. I told him that I was not willing to be a sacrificial lamb.

Days later Dominic went to Niagara Falls to nominate Hugh Carey for governor. He bet on the right horse. Carey won the ensuing state Democratic primary against Howard Samuels—who was the bosses' choice—and beat the Republican gubernatorial candidate, Malcolm Wilson, to become the first Democratic New York State governor in 17 years. He rewarded Dominic for not supporting the bosses' candidate by making him the state Democratic Party leader.

The day before Dominic nominated Carey, I ran into Marty Burgess in the little coffee shop in the county courthouse in Riverhead. I had just settled a small automobile accident case and started to chat with him. Marty was a lawyer who represented insurance companies. He also was the chairman of the Suffolk County Conservative Party. Over the years I had settled a number of negligence cases with him. I liked him a lot. He was always a straight shooter, and we got along well with each other. We started to talk politics. He told me that he thought that Dominic was not really serious about working out a deal with the Conservative Party. He also told me that he could not broker a deal with the Republican Party because it thought that the Conservative Party was getting too greedy in its demands.

I then told Marty that Dominic had asked me to run but had said that the Conservative Party would not support me because I was Jewish. Marty was astonished. His Irish face turned beet red. He told me that he was an ardent supporter of Israel and was furious that anyone could think that he or his party was anti-Semitic. The Conservative Party's convention was the next night, and he wanted me to be its D.A. candidate. Dominic presumably would still give me the Democratic nomination, and the Republican Party would get its comeuppance. I told Marty that I was hardly a conservative,

79

but wresting the powerful office of Suffolk County District Attorney from the grip of the Republican Party was paramount. I reasoned that since the D.A. was not a legislative office, I would have no ideological problem being the candidate for the Democratic and Conservative Parties. I would run the office in a totally nonpolitical professional fashion just like the eminent D.A. Democrat from Manhattan, Frank Hogan, who prided himself on being returned to office for decades as the unanimous candidate of all the political parties, including the Conservative Party.

I would not tell Dominic. I thought that he would be preoccupied with Carey and that I would surprise him. I was not sure what his reaction would be but figured that he would be practical and support me since we could win. After all, he was willing to let me be the Democratic candidate.

I could not have been more wrong. I got the Conservative Party nomination while Dominic was delivering a fiery nominating speech for Carey. The next day he flew back in a rage. I figured that he might be annoyed that I did this behind his back but never thought that he would be that angry. The first thing he did was to tell O'Brien that he had to be the Democratic D.A. candidate. I was dismayed. I could not understand why Dominic would be willing to commit political suicide and hand the D.A. election to the Republican Party on a silver platter. I would eventually find out.

Since I could not win with only the Conservative Party line, I had no choice but to run against O'Brien in a primary. It was now an all-out war. The Democratic Party Executive Committee was also puzzled. They were my friends and could not understand why Dominic was doing this. Dominic made it personal, telling all of the Democratic committeemen that they had to do everything in their power to beat me; they simply had to do this for him—without question. Most followed like sheep, but many thought that Dominic was being unrealistically vengeful and would not go along. The campaign was ugly, but Dominic marshaled enough of his forces to narrowly beat me. I was able to raise a sufficient amount of money to mount a credible campaign, but Dominic pulled out all of the stops and seemed to have unlimited funds to fight me with.

Ironically, Henry O'Brien narrowly upset the Republican candidate and became Suffolk County's first Democratic District Attorney. The margin of difference was the vote that I pulled on the Conservative line; he would not have won otherwise.

Years later Buzz Schwenk stopped by my office. He was the Suffolk County Republican Party Chairman when I ran for D.A. He had since left the political world to fully devote his time to his milk business. I always liked him, and I think that he liked me, too. For whatever reason he told me what happened the night that I got the Conservative Party nomination. He had called Dominic in Albany and accused him of being a double-crosser. He and Dominic had decided that neither party would work a cross-endorsement deal with the Conservative Party. It was getting too big for its britches, and it was time to put a stop to letting them play one party against the other. While Dominic would not win the D.A. race, he would get a number of bipartisan judgeships in the future as his reward, in addition to a fair amount of patronage appointments in various Republican-controlled county agencies.

Schwenk told me that Dominic was able to convince him that he had nothing to do with my nomination by the Conservative Party and that he would do everything that he could to beat me in the primary. Schwenk, in turn, told Dominic that the Republican Party would secretly help him. To my astonishment he showed me two cashed $5,000 checks made payable to the Democratic Party which he told me that he gave to Dominic to help him finance his campaign against me. The Republican Party had joined forces with Dominic to beat me in the Democratic primary.

Before I learned this, I had one other misadventure with Dominic. He was a complex person, possessed of an inordinate intellect but a mordant view of the human condition. When I was his partner, I would invariably playfully ask him every day how he felt, knowing that his response would always be: "How good can you feel knowing that you're on a conveyor belt?" I think that he knew down deep that he had not been level with me throughout our relationship and in his own way wanted to make amends. Two years after the D.A. fiasco, he told me that he had a bipartisan deal for a local Town of Brookhaven district court judgeship and offered it to me. I do not know what I was drinking that day, but I told him that I would take it. The next day he told me that the Town Democratic leader, Burt Friedman, had promised it to someone else and that he felt that it would be politically inappropriate to override him. How fortunate for me. In retrospect I would have been miserable just handling misdemeanors and small commercial cases. More significantly, it would have buried me in the lowest level of the local judicial world and as a practical matter would have ruled out any chances that I could someday become a different district court judge.

Schwenk's revelations soured me against politics. I would be content with building up my law practice and confine my extracurricular energies to becoming active in the Suffolk County Bar Association.

* * *

On December 20, 1974, New York's high court came down with its decision in a sex scandal case that I had been handling during the last year for Gary Goldin, who was a 28-year-old guidance counselor at a local high school. Gary had been brought up on disciplinary charges by the school district for having an affair with an 18-year-old former counselee. He was charged with sleeping with her at her home during the summer when her parents were away after she had just graduated. The school did not think that this was an appropriate graduation present. It assumed that the affair must have been going on when Goldin was her guidance counselor. When Goldin was questioned by the school officials, he flat-out denied the charge; therefore, they also charged him with lying to them.

The school wanted to fire Goldin, but because he was tenured, he had the right to a hearing before an internal hearing panel. We went to court to enjoin the hearing, claiming—without admitting—

that even if the charges were true, Goldin's constitutional rights to privacy and freedom of association "prevent[ed] inquiry or punishment for his private, consensual sexual acts with a former student."

Justice DiPaola of the Suffolk County Supreme Court agreed because there was no "allegation or proof before the court that the plaintiff's consensual exploits with his former pupil on the night of August 8 and the morning of August 9 in the privacy of her home were the continuation or culmination of an association commenced or an influence exercised while the plaintiff and the young lady maintained the relationship of teacher and pupil." He reasoned that "[t]he private association of a teacher with a member of the opposite sex, is not by itself the concern of the [school district] except on a showing not here made that it may interfere with his responsibilities to his students and his ability to teach."

The judge would not, however, dismiss the lying charge. The hearing could go forward on that single issue. Even if proven, however, it could only establish that Goldin did not tell the truth when he denied being with his ex-student on the night in question. However, since the other charge had been dismissed, the hearing could not delve into whether there was any sex between them when he was her guidance counselor. While Goldin could be subject to some form of discipline for lying about being in his former student's home, it could not warrant firing him. His job and career had been saved.

There was one collateral aspect of the case that was before the court. When the school district filed the charges, it simultaneously suspended Goldin without pay. I had argued that it was illegal to strip him of his salary while the proceeding against him was pending. Justice DiPaola disagreed because he "anticipated" that the hearing would proceed "expeditiously."

Instead of holding the hearing without the right to question Goldin about his behavior while he was the ex-student's guidance counselor, the school district appealed to the appellate division. We cross-appealed, claiming that the lying charge should also be dismissed and that, in any event, Goldin could not remain suspended without pay. On July 22, 1974, the majority of the appellate judges held that "there was no basis, constitutional or otherwise, for barring a hearing and further proceedings on the first charge." While acknowledging that there was no specific charge that Goldin had slept with the student while she was his counselee, it reasoned that if it was established at the hearing that he had gone to bed with her just a few months after she had graduated, "[s]uch conduct might be susceptible to the presumption that the intimate relationship did not develop overnight." If so, the incident "conceivably could so upset the community as to undermine the confidence of students and parents of students who now seek plaintiff's guidance."

One justice dissented. Justice Brennan believed that there was "no warrant for permitting an inquiry for the avowed purpose of establishing a meretricious relationship between the teacher and the young lady involved while she was a student under his guidance." He reasoned that such an inquiry "would be an exercise in futility, since it is apparent that proof of such a prior relationship is not available to the [school district] or it most certainly would have been the subject of another and separate charge."

All of the judges agreed that the hearing could explore whether Goldin had lied, but they split again on the back pay issue. The same majority which held that the school could go forward on the sex charge held, however, that it could not suspend Goldin without pay for more than 30 days. Once again Justice Brennan broke ranks, believing that the school had to pay Goldin all of his past and future salary while the hearing was pending.

Everyone appealed to the state's high court. I did not pursue the argument that a hearing was not warranted on the charge that Goldin had lied. I concluded that it was a loser and did not want to distract the Court of Appeals from focusing on the issue that a hearing on the sex charge would violate Goldin's constitutional rights, as well as on the pay suspension issue.

By the time of oral argument, the sex aspect of the case had gotten a lot of press. Word of the affair was the talk of the town. In addition, the issue of whether teachers brought up on disciplinary charges could be suspended without pay pending the conclusion of disciplinary hearings became a cause célèbre for the New York State Teachers' Association because these hearings would often not be concluded for many months and the teachers would be financially hung out to dry in the meantime.

All of the seven judges of the state's high court agreed that there was no constitutional impediment to delving into Goldin's relationship with the young woman when he was her guidance counselor. They recognized, as had Justice Brennan, "that the charge as phrased did not explicitly link the alleged conduct with the school-year performance of the teacher's responsibilities as guidance counselor." However, they echoed the rationale of the majority of the appellate division in writing that "[n]onetheless, the period of time since the former student was graduated (less than two summer months) was so short that, without clear evidence of no prior association, the availability of practical, realistic inferences is such as to make judicial foreclosure of further inquiry inappropriate, particularly at the threshold, prehearing state of the disciplinary proceedings."

As to whether the school district could withhold paying Goldin pending final resolution of the hearing, the judges split in Goldin's favor by the barest 4-3 vote. Thus, although the hearing would go forward, Goldin would be entitled to receive all of the pay that had been withheld from him since he was suspended as well as his future salary until the hearing was concluded.

Gary Goldin never subjected himself to a hearing. After the Court of Appeals came down with its decision, he got a new job heading up a unit in a psych hospital—for more money—and resigned before the hearing was scheduled. The school district never had the chance to try to prove that where there was smoke there had to be fire. Moreover, it had to pay Goldin over $80,000 in back pay.

Because teachers in New York State could never again be suspended without pay—and deprived of the financial means to support themselves during the pendency of disciplinary proceedings—

the New York State Teachers' Association hailed the *Goldin* case as a landmark decision for teachers' rights.

As for Gary Goldin, several months later he dropped by my office to introduce me to his new girlfriend. She seemed like a pleasant lady, but at 48 she was 20 years older than him—and not nearly as good-looking as his former teenage student. I guess that he could never be accused of age discrimination in his love life.

* * *

I had two other cases during the rest of the '70s that stand out after all of these years. One was a murder trial. The grand jury had indicted Ronald Faines, James Culpepper, and Ira Lee Marsh for holding up a liquor store. The owner was shot to death. The defendants were indigent, and the Suffolk County Court assigned separate counsel to represent them. I got Faines. He was a mean-looking, heavy-set career criminal who had guilt written all over his face. Even though he and his two codefendants were indicted together, they could not be tried together because Ira Lee had given a written confession which implicated the other two. In it he said that he was only the driver and pinned the blame for the murder on his two buddies. According to Marsh, Faines took the money out of the cash register and Culpepper did the shooting. He said that he was innocent because he never knew that Culpepper would do that.

If Marsh had gone to law school instead of dropping out of high school, he would have learned about the law of felony murder. Those who join together to commit a felony are all in the soup together. They are each equally responsible for the criminal misdeeds of their cohorts. Thus, even though Marsh was in his car while the murder was unfolding, he could also be prosecuted for the murder. Because he did not know this, he foolishly thought that he was asserting his innocence when he said that he had only driven his friends to the liquor store and fingered them as the culprits.

In a seminal Supreme Court case, the high court of the land had made it clear that if a defendant's confession had implicated codefendants in the commission of a crime, they could not be tried together because while the confession could be introduced into evidence against the one who confessed, it would be constitutionally impermissible to also use it as evidence against the others. Faines, Culpepper, and Marsh would have to receive separate trials before three different juries.

The trials took place during January, February, and March of 1976. Poor Ed Flaherty, the Suffolk County Assistant D.A. assigned to handle the cases, had to try them all back-to-back. Marsh was the first batter up. Faced with his confession, there was little that his lawyer could do. Even though Ira Lee was only the driver, he was convicted of felony murder and sentenced to 25 to life.

I thought that Faines was also a cooked goose. His fingerprints were all over the cash register, and the poor liquor store owner's body was sprawled in front of the counter. However, for reasons which I have a hard time fathoming to this day, the jury only convicted him of robbery. My best guess is that it concluded that Culpepper was the killer but did not fully comprehend the law of felony murder. Ronnie was ecstatic. He had beaten the murder rap. He got out of jail after doing 10 years for the robbery.

Culpepper was the last to be tried. Amazingly, he was acquitted. There were no fingerprints of his in the store. While Ed Flaherty had an eyewitness testify that he saw someone looking like Culpepper in the store, Culpepper's lawyer, Vince Berger, did a terrific job of casting doubt as to the reliability of the testimony. The jury never heard Marsh's confession and statement that Culpepper was the shooter. It apparently had reasonable doubt as to whether Culpepper was anywhere in sight.

The improbable upshot of it all was that the only one convicted of murder never was in the store. It was a poignant example of the realities of our criminal system of justice.

* * *

The second case was a lulu. In 1973 a mother, father and four of their six children were found brutally murdered in their home in

87

Amityville, a small village in the western part of Suffolk County. One of the surviving children, Ronald DeFeo, was tried and convicted for the murders. He had claimed that the house was haunted and that paranormal events were responsible for his family's misfortune. His fanciful story captured the interest of George and Kathy Lutz, who sought to capitalize on all of this by buying the DeFeo house and spinning tall tales about how the house was indeed haunted. Out of this came a bestseller book and hit movie, *The Amityville Horror,* which were billed as true stories. Over 10,000,000 copies of the book were sold, and the movie made millions. They spawned an Amityville Horror cottage industry: house tours, TV shows, lots of magazine articles, eight more movies, and many more books.

The Lutzes moved into the house with their three children on December 19, 1975, 13 months after the murders. They moved out two years later, just long enough to collect their horror tales. For example, they told of hearing voices and a German marching band and of seeing blood dripping from the walls and a demon with half of his head ripped off. Kathy said that she levitated two feet off of her bed. George said that he saw Kathy transformed into a 90-year-old woman with saliva dripping from her toothless mouth. After they moved out, they went to live with Kathy's mother, where they saw "green slime coming up the staircase toward them."

In the meantime, Billy Weber thought that he would financially capitalize on being DeFeo's assigned counsel—which did not pay him very much—and he and a legal colleague contributed to a number of articles which appeared in magazines like *Good Housekeeping*. In them they recounted stories that Weber claimed DeFeo had told him about the spooky things that happened when he lived there, as well as stories told to him by the Lutzes. He had met with them on a number of occasions. Unbeknownst to Weber, the Lutzes had entered into a book deal with a professional author, Jay Anson, and *the Amityville Horror* was on the verge of being published. The Lutzes thought that Weber's stories would take away from their book and sued him and his colleague in May 1977 for $4.5 million, claiming that they had no right to use their material.

The Amityville Horror was published three months later. Weber countersued for $2 million. He claimed that when he had met with the Lutzes he had shared in confidence the stories that DeFeo had told him and that the Lutzes had agreed that they would join forces with him for a book that would be written by a writer whom Weber had hired. Weber claimed, therefore, that the Lutzes had welched on their deal and that the Lutzes' book contained information that they could only have learned from him. The countersuit was, therefore, for breach of contract and fraud.

At first Weber represented himself. He had a high opinion of his legal talents and did not want to pay for a lawyer. He took the Lutzes' depositions and did all of the pre-trial work. Since he would be a witness at the trial, however, he needed a lawyer to try the case. He asked me if I would do it. Since he forgot to demand a jury trial, it would be a bench trial, meaning that a judge would decide the case. It would be tried in the New York Eastern District federal courthouse in Brooklyn. The case was in federal court because when plaintiffs and defendants reside in different states—Weber and his colleague were from New York and the Lutzes had moved to California—the party initiating the case can bring it in either state or federal court. It was in Brooklyn because at that time it housed the only federal courthouse in the Eastern District of New York (EDNY); cases like this one which emanated from Suffolk County would be tried there.

The case was randomly assigned to District Court Judge Jack Weinstein. Judge Weinstein was fast becoming a legendary judge. He was appointed in 1967 by President Johnson. He had been a distinguished professor at Columbia Law, and his multivolume treatise on evidence was considered the bible. He had pioneered the procedures for handling mass tort litigation and was renowned as a creative and inventive judge. He had his own unique, iconoclastic style for handling cases. In nonjury civil cases, he would preside by having the lawyers and witnesses sit with him around a large conference table in his courtroom. He was an imposing figure, tall and athletic. He was always polite and courteous to lawyers and witnesses alike, but you never knew what he was thinking and when he would pounce. No one messed with him. Little did I know that 15 years later I would become his colleague.

The challenge of trying this weird case before Judge Weinstein was too much to resist. It was tried over a two-week period in January 1979. The courtroom was packed each day. It was the judicial entertainment event of the year.

The trial was in keeping with the comedic nature of the case. Judge Weinstein quickly realized that this was not a remake of *Marbury v. Madison* but sat stone-faced as George Lutz, under oath, ticked off all of the phantasmagorical happenings. At one point, in his inimical way, the good judge joined in the fun. Lutz started to testify about how he had enlisted the services of a Father Pecorora to bless the house and how when the putative priest came he had said that he heard a voice say, "Get out of here," and quickly left. I objected because this was classic hearsay; Lutz could not testify about what Father Pecorora said because I could not cross-examine this missing person.

Judge Weinstein, of course, agreed but asked the Lutzes' lawyer if he knew where the Father was. The lawyer said that he probably was in California. Judge Weinstein ordered him to get him on the phone. A few minutes later, the lawyer reported that he was able to contact Father Pecorora in Los Angeles. Judge Weinstein brought the lawyers into his chambers and made the Lutzes' lawyer dial up Father Pecorora on his office speakerphone. When a voice boomed, "This is Father Pecorora," Judge Weinstein said, "Mr. Block, cross-examination."

To this day I have no idea who I was talking to. I doubt if it was Father Pecorora because no one, other than the Lutzes, ever claimed to have seen such a person. Judge Weinstein—as the esteemed expert on the rules of evidence—obviously knew that this was not the right way to question a missing person, but it was literally and figuratively in keeping with the spirit of the trial.

Ultimately Judge Weinstein tossed out the Lutzes' lawsuit. He simply ruled from the bench that "[b]ased on what I have heard it appears to me that to a large extent the book is a work of fiction, relying in a large part on the suggestions of Mr. Weber." The judge never passed upon Weber's countersuit. A few days later, while Weber was testifying, he commented that, "there is a very serious ethical question when lawyers become literary agents." I had observed during the trial that Judge Weinstein spent a good deal of time reading Drinker's seminal textbook on legal ethics and was fairly convinced that he was going to take Weber to the woodshed in a virulent written opinion. As his lawyer, I cautioned him that this might trigger disciplinary proceedings and that it might be in his best interest to bail out. The next day we were able to settle the counterclaim. A confidentiality agreement prevents me from disclosing the amount. Weber paid me a few thousand dollars, and I closed my file.

In October 2000, the History Channel marked the 25th anniversary of the *Amityville Horror* by broadcasting a two-part series, *The Haunting and Amityville: Horror or Hoax.* Commenting on the program, George Lutz, sticking to his guns, said, "I believe this has stayed alive for 25 years because it is a true story."

Debate as to its accuracy continues. It remains one of the most popular haunting accounts in American folklore. As for me, looking back, I realize that Judge Weinstein's instincts were right: A lawyer assigned to represent a criminal defendant should not try to use it as a commercial vehicle for making money. Although Weber did need a lawyer to defend him against the Lutzes' lawsuit, I was lured by the high profile nature of the case. I probably should not have represented him unless he dropped his counterclaim, but it was a lot of fun.

* * *

In the spring of that year I was nominated to be president of the Suffolk County Bar Association. When my son Neil—who has a witty and cynical sense of humor—learned that I would be running unopposed, he told me that since I had lost every race I ever ran in, he gave me a 50-50 chance of getting elected.

After I had my fill of local politics—and Dominic Baranello—I decided that the bar association would be a more productive way to render some public service. I was friends with Merton Reichler, a liberal arts professor at the State University of New York (SUNY) at Stony Brook, who thought that it would be a good thing for both the college and the association to join forces to offer continuing legal education courses. With the help of another SUNY professor and friend—Marshall Cohen—we put together a pilot program which was held on the campus. It was a success. Over 50 lawyers came. We soon followed up with a few more programs, and many more lawyers came. I was made chairman of the bar association's new continuing education committee. I was rewarded for my efforts by being made a director and then the vice president of the association.

At that time continuing education for lawyers was strictly voluntary. Curiously, it seemed as if only the best lawyers would show up. The ones who really needed it would be nowhere in sight. We were pioneers. Continuing education for lawyers was not in vogue. The Suffolk bar became leaders in the cause. Several years later, in 1997, the State of New York made it mandatory for lawyers to take 24 hours of legal education courses every two years. In the meantime, our continuing education committee was institutional-ized as the Suffolk Academy of Law. Today the academy is the financial and educational mainstay of the Suffolk Bar Association. It is one of the things that I am most proud of.

The presidency was a one-year term. I would hold office from June 1979 through May 1980. The first thing that I had to do was to appoint committee chairpersons. One of the committees was the civil rights committee. The existing chairman suggested that it be disbanded because it never did anything. I mentioned this to Tom Boyle, who was a tenant in the small office building that I had bought in the Town of Smithtown, and asked him if he would be willing to revitalize the moribund committee. Tom had been an active civil liberties lawyer—he had worked on a death penalty case in Mississippi—and I had a high regard for his passion for the cause of justice. He agreed, and we brainstormed what might be a good project to take on.

Soon the idea struck. During the last few years, the New York State Court of Appeals had thrown out a number of murder convictions from Suffolk County because they were coerced by the Suffolk police. I thought about Clayton and wondered whether anything had really changed since the courts ruled that his confession was involuntarily extracted from him. Tom and I would spearhead a reborn civil rights committee that would look into what was going on. We worked diligently throughout the rest of 1979 to flush out the facts. On January 28, 1980, the Suffolk County Bar Association rendered its *Police Brutality Report*. It was an auspicious way to start the next decade of my legal career.

Chapter
4

Practicing
The Eighties

Investigating allegations of police brutality was not the type of activity that was the usual cup of tea for the bar association. By its nature it was a conservative type of organization focused primarily on defending against public attacks on the legal establishment. It was basically reactive, not proactive. It had a board of directors which met monthly. It spent a lot of time dealing with its budget and planning dinners to honor prominent lawyers and judges. The board mostly resembled a debating society rather than an activist group bent on taking the lead in promoting needed changes to the legal order.

I wanted to try to change this during my presidency. Days after I took my oath of office, I read an article published in the *National Law Journal* titled, "When Suspects Are Abused; Allegations of Beatings, Forced Confessions in a N.Y. Suburb Are Widespread." It concluded that an "apparent pattern" of police beatings of suspects by members of the Suffolk County Police Department existed in Suffolk County. I wondered whether anything had changed since *Clayton*.

I was able to prevail upon the officers and directors of the bar association to delegate to Tom Boyle's newly constituted civil rights committee the task of examining the allegations of police brutality in Suffolk County and, specifically, to report on three main issues:

1)   Is there "validity" to the complaints of police brutality in Suffolk County that the *National Law Journal* article addresses, and, if so, do such complaints warrant further bar association activity?

2)   Are procedures presently followed by the Police Department, the District Attorney's Office, and the United States Attorney's Office adequate for rendering a proper, fair, and impartial determination of issues involving police brutality in Suffolk?

3)   What, if any, role can the bar association play in this area?

To draw attention to our mission and to gather the facts, Tom and I decided to conduct public hearings. Since we had no subpoena power, we wondered whether anyone would voluntarily come; the bar association had never done anything like this before. To our surprise, they did. During a two-day period, the committee took the testimony of a broad spectrum of interested parties. In addition to lawyers who had represented clients mistreated by the police, we heard from a representative from the D.A.'s Office, the president of the Suffolk Police Benevolent Association, the coordinator of the Black United Front, the author of the *National Law Journal* article, a spokesperson for the F.B.I., the head of the Suffolk County Legal Aid Society, representatives from the county's civil liberties union and economic opportunities council. We also took the testimony of the executive director and chairperson of the Suffolk County Human Rights Commission and the inspector of internal affairs of the Suffolk County Police Department.

As soon as it was issued, the 59-page *Police Brutality Report* created a firestorm. It pulled together in one document disturbing information from those who testified at the hearings. Amongst the most troubling were statistics that had been gathered since 1972 by the Suffolk County Human Rights Commission. They reflected that 75% of all police complaints funneled through the commission occurred in the areas containing the county's largest minority and poverty-level population. While blacks made up approximately 7% of the county's population, 50% of all complaints against members of the Suffolk County police were from black citizens. The commission also reported that of the 311 complaints that it had screened and referred to the police commissioner, 97% were returned as unfounded or without sufficient cause for any disciplinary proceeding. It concluded that the evidence indicated that police misconduct was a serious and continuing problem in Suffolk County and that the victims were "usually poor and powerless" or were "perceived in that light."

The *Police Brutality Report* also contained statistics supplied by the police department's internal affairs unit reflecting an increasing number of citizen complaints against the Suffolk police. The report also recounted that in 1976 Judge Weinstein had made a number of findings in the course of a class action lawsuit brought in federal court by the NAACP. He concluded that there were a substantial number of cases where the Suffolk police used excessive force, that there was evidence of racist remarks by Suffolk police officers, and that internal discipline in police brutality cases was lax. The report also analyzed seven recent cases where the state's high court reversed Suffolk County convictions—five involving homicides—and detailed deficiencies in the existing procedures for handling complaints of police abuse. In particular, it chastised the Suffolk District Attorney's Office for not acting as "an adequate check against police brutality." It noted that the D.A. was not inclined to thoroughly investigate and prosecute police misconduct and that if this were not made a priority, "the situation will worsen."

There were a number of recommendations which the bar association promulgated in its *Police Brutality Report*. They included the creation of a "law enforcement appeal panel" to investigate brutality complaints to be composed of members appointed by the police commissioner and the county executive, more stringent sanctions against police found guilty of brutality, an improved minority training program for the police, and the videotaping of interrogations.

Anthony Noto, the presiding officer of the county legislature, called the report "hogwash" and said that he would consider ordering the legislature's public safety committee to investigate how and why the bar association compiled the report. Its chairman, John

97

Wehrenberg, a self-described "police buff," was quoted as saying that he was "not going to let 2,500 cops be chastised for the acts of a few." Other officials described the report as "garbage" and a "cheap media trick." Not surprisingly, the District Attorney, Patrick Henry, took personal offense to the attack against his office and decried, as reported in the press, that he "saw nothing in the bar association report that will cause him to change any of his present policies." I defended the report by noting that it was "the absence of objectivity and accountability in the investigation of police brutality cases that is at the root of the problem in Suffolk County."

Noto and Wehrenberg never carried through on their threats. The bar association's gutsy and unprecedented action started to get a lot of positive national attention and press. Later that year, the American Bar Association gave the Suffolk Bar Association its coveted awards for both the best bar association project in the country that year and the country's best local bar association.

Sad to say, no changes were made by the police or the District Attorney, and matters got worse. In 1985 my former partner Stuart Namm, who was now a Suffolk County Court judge, asked the Governor to appoint a special prosecutor to pursue allegations of misconduct in two widely publicized Suffolk County murder trials which had occurred that year. He noted that he had "witnessed among other things, such apparent prosecutorial misconduct as perjury, subornation of perjury, intimidation of witnesses, spoliation of evidence, abuse of subpoena power," and attempts by the police to intimidate him.

Out of this came a four-year investigation by the State Investigation Commission (SIC) culminating in a searing report in 1989 finding "grave shortcomings in the leadership and management" of Suffolk County's District Attorney's Office and Police Department. The SIC described its main goal as "nothing short of a major reform of Suffolk law enforcement," calling for sweeping reform "which seeks justice and integrity, in place of an attitude of '[y]ou do what you've got to do to arrest and convict.' " The report railed against "the day-in, day-out manner in which the Police Department (through 1987)

98

and the District Attorney, to date, have conducted the business of law enforcement in Suffolk County so badly." It took particular shots at Patrick Henry, who was still the D.A. seven years after attacking the Suffolk Bar Association's *Police Brutality Report:*

> Furthermore, while the Suffolk Police Department, with its new Commissioner and almost entirely new top staff, offers promise for reform, no such promise is yet offered by the District Attorney's Office. Quite the contrary, District Attorney Henry, who most charitably can be described as having ignored the grave and demanding responsibilities of his Office, despite clear danger signals and warning, has exhibited increasing intransigence as the Commission's investigation uncovered ever more serious misconduct. He has become increasingly resistant, resorting to vituperative press statements, and even to litigation, in an unsuccessful effort to block this very Report. In the Commission's view, Mr. Henry has shown himself as unwilling to reform his own Office and to exert proper authority as the highest law enforcement officer of Suffolk County.

To my immense gratification the SIC report credited the bar association for first calling for reform, including videotaping confessions. It noted, however, that "[f]ew, if any, of these recommendations were instituted by the Suffolk County Police Department or by Mr. Henry," and that the bar's prophesy that the situation will worsen "did indeed prove correct."

After the SIC report Patrick Henry announced that he would not seek reelection to a fourth term. A new D.A. was elected, and sweeping reforms came to pass. It was not until 2010, however, that the bar association's recommendation 20 years earlier that all confessions be videotaped came to pass. District Attorney Thomas Spota supported it as "the natural evolution of the interrogation process." He was largely prompted by jurors' requests for more transparency in the taking of confessions, especially in light of Suffolk County's 94% confession rate in homicide cases.

By that time videotaping had become commonplace by responsible law enforcement personnel. Stephen Saloom, the policy director for the Manhattan-based Innocence Project reported that more than 500 police departments throughout the nation had embraced it and "[t]o a man, they're glad they're doing it." In Suffolk County, its advent was heralded by the supporters of Martin Tankleff, who had recently been freed from his notorious 1990 convictions in his parents' murders in their home in Belle Terre, a bedroom community next to Port Jefferson, based in part on his unsigned confession. A family spokesman for Tankleff pointedly commented that "[i]f Marty had a video recording of his complete interrogation then he would not have had to spend half his life imprisoned for a crime others committed." The same could be said for Robert Clayton.

* * *

Recently I read a book review in the *New York Times* Sunday book review section that caught my eye. The book was written by a Virginia Law School professor, Brandon Garrett, and was appropriately titled *Convicting the Innocent.* Professor Garrett pointed out that since the late 1980s DNA testing has exonerated 250 wrongly convicted people who spent an average of 13 years in prison for crimes which they did not commit. Seventeen were sentenced to die, and 80 others were sentenced to life. After digging into the files in each of these cases and interviewing the lawyers, prosecutors, and court reporters, Professor Garrett concluded that 90% of these innocent people were falsely convicted of rape or rape and murder and that 40 of them actually confessed to committing these heinous crimes. Furthermore, in addition to false confessions, eyewitnesses wrongly identified the accused in 76% of the 250 cases. The misidentifications were mostly caused by police misconduct like suggesting which suspect in a lineup should be selected or conducting lineups where one suspect obviously stood out from the others.

Professor Garrett also leveled some blame on the courts. He pointed out that in 10% of the 250 cases, appellate courts called the evidence of guilt "overwhelming," while the Supreme Court summarily dismissed requests to review 37 without giving reasons.

The book reviewer, Jeffrey Rosen, a distinguished law professor at George Washington University and the legal affairs editor of *The New Republic,* praised Professor Garrett's book as "a gripping contribution to the literature of injustice, along with a galvanizing call for reform." He hoped that the book would "mobilize a broad range of citizens, liberal and conservative, to demand legislative and judicial reforms ensuring that the innocent go free whether or not the constable had blundered."

Professor Garrett's book only focused on a small segment of cases where DNA evidence was available to exonerate innocent people falsely convicted of violent crimes due to false confessions or misidentifications. Surely there are many more. As I read Professor Rosen's book review, I naturally thought about Clayton. I also thought about the Faines and Culpepper trials where guilty people were not convicted. On one level, Professor Garrett's stories are not revelations. As long as human beings are called upon to decide the guilt or innocence of those charged with crimes, innocent people will be found guilty, and guilty people will be set free. On another level, however, they show that the justice system should always strive for reforms to minimize the chances for these injustices to happen.

In retrospect I am so proud of the Suffolk County Bar Association that it had the guts in 1980 to take on the Suffolk Police Department and the vaunted District Attorney's Office, as well as to take the lead in the reform efforts that ultimately came to pass after the SIC backed up its *Police Brutality Report.* Hopefully, fewer innocent people are now convicted in Suffolk County and fewer guilty people are acquitted. The *Clayton* case and the revelations of the police misconduct documented in the *Police Brutality Report* and in the subsequent State Investigation Commission's report made me realize how critical it would be—if I ever were to be a judge—to guard against the conviction of an innocent person.

* * *

The Suffolk County District Court had been created by the state legislature in 1964. In that same year it gave birth to the Nassau

County District Court. Nassau and Suffolk were adjoining counties. Together they constituted what is commonly called Long Island, stretching 140 miles from New York City to the end of Suffolk. In addition to handling misdemeanors and civil cases up to $10,000, these new courts replaced the justice of the peace courts and took care of traffic offenses and small claims. Thus, they were the lowest rung of the judiciary in those two counties. The state statute which established these local courts provided that the judges would be elected from each of Nassau's towns and Suffolk's five western towns; there would be no district courts in the five eastern towns. Each town would have two judges. In addition, a presiding judge would be elected at large from all of these towns. All of the judges would be elected for six-year terms. They could run for reelection.

Prior to 1977 both courts were funded by their respective counties. Nassau paid its district court judges about $1,000 more than the more parsimonious Suffolk Board of Supervisors. This changed in that year, when the state legislature decided to consolidate all of the state's courts under one umbrella administrative agency to provide uniform management and supervision. As part of the establishment of this new statewide uniform court system, the state took responsibility for funding all of the courts and established a uniform salary classification plan for all nonjudicial personnel. It also fixed the salaries for all of the state's judges. In 1980 the Suffolk District Court judges were being paid $49,000 a year. Their Nassau counterparts were getting $50,000.

This salary disparity irked Morty Weissman, who was rewarded in 1963 for his support of Boss Zeidler by becoming a Republican candidate for one of Brookhaven Town's first district court judgeships. Since at that time Republican Brookhaven Town candidates were virtual shoo-ins for election, Morty easily defeated his nominal Democratic opposition. Even though a district court judgeship was the lowest level judgeship in the county, Morty always wanted to be a judge, and he took the job as a stepping stone. The Boss told him that he would try to get him on a higher court when there was an opening. He kept his word, and Morty was elevated from the district court to the Suffolk County Criminal Court in 1978.

Morty always tried to get me to see the light and become a Republican. He could not understand why I was killing any chances of ever joining him on the bench by being pigheaded and staying a Democrat. Nonetheless, we had become good friends. We lived in the same community. Our kids went to the same schools.

While Morty was still a district court judge, he had asked me whether I would be willing to represent all of the Suffolk District Court judges in a lawsuit against New York State to eliminate the salary disparity between the Suffolk and Nassau District Court judges. I agreed. It seemed to us that now that the state was fixing all judicial salaries, there was no justification for treating the judges of the state's two district courts differently. It would be the first judicial pay parity lawsuit ever brought in the state. It was a gutsy thing to do. Judges just did not sue. Nonetheless, Morty was highly principled and could not fathom that the State had thought that the Suffolk judges were less worthy than their Nassau counterparts. He thought that since my handling of the reapportionment case had shaken up the legislative establishment, I would be the right lawyer to shake up the judicial establishment.

Since we thought that a Suffolk judge should not be asked to decide a case involving a fellow Suffolk judge, the lawsuit was brought in the Westchester County Supreme Court. It was based on the equal protection clause of the 14th Amendment of the Constitution which prevents the states from passing legislation that treats similarly situated people differently. We argued that judges do not shed their constitutional rights when they don their judicial robes. We presented statistics showing that the two contiguous Long Island counties had similar populations and formed one economic unit. We also showed that the Nassau and Suffolk district courts did the same judicial work and had essentially the same caseloads. The only difference was their salaries.

On May 21, 1980, two years after we brought the lawsuit, Supreme Court Justice Rubenfeld agreed that this was constitutionally impermissible. He gave the State until October 1 of that year to pass legislation equalizing all of the judges' pay. The State appealed to the appellate division. We also appealed because we had asked for retroactive pay back to 1977, when the State first decided that the Suffolk judges would be paid less. Even though Morty was now a county court judge, he would be entitled to about a year's back pay for when he was a district court judge. It took several months for the appellate papers to be prepared and filed with the court. In the meantime my old partner and nemesis, Dominic Baranello, and the governor he nominated in June 1974 came back into my life.

* * *

Because of Dominic's fiery nominating speech and the support he was able to garner from the suburban counties, Hugh Carey had received enough votes at the 1974 Democratic nominating convention to challenge the bosses' candidate, Howard Samuels, in a primary. The Democratic rank and file did not care for the bosses' choice. Carey handily beat Samuels. On November 4, 1974, Carey defeated the Republican gubernatorial candidate, Malcolm Wilson, and became New York's 51st governor.

Carey was a good governor. During his first term of office—from 1974–1978—he was the architect of the financial plan that averted the bankruptcy of New York City and instituted the *I Love New York* campaign. He was a spokesperson for regional concerns and a proponent of comprehensive programs for urban and industrial revitalization. He was easily reelected in 1978 for a second four-year term, doing what I was not able to do 14 years earlier: beat Perry Duryea. However, the Governor was developing a reputation for living the high life. The prominent columnist Jimmy Breslin nicknamed him Society Carey. Worst yet, he started to fall prey to the disease that often inflicts those in power for a long time—the belief that they pretty much can get their way any time they want.

On November 6, 1980, Philip D'Arrigo called me. I think he was referred by ex-Judge Sarisohn. He was obviously agitated and wanted to see me at once. When I met him in my office later that day, he told me that he had been served with papers that morning notifying him that the State had condemned the property which he owned in Shelter Island. I thought back to the reapportionment case when tiny Shelter Island was the focal point of the one person, one vote lawsuit. Nevertheless, Shelter Island—sitting in the middle of Gardiners Bay at the end of Suffolk County—in addition to being one of Suffolk's 10 towns, was a beautiful, bucolic island that attracted many prominent people who coveted it as a great place for a vacation home. One of its most prominent at that time was Governor Hugh Carey.

Phil D'Arrigo was a 45-year-old dentist who had worked hard to build up an everyday dental practice in the poor section of the Bronx. He had fallen in love with Shelter Island while he was a struggling dentist. By 1979 he had saved enough money to buy an empty lot on Shelter Island for $48,000. It had a beautiful view of the Great South Bay. Dr. D'Arrigo dreamt about the time when he would be able to afford to build his dream vacation house there. He could now afford to do it; he was then living in Scarsdale, an affluent community in Westchester County. Moreover, he would have a celebrity next-door neighbor. In 1969 then-Congressman Carey had bought an old, rambling house next to the dentist's property. It became the Carey family's summer retreat. The Governor could have picked up the empty adjoining lot for a song long before Dr. D'Arrigo snatched it up, but passed on it.

When Dr. D'Arrigo had started to build his house in early November, he was notified that the State had decided to condemn his property and was preparing the necessary paperwork. He was told that the Governor thought that the house he was building would pose a security risk since it was so close to the Governor's. He showed me all of the papers that he had just received. I was shocked. I had handled a number of state takings. While the state has the power to condemn someone's property if needed for a public purpose, the condemnation process, from beginning to end, usually takes many months, if not years. The State had condemned Dr.

D'Arrigo's property in one week. He was willing to sue to get it back. I was happy to be his lawyer.

I immediately started to prepare the court papers that same day. I thought, however, that the best way to handle the matter might be to first go public with the story. It seemed to me to be an incredible abuse of power. I believed that once the papers got wind of it, pressure would likely be placed on the Governor to change his mind and let Dr. D'Arrigo finish building his home.

Phil D'Arrigo was not looking for publicity. He was a decent man and had no political axe to grind with the Governor. I convinced him, however, that this was one of those unique cases which should be tried in the press. It would save him a lot of money in potential legal fees and was likely to produce a quick knockout. However, true to his character, he asked me if there might be a way for the Governor to relent before we went public. I thought of my ex-partner. Dominic Baranello was still the Governor's state Democratic leader. Though I did not relish having to deal with him again, it was in my client's best interest to tell him what was about to happen.

Dominic thanked me for calling. He agreed that this could be very embarrassing for the Governor and asked if I could hold off until he was able to speak to the powers-that-be. The next day he called me back. He was distraught. He told me that he had spoken to Robert Morgado, Carey's closest advisor, and that Morgado had spoken to the Governor to tell him what was about to happen. The Governor had a stubborn streak and would not give in.

On Saturday, November 8, 1980, I called a reporter friend of mine at *Newsday*—Long Island's leading newspaper—and spilled the beans on the Governor. *Newsday* broke the story the next day. On Monday it appeared all over the state. A resident of Shelter Island commented—she was typical of those who expressed concerns about the matter—that "it looks like he misused his office to protect his privacy." Many of the locals thought that the real reason for the Governor's high-handed behavior was because he was annoyed that Dr. D'Arrigo's house would block his view of the Great South Bay.

Editorials were just as critical. The *Staten Island Advance,* for example, ran a headline stating that the "Governor's 'security' claims are weak."

The Governor blamed the Republican Party. He accused it of getting a local Republican lawyer to do a hatchet job on him. Obviously no one, including Dominic, had told him that I was the former law partner of his state Democratic Party chairman. Apparently Dominic also had never told him that I had called his chairman so that he could get word to the Governor that if he changed his mind about taking Dr. D'Arrigo's property, then the matter would not hit the press.

The Governor's inner circle had begged him to cancel the condemnation. His own transportation commissioner, William Hennessy, was later quoted as telling him that his hope that he could convince the public that the takeover was justified was wildly optimistic. The Governor's aides knew that he had a deep emotional attachment to Shelter Island—he had lost his temper when the state's Office of General Services had bulldozed one of the shrubs on his lawn to construct a gate for a security guard—but they informed him in no uncertain terms that to protect his privacy and waterfront view by taking his neighbor's property was politically disastrous. They were right. The press would not let up. Jimmy Breslin came to my office to get my first-hand take on the Governor's fiasco and vilified him in his widely read column in the *Daily News.* His fellow columnists were also all over the story. The Albany *Times Union* columnist Barney Fowler dubbed him "The Squire of Shelter Island."

The Governor finally saw the handwriting on the wall. On November 12, less than a week after Dr. D'Arrigo received the notice saying that he would have to stop building his home, the Governor rescinded the takeover. However, the horrific press that he had gotten triggered an avalanche of negative newspaper articles during the remainder of his second term. While Hugh Carey was a talented and effective governor, the public saw him as imperious. When it was time for him to decide whether to seek reelection to a third term, his approval rating had sunk to an all-time low. On January 15, 1982, he announced that he would not run again. With respect to his Shelter Island fiasco, he had humbly acknowledged that "I got the punishment I deserved by paying in notoriety for what I tried to do in the name of privacy."

* * *

Some months after Dr. D'Arrigo got his property back, I was invited by Alex Forger to be part of an ad hoc committee to champion the cause for reforming New York's courts. Alex was a past president of the New York State Bar Association and was chairman of the Fund for Modern Courts. He was tall and patrician. As the senior partner of one of the world's mega law firms, he represented the epitome of the establishment. I felt insecure in his presence, especially when I learned that he was Jackie Kennedy's personal lawyer, but Alex liked me. I was then the ex-president of the Suffolk Bar and had become a delegate to the New York State Bar. I also had founded a movement to give the bar associations in suburban and rural communities a bigger voice in the state bar's affairs. It led to the establishment of the New York Conference of Bar Leaders. I arranged for the leaders of these bar associations to have periodic meetings to discuss issues that were of unique importance to them. We would then bring them to the attention of the full state bar association, which we thought was too dominated by the big-city firms.

I was recognized for my efforts by being appointed as the first chairman of this new organization. The Conference of Bar Leaders would become an important part of the New York State Bar Association and to this day continues to give the smaller, non-city bar associations an important voice in its affairs. I guess that Alex thought that as the founder and leader of the Conference of Bar Leaders, I should be part of an elite group that he had assembled to try to reform the courts. It truly was an elite group. The chairman was Cyrus Vance, who had been the Secretary of State in the Carter administration. The other members were Charles Breitel—recently retired as the chief judge of the New York State Court of

Appeals; Richard Bartels—a powerful Republican leader of the New York State Assembly; Haliburton Fales—another mega-law firm big shot and the president-elect of the New York State Bar Association; Michael Cardozo—a prominent New York City lawyer who would later head the City's law department; and Judah Gribetz, who had been Governor Carey's legal counsel during his first term.

Court reform was a worthy cause to tackle. Although New York State had taken over the funding of the courts, there was no consistency to the organization of the state's far-flung court system, nor to the way in which its judges came into being. It was historically the playpen of the politicians, who had a vested interest in perpetuating an outmoded judicial system that was sorely in need of change. Its structure was a crazy quilt of supreme courts, county courts, family courts, surrogate courts, and local district courts, municipal courts, and civil courts. Their jurisdictions often overlapped. Reorganization into a cohesive, streamlined statewide system was sorely needed.

As for the judges, they were beholden to the politicians. While most were elected, they were in reality the handmaidens of the bosses, who controlled the archaic nominating processes that placed them on the ballot. Unless there was a politically engineered cross-endorsement deal, you could not become a judge in places like Suffolk County if you were not a Republican or in places like New York City if you were not a Democrat. Independents need not apply.

There were inexplicable inconsistencies. For example, in New York City the family court judges—unlike the elected family court judges elsewhere in the state—were appointed by the mayor. The City's municipal court judges—which handled small criminal matters—were also appointed by the mayor, but not the City's civil court judges—which handled small monetary cases—who were elected. Historically, the quality of the New York City judges who were appointed to the bench would vary greatly, depending on the predilections of the mayor. To his credit, Mayor Koch had recently put in place a bipartisan, merit-based judicial selection committee of reputable lawyers and community leaders. He would not appoint

109

anyone who was not recommended by his committee. Subsequent mayors followed his lead. As a result, the City has been blessed with a fine cadre of family and municipal court judges.

As chairman of our ad hoc committee, Cyrus Vance would be our spokesperson and personally press the need for court reform to State Senator Barrett, the omnipotent head of the State Senate Judiciary Committee. Without his support, court reform would be dead in the water. Cy Vance, as the former Secretary of State, was an internationally respected diplomat. He had brokered complex international treaties and resolved hot-button disputes between warring nations. Certainly he could convince Senator Barrett that it was time to take the high road and bring the New York judicial system into the modern age.

President Carter's Secretary of State wanted to lay out the approach he planned to take with Senator Barrett to our committee and get our input. He also wanted to enlist the support of Governor Carey. We met at the Governor's offices in Manhattan. At the end of our discussion, the Governor came into the room and gave us his blessings. After his remarks, he had a photographer memorialize the meeting. The picture that was taken of our group sitting around the Governor's conference table—with the Governor at the head—hangs in my judicial chambers today.

After the photo shoot, the Governor went around the room to shake hands with the members of the committee. He spoke familiarly to each one before he came to me: "Glad to see you again, Mr. Secretary of State"; "How are you enjoying your retirement, Mr. Chief Judge?"; "How's the esteemed Assemblyman doing these days?"; "How's Jackie behaving, Alex?"; "Nice to see you again, Michael"; "How have you been, Hal?"; "Glad to see my former counsel is here to help the cause."

I was next. I froze. The press was still writing about Dr. D'Arrigo. The Governor stared at me. Judah Gribetz introduced me as an active member of the Suffolk County and New York State bar associations. It seemed an eternity before the Governor spoke. He asked Judah my name again. After Judah told him, he blurted out,

"Where have I heard that name before? It sounds awfully familiar."
He then moved closer to me and with a puzzled look inquired, "Do I
know you from someplace, Mr. Block?" I assured him that he must
be mistaking me for someone else. The Governor was scratching his
head as he walked out of the room. I wiped the sweat from my
brows.

When I was sure that the Governor was nowhere in sight, I
walked into the hallway to grab the first elevator I could get. Judah
Gribetz was next to me. He was smiling. He told me that if he had
remained as the Governor's counsel he would have told him that he
was nuts for taking Dr. D'Arrigo's property. He assured me that the
problems that befell the Governor were not my fault. Little did I
know that 12 years later Judah Gribetz would be the chairman of
Senator Daniel Patrick Moynihan's merit-selection committee
when I appeared before it as a judicial candidate for the federal
district court.

Nothing came of Cyrus Vance's meeting with Senator Barrett.
The Senator was courteous to his esteemed visitor, but President
Carter's Secretary of State was on a fool's errand. When all was
said and done, Senator Barrett would not support any legislation
that would consolidate the courts and encroach upon the power of
the bosses to anoint the state's judges. To this day, the New York
State judicial system is stuck in the past.

* * *

On August 14, 1981, the appellate court came down with its decision in the Suffolk County District Court judges' judicial pay parity
case. It unanimously agreed that the judges of Long Island's two
district courts should be treated the same. It disagreed with the
State that it could constitutionally provide different salaries for
judges from different counties, holding that "a territorial distinction, without any rational basis, cannot withstand constitutional
scrutiny." However, it would not award back pay. Moreover, it
extended the time for the State to take corrective action until April

111

2, 1982. Both sides appealed again. The high court of the state would decide the issues.

On July 2, 1982, the Court of Appeals unanimously agreed with the appellate division that the Suffolk District Court judges should be paid the same as their Nassau counterparts. It reasoned, as I had argued, that the two courts were part of a judicial district—comprising Nassau and Suffolk Counties—that constituted "a true unity" of judicial interest indistinguishable by separate geographic considerations and that "the jurisdiction, practice and procedures of each of the District Courts and their functions, duties and responsibilities of their Judges are identical." It recognized that there may be situations where geographical differences could make a difference but that this was not such a case because the State had failed to demonstrate that providing separate salaries for courts so similarly situated was "neither capricious nor arbitrary."

The court then addressed our back pay argument and held that "fixing October 1, 1978 as the date from which to measure the accrual of plaintiffs' rights would accord with simple equity and fairness." The Suffolk County District Court judges would, therefore, be entitled to back pay from that date. It was a great win. It established the principle under the Equal Protection Clause of the United States Constitution of pay parity for the judges of the state's courts who were being paid less than their colleagues solely based on arbitrary geographical differences.

I did not get paid for my legal work. I had never discussed fees with the judges. I was happy to champion the cause. It also did not hurt my legal reputation to be the judges' lawyer. The New York State Controller correctly calculated the back pay for the judges who had been on the bench since October 1, 1978, and sent me the checks each was entitled to receive. I sent them on to the judges. They did not amount to a lot of money since the pay differential between the two district courts had annually averaged only a little more than $1,000.

* * *

At about the same time that I was in the throes of helping the Suffolk District Court judges get pay parity, I was also handling a lawsuit for Theatre Three, a little community theater in Port Jefferson. I had incorporated the theater years ago and it was now being sued by United Artists Film Corporation. Theatre Three started out putting on plays in the basement of the local Presbyterian Church. United Artists owned a little movie theater on Port Jefferson's Main Street. It only used it during the summertime to show art films. The building had a lot of charm and a rich history. In the early 1900s Frederick Griswold had invented the film splicer in its basement. Bradley Bing, a local high school English teacher, was the executive director of Theatre Three. He was able to get United Artists to let him have full-time use of the basement of the movie house. He would also be allowed to use the theater upstairs, except during the summertime when UA was showing movies there.

Bradley converted the basement into a small, charming space and used it to put on best-of-Broadway musical revues on the weekends. He named it *Griswold's Cabaret*. At the same time he used the larger theater upstairs for plays when it was not being used by UA as a movie theater. The public embraced Theatre Three as its local community theater. It crowded into *Griswold's Cabaret* every Friday and Saturday night to listen to the local talent belt out the songs of Gershwin, Irving Berlin, Cole Porter, Rodgers and Hammerstein, and the other great songwriters of the 20th century. Many times it also filled the seats of the 400-seat theater upstairs to see good amateur productions of the latest Broadway plays.

The theater company was having growing pains and the usual financial problems that beset local community theaters. In order to survive it needed to use the upstairs theater during the entire year, especially during the summer, which was the height of the tourist season. When, in the summer of 1991, it would not turn the theater over to United Artists, the big movie company sued. Bradley asked me to help. I did not know what kind of defense could be mounted. It seemed like United Artists had a pretty open-and-shut case, but

113

the survival of Theatre Three was at stake, so I said that I would see what could be done.

Bradley knew that I was a soft touch and had music in my blood. I had taught myself to play boogie-woogie on the piano when I was a teenager and could play pretty good boogie beats from the likes of Meade Lux Lewis and Jelly Roll Morton. I would also make up silly little satirical songs about such things as life in suburbia. I conjured up some defenses to the lawsuit. There was no doubt that Theatre Three was in breach of its lease agreement with United Artists, but I claimed that UA had also breached the lease because it failed to live up to its end of the bargain and repair the heating and ventilating systems. While the case was being prepared for trial, I tried to talk United Artists into allowing Theatre Three to use the entire building year round. It did not seem like a big deal for it to do this for the community. It would be a nice goodwill gesture. Unfortunately, UA was not interested in charity, and it wanted to keep making the few bucks it brought in during the summer months.

The case was tried in the Suffolk County Supreme Court before Justice Paul Baisley. UA's lawyer was Bernie Smith. He and the judge were both from the Town of Huntington and were close Republican political allies. We tried to insulate ourselves by having a jury, but Justice Baisley refused to let the jurors decide whether UA could not evict its tenant because it had also breached the lease by failing to make the promised repairs. The jury was sympathetic to our cause but had no choice but to hold against us. Justice Baisley was wrong. He basically charged us out of court. There was no doubt in my mind that he would be reversed on appeal.

That's exactly what happened. On December 6, 1982, the appellate division sent the case back for a retrial because Justice Baisley had refused to submit the issue of United Artists' breach to the jury. During the second trial, in the spring of 1983, United Artists gave in and for just $10,000 agreed to let Theatre Three buy the building. Port Jefferson would have—and still has after all these years—its own community theater.

114

* * *

While all this was going on, I would play for Bradley Bing all of these little songs I was writing about my suburban life. It was great therapy. I never took it seriously. However, Bradley was amused and came up with the idea of packaging them and having them performed in *Griswold's Cabaret.* He introduced me to two of his theater friends, Peter Winkler and Ernie Muller. Peter was a music professor at the SUNY Stony Brook. Ernie had been a high school English teacher. He was a local community theater guy and had a gift for writing funny sketches. Out of this came a satirical musical review about life in the suburbs, appropriately called *Suburbia.* We wrote songs and sketches about such things as wives driving their husbands to the train, shoveling their kids off to school, shaping up at health spas, and watching their husbands fall asleep soon after they came home from work. There were some funny parts, but I did not think it was bound for Broadway. Nevertheless, the public loved it, and it packed *Griswold's Cabaret* every weekend for months. Because it was so successful, I started to write silly satirical songs about the professions. The first one I did was a parody of one of Shakespeare's famous lines. Bradley laughed the first time that I played it for him.

First let's kill all the lawyers

Hang 'em from the highest tree

We won't have relief

Until that final brief

When we're set legally free

No more subpoenas

No misdemeanors

Never a summons or complaint

Oh how happy we will be

When we never pay a fee

When all the lawyers ain't

Out of this nonsense came *Professionally Speaking.* It was a *Griswold Cabaret* hit. It played to packed houses for all of 1984. The show was reviewed in the Long Island edition of the *New York Times.* Leah Frank, the reviewer, praised it as "a delightful new musical review that takes a wry look at the careers of the army of doctors, lawyers and teachers," calling it "crisp, biting and often very funny."

After it closed, we took the show on the road. It played during that summer at the Spinning Wheel, a dinner theater in Ridgefield Connecticut. One Sunday morning I got a telephone call from a stranger who told me that he had seen the show there the night before and thought that it had great off-Broadway potential. I was flabbergasted. He introduced himself as Tony Tanner. The name sounded familiar. As soon as he told me that he had been the costar with Anthony Newly in the successful Broadway musical *Stop the World—I Want to Get Off,* I remembered seeing his name. He also reminded me that he had been nominated for a Tony award for directing the original *Joseph and the Amazing Technicolor Dreamcoat* on Broadway. He asked whether I would be willing to meet him at his Upper West Side flat in Manhattan to talk about bringing *Professionally Speaking* into the Big Apple.

On the following Tuesday I had a morning meeting in New York City of the executive committee of the state bar association. I had been chosen by the Nassau and Suffolk bar associations to be the Long Island representative to the state bar as one of its vice presidents. I was then in the middle of my two-year term. The meeting was held at the Harvard Club on West 44th Street. I was appropriately dressed for this stolid group at this prestigious establishment place. Later that afternoon I walked up two flights of stairs in a brownstone building on West 93rd Street to meet Tony Tanner. When the door opened, I was met by a middle-aged man in an orange bathrobe. As he gazed at my black pin-striped suit, starched white button-down shirt, and red, white, and blue tie, he sighed and said, "Darling, you're terribly overdressed for the occasion." He introduced me to his masseuse, who was rubbing his neck, and invited me into the living room. *Professionally Speaking* would open at the St. Peter's Theatre in the Citicorp building in Midtown Manhattan on May 22, 1986.

* * *

It took 18 months to mount the show. In addition to working on improving it, I also took on the responsibility of being the principal producer. I raised most of the $175,000 that we needed to get us a few months past opening night. I hired Neil Simon's lawyer, Al DaSilva, to do the necessary legal work, negotiated the contracts with the actors' union, Actors' Equity, for the six-member cast which Tony Tanner picked, and retained one of the theater's top public relations firms—Shirley Herz & Associates—to do the PR. It was heady stuff.

While all this was happening, I learned during the winter of 1985 that Senator Daniel Patrick Moynihan would be picking a candidate to recommend to the President to fill a vacancy on the federal district court bench for the Eastern District of New York.

The federal judiciary is divided into 94 districts, correlated to some degree to population. For example, New York has four districts, two of which—the Southern and Eastern—cover the megalopolis of New York City and its surrounding counties. Having lived and practiced law in Suffolk County, I was a product of the Eastern District, which takes in three of New York City's five counties—Kings (Brooklyn), Queens, and Richmond (Staten Island)—plus the two counties comprising Long Island—Nassau and Suffolk. It currently covers a population of about 8 million people, stretching from the urban sprawl of Brooklyn 140 miles eastward to the sandy beaches of Montauk.

The Eastern District of New York (EDNY) was established by Congress in 1865 with one judge. In 1985 it had 14 judges.

Although the President nominates and the Senate confirms all federal judges, the process usually begins at the local political level. The generally understood practice is that the senators from the same political party as the President agree amongst themselves to recommend a candidate to the President whenever a vacancy occurs in their state. When the senators are from different political parties, they usually agree amongst themselves how to divide the recommendations.

If, however, there is no senator from the President's political party, the White House will either turn to other state political sources from the President's party, such as a governor or congressional leader, or directly solicit potential candidates from other sources. At the time there was a Republican, President Reagan, in the White House. Alphonse D'Amato, a Republican, and Moynihan, a Democrat, were New York's two senators. They had an understanding that they would divide their recommendations three to one, with the senator whose party was then occupying the White House having the dominant number. This did not mean that the White House would necessarily accept the recommendations, but most times that was the case.

Since the country was born, back in the 18th century, Suffolk County had never had a Democrat appointed to a federal judgeship, and it only had a handful of Republicans who made it. Nassau County did not fare much better. The two Long Island counties were truly the stepchildren of the EDNY. All of the action was centered many miles away in Brooklyn where the only courthouse for the district and the district's United States Attorney's Office were located. Suffolk and Nassau, though, now each had well over 1 million people and comprised 40% of the EDNY's population. If Long Island had been located in any other part of the country, it would have had its own courthouse and many judges.

It would take a lawyer from Long Island from three to seven hours to make a round trip to the Brooklyn federal courthouse—depending on where the lawyer's office was located. Because an appearance in federal court for something as simple as a 10-minute status conference would kill the lawyer's entire day, bringing a case in federal court by a Long Island lawyer was an economic burden and a luxury which the lawyer could ill afford; thus, the trial lawyers from these counties, especially those from the more distant Suffolk County, would often avoid litigating in the federal court.

I found out who was on Senator Moynihan's judicial selection committee. While they were a group of distinguished lawyers, professors, and citizens, none were from Nassau or Suffolk. They probably had no clue how difficult it was for the Long Island lawyers to practice in the Brooklyn federal court and how woefully underrepresented they were on the bench. There was a cause to champion. I would tell all of this to Senator Moynihan's blue-ribbon committee if I were selected to be interviewed. There was no guarantee that this would happen. Coming from Suffolk County, I was not known to this New York City group; moreover, because there were so many applicants, not all could realistically be interviewed. They had to be winnowed out.

I thought I had a chance. As the Vice President of the State Bar Association and as a leader of the Suffolk bar I was knee-deep in the establishment phase of my legal career. Moreover, thanks to Dean Thoron, I had also just been appointed to the New York State Bar Ethics Committee. The Dean—as I always would call him— was now the ex-Dean of the Cornell Law School but was teaching Professional Responsibility at the school. He was also a member of the ethics committee. I had had no contact with him since I had graduated from Cornell. Out of the blue he had called me several months before and asked whether I would like to join the committee. He must have still felt guilty about the way he treated me when I was in his Conlaw class almost 20 years before.

The Dean also had another reason for bringing me back into his fold. After I became a member of the ethics committee, he would periodically invite me to return to Cornell to speak to his Professional Responsibility classes. He would also invite Milton Gould. We had both graduated from the law school, but while I had been a solo practitioner or had small partnerships with one or two other lawyers in the Suffolk boondocks, Milton Gould was one of New York City's most prominent mega-firm lawyers. We would be a matched pair. I would extol the virtues of being a small-town prac-

119

titioner, while Milton Gould would talk about life as a major lawyer in the Big Apple.

I got the interview.

* * *

Senator Moynihan's committee, like other merit-selection committees, required those wishing to be considered to fill out a detailed, multipage questionnaire. I had to list all of the trials and appeals which I had handled over the prior five years; the names, addresses, and telephone numbers of my adversaries; the names of the trial judges; any grievance filed against me; all of my political, professional, and civic activities; any country clubs that I had belonged to; any courses which I had taught; anything that I had published; and every organization that I had joined. It was, in other words, a "this is your life" disclosure designed to give the committee a comprehensive sense of who you were. It also required me to reflect on my life and legal career.

I was surprised that I was able to comprehensively answer all of the questions and felt good about a number of things which I had done over the years; nonetheless, coming from Suffolk County, I was also surprised to be selected to be interviewed. I told the committee about how shabbily Long Island had been treated. I then took a deep breath and pointed out that not one member of the committee was from Long Island.

I also told the committee that I had no expectation of being recommended to the Senator and thanked the members for giving me a forum to speak my piece. I recognized that Ed Korman, the district's United States Attorney—who had just successfully prosecuted the chairman of the Nassau Republican Party for requiring his cronies to kick back to the party 1% of their salaries for county jobs he got for them—was deserving of being elevated to the bench. He was considered by the bar as a shoo-in.

I was shocked, therefore, to receive a phone call a few days later from Senator Moynihan's office asking me to meet with him. In addition to Ed Korman, his committee had also recommended me for the judgeship.

I will never forget my meeting with the Senator. It was in his New York City office on Third Avenue and 45th Street. It lasted two hours. Most of the time was spent listening to him wax eloquent about the Constitution and the history of the 19th century in the United States. The Senator was an imposing physical presence with a rich reputation as both an intellectual and a grassroots politician; he was the author of many books, most notably the one which he wrote while a Harvard professor exposing the failings of the welfare system. I was trying hard not to appear in awe.

I had heard that the Senator was a provocateur and, true to form, toward the end of the interview he called for his secretary to bring in a copy of the Constitution. When she gave it to him, he knew exactly what he was looking for. He read to me—in his sonorous voice—the Establishment Clause of the First Amendment: "Congress shall make no law respecting an establishment of religion[.]" A practicing Irish Catholic, he then entered into a diatribe against those Supreme Court decisions striking down legislation that arguably blurred the line between church and state, after which he asked for my opinion. To this day I am not entirely sure how I got the courage, but I blurted out that I disagreed with him and told him that I thought that the Supreme Court had gotten it right. He smiled.

Three days later, someone from Senator Moynihan's office called to tell me that the Senator had decided to recommend Ed Korman; the Senator did not want me to read about it in the newspaper and wanted me to know how much I had impressed him. To Senator Moynihan's credit, he would not cave in to the pressure being placed upon him by a number of his Republican colleagues who would not have been unhappy if Korman were denied the nomination for the wounds his successful corruption prosecution had inflicted on the vaunted Nassau County Republican Party. The next day, April 18, 1985, I received this letter from the Senator:

May I repeat what my administrative assistant told you last evening:

121

my recommendation for the Eastern District vacancy was an extremely close decision. I was supremely impressed by your qualifications and our conversation in New York.

In the end, it was experience with the Federal judiciary that weighed most heavily in my choice.

The members of my judicial selection panel had commended you to me in the highest terms. And I found them to be right, as always. I would hope another occasion might arise for me to recommend you for the judiciary.

You have my deepest respect, sir.

I framed it, hung it on the wall in my study as the booby prize, and assumed that this would be as close as I would get to becoming a federal judge. It was time to get back to my law practice—and *Professionally Speaking*.

* * *

Opening night was a triumph. The audience laughed and laughed. When the curtain went down, we got a standing ovation. Celebrities were everywhere. Shirley Herz had arranged for the traditional opening night party to be held at the Limelight—the hottest club in the City at that time—while we waited for the reviews. I got drunk.

Two reviews came in that night. Both the *Associated Press* and the *Daily News* praised the show. Don Nelsen, the *Daily News* theater critic, called it "one of the keener entries in the satire stakes," but we would have to wait for the all-important *New York Times* review. It came on Sunday, May 25. It was mixed. Stephen Holden, who is still with the *Times*, wrote that "the material displays a frisky verbal energy as it takes a bleak, cold-hearted view of the professions." In several respects he damned the show with faint praise, referring to its "cleverer songs" as having "the brittle formality and verbal precision of Tom Lehrer," but missing his "knack for going for the jugular." He also compared one of the songs as "affect-[ing] a Stephen Sondheim-like urbanity but lack[ing] Mr. Sondheim's psychological acuity and depth of feeling."

Other reviews were equally mixed. Clive Barnes of the *New York Post* hated it. On the other hand, Edith Oliver, the highly regarded critic for *The New Yorker* magazine, referred to it as a "cocky little review." She described much of the material as "funny and charming" and many of the songs as "fresh and sensitive and lively." On balance, we had stronger reviews than another off-Broadway show that opened that week, *Nunsense.*

Nevertheless, *Nunsense* had one thing going for it that we did not: money. Shirley Herz told us about a number of off-Broadway shows like ours—with a small cast—that had become very successful in the face of comparable reviews and had traveled throughout the country after their New York City debut. However, they each required lots of capital for promoting them through their infancy. We did not have it; *Nunsense* did. It became a mega-hit and still plays throughout the world.

We did, however, get some mileage out of *Professionally Speaking.* It had a successful two-week run at a beautiful theater in Fort Lauderdale, and it played for a limited engagement in Portland, Oregon. Nevertheless, without the financial wherewithal to promote it and facing financial pressure from the actors' union to commit ourselves to long-term contracts for the performers and stagehands, we had to close the show six weeks after it opened. Sad to say, only a handful of people got to hear such memorable hits as *The Best Part-Time Job in Town; Who the Hell Do These Wise Guys Think They Are; Three Little Doctor's Wives;* and my personal favorite, an operatic send-up called *I Professionisti*—in English, "The Sick Professionals."

Once I had cleared the stars from my eyes, I went back to my day job.

At that time Richard Hamburger was working for me. He had been looking for a job in Suffolk County and dropped by one day since he had heard that I might be in the market for some help. I told him about *Professionally Speaking,* which had then been playing at Theatre Three for the past few weeks. I invited him to the

123

show. He came that Friday night with his wife, Lisa. He loved the show. I offered him the job.

Richard would soon become my partner and for the next decade—until I got the judgeship—we had lots of fun practicing law together. We also won a lot of cases. Richard was, and still is, a terrific lawyer. After I got the judgeship, Richard took our little office—consisting then of a wonderful associate, Lane Maxson, our loyal long-term receptionist, Fran Erlich, and our two secretaries, Tina Farrell and Caroline Pumilia—and relocated to a high-end commercial corridor in the Town of Huntington. Today he presides over a large, highly regarded law firm specializing in all types of exotic litigation and commercial matters. I count him as one of my closest friends.

* * *

The first order of legal business was to take an appeal to the appellate division in what I called *Weissman II*. Soon after we got pay parity for the district court judges, the county court judges came to me and asked, "Why not us also?" They had a pretty good point. Their salaries were $4,000 less than the county court judges in Nassau County. It seemed like a sure thing. Morty Weissman was now a Suffolk County Court judge. He would be the lead plaintiff. Once again—to avoid the awkwardness of asking a Suffolk judge to pass upon the issue—we brought the case in Westchester County Supreme Court. There was no doubt in my mind that we would get the same result there that we got in the district court judges' case. I was surprised, therefore, when on May 1, 1986—while *Professionally Speaking* was in previews—Justice Buell threw the case out. It had to be reversed—and it was.

A year would pass, however, before the appellate court spoke. Finally, on June 29, 1987, the court handed down its decision. Justice Kooper wrote a lengthy opinion for a unanimous four-judge appellate bench. She recognized that the state's high court had decided five years before in *Weissman I* that the salary disparity in the district court judges' case "was premised upon precisely the same geographical classifications" and saw "no reason on this record to differ from the Court of Appeals assessment" in that case. In commenting on the data we had submitted, Justice Kooper concluded that our facts "clearly demonstrate that the functions, duties and responsibilities of County Court Judges serving Nassau and Suffolk counties are identical; that, for all practical purposes, their caseloads are the same; that there is no meaningful difference in county-wide populations; and that there are absent significant economic distinctions between the two contiguous counties upon which to rationally ground the salary disparity." The appellate court also tracked the Court of Appeals in *Weissman I* by giving the judges back pay to October 1, 1978.

The State did not think that the Court of Appeals would overrule Justice Kooper's carefully analyzed opinion and decided that there was no basis for an appeal. I handed out back pay checks to the 11 Suffolk County Court judges totaling about $250,000. Under a special statute allowing for counsel fees for bringing successful constitutional challenges against a state, I received a modest fee.

The Suffolk County Court judges pay parity case turned out to be small potatoes, however, compared to what was about to happen.

* * *

As the last year of my third decade of practicing law was coming to a close, I got a call from Leon Deutsch. He introduced himself as a family court judge from New York City. He told me that he ran into Judge Weissman at a New York State judges' conference who had told him that I was the lawyer who had successfully handled his two pay parity lawsuits. He wanted to talk to me. When I met with him he told me that he had been asked by his colleagues to take over the leadership of the New York City Family Court Judges Association. Judges were not allowed to unionize, but they could band together to address common concerns. At the time, their main beef was that they were being paid several thousand dollars less than the family court judges of Nassau County. Their pleas to the state legislature to give them the same pay as their next-door neighbors had fallen on deaf ears. He asked me if I would speak to

125

his colleagues to see if litigation might be warranted. He cautioned me, however, that he was not at all certain that the judges would be willing to sue the State because of the *Cass* case. I was familiar with *Cass* because the State relied on it—unsuccessfully—to try to prevent us from winning in *Weissman II.*

In *Cass,* many of the New York City Family Court judges had banded together with other family court judges throughout the state, as well as with many of the state's county court judges and surrogates, claiming that under the equal protection clause, all of the state's judges of these courts should be paid the same. They lost. As recounted in a footnote in Justice Kooper's opinion in *Weissman II,* the state's high court had ruled against the state judges in *Cass* because it noted, in Justice Kooper's words, "that there were evident distinctions in caseload, population and cost of living among the wide range of counties in which the plaintiffs' served, thereby establishing a rational basis for the salary disparities." By contrast, as Justice Kooper further explained, the Court of Appeals in *Cass* "specifically distinguished" its prior Suffolk County District Court decision in *Weissman I,* "stating that *Weissman* involved one class of judges serving in two adjoining counties where differences in caseload, population and cost of living were not evident."

Before I met with the judges, I did some homework and concluded that, just like the Suffolk County District Court judges' and County Court judges' cases, there was no rational basis to pay the New York City Family Court judges less than the Nassau Family Court judges. The judges were skeptical, however. They had lost in *Cass* and did not think that they could get a second bite of the apple. A number of them were also not comfortable with suing the State again. They also told me that Murray Gordon, a prominent New York City lawyer who had unsuccessfully represented them in *Cass,* had advised them that a second lawsuit was doomed to fail.

Nonetheless, a majority of the judges decided that if some lawyer from the sticks was willing to embark on a fool's errand, they would let him do it. They would not, however, throw good money after bad and pay a legal fee. I said that I would not charge them a penny and would finance the litigation. They agreed that if by some stroke of magic I won, they would be happy to give me one-third of any monies I would get for them. I jumped at the opportunity.

The New York City Family Court—covering all of the five boroughs—had lots of judges. Forty-two were willing to sign the contingency fee agreement which I had prepared, including Judge Judith Sheindlin, who was then the court's supervising judge. Little did I know, as the '90s loomed, that I would be representing Judge Judy.

Chapter
5

Practicing
The Nineties

Much to the dismay of most of the family court judges—but not to me—Westchester Supreme Court Justice Delaney held, on May 29, 1990, that all plaintiffs, including those who were plaintiffs in *Cass,* should be treated the same as their Nassau colleagues. He also ruled that they were entitled to back pay from October 1, 1978— just like the Suffolk judges in the *Weissman* cases—and awarded counsel fees. Justice Delaney was satisfied that the facts which we submitted clearly showed that there was no rational justification for New York State to pay the busier New York City Family Court judges less than their Nassau counterparts. The State appealed. The appellate division would have yet another pay parity case to decide.

In the appellate court, the State shifted gears. It did not challenge the lower court's finding that the salary statute was unconstitutional. Instead it argued that the family court judges who were plaintiffs in *Cass* should be tossed out of court because they had there unsuccessfully "challenged the same statute on the same grounds, namely, that the disparity in salaries denied them the equal protection of the laws." The State argued that, in any event, neither back pay nor counsel fees were warranted.

On March 25, 1991, the appeals court rejected all of these contentions. As for *Cass*, it pointed out that there the plaintiffs challenged the salary statute as being unconstitutional "on its face," whereas here the plaintiffs challenged the statute as being unconstitutional "as applied." It explained, therefore, that "the material evidence necessary to support the claim at bar is very different from the evidence required in the *Cass* trial." We were entitled to win because we had submitted "hundreds of pages of statistical information and articles to demonstrate the similarities between the City of New York and Nassau County." The appellate court also agreed with the lower court that the plaintiffs were entitled to receive back pay from October 1, 1978, and counsel fees. Because the salary disparities were so large and many of the judges had been on the court since that date, the State had to fork over more than $4.5 million. I made a million and a half bucks. It was a huge win.

Murray Gordon never called to congratulate me.

* * *

The back pay checks that the judges received varied. Those who had been on the family court bench since October 1, 1978, received in excess of $100,000. I billed the judges separately for my one-third fee. Many were very grateful and called to personally thank me. Three of the 42 were not so gracious. They refused to pay. Two of them changed their minds after I told them that I would have to sue. The third called my bluff. I guess he thought that no lawyer would ever sue a judge. I tried to reason with him that he was simply a client. I told him that it was inappropriate to try to use his judicial status to avoid paying a just debt. He was arrogant. I sued him. Within days after he was served with the summons, his lawyer called and apologized profusely for the judge's bad behavior. Two days later I got his check in the mail. I thought that if I were ever a judge I would hope that I would never hide behind my robe for my own personal advantage.

I had one other unpleasant experience with a member of the bench. I got a phone call from a federal district judge from Manhattan who told me that she had been a New York City Family Court judge before she got on the federal bench. She wanted to know why I had not included her in the lawsuit. I told her that I had no idea that she had been a family court judge. In any event, even if I had known, she would not have been one of the plaintiffs. I explained in a calm, respectful way that the statute of limitations was six years. That meant that the only judges who could be plaintiffs had to have been family court judges within six years from the time when we brought the lawsuit. She would not have made the cut. The judge was not happy. She made it perfectly clear that I was talking to a federal court judge. She berated me and was just plain rude. I ended the call as soon as I could.

Nonetheless, the worm usually turns. When it was my turn to become a federal judge, three years later, I was invited to a reception sponsored by the Federal Bar Council for new judges. All of the district court judges from the Southern and Eastern Districts of New York were also invited. I hardly knew anyone. Judge Korman was kind enough to take me around and introduce me to many of the judges. There she was. "This is my new colleague, Judge Block," he said. "Have you met?" Before she could speak, I said "Yes, but not in person." She never said a word. I walked away.

I remember that telephone call whenever I talk to someone who is not fortunate enough to have the job I have, regardless of that person's station in life.

* * *

While I was writing about the family court judges' case, I asked Alex, my law clerk, to try to find out how I could speak to Judge Judy. I assumed that since she had just been given a two-year extension for her wildly popular TV show—at $45,000,000 a year— she might be difficult to get a hold of. I wanted to find out how much money I had given her as one of my 42 family court clients. I had not saved the file.

Alex, like most smart guys his age, was a whiz at the Internet and found the telephone number for Judge Judy's New York office. The woman who answered when he called did not give her name.

131

He told her why he was calling. She said she would call back. A few minutes later Alex told me that while I was in the courtroom he got a call from Judge Judy's secretary, who told him that she would like to speak to Judge Block. I called her back and explained why I wanted to talk to her boss. She was as friendly as could be and said that she would get back to me.

I did not know it would be within minutes. I had gone down the hall to talk to Chief Judge Carol Amon when one of her law clerks came into her office to tell us that Judge Judy was on the phone looking for Judge Block. I told the law clerk to take her number and tell her that I would call her back. I think it must have been her private phone because she answered it directly when I called her after I had finished talking to the Chief.

Judge Sheindlin, as I called her, was open and friendly. I was struck by the fact that she had no celebrity affect. We spoke for about 20 minutes. She remembered that she was one of my clients in the family court judges' case but did not recall how much back pay she got. I told her that I would try to find out. She was in no hurry to hang up. She told me how blessed she was that her life turned out so well. I told her that I felt the same way even though I was making $43,826,400 a year less than she was. She laughed. I explained why I was writing my book. She asked me whether I had a title for it yet. I said that I was thinking of calling it *Disrobed*. She shot back that it was pretty good, but not as good as the name of her first book, *Don't Pee on My Leg and Tell Me It's Raining*. I told her I would send her a draft of what I would be saying about her in my book. I thought that it would be the right thing to do. She thanked me and told me to send it to her secretary. She would read it after she got back from taking her grandchildren to Europe. I told her that I would also send the entire book to her before it was published and would be happy to get whatever feedback she might be willing to give me.

Subsequently I found out from court records that I got Judith Sheindlin $35,368 in back pay, plus 9% interest from 1983—the year when she had become a family court judge. I guess it did not dissuade her from trying to earn a little more.

* * *

At the time when I was handling the family court judges' case I was practicing law in Smithtown. I had bought a small building on Main Street. Across the street was Dr. Phillip Levitan's medical office. He was a highly regarded local surgeon. I knew that he also had a showbiz hobby. He produced a couple of made-for-TV movies. I told him about *Professionally Speaking*. We had a common bond outside of our professional lives and became good friends.

Phil Levitan would brag about his son Kenny, and for good reason. Kenny Levitan had become a big shot agent in Nashville, Tennessee for many country music stars. I told Phil that after *Professionally Speaking* I had started to write country songs. I played a bunch of them for him. He liked one in particular, *She Was a Cheap Date, but Look What She's Costing Me Now*. He invited me to come to Nashville with him to meet his son. I had never been there before. I took him up on his offer.

Naturally I went to the Grand Ole Opry. Kenny arranged for us to go back stage and introduced me to a bunch of the performers. Afterwards, Phil took me to Nashville's big outdoor amphitheater to see Frankie Valli and the Four Seasons. Phil told me that he had gone to Nashville's great medical school at Vanderbilt and had at the same time another life representing some struggling wannabe music stars. Somehow he met Bob Gaudio—who would write most of Frankie's hits—and became his agent, but before Frankie and Bob created the Four Seasons, Phil had moved on with his medical career. He did, however, remain friends with them throughout the years.

After the show we went back stage and hung out with Frankie for a while. He told me that he could no longer hit the high notes and had a backup guy do it for him. He was terrific. I told him that I was going to try to peddle some of my country songs. He said that it was not his thing and wished me good luck. I remembered this special night years later when I saw *Jersey Boys*.

While I was in Nashville, Phil introduced me to some country music producers that he and Kenny knew. One of them also liked *Cheap Date* and said that he would try to get it recorded by one of his boys. It never happened. I did, however, put together a demo of 10 of Tex Block's greatest country songs. Sad to say, none of them ever got performed. The demo did get me picked, however, as a student by Hugh Prestwood for the country music song writing class he taught in Manhattan at the New School. He had written most of Randy Travis' hits, who was then the top country music singer in the country. I showed up for the first class the same day that I had argued the family court judges' case in the appellate division. It was shades of Tony Tanner all over again. Hugh was dressed in his boots and 10 gallon hat. As I walked into the class, he looked at me in my pin-striped lawyer's uniform and told me that I did not have to dress like that for him.

I had a great time in Hugh Prestwood's class. He would play the latest country song that he was composing. It would become another one of Randy Travis' hits. He also listened and critiqued my songs as well as the other six students'—who also wore boots. I was the oldest by 35 years. Hugh liked my songs but said that they were a little dated. I took his assessment to heart and realized that I was doomed to forever be a lawyer.

Nevertheless, I was getting burnt out with private practice. I was doing a lot of work for some wealthy clients, and though I was now making a decent income, I was getting tired of using my legal talents to make rich people richer. I was approaching my 60th birthday. I wanted to do something else. It would probably be law-related but in the public sector. Perhaps I would become a full-time law professor—if that were possible at my age. I was then a part-time adjunct professor at Touro Law School. If nothing interesting materialized I would volunteer for the Peace Corps. It was time for a change.

* * *

When, in 1993, I learned that Senator Moynihan had another chance to recommend a candidate for a district court judgeship on the Eastern District bench, I thought that I would give it another shot. Since I was last before his merit-selection committee eight years before, I had tried a number of federal cases in the federal courts. There now was a small makeshift federal court facility in a converted office building in Suffolk. It was not a courthouse, but we were able to try cases there. I had also written a few articles for law journals. With my heightened federal trial credentials, my teaching and writing, and the notoriety that I got from representing Judge Judy and her family court colleagues, I thought that I had stronger credentials than when I lost out to Judge Korman in 1985.

I did not get the judgeship. It went to David Trager. It was well-deserved. He had been the Eastern District's United States Attorney and was then Dean of the Brooklyn Law School. He was credited with transforming the U.S. Attorney's Office into a professional, nonpartisan shop. He expanded the law school and presided over a top faculty. He was the head of the New York State Investigation Committee that had investigated the conduct of the Suffolk County police and District Attorney back in the late '80s. He also was the chair of Mayor Koch's judicial selection committee.

I should have realized that Dave Trager would be the next EDNY district judge and not have tossed my hat in the ring again. Still, since I had been recommended to Senator Moynihan the last time, I thought that I should give it a shot. The members of the committee were friendly to me. Many had been there when the committee had sent me and Judge Korman to the Senator, but Dave Trager was a lock. The committee had apparently already decided that he should get the nod. I felt some discomfort in the room when it went through the formality of interviewing me.

The next year Clinton succeeded George H. W. Bush as President. There now were three vacancies on the EDNY bench and many in the Southern District, as well as others throughout the state. Judgeships usually backed up during the last year of a President's term. Senator Moynihan would now have three out of four picks, including all of the EDNY openings. I thought about trying again, but initially decided not to. I was a two-time loser. It would be embarrassing to go before Moynihan's committee again. Nevertheless, John Bracken talked me into it. John had been president of the Suffolk Bar Association and was now the president of the New York State Bar Association. He had friends in high places, including some who were members of the Senator's committee. They told him that I was held in high regard and had a really good chance of being recommended to Senator Moynihan once more. I also had the support of Nick Robfogel, a Cornell Law School classmate who was a highly regarded lawyer from Rochester. He told me that he had put in a good word for me to a good friend of his, David Hoffberg, who was a member of Moynihan's committee.

Chapter
6

Payoff

This time things were different. Judah Gribetz—who was now the committee's chair—set the stage by asking me how the Shelter Island dentist was doing. Herb Rubin said that he had seen *Professionally Speaking*. It was almost like a lovefest. When it was over I was confident that I would be one of the committee's recommendations.

In addition to me, five others were recommended for the three slots. There was only one other from Long Island: Jeffrey Stark. He would be my competition if the Senator were inclined to pick one from the suburbs. I did not think that I had much of a chance. Jeffrey was the senior litigation partner at Nassau's most prestigious law firm, Meyer, Suozzi, English & Klein. John English had died a few years before but had been a powerful national Democratic leader. He was the architect behind Robert Kennedy's successful New York senatorial campaign. Thomas Suozzi, also a Democrat, was a major player in Long Island politics and had been a judge of the appellate division. His son would become the Nassau County Executive. Basil Patterson was a Democratic power broker in New York City and the father of a future governor of the State of New York. Yet another partner of the firm, Harold Ickes, was a mover and shaker in Democratic politics on the national scene. They all had close ties to Senator Moynihan. I had nobody. I also had to worry about my old nemesis and former partner, Dominic Baranello, who, although no longer the chairman of the state Democratic

Party, was still the head of the Suffolk County Democrats. He, too, knew Moynihan.

I was surprised when the Senator picked me over Jeffrey Stark. His two other choices were assistant U.S. Attorneys from the Brooklyn office. Allyne Ross came from the appeals bureau. John Gleeson had just successfully prosecuted John Gotti. The Senator obviously thought that all three of his candidates should not be prosecutors or come from Brooklyn. His third choice would, therefore, come from Long Island.

Daniel Patrick Moynihan was one of a kind. Although he was a Democrat, he was fiercely independent and appealed to voters of all persuasions. He truly believed in merit appointments to the federal bench. He would not be influenced by politics. He was so different in that respect from other senators.

The federal judges do have to have threshold qualifications for the job, and the system is geared to weed out those who do not measure up. From my observations over the years, however, the surest way to becoming a federal judge is to be the best buddy of a senator. Other times it makes good political sense for a senator to support the judgeship candidacy of someone who has been a thorn in the side of his political party. Most often the dominant concern motivating the recommendation to the President is pure politics: Does it make good political sense? Is there a particular constituency that I want to curry favor with? Do I "owe" it to a major contributor to my campaigns? Those who get to be judges this way are often asked, "Who was your rabbi?"—a common expression, at least in New York, meaning, "Who *really* got you your job?"

No one believes me when I tell them that I had no rabbi. I had only met Senator Moynihan once, when he picked Judge Korman. I did not know him. I never gave him any money for his campaigns. Years after I was on the bench Judah Gribetz told me that the Senator had simply asked him which of the committee's six candidates he should pick. Judah said that I was number one. That is all that there was to it. If not for Senator Moynihan's disdain for political appointments and his commitment to pure merit selection, I would never have become a federal judge.

Senator Moynihan's impact on the federal judiciary would be profound. He was a United States Senator for 24 years. He was responsible for putting more judges on the federal bench than any other senator in the history of the nation: 43. His New York judges dominate the judiciary to this day. They are all highly qualified and are considered to be amongst the best in the country. The most prominent is, of course, Supreme Court Justice Sonia Sotomayor.

* * *

I remember the date that the Senator called to tell me that he had chosen me—April 17, 1994—and, in particular, the embarrassing circumstances. It was Sunday, and I had to be in my office with my secretary, Tina, to finish a brief that had to be filed the next day. While Tina was typing away, her 17-year-old son had called a number of times, pestering her with all sorts of idle chatter. Unbeknownst to both of us, Senator Moynihan—who was known by his friends as "Pat," the same name as my secretary's son—had called my home, and Cooky had given him my office number. When Tina's phone rang the next time, I overheard her scream, "Pat, what the hell do you want now?"

The Senator was not deterred. We laughed. He asked me whether I still wanted to be a judge. We met at his Senate office in Washington two days later. I took my son with me. Neil was then in law school. We waited nervously in the Senator's main office for him to arrive. When he did, he told Neil that he wanted to speak to his father alone. He took me down the corridor to his private office and sat me down in a winged chair. He told me that Yasser Arafat had sat there the day before. True to his intellectual bent, he took from his desk a copy of his latest book, *Pandaemonium*, and asked me whether I had read it. I told him I had. I read all of this books, just in case he asked me about any of them.. It paid off. He took out his pen, wrote something on the inside cover, closed the book, handed it to me, and told me that he never expected to see me again unless he was a defendant in my courtroom. He then walked me back to his main office and told Neil to take his father to the pub across the street and buy his dad a martini; the Senator was known to down a few from time to time. Neil dutifully obeyed. After the first sip, I opened up the book and read what the Senator had written: "To Judge Frederic Block. With great respect."

* * *

Being recommended to the White House by a senator, however, does not guarantee that you will be nominated by the President and confirmed by the Senate. The road from recommendation to nomination to confirmation is long, arduous, and full of potential pitfalls. I was nominated in June and confirmed by the Senate in September, about six months from the date that I received Senator Moynihan's call. I was told that this was a relatively quick turn-around, but the delay was difficult to live with. My small firm practice was very much dependent on my generating business. Once the news spread that I was likely to become a judge, the clients stopped coming, believing, quite logically, that I would not be able to handle their cases.

In the meantime, here is what was happening: The American Bar Association has a 13-member judicial screening committee, each of whom individually rates federal judicial candidates as either highly qualified, qualified, or unqualified. The members are appointed by the president of the association from across the nation and generally are recognized as highly regarded lawyers. One is assigned to personally interview the candidate and render a full report to the committee. Before doing so, the candidate must complete the committee's own extensive questionnaire—somewhat similar to the one that I had to submit to Senator Moynihan's committee. The interviewer is expected to conduct a "due diligence" investigation—checking references, obtaining the opinions of prior adversaries and judges who had presided over the candidate's trials, and, in general, trying to get a sense of the candidate's professional and personal reputation.

I was interviewed by Arnold Burns, a prominent large-firm lawyer from New York City and a former United States Deputy Attorney General. He insisted on coming to my modest office in Smithtown, although I offered to meet him in New York City. Instead he wanted to make the three hour trek to the middle of Suffolk County. I guess that he wanted to see my office and get a sense of what a small-town practice was all about. I was somewhat intimidated.

I guess Mr. Burns gave me a good report since 11 members of his committee found me highly qualified; two gave me the lesser qualified rating. While I would have loved to have been unanimously found highly qualified, I was happy that no one thought that I was unqualified.

Although there is no law requiring a candidate to cooperate with the ABA and nothing that precludes a candidate from becoming a judge if found unqualified, it used to be that a President would not, with rare exceptions, nominate a candidate who was not found qualified by it, given the ABA's place as the leading organized bar association in the country and the meticulous way in which it passed upon a candidate's qualifications. This changed with the presidency of George W. Bush, who believed that the association was biased against his type of jurist; he decided, therefore, that he would not wait for the ABA's rating before placing a candidate's name before the Senate for confirmation. To be sure, there were senators who still took the association's ratings seriously, but there would then be more candidates found unqualified by the American Bar Association who became federal judges.

The ABA was not the only bar association that screened candidates. The prestigious Association of the Bar of the City of New York wanted to have its say as to whether it believed the candidates from the two district courts covering the City would be capable of handling the City's judicial business. Given the practical clout of the City bar, the candidates generally went along with submitting themselves to its judicial screening process. This meant filling out yet another elaborate questionnaire and an interview by its full judiciary committee, which rates candidates either qualified or unqualified. I was told that I was found qualified. I do not know what the vote was.

Next came the F.B.I. and the Justice Department. I had to fill out two more questionnaires. The one for the F.B.I. had a question that gave me a headache. Question 17 asked for the names, addresses, and telephone numbers of any shrinks that I had ever seen— including marriage counselors. I had to name all seven. In addition, I would be interviewed by two F.B.I. agents. I thought that it would be curtains.

As I walked into the interview room at the F.B.I.'s offices in lower Manhattan, I was greeted by an officious, stern-looking male agent. The other agent was a slightly overweight, pleasant-looking female. Sure enough, as soon as I sat, the man picked up my questionnaire and bellowed: "Mr. Block, let's talk about Question 17." The good Lord must have wanted me to become a federal district judge, however. I started to explain that Cooky and I had been in marital counseling for a number of years. However, before I could elaborate, the female agent abruptly put an end to it: "I don't think Mr. Block has to say anything else. I've been in therapy myself. I think it has made me a better person. Mr. Block will probably be a better judge because of it." I wanted to kiss her. The rest of the interview was uneventful. They were satisfied that I did not pose a security risk, was a good citizen, and was loyal to the country.

The Justice Department had two functions: First, to make sure that there were no skeletons in my closet that could embarrass the President if he were to nominate me. Once nominated, it was to shepherd me through the Senate confirmation hearing.

The Department had a separate office just to deal with judicial candidates, and it assigned one of its attorneys to look for the skeletons. The office was headed at that time by Eleanor Dean Acheson, the niece of the late Dean Acheson, President Truman's Secretary of State. Tim Macht, a brilliant recent graduate from Harvard Law School, was my skeleton-seeker. The Justice Department's questionnaire was more extensive than any of the others, but, to my great relief, there was no Question 17. I had to disclose every one of my writings that had ever been made public. It was Tim's job to follow up on all of the information which I provided and to make sure that nothing was left out. It seemed that he called me every day, and when my secretary would tell me that "Mr. Macht was on the phone," I took a deep breath and wondered, "What now?"

Actually, Tim was only doing his job, and he did it extraordinarily well. I remember the day that he called asking for a copy of the libretto of *Professionally Speaking*. I never wrote anything about *Professionally Speaking* in any of the questionnaires since I did not think it bore upon my qualifications for judicial office. I also was concerned that I might be thought of as more interested in show business than the law. I was wrong on both counts.

I do not know to this day how Tim Macht found out about the show, but he told me that he had to have *everything*. I sent the entire score to him, wondering whether the few scatological lyrics—fit for the theater, but not for the courtroom—would doom my nomination. I was apprehensive when a few weeks later I had to go to Washington to be interviewed by Eleanor Acheson's office, even though this was a normal part of the vetting process. When I arrived, I met Tim Macht for the first time. He was serious, but friendly. He took me into a large conference room. I was greeted by Ms. Acheson and a number of Justice Department lawyers sitting around a large, oval-shaped table. As I sat, my worst fears were realized. The first thing that they wanted to know about was *Professionally Speaking*.

Much to my surprise, they were genuinely pleased that there was more to me than the law. They told me that many candidates took themselves too seriously and that they looked favorably upon those who might add a human touch to the bench, a perspective which helped shape my approach to how I should act as a judge.

On July 22, 1994, just a few weeks after the interview, I was nominated by the President, and my name was sent to the Senate for confirmation.

* * *

The confirmation process is fraught with peril. The Senate never gets to vote on your nomination unless you first get voted out of its Judiciary Committee. Not everyone makes it. The stories are legion about all sorts of casualties for all sorts of political reasons having nothing to do with the candidate's qualifications. Any member of the committee can veto the nomination. The committee has its own questionnaire—the fourth I had to do—and conducts a hearing on all nominees.

Once nominated by the President, the Justice Department becomes your advocate and guides you through the hearing process. It will find out if any senator has a particular question for you to answer and will generally counsel you on how to handle yourself at the hearing. I was told that there did not appear to be any problem with my candidacy and that I should try to relax and get a good night's sleep the night before the hearing. I also drew comfort from the fact that Senator Moynihan was held in high esteem by his fellow senators. He was also chair of the powerful Senate Finance Committee, making it even more unlikely that any of his colleagues would rebuff him.

A few days before the hearing, I decided to pay a courtesy call to Senator Moynihan's New York Republican counterpart. I met Senator Alphonse D'Amato at his office next to Penn Station. He told me how pleased he was that I stopped by. I told him that I thought it was the right thing to do since I strongly believed that judges must truly be perceived as nonpolitical. We got along well. He kept me there for over an hour telling me wonderful stories. I was glad I went.

There probably never will be two senators from the same state at one time so different than Senators Moynihan and D'Amato. While Pat Moynihan was the resident intellectual of the Senate, having taught at Harvard and authored five books, Al D'Amato was a nuts and bolts regular guy priding himself on being a people person and delivering on the most basic constituent needs—earning the name "Senator Pothole." Still, one thing they had in common: they both prided themselves on putting highly qualified lawyers on the bench and even occasionally crossed party lines to do it. Senator Moynihan selected Judge Trager even though he was a Republican, while Senator D'Amato picked my colleagues Judges Arthur Spatt and Sterling Johnson—both Democrats.

When I arrived in Washington the day before my confirmation hearing, I did not hear from Senator Moynihan; I imagined that he might be working on his next book and took no offense, but true to form, Senator D'Amato had his office call to make sure everything was alright. It was his considerate way of assuring me that I had his support.

All went well the next day. There was only one Judiciary Committee member present, its chair, Senator Howell Heflin from Alabama. After Senator Moynihan presented his Eastern District court candidates to him, Senator Heflin just asked each of us a few softball questions in his Southern drawl and wished us good luck.

On September 14, 1994, I was unanimously voted out of the committee. Two weeks later, while I was at a Mazda dealership trying to lease a car, the saleswoman, who was in the midst of checking my credit rating, received a call from the White House; my office had said that I was there. With a look of incredulity, she handed me the phone. When I hung up I told her that I had just become a federal district judge. She leased me the car.

Over the next few weeks I cleaned up my office, tried to deal with a few pending cases, notified my clients that I could no longer be their lawyer, and bought a robe (the government doesn't give you one). I was sworn in on Halloween, October 31. It struck me as an appropriate day to wear my judicial costume for the first time.

Chapter
7

Reflections

On June 7, 2011, I was at Citi Field watching the Mets get blown out by the Pirates. My stockbroker, Brendan Walsh, had invited me to be his guest. He had two extra tickets. I asked him whether I could bring Neil and his son, Jordan. He had never met them and insisted that we all have dinner before the game in the ballpark's fancy dining room. My grandson had just finished his second year of college at Cornell and was about to start a summer internship with one of the largest law firms in the world, Skadden, Arps, Meagher & Flom. He liked Mr. Walsh and listened intently as Brendan told him about what was going on in the stock market. Suddenly Jordan asked: "Mr. Walsh, if I gave you $1,000 today how long would it take before I would have $2,000?"

I have a habit of lecturing my five grandkids about values. I always jump at the opportunity to drive home the point that there is more to life than money. Jordan's question to my stockbroker caused me to reflect about what I had written in the first part of this book. I realized that what had made me a viable candidate for the bench were all of the things that I had done for little or no money—other than the family court judges case. I thought about the re-apportionment case; the Sarisohn and Clayton cases; my battles with United Artists to save Theatre Three; the *Police Brutality Report*; continuing legal education; my local and state bar association activities; my teaching and writings. I also reflected upon the elections that I lost and not taking the easy way out by becoming part of what I saw as a corrupt political establishment. Then there was, of course, *Professionally Speaking* and my country songs.

So I told Jordan that while you have to take care of business and make a living, at the end of the day it is the other things that you do that make the difference in the quality of a life, and I ended my little lecture by telling him that if it were not for those "other things," I would not be having the enriched life that I now have as a federal judge.

While I was driving home from the ball game that night I thought about how I did take care of business and make a living. Although it was not the stuff that got me on the bench—and would not make interesting reading—I did not want anyone who might read my book to think that my everyday life as a lawyer was all roses. What I had written were the highlights. The book needed some balance.

* * *

Until I became a judge, the chest pains never entirely went away. If the office was quiet and the phone was not ringing with new business, I would get anxiety attacks. I dealt with them by doing some deep-breathing exercises and just literally walking out of the office. I would not go there unless I had to see a client or give work to my secretary.

While I was doing the special things that I have written about, I made most of my money by taking care of ordinary things that make up the general practice of a suburban lawyer: wills, real estate closings, simple negligence cases, small commercial matters, and divorces. It was not until the late 80s and early 90s that I started to make some real money, thanks largely, once again, to the family court judges' case and some litigation I was handling for some wealthy clients. I remember having dinner in Port Jefferson with Gus and Sylvia Kogel in the mid-'70s when I had just turned 40. They owned a successful lumber business and let me handle some collection work. While we were having our coffee at the end of the dinner Sylvia commented on how well their business was doing and made the offhand comment that some people do not even have

$1,000 in their bank account. I was too embarrassed to tell her that I was one of those people.

* * *

Some of my everyday experiences stand out because they represented the human condition that is the stuff of a local, small-firm suburban law practice. One involved a successful businessman who was a kleptomaniac. He had a specialty. He would walk into a shoe store and exchange the shoes he was wearing for a new pair from the rack. He was stopped one day and arrested while walking out with his new shoes. After he apologized to the store owner—and paid for the shoes—the charges were dropped. Being a true kleptomaniac, he did this several more times at different shoe stores until he was caught again. This time he was not so lucky. The owner would not drop the charges, but it was a blessing in disguise. He got a conditional discharge. The condition was that he had to seek professional help. He did. He made do afterwards with his old shoes.

I had another kleptomaniac. He was a successful insurance salesman. He had just earned a $100,000 commission and had the check in his pocket when he walked into Bloomingdale's to buy a gift for his wife. He walked out with a man's mink coat on his back. The check was still in his pocket. He did not have a clue as to why he did that. He had never done anything illegal before. We explained it all to the judge and prevailed upon Bloomingdale's to drop the charges.

Domestic matters were a fertile ground for strange happenings. I remember handling a divorce for a young couple in their early 20s. She was a knockout—tall and blond—and reminded me of Daisy Mae except that when she spoke she sounded like an idiot. He struck me as a bright guy. Within weeks after the ink had dried on the divorce decree he came back to introduce me to his new wife. She was at least 50 and hardly resembled Daisy Mae, but she was well-spoken and they seemed to be very happy. When I recount this story, I think about another book that Judge Judy has written, *Beauty Fades but Dumb Is Forever.*

One day a middle-aged man came to see me. He was obviously distraught. For many years he had owned a second-hand clothing store in Harlem. It was strictly a cash business. Over the years he had stashed away about $2 million in a safe deposit box in the Roslyn Savings Bank. Only one other person had the key—his loyal wife of 25 years. Both the money and the wife had disappeared. He suspected that she took off with the French house painter. What should he do? The choice was simple. Either he reported it to the authorities, admitted to cheating the IRS for two decades and risk going to jail, or say c'est la vie and chalk it up to one of life's little surprises. He said c'est la vie.

Then there was the prominent businessman who really had a bad hair day. He had been celebrating a big deal that he had put together and had had a little too much to drink at a local gin mill. The next thing he remembered was driving to Maryland with some floozy he had picked up. Fortunately, she did the driving. He told me that they had stopped at a Justice of the Peace house late at night and got married. I had heard that you could do quickie marriages in that state, but this took the cake. When he awoke the next day, his bride, car, and wallet naturally were gone.

It was an incredible story, and I had a hard time believing it. However, he had sobered up, was meticulously dressed, and was totally coherent and convincing. He was ashamed of himself. He told me that he was happily married with two wonderful teenage boys. He asked me whether he should fess up to his wife—who was wondering why he never came home that night—and tell her that he was a bigamist. I hate to tell people to lie, but I made an exception in his case. I told him to chalk it up to a bad dream and sent him on his way. I do not know, however, how he explained the loss of his car to his family and why he did not come home that night.

There were interesting episodes with names. I had to petition the court to change Ellen Cooperman's name to Ellen Cooperperson. She really took women's lib to heart. The pièce de résistance, however, was the recently married couple who wanted to buy two homes. I was happy to handle the double house closing. They were academics with a strong independent bent. They thought it best for each to have their own house so that they could concentrate on their intellectual pursuits during the week. They would get together in one of their new homes on the weekends. That was strange enough, but they had their new baby son with them at the closings whom they had yet to name. When I asked why, they told me that they thought that they would wait to see how his personality developed. A year later they came back to make out wills. Their son was with them. He was now a chubby little boy. I could not wait to learn his name. They told me that they had recently named him Joseph. I never could understand why it took them so long to name him Joe.

My own son would occasionally hang out with me when I went about my legal business. When Neil was a teenager, he came with me one night to the gymnasium of the Comsewogue High School. I was still the lawyer for the school district. I had to be there to supervise the voting that was taking place on the budget and for school board elections. Neil watched from a distance as I was opening up the voting machines. Afterwards I took him out for a bite to eat. Neil told me that some guy had come up to him and told him that he was one of the candidates for the school board. He did not know that he was talking to my son. He told Neil that if he were elected the first thing that he was going to do was fire the lawyer. Fortunately, he lost.

When Neil was in law school he came to court with me one day while on spring break to watch me pick a jury. As we were looking over the jury pool, he told me that he had learned in his trial practice class that if you did not like the way that a prospective juror looked, then you could rest assured that he did not like you either. I asked Neil what I should do if I did not like the way any of them looked. He said, "Settle the case." I knew right then that he would become a good lawyer, and he did.

I lost my fair share of cases. One in particular still haunts me.

151

Dorothy Steckel got stuck in an elevator at the health sciences building at the SUNY Stony Brook. It plummeted 10 floors. She was badly hurt. Her case was easily worth six figures. The elevator company did not offer her a decent settlement, and we went to trial. I thought that it was a slam dunk, but the insurance carrier produced records from the elevator company showing that it had regularly inspected the elevator and that there was nothing wrong with it. I took the case for granted. I did not think that I had to have an expert check it out to explain to the jury how this could have happened. I was wrong. I was shocked when the jury came back with a defendant's verdict. I remembered Neil's advice. I guess there were a lot of jurors whose faces I did not like. The lesson served me well. I would never go into the courtroom again—whether as a litigant or judge—unprepared.

* * *

I finished the first part of *Disrobed* as firecrackers were going off on July 4, 2011. As I wrote the last paragraph, I thought that if that young lawyer whom I sat next to at the Waldorf during my first week on the bench 17 years ago were to someday read it, he would then know the full story of how I became a federal district judge from that first day that I hung up my shingle as a solo small-town lawyer.

PART II

BEING THERE

Chapter
1

The Start

Right out of the box I had to make an important professional decision. The EDNY now had two federal courthouses. I could sit in the new Long Island courthouse in Central Islip—the middle of Suffolk County—or return to the place of my birth and be a judge in the Brooklyn courthouse. At that time there were five judges in CI and 15 in Brooklyn. The differences between the two courts were significant. The CI cases all came from Suffolk and Nassau. The Brooklyn cases mostly had their roots in New York City. It was where the Mafia was prosecuted—John Gotti had just been convicted there. It was where the action was.

However, I would then be playing on the big-city stage. I was well known in Suffolk County, but unknown to the City's law firms and the Brooklyn U.S. Attorney's Office. I was not part of that world. Since Judge Korman was put on the bench in Brooklyn in 1985, seven others had come on board there. Judges David Trager, Raymond J. Dearie, and Reena Raggi—like Judge Korman—had been EDNY U.S. Attorneys; Judge Carol Amon had been an AUSA;

Judge Sterling Johnson had been Special Narcotics Prosecutor for New York City. Together with Judges Gleeson and Ross, they shared one thing in common: they were all prosecutors from the City. I could stay in the cozy confines of my home turf or venture forth into the Big Apple as a fish out of water.

I chose to be the fish. I thought that since I was the only one of this recent crop of EDNY judges who had mixed it up in the regular, everyday practice of law that I had something different to offer. Moreover, after three decades of being a Suffolk County lawyer, I was ready for a change of scenery. I was, however, apprehensive. I would be leaving my reputation behind and starting all over in a strange environment dominated by colleagues who were entrenched in the New York City establishment. They were all known to, and respected by, the government prosecutors from the Office. I would be odd man out.

My fears were not unjustified. During my second year on the bench a new prosecutor from the Office—John Kroger—had his first trial before me. He left the Office shortly after and has had a distinguished career; he was recently elected Attorney General of Oregon. In 2008 he wrote a book, *Convictions*. In it he recounted how apprehensive he was when he learned that his case was assigned to me. Here's what he said about my judicial colleagues and the new judge:

> When the President appoints a new federal trial judge, the last thing he wants is controversy. Most presidents choose safe, solid nominees, the kind that flies through the Senate approval process. The result, for better or worse, is a bench with a uniform, socially conservative outlook on life. The federal judges on the Eastern District bench, for example, tend to be pretty stodgy. Many are former prosecutors, and the rest typically practiced at large Manhattan corporate law firms. These judges may not always rule in the government's favor, but they understand and respect what the government prosecutors are trying to accomplish, and they usually give them a fair hearing. Many defense attorneys believe they have a pro-government bias.

Judge Fred Block was cut from a different cloth. Appointed to the federal bench in 1994 by President Clinton, Block had worked out on Long Island for his entire career, in solo practice and in very small firms. He was a lifetime member of the NAACP and had been active in various arts organizations. He had no prosecutorial background. He was often seen, friends told me, in Manhattan nightclubs, dressed in leather, drinking martinis.

As a rookie I had never appeared before Judge Block, but I had heard many rumors about him. Block, senior prosecutors told me, was anti-government, viewing many of the office's prosecutions with deep-seated skepticism. He also had a reputation for lawlessness. Instead of making decisions based on the *Federal Rules of Evidence* and the *Sentencing Guidelines*, he was often guided by his own sense of fairness and decency, turning court proceedings into unpredictable free-for-alls. I later concluded that these stories were exaggerated, but they overstated the case only to a degree. Block was not your typical federal judge.

Lest the reader think that the new judge was some kind of kook, rest assured that the rumors did not track reality. Kroger never read the profile of the judge in the Brooklyn Barrister—the official publication of the Brooklyn Bar Association—written by the president of the association:

> Since his appointment by President Clinton in 1994, Hon. Frederic Block has been presiding with patience and distinction from his judicial perch at the downtown Brooklyn Courthouse, processing over a docket of significant cases and controversies which have earned Judge Block high marks from the Court's keen eyed litigation bar.

Kroger's take on me through his rumor mill—and his view of the nature of the Brooklyn federal bench—convinced me that I made the right decision in choosing to be a judge in Brooklyn. After all, not every judge should be "cut from the same cloth," and if being a "typical federal judge" meant that you had to be "stodgy" and had been a prosecutor or had come from a Manhattan corporate law firm, I was glad that I was not a typical judge.

Nevertheless, Kroger's comments crystalized what I was up against. Most of the trials that I would have would be criminal cases. They all would be prosecuted by assistant U.S. attorneys from the Office. Since I was not a former prosecutor and "one of them," they would not be as comfortable trying cases before me as with one of my colleagues. As Kroger put it, the other judges understood and respected "what the government prosecutors are trying to accomplish." Although my new colleagues were a terrific bunch of judges—and they greeted me with open arms—I was convinced that there was a need for at least one judge who was not part of Kroger's world. Contrary to his perception, I was neither anti-government nor pro-defendant. I thought that my job would be to call the shots down the middle and be fair to both sides. That is exactly what I would try to do.

* * *

Before I showed up for work the first day, I had found an apartment to rent in Greenwich Village in Manhattan and moved in. I also immersed myself in mastering the *Federal Rules of Evidence* and reading exhaustively anything that I could get my hands on about the federal judiciary. In particular, I thought that while I was getting started I should learn more about how the federal judiciary got started. I knew that the Founding Fathers created the judicial branch in the Constitution, but I wanted to know exactly how it happened. This is what I learned.

After our country had achieved its independence in 1776, the colonies had banded together under the loose-knit Articles of Confederation. It left a lot to be desired. Eleven years later, the new states decided that it was time to try to create a Constitution. They called for the convening of a Convention to be held in Philadelphia. It officially opened for business on May 14, 1787. All of the states except Rhode Island agreed to send delegations. Seven would be needed for a quorum. There would be 55 delegates, but the number that arrived on that scheduled date were too few to conduct business. A quorum was not obtained until 11 days later.

The delegates were some of the greatest political thinkers of the time. While there were no Founding Mothers and all of the delegates were white, they were a talented bunch. They attended some of the world's finest universities, including Harvard, Yale, Princeton, Columbia, and Dartmouth. Each had some experience in the world of politics or in the military. Twenty-nine were lawyers; 44 had served their state legislatures; seven were state judges; seven were even state governors; eight had served in the military; and 37 were also members of the Congress of the Confederation. They ranged in age from 26-year-old Jonathan Dayton of New Jersey to Pennsylvania's Benjamin Franklin, who was then 81. Nine were from New England, 16 from the middle colonies of New York, New Jersey, and Pennsylvania, and 30 from Maryland and the Deep South. George Washington was chosen as the Convention's president.

Alexander Hamilton, James Madison, and George Mason were also delegates. Jefferson and John Adams were not—they were overseas. Patrick Henry—ever the patriot—chose not to have anything to do with the Convention, stating that he "smelt a rat in Philadelphia tending toward the monarchy."

The Constitution was not signed until September 17, 1787. Most of the delegates' time had been devoted to the creation of the executive and legislative branches. By comparison, the judiciary got short shrift. To make matters worse, the summer of '87 in Philly was a scorcher. The heat in the Pennsylvania State House was unbearable. Tempers often flared, and fatigue sapped the delegates' energy. Conditions were so oppressive—and progress so slow—that on June 28 Franklin would "call for prayers" because he was so disheartened by the heat and pace. On July 10, George Washington wrote to Hamilton that he "almost despair[ed] of seeing a favourable issue to the proceedings of our Convention, and do therefore repent having had any agency in the business."

When the delegates turned to the judiciary, there was general agreement that the Constitution should guarantee the right to a trial by jury in serious criminal cases and that there should be a supreme judicial tribunal, but the question of whether there should be a system of lower federal courts was hotly contested. The memory of tyrannical centralized British government led many delegates to fear the power a federal judiciary might wield against the states. In the end, a compromise was struck. In order to get the Constitution passed, the legislative branch was given the *right*, but not the obligation, to create federal courts inferior to the Supreme Court. The battle lines had been drawn. The shape of the federal judiciary would have to be resolved by Congress.

The Judiciary Article—Article III—therefore, was bare-bones. It has never been amended. It had only three sections: Section 1 contained the language that reflected the compromise which the delegates had reached over the composition of the judiciary:

> The judicial Power of the United States shall be vested in one supreme Court, and in such inferior courts as the Congress may from time to time ordain and establish. The Judges, both of the supreme and inferior Courts, shall hold their Offices during good Behaviour and shall, at stated Times, receive for their Services, a Compensation, which shall not be diminished during their Continuance in Office.

"Good Behaviour" meant that the judges could serve for life. The second section addressed the types of cases that could be brought before a federal court. They would be all cases arising under the Constitution, federal laws, and treaties. In addition, federal jurisdiction would extend to cases related to foreign diplomats, admiralty and maritime issues, disputes between states, and disputes between citizens of different states. The section also guaranteed the right to a jury trial for felony cases, but left it to Congress to fill in the details—including the number of jurors.

The last section gave Congress the power "to declare the Punishment of Treason," but only for those who levied war against the United States or gave "Aid and Comfort" to the country's enemies. It also provided that, "No Person shall be convicted of Treason unless on the Testimony of two Witnesses to the same overt Act, or on Confession in open Court."

There were a few other Articles of the Constitution that related to the judiciary. The delegates agreed that federal judges would be appointed by the President with the advice and consent of the Senate and that they could only be removed from office—like the President—through impeachment by the House of Representatives and conviction of "high crimes and misdemeanors" in a trial by the Senate.

The Constitution had to be ratified by two-thirds of the states. This did not happen until June 21, 1788, when New Hampshire became the ninth to give its approval. It took until March 4, 1789, before the new government started to function. It was not until the following year, however, that on May 29, 1790, the last of the 13 states, Rhode Island, voted for ratification.

* * *

Congress did not wait for all of the 13 states to ratify the Constitution, and on September 24, 1789, it passed the Judiciary Act. Appropriately titled an "Act to Establish the Judicial Courts of the United States," it put in place the basic three-tier structure of the federal courts that remains in existence to this day—as well as their jurisdiction—and ended the ongoing debate as to whether the country would have a system of lower courts.

The Act set the number of Supreme Court Justices at six: one Chief Justice and five Associate Justices. It did not reach its present size of nine until 1869. It created 13 judicial districts, each with one district judge. It also established 13 circuit courts, one for each district. The circuit courts each consisted of a district judge and two Supreme Court Justices. The Act fixed the number of jurors at 12, but only in cases punishable by death. The Supreme Court subsequently held, however, that the constitutional guarantee of a jury trial embraced the common-law right to have 12 jurors in all criminal cases, other than for petty offenses.

Two other parts of the Judiciary Act were of particular importance. The Supreme Court was given jurisdiction to review state court decisions where federal law was at issue. Congress also authorized a mechanism to remove state lawsuits between persons from different states to federal court.

Remarkably missing from the Constitution and the Judiciary Act were any qualifications for serving on the Supreme Court or the lower federal courts. The creators of the country's judiciary did not insist on an elitist federal bench. There were no exams to pass, no minimum age requirements, no need for judges to be native-born citizens or legal residents, no requirement that judges even have a law degree. Nor are there any today. Although I know of no federal judge who does not have a law degree, it is simply the responsibility of the President and Senate to put qualified people on the bench.

The passage of the Judiciary Act was no piece of cake. Anti-federalists were incensed. Of the Senators from the ten states that participated in the vote, 4 voted for the Act and six voted against it. From that beginning, the Article III federal judiciary has grown to its present size of 94 judicial districts and 12 geographic circuits, plus the federal circuit.

* * *

In addition to boning up on the history of the federal judiciary, I did a few other things while I was preparing to start my new job. I learned that a district court judge was entitled to have four employees to help him to do his job. One would be a permanent clerk who would be the judge's administrator. The chief clerk of the court would assign this person—subject to the judge's approval—from the pool of full-time clerks on his staff. The other three could be hired by the judge. The general practice at that time was to have one as the judge's personal secretary and the others as his law clerks. I asked Tina Farrell whether she wanted to continue to be my secretary. She was happy to come on board.

I wasn't sure how I would get my two law clerks. They would be critical. A judge's law clerk assists the judge in many important ways. The judge is not always trying cases. Most of the criminal cases wind up with pleas, and only a small percentage of the civil cases make it to trial. Most of the judicial business takes place in chambers, where the judge must weed out which civil cases should be tried. Only those that raise material disputed issues of fact go to trial. This requires deciding written motions to dismiss. The principal job of the law clerk is to review these papers from the lawyers, check out the applicable law, and prepare either a written memorandum or a draft decision.

Most law clerks have just graduated from law school or have been practicing with a large firm for a short period of time. They have invariably done very well in law school. The job is demanding. The general practice in the federal courts is to have one-year clerkships. For the clerks it is a great opportunity to jump-start their legal careers. For the judge, getting new young blood every year keeps the judge's chambers fresh and vital. Some judges, however, keep their clerks for longer periods. A few even have one or more as permanent clerks.

The general protocol is for the judge to select his law clerks in early September for the following fall. A new judge would not have that opportunity. He would need to find clerks right away. I was lucky. Shortly after I was nominated and waiting to be confirmed by the Senate, Ken Ashman called me at my home in Port Jefferson. He had been working for a few years as an associate with a major New York law firm and wanted out. The mega-firms are known for making their money off of the backs of their bright young lawyers. They work ungodly hours and are at the beck and call at all times of senior associates and partners who control their lives. Their work is often pure drudgery. They do the grunt work and rarely get into court.

I never wanted to be part of that world. I thought that it was a form of legal slavery, but the pay is the lure. A second-year associate makes more money than the federal judge. Most new lawyers are heavily in debt. They are willing to give up their lives for a few years to pay off their student loans. Many are then happy to land a federal court clerkship even though they have to take about a $100,000 pay cut.

To be fair, some young lawyers are drawn to the big firms for reasons other than money. A few become partners—usually after many years—and represent major corporate clients. Although they now make millions, many also become leaders of the legal community. Some become federal judges, but most fall out and usually wind up as in-house counsel to one of the firm's corporate clients. Others join small law firms or segue into public service.

Ken Ashman dreamed about someday establishing his own law firm. I was impressed by his excellent academic credentials but equally impressed by the smarts he displayed in finding me. He knew that I had just been nominated and would probably be confirmed. I told him that if the Senate did not reject me, then he had the job. I wondered how many other young lawyers who wanted to get a coveted federal court clerkship would be as clever and assertive as Ken.

My second clerk also jumped into my lap. George Pratt, who was a federal circuit judge on the Second Circuit, called after I had been confirmed and asked whether I would hire Mitch Drucker. Mitch had graduated number one in his law school class, and Judge Pratt had offered him a clerkship. However, the judge had suddenly decided to resign from his lofty judicial perch and return to private practice. I knew George from the days when he was a highly regarded Nassau County lawyer. I also had a few trials before him when he was a district judge—before he was elevated to the appellate court. He was an outstanding trial judge. He did not take, however, to the monastic existence of a Court of Appeals judge. He found it confining and missed the action of the trial bench. Judge Pratt felt badly about not being able to keep his commitment to Mitch and asked me whether I would take him on. I was thrilled to have him as my other law clerk.

Armed with my two law clerks and my secretary, I was now ready to start my judicial career.

Chapter
2

Breaking In

I did not stay out at a nightclub or drink martinis the night before I walked into the courthouse on October 31, 1994, as a newly minted federal district judge. However, I did have a hard time sleeping and got up at 5:30 that morning. I could not get back to sleep. I made a cup of coffee and decided to go to work. The courthouse was right next to the Brooklyn Bridge. I had checked the place out a few weeks before and knew how to find my chambers. It was 7:00 a.m. The place was deserted except for a janitor who was vacuuming the carpet in my office. He knew that I was a new judge. I asked him his name and engaged him in some small talk for about 10 minutes as he went about his work. When he finished, he said, "Judge Block, you're gonna be a good judge." I asked him how he could tell. He said, "Cause you talk to me."

I never would forget that moment. Everyone likes to be acknowledged. Especially if the acknowledgment comes from someone who is perceived to be an important person—like a federal judge—it makes a big difference. I asked myself what would be the best way to interact with the courthouse personnel—the clerks, security officers, cleaning people. It might make them uncomfortable if I were overly friendly, but I would try to learn their names, say "hello," and say a few friendly words.

After the janitor left, I was at a loss as to what to do. I checked to see if the phone was working; found out where the bathroom was; and checked out the adjoining offices where the clerks would be working, as well as the courtroom where I would be trying my cases. Then I waited for Tina to show up. I had opened up the letter from the Federal Bar Council inviting me to the Waldorf, and her first assignment would be to fax my acceptance. While Tina was getting organized, I spent the next few days meeting with my new law clerks and the court clerk who had been assigned to me. We would have to decide how we would run the shop. There were lots of things to think about.

My first courtroom action happened later that week. Judge Johnson, who had been on the bench for four years, was trying a big criminal case. I had no idea what the case was about at the time that the judge invited me to join him on the bench while he was presiding over the trial. I did not know Judge Johnson, and no one had warned me about his unique sense of humor. While I was sitting next to him, he told me that the defendant was a Colombian drug kingpin charged with murdering at least 20 people and asked me if his clerk had given me a bullet-proof vest to wear under my robe.

The next week I got a call from Judge Weinstein. He had now been on the bench for 27 years. I wondered whether he truly believed that the person whom I was cross-examining in his office during *the Amityville Horror* trial was really Father Pecorora. Judge Weinstein said that he wanted to give me my first trial. He told me that he had an easy criminal case ready to go. He flattered me by telling me that he knew that I had a lot of trial experience and would have no problem breaking in with this simple case. I took it. Most new judges ease into their new world. Many do not try their first case for many months. Some do not even get their feet wet during their first year. I was not going to flinch before this legendary judge.

I did not then fully appreciate Judge Weinstein's good-natured devilish ways. He, like Judge Johnson, also prided himself on breaking in a new judge. The case turned out to be a three-defendant, 16-count mafioso trial involving extortions, racketeering conspiracies, and all sorts of other bad things. It was anything but a simple case for a new judge to cut his teeth on. The trial lasted three weeks. I stayed up to the wee hours of the night rereading the *Federal Rules of Evidence*. There were many objections on hearsay grounds and other evidentiary issues. When I made my rulings, I felt like I was walking through an Iraqi minefield.

Miraculously no bombs blew up. I charged a jury for the first time. The defendants were all justly convicted. The circuit court of appeals upheld the convictions. Thanks to Judge Weinstein, I was on my way. I thought that I could handle the job from the get-go because I had had a broad exposure to the everyday practice of the law on both the civil and criminal levels as a general practitioner and because I had tried many garden-variety types of cases. I wondered what I would have done if I only had tried a few cases or if I had only been a prosecutor and knew nothing about the civil law.

* * *

There is no formal training that a new judge gets. It's pretty much a learning on the job thing. The Administrative Office of the United States Courts (AO)—which is the administrative agency of the federal court system—sends you to "Baby Judges School" for a week's indoctrination. Otherwise, you're on your own.

The Baby Judges School usually takes place shortly after you have been let loose on the unsuspecting public. I went there soon after I had tried the mafioso case that Judge Weinstein sent me. The "School" moves around the country. That year, as I recall, I was one of 13 new judges who were sent to Atlanta. There was a natural bonding. All of us were in the same boat. We wanted to learn as much as we could as fast as we could about how to be a good judge. The AO picks an experienced judge to break in the rookies. Our leader was Judge Michael A. Telesca, a seasoned district judge from Rochester, who would later become the Chief Judge of the Western District of New York. He was warm, caring, and wonderful.

Most of the time was spent on sentencing. In 1984 Congress had passed a law which took away unbridled sentencing discretion from the judges. It created the United States Sentencing Commission to prepare sentencing guidelines—subject to Congress' approval—in an effort to create sentencing uniformity so that similarly situated defendants throughout the country would be given similar sentences. Basically, the new sentencing regime created a point system. Each crime carried a certain number of points. For example, if it involved murder, you got 43 points. If it was a less serious crime, you might start with 10 points. To this base level you might have to add additional points. For example, if the defendant was a leader or organizer in the criminal activity, he might qualify for up to three more points. There were a host of other possibilities for stacking up points. If the defendant had pled guilty—sparing the government of a trial—he could get two or three points deducted for his acceptance of responsibility.

Once you arrived at the total points associated with the crime, you would then have to determine what criminal history category the defendant fell into. If the defendant had no prior criminal brushes with the law, then he would be in category I. If he had prior convictions, he would get criminal history points. For example, a serious prior felony would give the defendant three points; a less serious crime might only carry one point. The criminal history categories ranged from I through VI—correlated to the total number of points. For example, if the defendant had more than 12 points, he would get the top prize—category VI—reflective of a real bad apple.

Once you calculated the correct number of points associated with the crime and the appropriate criminal history category, a grid would tell you what the range of punishment should be. For example, 17 points and a criminal history category of III would carry a sentencing range of 30–37 months. The judge could sentence the defendant to any point within that range. It was only in picking that point that the district judges were given any discretion. Downward departures were available in only a very limited number of exceptional circumstances.

In short, it was complicated stuff. None of the new judges had ever sentenced anyone, of course, and most were not on top of the intricacies of these sentencing guidelines. It would be a little while before I would have my first sentence, and I would study the 370-page *Sentencing Guideline* book almost every day I until I mastered it.

When I returned from Baby Judges School I had lots to do. Every judge has his own set of rules to govern the way that the judge handles his judicial workload, and I had to decide what mine should be. I checked out the rules of the other judges. I thought that many of them were too demanding and picky. I would try to keep mine simple. In the meantime, there were cases to be tried.

Before I tried my next case, I decided to take a two-day course to learn how to use the word processor. In private practice I dictated everything. I thought it was time to jump into the current technology. The course was given in the federal courthouse in Manhattan and was open to all EDNY and SDNY personnel. A handful of judges were there. I was astonished to sit next to Judge Whitman Knapp. He had been a prominent district judge in the Southern District for many years. He thought it was time to get with the modern times. He was 90 years old.

Judge Knapp was an inspiration. I vowed not to get stuck in the past. Like Judge Knapp, I would strive to stay technologically current.

* * *

I was told by a number of the old judges that the worst experience for a new judge would be for his first trial to be with a pro se criminal defendant—meaning that the defendant would be his own lawyer—or a patent case. Thanks to Judge Weinstein, I had dodged the bullet, but I struck out on my next two trials during the next few months.

Darrell Fulton was charged with holding up a bunch of people and insisted on representing himself. As with all criminal defendants charged with serious crimes, he had the right to be tried by a jury. The problem with pro se defendants is that they are not bound by professional rules of conduct (as are lawyers), do not know the rules of evidence, and are not knowledgeable about the law. They are loose cannons, and the judge usually has a hard time reining them in and controlling the courtroom. It is a challenging cup of tea for an experienced trial judge, let alone for a brand new one.

Fulton's trial lasted three weeks. It was easier than I thought it would be. He was a bright, articulate young man who regrettably took a wrong turn in the road. He did not give me a hard time. The trial was remarkable in one way: Fulton only had one leg. He would hobble around the courtroom with a crutch. I thought for sure that he would tell the jury during his summation that the government did not have a leg to stand on—but he resisted the temptation. Nonetheless, I think that the jury felt sorry for him. They did their duty, however, and appropriately convicted him; the evidence was overwhelming. Under the strictures of the sentencing law, I had to sentence him to jail for 240 months.

Patent cases are difficult because they are highly technical. In order to decide whether a patent is valid, the judge has to understand the technicalities of the patent process and the engineering underlying the invention for which the patent is sought. It is a speciality unto itself. The patent lawyer usually has an engineering degree to go with his law degree. The words that are used to describe a patent and the legal text of the laws that govern its validity are so dense and abstract that it is like learning a foreign language. I listened to dueling experts for days argue for and against the validity of the patent. I was totally confused. I spent days trying to figure out what to do. Eventually I wrote a lengthy, complex decision and invalidated the patent. I was surprised that there was no appeal.

The highlight of my first year on the bench was my first high profile case.

A partially clad 29-year-old barmaid had been found brutally stabbed to death in the hallway of an apartment building in Queens during the chilly early morning hours of March 13, 1964. In canvassing the neighborhood several weeks later, detectives learned that 38 people had heard Kitty Genovese scream for help as she was being stabbed and raped in the hallway—but did nothing. Consequently, the case came to symbolize urban apathy and reinforced New York City's image as a place where cold, uncaring citizens would do nothing while a helpless victim lay dying.

Winston Moseley was arrested and tried for the murder. His defense was insanity. To try to convince the jury that he indeed was insane, he testified at his trial and recounted the gory details. He told the jury that since no one was responding to Kitty's screams, he decided to remain in the hallway to rape her. He testified that he removed his victim's undergarments, but upon discovering that she was menstruating, took his knife and "st[u]ck it in her vaginal tract." He said that he "would have pulled the knife straight up, but the bone [had] stopped [him] from being able to do that."

The jury rejected the insanity defense. At that time New York had the death penalty. Given the heinous nature of the murder, it was no surprise that the jury sentenced Moseley to death, especially since he also confessed to numerous other rapes and murders. After the conviction, the trial judge said that although he did not believe in capital punishment, "when I see this monster, I wouldn't hesitate to pull the switch on him myself." Moseley was not put to death, however, since on appeal the state's high court reduced his sentence to life because it determined that the trial judge had improperly excluded significant evidence bearing on Moseley's mental condition during the sentencing phase of the trial.

In 1990, 25 years after he had murdered Kitty Genovese, Moseley brought a pro se habeas corpus petition in the Brooklyn federal court seeking his freedom. He claimed that his trial lawyer, Sidney Sparrow, had a conflict of interest at the time of the trial because Sparrow had also been Genovese's lawyer. Moseley's habeas petition lingered in the court for the next five years. I do not know which judge was assigned the case, but I could surely understand why no judge would want to touch it. Nonetheless, it had to be disposed of. The courthouse is open to all, even deranged, pro se, convicted criminals.

When a new judge comes on board, he has to be assigned a docket of cases. Each existing judge is asked to give up some of his cases. In many district courts—but not in the EDNY—some use the opportunity to unload their dogs and hot potatoes. I got the *Moseley* case. After Moseley had been convicted, the United States Supreme Court had decided a number of cases making it clear that a criminal defendant was entitled to be represented by a conflict-free lawyer. Sparrow had represented Genovese when she had been prosecuted on gambling charges. Moreover, I had read the transcript of Moseley's trial and was shocked that Sparrow had told the jury during the sentencing phase—to determine whether Moseley should be put to death—that "I didn't try this case involving Kitty Genovese objectively, calmly, just as a lawyer defending a client because I knew Kitty Genovese and represented her for years." Under Supreme Court law, Moseley was entitled to a factual hearing before a judge—without a jury—to determine whether Sparrow's conflict and comments would require a new trial. I had no choice.

I conducted the hearing on July 24, 1995. It was the first time a case of mine would make big news and that my name would hit the papers. The press reported that I had said in court that, "I have a responsibility as a federal judge to not let [the government] sweep this under the rug." Nonetheless, as a new judge I needed this case like a hole in the head. I anticipated that I would be vilified in the press. I had doubts that people would be able to detach their emotions and accept the fact that a judge is bound to adhere to the rule of law. I was right. The *New York Post*, for example, wrote that "the very fact that this absurd appeal had actually made it into court demonstrates, in graphic terms, the sorry state of the criminal justice system: The mythical man from Mars would shake his head and marvel at the prospect that Kitty Genovese—a full 31 years after she was murdered—stands to be denied justice."

During the hearing, three of Kitty Genovese's brothers and a sister sat in the first row and stared down at their sister's killer. Kitty's sister later told the press that she "was shocked to hear that this case would be reopened." Her brother Frank added that, "The whole thing is kind of surreal." The courtroom was packed. Sparrow, who was then 82, testified about the way in which he handled the case. He had kept copious notes. I was impressed. In a lengthy, 28-page decision I denied Moseley's habeas petition, concluding that, despite Sparrow's statements to the contrary, he gave Moseley "effective, competent and capable counsel under difficult circumstances." I noted, however, that "Moseley's quarter-century delay in bringing his *habeas* petition poignantly support[ed] those who would argue that Congress should establish a *habeas* statute of limitations," but "Congress ha[d] yet to do so."

Moseley appealed to the circuit court of appeals. As a new judge, I was thrilled that the appellate court summarily affirmed "for substantially the reasons stated in the district court's thorough and well-reasoned opinion." A few years later, Congress established a one-year statute of limitations for habeas cases. Moseley would have to die in jail, and stale cases like his could never come to court again.

Nevertheless, the Kitty Genovese case lingers on. For many people the question still centers on those 38 New Yorkers who failed to act. After the hearing, Professor William DiFazio, chairman of the sociology and anthropology department at St. John's University, suggested a reason. He viewed the apathy as a coping mechanism: "In the city, human beings are confronted with so much stimuli that there is no way they can process it all. What you have to do is shut yourself off a bit—if you don't you can go crazy." However, on the positive side, he thought that as the legacy of the horrifying Genovese murder lingered in the City's psyche, it might subconsciously cause some good Samaritans to act. He thought that it was good that the case came back to court years later because "it remind[ed] us we should get involved."

* * *

My first three cases—Darrell Fulton's trial, the patent case, and the Kitty Genovese hearing—made me realize that the work of a federal trial judge is diverse and all-encompassing. It seemed to me that you had to know everything. How would one human being be able to do it all? In the New York State courts, there were judges who just handled family matters; others just handled crimes; others just handled tort cases; others just handled commercial matters. The differences between the state and federal systems were profound.

Each state has its own court structure and judicial system. In many of the states the judges are elected for a stated term. There are many variations on the theme. In New York, for example, the judges of the supreme court—the general trial court—are elected for 14-year terms. They have to run for reelection, and if given a clean bill of health, can serve until they are 76. In other states where judges are elected, they are periodically subject to an up or down retention vote. In some states, such as Arizona, the trial judges are appointed by the Governor through a merit-selection process. Unlike the federal system, none of the states give their judges lifetime tenure.

In addition to handling federal cases, the federal judges oftentimes preside over state law cases as well. This is because the Founding Fathers had provided in Section 2 of Article III of the Constitution that lawsuits between litigants from different states can be brought in federal court. For example, if a person resides in New Jersey and has an automobile accident on the New Jersey Turnpike with someone from Brooklyn, the plaintiff can sue in the EDNY. However, since the accident happened in New Jersey, the federal judge in Brooklyn would likely have to apply that state's substantive laws. This is called diversity jurisdiction; Congress has required, however, that the case must be worth at least $75,000.

In addition to dealing with state law, the federal judge has to master the Constitution and be able to deal with all of the civil and criminal statutory laws that Congress has enacted. Unlike in many states—such as New York—where civil and criminal cases are handled by separate judges in separate courts, the federal trial judge has to do it all.

Moreover, the cases cover the waterfront. In the criminal world, while the states have jurisdiction to try all state crimes committed in the state, if the crime has a federal hook, it can also be tried in the federal courts, and this is often the case. For example, while murder cases are typically state law cases and can only be tried in the state where the murder occurred, if the murder was carried out in the course of a drug-related federal crime, it can be prosecuted in federal court. As another example, if a robbery occurs that has any effect upon interstate commerce, regardless of how slight, it can be prosecuted in the federal court. Thus, when Darrell Fulton took money from the people he held up, he could have been prosecuted for robbery in New York State. But he was also appropriately prosecuted in federal court because his robberies affected interstate commerce. If the crime is plotted by the use of the mail or wires—such as the telephone or Internet—a federal crime has been committed because they are interstate in nature. The use of wiretaps on the Mafia is a case in point.

On the civil side, there is only one category of cases that are immune from federal jurisdiction: domestic relations. Divorces and custody cases are truly state matters. There is no federal hook. Otherwise Congress has blanketed the law. For example, in addition to patent cases, the federal courts have exclusive jurisdiction over bankruptcy cases, torts committed by federal agents and employees, violations of the country's anti-trust and securities laws, admiralty law cases, and violations of international treaties to which the United States has subscribed. Congress has also passed a host of anti-discrimination laws which make up a significant part of the federal courts' dockets. While the Constitution outlaws discrimination based on race, color, and national origin, Congress has also outlawed discrimination based upon sex, age, and disabilities. Congress' reach is pervasive. I cannot think of any area of the law—other than family law—that it has left untouched.

The breadth of the cases which a federal trial judge has to deal with—on both the criminal and civil side—is, therefore, daunting. The judge is a jack-of-all-trades.

* * *

Each year the judges from each of the country's 13 circuits hold a judicial conference. The purpose is to bring the judges together to discuss the business of their courts and new developments in the law. It is also a social event. The circuit and district judges of the Second Circuit usually meet for three days during the first week of June. My first judicial conference was in June 1995 at the beautiful Sagamore resort in upstate New York. While I knew the judges from Brooklyn, I did not know the judges from the rest of New York or from the other Second Circuit states: Connecticut and Vermont. It would be something like a coming-out party.

The judges were allowed to bring their spouses. Cooky came with me. The first event was a fancy cocktail reception. Cooky told me to introduce her by her real name. We would be on our best formal behavior. After we each got a glass of red wine, we met our first new couple standing next to us. I took the lead and introduced myself and Estelle. Fred Scullin told us that he was a district judge from Syracuse and introduced his wife, Cricket. Without missing a beat, Estelle told them to call her Cooky. We all laughed, and I started to relax.

It is traditional to introduce the new judges who came on board since the last conference at a formal dinner on the second night. One of the senior judges would be the master of ceremonies and would do it in alphabetical order. He simply told the audience that Judge Block had gone to Indiana and Cornell and had been a general practitioner in Suffolk County. He asked me to stand, and I got a polite, perfunctory round of applause. Next was Guido Calabresi. He had just been appointed to the Second Circuit Court of Appeals. My introduction lasted about three minutes. His was 20. Everyone knew that Judge Calabresi had been the Dean of Yale Law School. However, the audience was also told about the many books which he had written and that he had graduated first in his class from law school, college, and high school.

As I listened, I assumed that Judge Calabresi also was first in his Kindergarten class. I shrunk in my seat and thought that maybe

174

I did not belong here. However, when I got back to Brooklyn, I went to work and tried to put him out of my mind. I hoped that most of the other judges did not have similar credentials and were not as intimidating.

I sat next to a female judge that night who had become a district judge for the Southern District three years before. She comforted me and assured me that she, too, did not have Judge Calabresi's credentials. Little did I know that Sonia Sotomayor would become even more famous than Judge Calabresi.

The highlight of the conference each year takes place on the last morning. At 9:00 a.m. sharp, Supreme Court Justice Ruth Bader Ginsburg reports on the doings of the high court during the past year. Each Supreme Court Justice is assigned to a circuit. Justice Ginsburg is the Second Circuit Justice. Her comments that day were pithy and well-measured. She shared little tidbits about her colleagues and talked about some of the major cases decided by the Court during the last Term. She sounded super smart.

Justice Ginsburg is tiny and looks frail. I was briefly introduced to her the day before. I was struck by the fact that she wore white gloves. She was not a chipper conversationalist and did not make idle chatter. I wanted to say something profound but was intimidated. I wished that I had something clever to say like I did when I had met John Steinbeck, but all I could muster was, "Nice to meet you." However, looks are deceiving. I was assured by those who knew her well that the Justice was a warm and caring person. She was just painstakingly shy, and despite her frail appearance, deceptively athletic. I could not believe my eyes when later that day, as I was sunning myself by the lake, I caught a glimpse of her water skiing.

* * *

Late in the afternoon of September 28, 1995, I was in the middle of sentencing a Muslim man when my clerk came into the courtroom to interrupt. I remember the day because he told me that Neil's wife had just given birth to twin boys. I apologized to the defendant

175

for the interruption and told him about my good news. He said marbook—which he told me meant congratulations in Arabic—and suggested that I should name the twins Mohammed and Malamed. I thanked him for his good wishes but still sentenced him to jail. When I told Neil, he said that it was too late. The boys had already been named Brandon and Ryan. I realized, however, as my first anniversary on the bench was approaching, that I was now totally comfortable in the courtroom and had broken in as a new federal district judge.

Chapter
3

The Judges

The number of district and circuit judges in the country varies from year to year due to vacancies created by death or resignations. However, at any given time there are about 950 district judges and 250 circuit judges. About one-third of the district judges are senior judges; about 40% of the circuit judges are senior. Congress has provided that all district and circuit judges can take senior status after meeting the age and service requirements of the Rule of 80—their age and years of service must add up to 80—provided that they are at least 65 and have been on the bench for at least 10 years. This status differs from "full retirement" and "resignation." Full retirement means that having satisfied the Rule of 80, the judge completely retires from the bench; he or she no longer performs judicial duties and is free to pursue other employment. The retired judge receives an annuity equal to the salary at the time of retirement. Resignation simply means the voluntary relinquishment of all judicial duties and a return to the private sector, prior to satisfying the Rule of 80; there are no retirement benefits, and all compensation ceases.

By contrast, judges who take senior status continue to perform the same judicial duties as active judges and receive the same salary, provided that they render "substantial service" to the court, which may be satisfied by simply doing the same work as an active judge for three months per year. Moreover, like active judges, they continue to serve for life and are barred from the practice of law. In other words, they are just like active judges except that they can decide to do only one-quarter of the work; therefore, the common assumption is that they are now semiretired.

Most senior judges do avail themselves of the opportunity to work less hard during their senior years. Nationwide they cut their workload on average by 50%. Still, they are invaluable assets to the federal judiciary, disposing of almost 20% of the courts' judicial business. The federal judicial system would be enormously burdened if senior judges were to retire rather than continue to serve even though there is little economic incentive to stay on the bench. Since they would continue to get the same amount as their salary if they were to retire, the public gets their services free of charge.

Congress has also provided for magistrate judges. They are selected by the district judges for a term of eight years and can be reappointed. In the EDNY, there are about half as many magistrate judges as district judges. They are the district judges' judicial helpers. They can try civil cases, upon consent of the lawyers, and manage all pretrial discovery. On the criminal side, they can handle criminal arraignments and pleas. They can try misdemeanor cases, but not felony cases. The district judges can refer a host of civil and criminal matters to them for reports and recommendations. The magistrate judges are exceptionally talented. A number of them have later become district judges. Judge Weinstein likes to quip that we should send as much work to the magistrate judges as possible because, unlike the district court judges, they are selected only on the basis of merit.

* * *

While I was breaking in, I got to know who the other EDNY judges were. There were then 20 of them; five were senior judges. Only four were women. All of the judges except Judge Johnson were white. This tracked the traditional composition of the federal judiciary. Although the country is about 51% female, judges have historically been almost exclusively white males. Until the presidency of Jimmy Carter (1977–1981), less than 2% of district judges were female, and even with conscious efforts to change this imbalance, only about 14% of Carter's district judge appointments were women. Carter also tried to correct the racial imbalance; 21% of his district judgeships went to racial minorities.

Things started to dramatically change during President Clinton's administration (1993–2001). Forty-nine percent of his judicial appointments to the district and circuit courts were either women or minorities. His successors, Presidents George W. Bush and Barack Obama, have followed his lead. So far, towards the end of his first term, nearly half of President Obama's confirmed nominations have been women; 21% have been black, and 11% have been Hispanic. Today the number of judges in my court has grown to 25—12 of whom have gone senior. Of the total, nine are women, three are African American, one is Hispanic, and one is of Japanese ancestry. The majority of the nonsenior judges are women, including Chief Judge Carol Amon.

Happily, times have changed, and the federal judiciary continues to become more diverse. Nevertheless, when I got on the bench—given the paucity of women judges at that time—the public's perception was that it was a male club. I remember when my new female colleague, Allyne Ross, and I decided to celebrate our good fortune. Judge Ross had heard of a new restaurant that had opened in my neighborhood. We thought that we'd give it a try. Little did we know that it was a place for lovers—not judges. We were seated at a cozy, candlelit table. There were other candlelit tables on each side. There was a young couple playing footsies under the table to the left, and a young guy groping a woman at the other table. Allyne and I were not deterred. We each ordered martinis. When they came, I told the waitress that we were both federal court judges and were celebrating our ascension to the bench. When she raised her eyebrows, I started to laugh, realizing that there was no way that she believed me. As I was leaving after dinner, she whispered in my ear—so Judge Ross would not hear—that it was the best story that she ever heard and comforted me by telling me that they got cheaters in there all of the time.

I also celebrated one night with Judge Hurley. Denis Hurley

had been a Suffolk County Court judge, and he beat me to the federal bench by two years. We were good friends. Denis sat in CI and lived way out east. He rarely came to the City but wanted to take me out on the town to welcome me as his new colleague. His wife, Patti, insisted that he sleep over at my place so that he would not have to make the two-hour trip back home late at night.

Denis did not know much about the City and asked me to arrange for a fun time. I mentioned that Judge Hurley was coming to town to Alan Pastore, and he had some suggestions. Alan was then my part-time, temporary secretary. Tina was financially hard-pressed because her government salary was much less than what she had earned in private practice. She was able to get a much higher paying secretarial job at a big-city firm. Alan was working part-time for one of the other judges and was able to help me out until I found a replacement for her.

Alan Pastore was a special, lovable guy. He prided himself on being a male secretary and was supportive of the gay rights movement. He also knew everything about New York City. Alan recommended a restaurant, and he thought that after dinner we would get a kick out of dropping in for a beer at Hogs & Heifers in the Meatpacking District. I had heard that it was a unique place and had it on my places-to-visit list. Alan also suggested that we should have an after-dinner drink at his favorite night spot. He said that it was open to the wee hours of the morning and gave me the address.

The restaurant was fine. Denis and I reminisced about old times, and he gave me a lot of practical advice about my new job. After dinner we checked out Hogs & Heifers. Neither of us had ever seen anything like it before. It was a country-western joint with bar-maids dancing on top of the bar in boots and very little else. While we were gaping at the scene from the end of the bar, the front door opened wide, and some bearded guy in a 10-gallon hat drove his Harley motorcycle into the place.

I thought that it was time to call it a night, but Denis said that he rarely got into the City and wanted to see more of the scene. He asked me where we could go for a nightcap and some music. It was almost midnight, and nothing came readily to mind—until I remembered that Alan had given me the address of his late-night club. I told Denis that I had no idea what type of place it was, but he said that it was too early to turn in and that we should give it a try. When we arrived, we were greeted at the door by a young man in black, skin-tight pants. I told him that my secretary had sent us there. He said that he knew we might be coming because Alan had called and told him that Judges Block and Hurley might be stopping by. He escorted us down a flight of stairs and to a front row table by a large dance floor. He could not have been more friendly.

The dance floor was packed. A female DJ played pulsating dance music. She was the only woman in the place. Denis and I had a drink and watched the guys dance for a few minutes before we left and grabbed a taxi. I was glad that John Kroger was not there. On the way home I told Denis that there was no need to worry. We would never meet anyone that we saw there again.

Two days later I was picking a jury for a criminal trial. In order to get a jury, I qualify 28 prospective jurors—called at random—by questioning them one at a time. The lawyers then usually exercise their full allotment of 16 peremptory challenges—the defendant has 10; the government six. The 12 remaining become the jury. When I got to prospective juror number 23, I asked her the same question that I had asked all of the others: "Do you know any of the lawyers or parties?" I thought that she looked familiar. My face turned beet red, however, when she said that the only person in the courtroom that she had seen before was the judge. She was the DJ at Alan Pastore's club. I told her not to elaborate, thanked her for coming, and told her it might be best if she were a juror in some other case.

* * *

I got to know and like all of my other colleagues. They were each dedicated to the law and hardworking. They were wonderful role models. A few special moments stand out. Just days after I got started, Judge Korman invited me to have dinner with him at his favorite restaurant near the courthouse, the Queen. He ordered his favorite dish—it was a breast of chicken with eggplant and fontina cheese on top. It was delicious. He chided me by telling me that it was fortunate for me that I had lost out to him nine years before; otherwise I would not have made all of that money off of the family court judges. A tradition had been established. Judge Korman and I return to the Queen every month. We order the same chicken dish.

I also had dinner during my first year on the bench with the late Judge Eugene Nickerson, another new colleague. Gene Nickerson was beloved by everyone, and I miss him terribly. He was one of the great EDNY judges. Before he got on the bench in 1977, he had been elected in 1961 as the first Democratic county executive of Nassau County since 1912. During the '60s, the Nassau Republican Party was viewed as the strongest in the country, having in 1972 given President Nixon the largest victory of any county in the United States. Gene Nickerson, who was adored by the public, was reelected to two more three-year terms—in 1964 and 1967. He remained a viable political force in Nassau Democratic politics during the 1970s and was a thorn in the side of the Nassau County Republican Party. Thus when County Executive Nickerson decided to accept President Carter's nomination to become a federal district judge, the Republican United States Senator from New York, Jacob Javits, at the behest of the powerful hegemony of the Nassau Republican Party, was more than willing to support his candidacy and ease his path through the Senate confirmation process.

Between our appetizers and entrees, Judge Nickerson told me how badly the Nassau Republican Party had wanted to get rid of him. He believed that they could have cared less whether he had the qualifications to be a federal judge. To drive home the point, he recounted the time when he appeared before the Senate Judiciary Committee for his confirmation hearing. Senator Javits was at his side while President Carter's representative was telling the Committee about soon-to-be Judge Nickerson's extraordinary qualifications—an editor of the Columbia Law Review, law clerk to the esteemed Judge Augustus Hand of the Second Circuit Court of Appeals, followed by a clerkship for Chief Justice Harlan Stone of the United States Supreme Court—after which the Senator whispered in his ear: "Gene, I didn't know you were a lawyer also."

Judge Nickerson and Judge Weinstein were the best of friends. They were towering judicial giants and enhanced the reputation that the EDNY enjoyed when I got on board as one of the strongest district court benches in the country. It still has that reputation, thanks in large part to the fact that Judge Weinstein—at the age of 90—remains on the bench 44 years after his appointment. He is as active as ever and is truly a judicial legend in his lifetime. He has handled some of the country's major mass tort litigations and is considered the leading authority on the *Federal Rules of Evidence.* He wrote the leading multivolume treatise on the subject.

Thus it was natural for me to seek him out when I had my first difficult evidentiary ruling to make during one of my early trials. I explained the problem. The good judge stroked his chin and said, "Do whatever you think is right." I have never asked him another question about evidence.

* * *

After we sat next to each other at my first judicial conference, Sonia Sotomayor and I became good friends. We found out that we shared a number of things in common. We lived in the same neighborhood, ate at the same restaurants, enjoyed jazz and Latin music, and were each neophyte district judges. However, we did not share the same thoughts about what the future might professionally offer. Being a 60-year-old white male, I was content with the reality that this was probably it for me. I knew, however, that no Latino woman had ever been appointed to the Circuit Court—let alone to the United States Supreme Court—and that political pressure was mounting in the Hispanic community to right this wrong. As a young, bright, articulate judge with a compelling grassroots life story, many of her judicial colleagues thought that she could very well be the trailblazer.

It also did not hurt that she was making her mark on the district court. One night during the spring of 1995, Sonia told me at dinner at our favorite West Village restaurant that she had just been randomly assigned to handle the case involving the dispute between the baseball owners and the major league ballplayers. It was a lucky draw. There's not a judge that I know who would not have supported the ballplayers and said "play ball." It's no wonder that when she made it to the high court she was asked to throw out the ball that year on opening day at Yankee stadium.

On June 25, 1997, Sonia was nominated by President Clinton to the Circuit Court of Appeals for the Second Circuit. Being a minority from New York—and a Democrat—she was perceived by a number of conservative senators as too liberal for their appetite. The Republican senators were also aware that the circuit court was a stepping stone to the Supreme Court. They wanted to put stumbling blocks in her path and delay her confirmation as long as possible. They succeeded in holding up her confirmation for well over a year. She did not make it until October 2, 1998. Fearful that she was on her way to the Supreme Court, 29 Republican senators voted against her. They had no legitimate basis to withhold their approval. Sonia had an impeccable academic and judicial background. She had also been a prosecutor for the New York County D.A. and was tough on criminals. Moreover, she was the nationally revered judge who had saved baseball.

* * *

It is the tradition of the Second Circuit to hold a public induction ceremony for its new circuit court judges in the court's beautiful ceremonial courtroom. The place was packed for Sonia's. If I had not been a judge, I probably would not have gotten in. Sonia talked about her humble upbringing and said that she owed it all to her mother. It was one of the most moving events I had witnessed.

Although my dinners with Sonia started to taper off after she became a circuit judge, we still kept in close contact. She threw herself into her new job. She was always a hard worker, but she was now totally immersed in her work. She wanted to prove that she could keep up with her new circuit court colleagues and write high quality opinions. It was rare that she would call me for dinner. Knowing how wrapped up she was in her new calling, I did not take it personally, but I did share my Ernie story with her one night over drinks.

Ernie Muller had been one of my collaborators on *Professionally Speaking*. He wrote the sketches and most of the lyrics. We would have dinner often and talk about how we had come close to having a big hit. However, I always had to initiate our get-togethers. Ernie was more than happy that I did this. We were good friends and always enjoyed seeing each other. One night I had a little too much to drink and lectured Ernie about our one-sided relationship. I told him that he had to take some responsibility and call me also. I said that I was going to conduct an experiment. The next call would be his. It never came. Three years passed. I gave in. When I called, I found out that Ernie had died the week before.

I would not do the same to Sonia, but when I called I always asked for Ernie. Sonia would laugh. She said that I should call her Ernestine. Our friendship survived. While she was still a circuit judge Sonia celebrated my 70th birthday with me and my family at a Chinese restaurant, and she invited me and Cooky to join her and her friends to celebrate her 50th at a festive rooftop party. She had been taking dancing lessons and had also invited her teacher. There was a DJ—not the same one from Alan Pastore's club—who spun Latin music. Sonia and her teacher did a mean salsa together.

A few months before Sonia was nominated to the Supreme Court by President Obama on May 26, 2009, she told me that the buzz was that she would be on the short list. She knew that if she were picked, her life would never be the same. She told me that she never believed it would happen and never dwelled on it. Moreover, she had misgivings about doing it. She was happy with her lifestyle. As a single woman, she enjoyed dating and taking her salsa lessons.

I did not hear from Sonia for many months after she became Madam Justice. I had tried calling and had e-mailed my congratulations. I never got a response. I was very disappointed. I thought that we were good friends and that I would be part of her inner circle that would be invited for her induction. Nonetheless, at the end of her first year on the high court, I got a call out of the blue from Ernestine's secretary. Sonia would be in New York the following week for a few days and wanted to have lunch with me.

We met at her New York office in the Manhattan federal courthouse and walked to the Peking Duck House in Chinatown. We were followed by two marshals. Sonia was the darling of the paparazzi and needed to be guarded at all times. There were rumors that she was having lunch that day with a handsome younger man. I was flattered but knew that they had the wrong guy since I was 20 years older than she. Still, I realized right away just how much of her privacy was up for grabs. Her life was no longer her own. I also wondered how much she had changed since she became a celebrity Supreme Court Justice.

We sat in a corner in the restaurant and ordered the restaurant's signature Peking duck. No one bothered us. We spoke about old times. She was the same old Sonia—warm, caring, and open with her feelings and thoughts about life. I reminded her of our last time together and her misgivings about becoming a Supreme Court Justice. She said that she had no choice. The pressure from the Hispanic community was too great. She was a symbol and role model for every Hispanic citizen. She could not turn her back on them. She was right. I told her that my Puerto Rican doorman, Carlos Valentin, cried when she got the nomination. It made him feel so proud to be Hispanic.

Sonia shared with me how her life had indeed changed. Her social life had crashed. The dance lessons had stopped. There was just no time. Almost all of her colleagues had been on the Court for many years. As the new kid on the block, she had to read their opinions and get up to speed. She thought that it would take a few years to catch up to them. Her immediate goal was to sharpen her First Amendment jurisprudence. In the meantime she had to deal with her celebrity, which she said took up about 40% of her time. While she was honored by all the attention that she was getting, it interfered with doing the work of the Court. She would bury herself in her office or home the other 60% of the time to work, work, work. There was just no time left over for much of a personal life. The music would have to wait until things died down and she mastered her new calling. She was truly in the service of our country. I thought about the autobiography that I had read that Justice Blackmun—of *Roe v. Wade* fame—had written after he left the Court. He equated being on the Supreme Court to going through basic training as a Marine. It was all-consuming. I also thought about a comment that a former district court colleague and friend of Sonia's made to me when I told her that I had not heard from Sonia: "We just have to accept the fact that our loss is our country's gain."

Ever the caring person, Sonia wanted to find out how I was doing. I told her that I was writing a book. She told me that she had just gotten a generous advance for a book that she was writing. She inquired as to how Cooky was doing. She knew that we had gone our separate ways a few years previously. Cooky and I had tried to work out our differences, but after 40 years we agreed that an eighth shrink would probably not make much of a difference. Sonia liked Cooky, and for good reason. She was happy to hear that we had maintained a cordial postdivorce relationship. Before she got on the Supreme Court, Sonia had also met Betsy—my current significant other—and asked how she was. After lunch we walked back to the courthouse together and promised that we would stay in touch.

Two things happened shortly after that that touched my heart and reinforced my belief that Sonia was a special human being. Three days later I got a big manila envelope in the mail. When I opened it, I saw a beautiful 5 x 7 photo of Sonia in her Supreme Court robes. On it she wrote "To Carlos with warm regards," and signed her name. When I gave it to my doorman, Carlos looked at it in disbelief, hugged me, and cried again.

Some weeks later, Cooky had to undergo serious surgery. I let

Sonia know. While Cooky was in the hospital, the nurse came into her room to tell her that someone was on the phone who had the same name as Supreme Court Justice Sotomayor. Sonia and Cooky spoke for a few minutes. Sonia was relieved to hear that she was on the mend.

I recently read in the paper that the advance that Sonia got for her book was $1.17 million. She deserved it. I'm sure that when it comes out the public will get to know all of the details about her extraordinary life's journey, from her humble roots in a low-income housing project in the Bronx to being the 111th Justice of the United States Supreme Court and the first Hispanic on the Court. I was a little jealous. Sonia's advance was $1.17 million more than mine.

* * *

While much is known about a judge's educational, professional, and political background before the judge gets on the bench, no one really knows how the judge will turn out once let loose on the public. Everyone has a different personality. Will the judge be tough on the bench, empathetic to the disadvantaged, courteous to lawyers, rigid or flexible in running the courtroom? No one can predict for sure. When I was asked by Senator Moynihan's committee whether I thought that I would have good judicial temperament, I candidly answered, "I hope so, but I won't know for sure until I am on the firing line." Afterwards, I wondered whether there was a way to get a sense of how a judge might turn out.

When I had been on the bench for a few years, I stumbled upon an article written by John W. Kennedy, Jr., *Personality Type and Judicial Decision Making*. He was the presiding judge of California's San Bernadino County's trial courts and taught a course for the California Center for Judicial Education designed to help judges examine their individual fact-finding and decision-making styles. He decided to use the Myers-Briggs Type Inventory (MBTI) as the most appropriate psychometric tool to get a sense of a judge's cognitive and judgment processes. The MBTI had been administered worldwide to several million people a year and was widely used

188

throughout industry, government, education, and religion. During the prior 10 years, Judge Kennedy had administered the MBTI to 1,302 judges across the United States in dozens of judicial training programs that he had taught.

As Judge Kennedy explained in his article, the MBTI is not a test—there are no right or wrong answers. It is simply a pencil-to-paper, self-administered inventory that counts the number of responses in various areas of cognitive and judgmental functioning. It consists of 126 items divided into three parts. The first and third parts are multiple choice questions; the second part requires the subject to choose from a pair of words. It takes about 30–45 minutes to administer.

The results of the MBTI are scored on four scales that identify and quantify preferences between: (1) extroversion and introversion; (2) sensing and intuition; (3) thinking and feeling; and (4) judging and perceiving. Judge Kennedy reported on what he believed the four scales meant within the context of judging. The MBTI has nothing to do with a judge's legal ability, but it gives a lot of insight as to how judges behave on the bench.

Extroverted and Introverted Judges: This scale differentiates between those who focus on the external—on other people and things—and those who focus on the internal—on their own thoughts and values. "Extroverted Judges" are the doers of the judiciary. They go to meetings and join groups. They tend to juggle busy schedules and oversee heavy calendars. They are keenly aware of public opinion, often to the point of becoming stressed when called upon to make unpopular decisions. They tackle problems with zest and enthusiasm and make popular administrative and presiding judges. "Introverted Judges" prefer written presentations over oral; are likely to make their decisions based on private reflection in advance of a hearing, and are unlikely to be significantly influenced by oral argument. To introverts, there is no reasonable excuse for failing to follow the law. They are likely to be brief and to the point. They become impatient with lawyers, litigants, or witnesses who ramble on, and often see extroverts as shallow chatterboxes. They may be characterized as stubborn and independent-minded.

Judge Kennedy's statistics indicated that approximately 60% of male judges expressed a preference for introversion. For female judges, the results were the opposite.

Sensing and Intuitive Judges: This scale is the most important with respect to fact-finding and decision-making. It measures the individual's preference in processing information. "Sensing Judges" pay attention to detail and give careful consideration to the facts of a case. They are traditionalists and have a deep respect for rules. They work systematically and realistically, and are resistant to change. They often see theoretical or philosophical discussions as impractical and irrelevant time-wasters. "Intuitive Judges" like change and challenges. They are bored by detail and, as a result, may not take many notes during trials. To intuitives, sensing judges can be seen as dogmatic, unimaginative, and preoccupied with rules and details. To sensing judges, intuitives can be seen as impractical rebels who refuse to follow the rules.

Once again, there was a significant difference between male and female judges. About 60% of the men reported a sensing preference. About 57% of women demonstrated a preference for intuition.

Thinking and Feeling Judges: This scale measures how people prefer to make decisions. In general, thinkers prefer to make decisions based on the impersonal application of objective rules. Feelers prefer to make decisions based on the human needs of the parties involved. Judge Kennedy found that the vast majority of judges are "thinking" decision-makers, whatever their gender.

Judging and Perceiving Judges: This scale measures exactly what the label says: preferences for judging and perceiving. "Judging Judges" prefer to live an organized, managed lifestyle. They seek resolution and closure, and are decisive and punctual. They can be impatient with lawyers or witnesses who are nonresponsive or take too long to get to the point. "Perceiving Judges" are naturally curious and have questioning minds. They can be extremely patient with lawyers' arguments, tolerant of rambling witnesses, and open to reconsideration of rulings. Judge Kennedy found that 72% of the both male and female judges scored as "judgers."

Judge Kennedy recognized, obviously, that no one shoe fits all and that there are many variations and permutations, but found that certain combinations of these four scales appeared to be the most prevalent among the judiciary. Moreover, there was a gender difference. For the female judge, the most common combination was ENTJ (extroverted/intuitive/thinker/judger). For the male judge, it was ISTJ (introverted/sensor/thinker/judger). He believed that ISTJs tended to fit the media's stereotypical expectation of a judge: quiet, reflective, traditional, predictable, decisive. The ENTJs, on the other hand, were often more verbal, argumentative, and unpredictable.

My curiosity got the best of me. I decided to take the MBTI to see whether it would give me any insights into the way I ran my court. I turned out to be an ESFJ, but there were significant differences in each category: Extrovert 100%; Sensing 81%; Feeling 62%; and Judging 52%. According to Judge Kennedy's statistics, only 2.3% of the judges he tested—30 out of 1,302—were in this category. I guess that the Oregon Attorney General was right when he said that I was not a typical federal judge. With the score came a brief summary of the type of person I am.

> Warm-hearted, popular, and conscientious. Tend to put the needs of others over your own needs. Feels strong sense of responsibility and duty. Value traditions and security. Interested in serving others. Need positive reinforcement to feel good about yourself. Well-developed sense of space and function.

I liked it, but wondered whether this book would have to be well-received in order for me to feel good about myself.

* * *

Regardless of the federal judges' individual personalities and characteristics, they can sit for life unless impeached by Congress.

191

Judge Wesley E. Brown sat as a district court judge in Kansas until he passed away on January 26, 2012 at the ripe old age of 104. His presence on the bench was seen as a daily miracle. His diminished frame was nearly lost behind the bench. A tube under his nose fed him oxygen, and he warned lawyers preparing for lengthy trials that he may not live long enough to finish them. He told them that, "At this age, I'm not even buying green bananas." Yet the consensus is that Judge Brown remained sharp and capable.

What happens, though, if a judge starts to lose it? The average life expectancy has more than doubled, to almost 80, since the Founders provided for lifetime appointments, and the number of people who live beyond 100 is rapidly growing. Impeachment is hardly the answer for dealing with those not as fortunate as Judge Brown who may linger on the bench after their mental faculties have seriously faded. Neither senility nor bad judicial temperament is a "high crime or misdemeanor." Therefore, only eight judges have been impeached since the judiciary came into existence—all for committing crimes. The most recent was in December 2010, when District Judge Thomas Porteous from New Orleans was impeached for falsifying financial disclosure forms, which concealed gifts he solicited and received from attorneys who had appeared before him.

Congress has tried to find some way for dealing with the problem of judges' poor behavior or diminished capacities—short of impeachment—without violating the Constitution. In addition to the legislation that it has passed to encourage judges to take "senior status," it has provided for disability retirement benefits for those no longer capable of serving. It also enacted, in 1980, the Judicial Conduct and Disability Act, requiring each circuit court to set up machinery to process complaints by any person claiming that a judge has engaged in conduct "prejudicial to the effective and expeditious administration of the business of the courts," as well as conduct reflecting a judge's inability to perform his duties because of "mental or physical disability." Rules have subsequently been enacted to govern the manner by which the circuit courts are to handle the complaints.

Thousands of complaints have been lodged against federal judges since the Act was passed. Most have charged the judge with being prejudiced or biased, or with abusing his judicial power. The overwhelming majority have been from disgruntled prisoners. Not surprisingly they were almost all found to be frivolous or without merit. Of the handful that reflected poorly on a judge, they were seriously investigated, and the judge was apprised of the results. Where warranted, the judge was "spoken to" by the chief judge of the circuit or a designee about the problem and what should be done to take corrective action.

Regardless of the grievance machinery put in place by the Judicial Conduct and Disability Act, the judges are generally well-aware of "problem judges" and realize that they have a moral responsibility to try to do something about it. There are things that happen that the public never knows about. It's an informal process, bottomed on the powers of persuasion, but it often works. For example, if a particular judge has a reputation for handing out very harsh sentences, the colleagues who are closest to the judge will have a heart-to-heart talk with him. This will also be the case if the chief judge receives a number of complaints about a judge's courtroom demeanor. Moreover, if a judge is getting on in years and is being challenged by his caseload, the chief will offer help, and the other judges will pitch in to take over the more difficult cases. The process is hardly foolproof—there are some stubborn apples—but the art of gentle persuasion goes a long way to compensate for the fact that the Founding Fathers did not provide for term limits.

Whether there should now be term limits for federal judges is a matter of fair debate. After all, even if Judge Brown could still function at the age of 104, his frail appearance on the bench with oxygen flowing through his nose must have been disconcerting to the lawyers and litigants. However, on balance I think that it should be left to the judge to decide if he should hang up his robe. I hope that I would be able to do that if my faculties start to seriously fade. At the present time, however, I feel that I can do a better job at my age than at any other time in my judicial career. If we had term limits,

Judge Weinstein would no longer be on the bench, nor would four other EDNY colleagues who are outstanding jurists in their late 80s.

Chapter
4

The Courtroom

My conduct on the bench is surely the product of my personality. Nevertheless, it is also influenced by my experiences with the Suffolk County state courts and their judges. I tried a lot of cases in those courts. Since the judges were picked by the political bosses based more on their loyalty to the boss rather than on merit, they were generally not of the same cut as the federal judges. While some happened to be very good, it was a mixed bag, and you had to be lucky to draw a strong judge.

The judges typically would not go out of their way to make the jurors feel very welcomed. They would read their remarks from a written script and never explain anything to them about the trial process. The system also was hardly juror-friendly. In civil cases in the supreme court courthouse, the lawyers would select the jurors in a dingy room in the basement without any on-site judicial supervision. The jury selection process was often contentious and many times would drag on for two or three days. Once the jurors were chosen, the trials often did not start for a number of days. Nonetheless, they had to come to the courthouse each day—and just sit in the general jury room—without knowing when the trial was likely to begin. They would understandably be impatient and angry. I would beg the judge who was assigned the case to talk to them and explain what was happening. The judge never would. By the time that the jurors were brought into the courtroom for the beginning of the trial, they would often be a hostile bunch.

The trials, both civil and criminal, rarely started at any particular time. Each day the judge would conference other cases before he turned to the trial. The lawyers and jurors just had to cool their heels. Lunch breaks would often last for up to two hours. Much time was also wasted over the introduction of evidence. Each proposed exhibit had to be marked by a bailiff and then shown to the opposing lawyer to find out if there was an objection. Oftentimes the jurors would have to sit and stare while the judge would talk to the lawyers for a long time at sidebar before deciding whether the exhibit would be allowed into evidence. Once the jurors started their deliberations—after the judge charged them on the law—they were not allowed to go home until they reached a verdict. They were put up overnight in a cheap motel.

I understand that things are much improved today, but that was what I often experienced when I was practicing in the Suffolk County courts. It made an indelible impression on me. I thought that if I were ever a judge, things would be a lot different.

* * *

Judges rarely invade their colleagues' courtrooms to watch them perform. While they are welcomed, there is a general feeling of discomfort in doing so. To some extent, they are like teachers who know their fellow teachers socially in the faculty room but have no idea what kind of teachers they are because they never see them in their classrooms. When I got on the bench, I decided to visit some of my colleagues' courtrooms while they were trying cases and sentencing criminal defendants. I'm glad that I did. I was generally impressed with their competence and command of their courtrooms, but was also struck by their different judicial personalities and the different ways in which they ran their fiefdoms.

The federal district judges' courtrooms are truly their fiefdoms. Unlike in many states, such as New York, there are no supervisors or bureaucracies that exercise control over them. While there is a chief judge—designated solely on the basis of seniority—who has general administrative and ceremonial responsibilities, the chief has no power over his or her fellow judges. The judges get their cases from a random wheel and are truly the kings and queens of their courts. No one can tell them when to show up for work, how many vacations they should take, how often they should be on trial, or control any other aspect of their world. It is up to the judges to decide how they should perform and comport themselves. It is, in reality, not a job, but a responsibility. It is what the Framers had in mind when they created an independent judiciary—and it works. The judges are aware of their responsibilities and take them seriously. Nevertheless, true to their different personalities—as shown by the results of the MBTIs collected by Judge Kennedy and their life experiences—they discharge them in different ways.

* * *

I decided to run my courtroom more informally than those who subscribed to the more traditional notion that strict formality is the best policy. The traditionalist belief can draw comfort from the way the Brits, our common-law brethren, run their courts. They are the epitome of rectitude and formality, complete with wigs and gowns for both the judges and barristers—the name given to their trial lawyers. I envy them in one respect. I would not mind having a handsome wig cover my mostly bald head.

Hewing to the British influence, the traditionalists run a tight ship. During a trial, lawyers can't stray from a fixed podium without asking for the judge's permission. They are admonished if they speak too loudly and do not behave with the utmost decorum. Everyone is expected to rise whenever the judge enters and leaves the courtroom. The judge always wears a robe. Little is left to chance. The judge usually reads from a prepared, written script whenever addressing the jury, and humor is considered inappropriate. In the courthouse, the traditionalists carry themselves with the utmost rectitude. They are courteous to all they meet but do not engage in idle chatter. They avoid mingling with the public. They always take the judges' private elevator and never eat in the public cafeteria. In short, they are "the judge."

This is not to say that the traditionalists are not good judges, and indeed there are variations on the theme, but one has to wonder whether they instill more fear than respect. I take a different approach. I believe that it is possible to create a less rigid and tense environment. I believe that humanizing the courtroom actually increases respect for the legal system. I have been bolstered in my beliefs by my experiences on the bench.

When it comes to the jurors, I try to make them feel like they are truly essential to the judicial process. Many have never been jurors before in either the state or federal courts. Before the trial starts, I speak to them informally for about 20 minutes. I give them a little sense of what the case is about, how long it is likely to last, when we will get started each day, and when we will be taking our lunch break and other periodic breaks during the day.

Most importantly, I explain our respective roles and responsibilities. I tell the jurors that we are truly partners—one without the other doesn't do it. I tell them that I am in charge of the law department. In that respect, I explain that I have to rule on objections that the lawyers raise, have to explain the law to the jurors after all of the evidence is in, and am responsible for keeping the trains running on time and conducting an orderly trial. I tell them, by contrast, that they are in charge of the fact department; therefore, it is their solemn duty to determine the facts and apply them to the law that I give them. I tell them that I have no place in that process.

In sum, I try to ease the jurors into the trial by explaining the ABCs of the process in a user-friendly manner. I do emphasize, however, the importance of coming to court on time and tell them how they should behave when not in the courtroom. With respect to being on time, I assume them that I will not be late and that if any of them are, they will just be imposing on everyone else. I use the biblical adage of "do unto others" to drive the point home as to how they should comport themselves when not in the courtroom. I explain how important it is to base their verdict only on what happens in court and to avoid any outside influences. I tell them, therefore, not to find out anything about the case from the papers, TV, or Internet. If they happen to hear or see anything, they must report it to my court clerk. I also tell them not to discuss the case with their loved ones or friends when they go home. I acknowledge that—given the naturally curious nature of the human animal—they will undoubtedly be asked a lot of questions and get a lot of off-hand input. I also acknowledge how hard it might be for them realistically to resist responding.

To get them off the hook, I tell the jurors that they should simply say that Judge Block told them that they can't talk about the case until it is over. I drive the point home by using humor for the first time. I tell them that all they can say is that Judge Block looks just like Brad Pitt and is a wonderful judge. I end by instilling a little guilt by telling them that no one will be monitoring their behavior and that they can get away with not following my instructions. However, I add that if they do, they will be violating the sworn oath they had just been given before I started to speak to them: "That they will truly try the case based only on the evidence and the law."

I also spend some time talking to the lawyers about how I want to treat the jury. I explain that I do not want the jurors to need-lessly cool their heels during the course of the trial and want to maximize the jurors' time in the courtroom. There will be no speaking objections and, unless absolutely necessary, no sidebars. They can talk to me all they want before the jurors come in the morning, after they have gone home, or during one of the daytime breaks.

To avoid the waste of the jurors' time that I had been exposed to when I tried cases in Suffolk County, I require the lawyers to give me a list of proposed marked exhibits before the scheduled trial date. If any lawyer has an objection to any of them, he or she must tell me about it at that time. If I can—which is usually the case—I then rule on their admissibility. Before the trial starts, the lawyers can place their objections on the record to preserve their clients' ap-pellate rights. At the trial, there is no need to waste the jurors' time by marking exhibits or discussing whether they can be introduced into evidence. When the lawyers use any of them during the trial, I

199

tell the jury that they are deemed in evidence. I tell the jurors what we have done to save them time and thank the lawyers for their professionalism.

During the trial, I educate the jurors whenever something happens that they might not understand. For example, when a lawyer confronts a witness with a statement made by the witness at a prior occasion—such as to a law enforcement officer or at a deposition—I explain what it is all about. I tell the jurors that it is impeachment material if they determine that it is inconsistent with the witness' trial testimony and that they can consider it in sizing up the witness' credibility. As another example, when objections are made to a question posed to a witness on hearsay grounds, I explain what hearsay is to the jurors after I make my ruling.

I do other things to educate and humanize the process before the jurors. I tell them that I might interrupt a witness' testimony and ask some questions if I think that the testimony is confusing or rambling. I tell the jurors that if I do not understand what the witness is saying, then I assume that they may also be confused. I tell them that the law does not permit them to ask questions and that I have to be their surrogate. However, I caution them that I am only doing this for clarification purposes and that they are not to draw any conclusions that I have any opinion as to the witness' credibility.

I also explain some anachronisms. I tell the jurors how we have mindlessly adopted some irrelevant practices and expressions from England, where our common-law traditions come from. I tell the jurors, as an example, that in London's Old Bailey criminal court, witnesses stand on an elevated platform when they testify and that in our courts we unwittingly tell witnesses to "take the witness stand." In a similar vein, when I and my colleagues are presiding, we are considered to be "on the bench," just like the Brits. I tell the jurors that I have searched high and low for a witness stand and a judge's bench but have yet to find one; in our courtrooms, the judges and witnesses sit in chairs.

Moreover, I always ask federal agents, such as F.B.I. witnesses, to tell the jurors why they are always called "special agents" and not simply "agents." They usually do not know. I tell them that I think the designation was the handiwork of the father of the F.B.I., J. Edgar Hoover, who always wanted his agents to be perceived as special. I ask them rhetorically why it is that the judges are not called "special judges."

When I deliver the charge to the jury after all of the evidence is in, I come down from the mount and stand in front of the jurors— just where the lawyers gave their summations. I got the idea from my colleague Judge I. Leo Glasser, who continues to be a warm, caring, and outstanding jurist in his 30th year on the bench. I think that Judge Glasser and I are the only EDNY judges that do this. I tell the jurors that I believe that they will concentrate better as I explain the law to them if I am closer to them. I try a touch of humor to put them at ease by telling them that when I delivered my first charge, I did in the traditional manner—from up high on the judge's "bench"—but I saw that juror number seven was sound asleep. I tell them that that has never happened since I got off my lofty perch. None of the jurors have ever dozed off while I was breathing down their necks.

I also tell the jurors that after they deliver their verdict, I will come into the jury room to give them the opportunity to ask me any questions they might have about what happened during the trial and to tell me how they were treated by the court personnel. Not all of the judges do this, but I find it another good way to humanize the process. I do not pry into their deliberations.

I am aware that the way in which I interact with my juries is the product of my own personality and background and that each judge has his own comfort level. Some do some of the same things I do; others do it differently. In the final analysis, there is no right or wrong way. Each must be comfortable in his own skin. However, I have been heartened by the letters I have gotten from some of my jurors. Two stand out:

Dear Judge Block—

I was one of the jurors on the Quinones & Quinnes case in Oct—Nov. I wanted to tell you that I have sat in on several criminal trials (on the State level). I was very impressed with your rulings and the way you ran the court room. I also appreciated how thoughtful you were toward the jurors. Most of all I was impressed with how much love and respect you have for the trial process. It was an inspiration, and sadly a quality that many judges seem to lack. I hope that you will continue to sit for many more years—we need you!

Sincerely, Barbara Salling

To your honor

"Special Judge"

Frederic Block,

You have made this time as a juror a pleasant experience. The very kind and reassuring manner in which you speak is comforting.

Lawyers, defendants, witnesses, and jurors were treated fairly and with great care.

The seat you possess is an honorable one. You serve this court with dignity, respect, humor & all the wisdom God has granted. It was an honor to sit in your courtroom.

God bless you in all you do.

Sincerely, Joan Schwick

* * *

I often think that while I did not have law enforcement, big firm, or academic establishment credentials like the rest of my Brooklyn colleagues, the practical experiences that I had knocking around in my everyday Suffolk County small-firm law practice better prepared me for the bench. I was exposed to so much of the real world. As for the lawyers, I went toe to toe with every type, got to know which ones to trust, who to reach out to for help, and how to settle a run-of-the-mill negligence case. I like lawyers. I was one of them.

While I was breaking in as a new judge, I had a sense that lawyers were not generally trusted by all of my Brooklyn colleagues to always behave properly. For example, none of them would allow lawyers to ask any questions to any prospective juror during the jury selection process. The judge did all of the questioning. If the lawyers had questions that they wanted to ask, they had to tell it to the judge and hope that the judge would ask it. This was very different from my experiences of the way we picked civil jurors in the basement of the Suffolk County courthouse, and it was different than the way my CI colleague Judge Leonard Wexler picked the jurors in the old days when Long Island only had a makeshift federal facility. Most of my federal trials had been before him at a time when he was being assigned all of the Suffolk County federal cases.

When it was time to pick my first civil jury, I thought Judge Wexler's way was the best way. I copied it. The lawyers would have a choice. They could let me do it all and ask all of the questions, or they could agree to let one of my law clerks preside over the jury selection process. I explained that if they opted for the law clerk, then the jurors would be given a standard set of written questions to answer dealing with basic information such as where they lived, their jobs, hobbies, etc. The lawyers would then be given about 20 minutes to ask the jurors whatever questions they had that were of particular relevance to their case.

In my 17 years on the bench, no lawyer ever refused the opportunity to talk to the jurors. Yet I have never had a single problem. No lawyer has ever abused the privilege. It has been a win-win-win. The law clerk is, of course, thrilled to be part of the process. I am free to attend to other judicial business—although I am in chambers in case a problem may arise. Moreover, the lawyers feel—and act—like lawyers.

I do not do this in criminal cases. There is something about a criminal trial which makes me feel that the judge should be present at all times and ask all of the questions to vigilantly guard against any possible prejudice that might inadvertently seep out. However, I am thinking of changing my mind to also allow the lawyers to pose questions to prospective jurors in criminal cases.

203

* * *

There are a few other practices I implemented early on to get across the message that I view and respect lawyers as professionals. I would hope that I am perceived as a "lawyers' judge."

In the courtroom, I do not require the lawyers to stand behind a fixed podium when questioning witnesses. They are free to move about and make themselves as comfortable as they wish—as long as they obey common courtesies. When they argue motions in front of me, I talk candidly to them about my concerns and do not simply sit silently while they make speeches. I recall how frustrating it was when I would be before a judge in the old days who would just listen to the lawyers give their pitches without saying a word. You never knew whether the judge had any clue about what you were talking about.

Moreover, I don't bombard the lawyers with rules. I have just one. If a lawyer wants to make a written dispositive motion—which is often the case—then he has to come visit me in my chambers and talk to me first. The only cases that go to trial are those where there are disputed factual issues that a judge or jury has to resolve. Many times the case can be disposed of on papers. At these conferences I have a candid discussion with the lawyers about the case to explore whether it can be resolved short of trial, or whether the issues can be narrowed, or whether realistically the motion has any chance of success.

I find this to be an invaluable way to avoid unnecessary motion practice and paperwork and to move the cases along. Many times the parties want to settle their case to avoid the uncertainties and expense of a trial. Realistically, only a small percentage of cases are ever tried. These informal, frank discussions have proven extremely successful. Patently meritless motions never get made, needless time-consuming paperwork is avoided, and cases get settled. Because of the informal nature of these conferences, I try to make the lawyers feel welcomed and break down needless communication barriers. Many times the lawyers have never seen or spoken to each other until they are sitting around my conference table. I try to make common talk about our lives and work. I will use humor. I will ask if there is any way I can help them work out their differences. Sometimes they might share with me the problems that they are having with their clients, and I'll ask them if they would like me to talk to them. I will explore alternative ways of resolving their problems, such as mediation. In short, I try to make myself useful in a friendly but firm way.

If my powers of persuasion and reasoning fail, the lawyers are simply told to work out their own briefing schedules and to send me their collective motion papers in one bundle when they are completed. I leave it to the lawyers to fix their own timetables. I do not micromanage their business. The lawyers appreciate that I trust them to act like professionals. I have never had any problems.

* * *

The use of humor by a judge is a controversial matter. Should the judge always be "sober as a judge" as the saying goes, or is there a place for some levity? Sir William Gilbert, author of the humor-packed librettos in the Gilbert and Sullivan operettas, was himself a lawyer, though he practiced only briefly. In the first act of the Mikado, the Lord High Executioner sings about various persons who should be executed because they never would be missed. Included in the group is "The Judicial Humorist." As Sir William wrote, "I've got him on the list."

In 1952 Dean William L. Prosser of the Harvard Law School—who was not known for his sense of humor—echoed Gilbert's sentiments in a preface to a book, *The Judicial Humorist,* which was appropriately named for the lawyer who Gilbert thought should be executed. Dean Prosser did not believe that the bench was an appropriate place for humor because the litigant's "entire future, or even his life, may be trembling in the balance, and the robed buffoon who makes merry at his expense should be choked with his own wig."

On the other side of the ledger stands the great Justice Benjamin Cardozo, who, although "preaching caution," did not believe a

205

judicial opinion "is the worse for being lightened by a smile." Justice George Rose Smith, a long-term justice of the Arkansas Supreme Court, aptly cautioned in his excellent article, *A Critique of Judicial Humor*, that a judge "must, without weakening the fabric of seriousness, weave into it a thread of playfulness. Not a simple feat."

I believe that judicial humor sometimes has its place, although I agree that it should not be used indiscriminately. With rare exception, I will not use it in my written opinions—which I think should be serious discussions about the law—but I believe that it can be employed effectively in the courtroom to make a point or provide an appropriate break from the dreariness of some trials which seem to be putting the jurors to sleep. Shakespeare's serious tragedies are not compromised because he always gave the audience some comedic relief. He knew what he was doing. That said, I am conscious of not using humor to make fun of lawyers or litigants. I try to make myself the butt of my humor. Moreover, I only use it when I think that it would serve a purpose, like telling jurors that they can only tell their loved ones that the judge looks like Brad Pitt. In that situation, I say that because I believe that the jurors are more likely to remember my instruction about how important it is to avoid outside influences.

I remember only one time when I used humor in a written opinion, but I did so to defend the honor of the lawyers who practice in the EDNY. There are certain times when a plaintiff is entitled to counsel fees, such as when he has successfully sued the government for a violation of his civil rights. The district court has to determine what the fee should be. In a recent opinion, the Second Circuit Court of Appeals ruled that in cases brought in Brooklyn, the legal fees cannot be the same as if the case were brought in Manhattan. The reasoning was that Brooklyn lawyers charge less for their services than Manhattan lawyers. Thus, if you decided to use a Manhattan lawyer instead of a less expensive Brooklyn lawyer, the losing party should not have to pay for the more expensive lawyer unless the case was truly extraordinary. However, the decision did not end there. In the concluding sentence the appellate court—which has only one of its 13 active judges from the EDNY—reasoned that the defendant "should not be required to pay for a limousine when a sedan could have done the job."

I considered this language to be ill-advised because I thought that it demeaned the lawyers who came from the EDNY. I could not resist the temptation to come to their defense. When I had the chance shortly after to fix legal fees for a Brooklyn lawyer, I wrote that I have had trials with many Brooklyn lawyers who "deserved to drive in limousines" and that I have had trials with Manhattan lawyers "who should have been driving clunkers."

Nevertheless, if you are going to stray from the straight and narrow, there are certainly risks that all may not go as you hoped. I recall one occasion when a psychiatric expert witness was testifying about a criminal defendant's mental status. He told the jury that the defendant had a low IQ and that IQs were "still considered to be a relatively good indicator of cognitive functions." My mind flashed back to the time when my principal, Mr. Richman, told me that I might have a hard time at Stuyvesant because of my low IQ. I should have kept my mouth shut, but could not resist jumping in. I told the shrink that I only had a 96 IQ and asked him, "What does a 96 IQ mean?" He answered that 100 is average, so mine would be a little below average. I then asked him whether that meant that "I would turn out to be an average Judge." He then got his revenge:

THE WITNESS: You would be an average person across the board. I think most people would want someone with more intelligence for a Judge.

I should have had the good sense to stop before matters got worse, but I kept the banter going and asked, "Should I consider resigning as a fraud or anything like that?" The psychiatrist comforted me by testifying that "I wouldn't say that you are obligated to, ethically." I thanked him for his professional consultation. He retorted, "Any time." Everyone laughed.

The repartee between me and the psychiatrist did, however, trigger further testimony dealing with the limitations of an IQ score. The witness explained that there were many variables, such as vision, fatigue, and reading abilities, and the jury took it all seriously.

There was one occasion when a humorous comment that I made was totally politically incorrect. A defendant's lawyer made a bail application for his Chinese client. The defendant had been in jail for a number of days. I was dubious about letting him out since I thought that he was a serious flight risk. Nonetheless, I set him free, but told him that I was giving him a break and that if he skipped "I will have egg foo young on my face." Everyone in the courtroom burst out in laughter. He thanked me profusely. He did not disappoint me. He faithfully complied with his bail conditions and showed up in court promptly whenever he had to appear. He pled guilty to a relatively minor crime, and I did not make him go back to jail.

I still periodically use humor to try to humanize the courtroom. However, these two examples of the misuse of it—early on in my judicial career—remind me that I should always be mindful of Judge Cardozo's sage advice to "proceed with caution."

* * *

There are also unintended humorous moments which remind me that the courtroom is, after all, a human environment. A very fine assistant U.S. Attorney (AUSA) had left the Office to go into private practice. This was hardly unusual. Most of the prosecutors do not make a career of it. They gain valuable trial experience as AUSAs and then usually make their living representing white-collar criminals for big law firms. However, some of them also get permission from their firms to be assigned by the judges to represent indigent defendants.

The Constitution guarantees the right to a trial by jury for criminal defendants charged with felonies. The Supreme Court has also held that it entitles them to a lawyer. In a series of landmark cases ending with *Gideon v. Wainright* in 1963, the high court interpreted the Sixth and 14th Amendments to require the federal and state courts to provide free counsel to indigent defendants who face jail time. In response, Congress established the office of the Federal Defender and many states have funded public defenders. Legal Aid Societies have emerged to try to fill gaps. Because most criminal prosecutions are against defendants who cannot afford a lawyer, these entities cannot handle all of the traffic, and the courts must step in by appointing private lawyers.

On the federal level, Congress has enacted the Criminal Justice Act (CJA) which fixes the fee for court-appointed counsel. Presently, an assigned lawyer gets $125 an hour for all of his time except in death penalty cases, where two attorneys must be assigned and the fees are higher. On the state level there are a lot of variations, and the fees vary greatly. The CJA also requires each district court to create a plan to assure that assigned counsel are competent criminal lawyers. The practice in the state courts is uneven, and there have been reports of assigned counsel falling asleep during a trial and other examples of inadequate representation.

The federal courts take their responsibility seriously. In the EDNY, the judges have created a CJA committee whose function is to see to it that only highly qualified attorneys become CJA lawyers. I chaired the committee for six years. The CJA lawyers get duty-assignment days. When an indigent defendant gets arraigned, the lawyer on duty that day gets the case. Many of the CJA lawyers are former prosecutors from the U.S. Attorney's Office. They have had lots of trial experience as AUSAs and make excellent CJA lawyers when they switch sides. Nevertheless, they have to recalibrate their brains so that they do not lose sight that they are now defending— not prosecuting—a criminal defendant. Sometimes the brain does not accommodate. Such was the fate of a former AUSA whom I had assigned as a CJA lawyer to represent a defendant charged with a serious drug crime. He had tried cases before me when he was an AUSA, and I was impressed by the way he handled them.

He did a wonderful job. He threw all of the passion and talent that he had displayed as a fine AUSA into representing his criminal client, but he lost it during his summation. After a fiery and brilliant argument, he wrapped it all up by pausing, looking the jurors squarely in the eyes, and telling them that the fate of the defendant was now in their hands. For his final flourish, he told them that he was confident that they would have no trouble finding the defendant "guilty as charged"—which they did.

I felt sorry for him and realized how embarrassed he must have been. I told the jurors that he had done a wonderful job representing his client and that it was an obvious slip of the tongue. When I spoke to the jurors after they rendered their verdict—which was clearly warranted—they assured me that they, too, felt for him and that it did not make a difference in their deliberations. However, the experience made me realize that you just do not know what is going on in the minds of those in the courtroom. From my perspective, I am focused on presiding over the trial and thinking about the law. The others in the courtroom are having different thoughts, and no one knows what they might be. A case in point poignantly drove this home.

The chief operating officer of one of the world's major public works construction companies was prosecuted for fraudulently obtaining government construction contracts. His alleged crime was that he did not parcel out some of the subcontracts to minority contractors, as required by the law. The trial lasted for three weeks. The defendant was represented by Gus Newman, who at the age of 84 was considered the dean of the New York City criminal defense bar and was still capable of trying a terrific case. Each day the defendant came to court on time. He was well-dressed and sat attentively at the defense counsel's table while the trial was unfolding. He was hardly a hardened criminal. He had never had any brushes with the law and was a well-respected leader in the public works construction world. He was responsible for the development and repairs of major highways and public works projects worth billions, such as the West Side Highway in Manhattan, the Brooklyn-Queens Expressway, and the John F. Kennedy Airport. His wife and his seven-months pregnant daughter came to court each day.

Gus Newman's defense was simply that his client was not in charge of handing out the minority contracts and had no knowledge that the law was not being followed. The jury did not agree. He was convicted. He sat expressionless as the foreperson read the verdict. I had no idea what was going through his mind. Because this was not a violent crime and the defendant was an upstanding citizen, he had been free on bail. The sentencing would not take place for a few months. I told him that I was not going to put him in jail now and that he might not be facing much time.

Two days later Gus Newman called to tell me that his client had committed suicide. We were both shocked. Mr. Newman told me that he had had lunch with him just a few hours before and had no inkling that he was thinking about taking his life; he had never shown any signs of depression at any time before, during, or after the trial. He left a suicide note. In it he apologized to his wife and pregnant daughter. He recognized that he would never see his grandchild but wrote that he did not believe that he had done anything wrong and could not go on living knowing that he had been convicted of a crime.

I remember this tragic episode whenever I walk into the courtroom and look at all of the people who are the players on the human stage in front of me.

211

Chapter
5

Sentencing

There is not a judge I know who does not think that sentencing is the most difficult part of the job. I believe that I do it responsibly, but I have never gotten used to it. There are so many different types of defendants and criminal scenarios. You just do not know how you will respond until you are face to face with the person whom you have to decide whether to put in jail—and for how long. However, at a time when we are cutting trillions of dollars from government spending, we are paying an enormous price to support our prison population. It is currently about 2.2 million. Ten percent—roughly 220,000—are federal prisoners.

Congress and the states pass lots of statutes criminalizing all sorts of behavior and providing for lengthy prison sentences. Many are warranted, but many are not. No politician wants to be seen as soft on crime. The net result, however, is that the United States proportionally puts more people in jail than any other country— even China—and at an enormous economic cost. The *New York Times* reported on March 3, 2009, that 7.3 million people are presently either in prison or on parole or probation in the United States. This translates to 1 out of 37, but the racial disparity is striking: One in 11of the people in prison is African American, and one in 27 is Latino. By comparison, one in 45 people in prison is white.

These figures do not account for the alumni—those who have already served their sentences. My guess is that about one out of every 15 people we pass on the streets each day is an ex-con. One has to wonder whether we have overcriminalized our society. Indeed, the United States, with 5% of the world's population, now accounts for 25% of the world's inmates.

As for the dollars we spend to punish so many people, the same *New York Times* article reported that the current annual cost of running our nation's correctional facilities is about $50 billion. This means, according to the *Times*, that our criminal corrections spending "is outpacing budget growth in education, transportation and public assistance." The Pew Center on the States—a reputable research group—reported that in 2009 "only Medicaid spending grew faster than state corrections spending, which quadrupled in the past two decades."

The Federal Bureau of Prisons is the agency in charge of running the federal prison system. It has to feed, clothe, house, and provide for all of the inmates' basic needs. Its 2011 budget for doing this is $6.8 billion. It operates and maintains 115 prisons. The cost per prisoner is about $28,000 per year.

The numbers do not lie. Our nation's priorities are focused on punishment. There is scant interest in rehabilitation. As Peter Greenwood, the executive director of the Association for the Advancement of Evidence Based Practice—a group that promotes rehabilitation—puts it: "Traditionally, probation and parole is at the bottom of the totem pole. They're just happy every time they don't lose a third of their budget."

While the politicians increase their prospects for reelection by talking tough on crime, society does not necessarily benefit by putting its head in the sand because the recidivist rate—those returning to jail—is staggering. In one study by the Bureau of Justice Statistics dating back a few years, it tracked 272,111 prisoners who had been released and found that within three years of the time they were let out of jail,, 67.5% had been rearrested at least once for a felony or serious misdemeanor. It's no wonder. The ex-cons cannot get jobs; given our current economic plight, even those without a checkered past are having a difficult time getting work. They are without hope. The prisons, therefore, are revolving doors.

I do not know if our society can ever solve the recidivist problem, but I share the sentiments expressed by Louisiana's governor, Bobby Jindal—no arch liberal:

> Without education, job skills, and other basic services, offenders are likely to repeat the same steps that brought them to jail in the first place . . . We cannot say we are doing everything we can to keep our communities and our families safe if we are not addressing the high rate at which offenders are becoming repeat criminals.

I feel sometimes like the traffic cop just waving on the endless traffic with no relief in sight. I wish that I had a magic wand to figure out how to change our culture to look at the bigger picture and take effective measures to reduce the prison population.

* * *

I get randomly assigned about 120–150 criminal cases a year. Over 95% of the defendants negotiate a plea disposition with the U.S. Attorney's Office and plead guilty. Most who go to trial are convicted. I sentence, therefore, about three defendants a week. Most are Hispanic or black. Of all of the defendants sentenced in 2010 by the 25 EDNY judges, 40% were Hispanic. The vast majority were for being in the country illegally. Thirty percent of those sentenced were black. Since there are only two black judges and one Hispanic judge, this means that of the total number of defendants sentenced, 7 of 10 were Hispanic or black and 22 of the 25 judges doing the sentencing were white.

Before the sentence, the Probation Department prepares a detailed presentence report, called a PSR, telling me about the defendant's personal history and any past criminal misdeeds. The district's U.S. Attorney's Office and the defendant's counsel usually make written submissions agreeing or disagreeing with the PSR. Most of the time the defendant's lawyer will send me letters from his client's family and friends. I read them all.

At the time of sentence, I have to calculate the *Guidelines* range by determining the points attributable to the particular crime and the criminal history category. I actively engage the lawyers in the process and usually ask them lots of questions. If the defendant's lawyer shows a lack of knowledge about the *Guidelines* and is not making a decent pitch for his client, I always jump in. I will tell him that he could do much better, explain why, and adjourn the sentence to give him the opportunity to make further submissions. This is always awkward since I must speak in the presence of the defendant. By law he is entitled to be present and to know if the judge does not think that his lawyer is properly representing him. The prosecutor may be unhappy when this happens, and the defendant's lawyer must hate me for embarrassing him in front of his client. However, I cannot sit silently by and allow a person whose liberty is at stake to be improperly sentenced because of a lawyer's inadequate representation.

This problem has never occurred when an indigent defendant is being represented by either the Federal Defender's Office or a court-appointed counsel from the CJA list. Because they are so highly qualified—and knowledgeable about the *Guidelines*—their sentencing submissions are excellent. It is ironic that oftentimes impoverished defendants think that they are getting inferior legal advice because they cannot afford private counsel. I often reassure them by telling them that if I ever have to be sentenced, then I would prefer to be represented by one of those fine free lawyers.

After listening to everyone, I impose the sentence. During my first 10 years on the bench, I was somewhat hemmed in by the mandatory nature of the *Guidelines*. I could only depart from the prescribed *Guidelines* range for extraordinary reasons. For example, I could not ordinarily consider the defendant's age, education, physical or mental problems, military service, prior good deeds, employment history, family or community ties, lack of youthful guidance, or socio-economic status. I could consider them, however, in deciding where within the range the defendant would be sentenced because I was allowed to assess "the nature and history and characteristics of the defendant."

There were some situations where I had absolutely no discretion. Congress had provided for minimum sentences for certain crimes.

Therefore, in those cases the minimum would have to be imposed even if the *Guidelines* range were lower. For example, if the range were 46–57 months but the minimum sentence for that crime was five years, I would have to sentence the defendant to 60 months. There were, however, two exceptions. In certain drug cases, a defendant with no prior record was allowed to be sentenced within the *Guidelines* range if he told the government everything he knew about the circumstances of his crime, including any others who were involved. If the defendant had entered into a cooperation agreement with the government, I had virtually complete discretion in fixing the sentence.

In 2005, the Supreme Court rendered its opinion in *United States v. Booker*. In this landmark decision, the majority of the Justices held that it was unconstitutional for Congress to have required that the *Guidelines* be mandatory. It recognized Congress' laudatory desire in 1984—when it put in place its mandatory sentencing regime—to eliminate sentencing disparity but reasoned that it could not constitutionally preclude the judges from exercising their discretion below a statutorily created maximum term of incarceration.

The Supreme Court, therefore, made the *Guidelines* advisory. The district judges still were required to consider all of the factors which they were required to take into account when they used to fix the sentence within the *Guidelines* range, but they now had the discretion—after doing so—to impose a sentence outside the range, provided that it was not a crime that required a minimum or maximum sentence. The circuit court of appeals could only disagree with the sentencing judge's out-of-guidelines sentence if it determined that it was unreasonable.

The district judge could now consider everything that was previously prohibited. Except for the mandatory minimum sentences, sentencing discretion was effectively restored.

* * *

Mandatory minimums were established as early as 1790, but

217

only for capital offenses. However, Congress began imposing them in earnest beginning with the 1956 Narcotic Control Act. By 2009 the United States Code contained 171 mandatory minimum provisions. They ran the gamut from drugs and firearms to obscure offenses such as bribing a Baltimore harbor inspector. According to statistics compiled by the United States Sentencing Commission, in 2010 they applied in 27.2% of all sentences. Drugs accounted for most of them—77.4%—followed by firearms. Nevertheless, they are often viewed as arbitrary and irrational and have become a source of controversy amongst the judges and the bar. The hard question is when, if ever, Congress should impose its will upon the courts and take away their sentencing responsibilities by establishing mandatory minimum sentences. A good example is child pornography. While every judge abhors it, Congress has decided in many cases that it—rather than the judges—is better suited to decide how those who collect and distribute dirty pictures of young children should be punished.

The child pornography industry has flourished through the Internet. As the number of federal cases grew, Congress increased the recommended prison terms and established a mandatory minimum sentence of five years for anyone convicted of simply receiving or possessing a large number of child porno pictures. It also provided for a mandatory 10-year prison term for anyone convicted twice for possessing even one picture. As Douglas A. Berman, a professor at the Ohio State Law School who studies sentencing issues, explained: "What has caused concern in courts across the nation is that we have a lot of relatively law-abiding individuals sitting in the basement downloading the wrong kind of dirty pictures facing not just prison sentences but incredibly long prison sentences." On the other side of the ledger, child advocates like Ernie Allen, the president of the National Center for Missing and Exploited Children, support dealing with the child porno possessors as criminals and locking them up for many years. As he sees it: "Real children are harmed in the production of these images, and these same children are harmed every time these images are downloaded and viewed."

A recent case of Judge Weinstein's—*United States v. Polizzi*—points out the problem. The defendant was a 56-year-old family man with a wife and five children. He was a religious person who attended church. He was well-respected by his community and was totally law-abiding. His problem was that he had a double-locked room in the attic of his detached garage where he collected and viewed a lot of child pornography through the Internet. However, he never sent these photos to anyone, nor did he enter teenage chat rooms or attempt online solicitations. Since Congress had criminalized the receipt and possession of child porno, he was convicted by a jury after a trial. His defense was insanity, which the jury rejected. Because of the large number of photos which he had privately collected, he faced a five-year minimum term of imprisonment.

Troubled by the harsh sentence which he would have to impose, Judge Weinstein asked the jurors after they had rendered their verdict if they would have made the same decision if they had known that the defendant faced a five-year minimum. A number of the jurors were shocked. They believed that he needed mental treatment, not a long jail sentence. They would have gone for the insanity defense. Judge Weinstein—ever the maverick—ordered a new trial. In doing so, he called attention to the strict punishment that Congress had called for—and its insistence on a lengthy minimum sentence—in a situation which he believed cried out for the exercise of sound judicial judgment and discretion.

I am hardly a fan of child pornography but—like Judge Weinstein and, I believe, most of my colleagues—neither am I a fan of mandatory minimum sentences. While I do not take issue with a few of them where violent crimes are involved, I am not at ease with the notion that Congress can at any time it chooses usurp the sentencing function of the judge and reduce him to a bean counter. Each defendant is different, and no two cases are alike. Taking stock of these differences and treating each defendant as a separate human being is at the heart of sentencing. It is the solemn and awesome responsibility of the judge—not the politician.

* * *

When it comes to sentencing, the main culprit is drugs. Our country is infested with them. About half of the roughly 220,000 criminals in the federal prisons have either brought them into our country, have distributed them here, or have otherwise associated themselves with this illicit activity. This means that probably half of the $6.8 billion of the Bureau of Prisons budget is eaten up by incarcerating the criminal druggies. Despite this, we do not seem to know how to stop the flow of drugs into the United States.

I remember sitting next to an elegantly dressed woman several years ago in an airplane on my way to visit my brother Leonard in Tampa. We started chatting. She was born in Colombia and was a drug counselor in New York. We talked about the Colombian drug lords, and I expressed my exasperation about all of the drug sentences that I had to hand out because of drugs brought into our country from her native land. The EDNY has more than its fair share of drug prosecutions because it has jurisdiction over the John F. Kennedy airport. Customs Officers pick up drug couriers every day there who are trying to smuggle drugs into New York from outside of the country. I told the woman that the majority of my sentences are for drugs. Her simple response was that if there were no demand, then there would be no supply. I told her that I did not understand why snorting coke, injecting heroin, and smoking marijuana was so rampant in the U.S.A. I asked her who these people were whom she was counseling. She said that I would not believe how many were kids from wealthy neighborhoods and that their parents never had a clue. I wondered what that said for our country and family values.

Drugs accounted for 43% of the sentences in the EDNY in 2010. Mandatory minimum sentences of five years must be imposed for the possession of large quantities of cocaine or heroin. Most of the sentences that I have handed out have been for smaller quantities of these drugs where I was not bound by mandated minimums and had considerable discretion—especially after *Booker* made the *Guidelines* advisory. They typically involved couriers smuggling the drugs into JFK from Colombia or the Dominican Republic. Usually they would risk their lives by swallowing pellets, just like the young girl in the movie *Maria Full of Grace*. They escaped detection more often than not. A customs officer once told me that only about 10% are caught. These swallowers do all sorts of things to avoid detection. I have had pregnant women, blind men, little children, and a dog before me. The poor animal almost died on the plane. The guy who came to retrieve him at the airport was arrested. Being bothered by cruelty to animals, I gave him a stiffer sentence than usual. He was upset when I told him that he would not be allowed to bring his dog to jail with him. The Drug Enforcement Agency saved the dog's life, named him Cokie, and trained him to be one of its best drug sniffers. Lots of couriers probably got nabbed because of Cokie.

* * *

All sentences must be rendered in open court in the presence of the defendant and his lawyer. The judge has to explain the reasons for the sentence—and reduce them to writing—so that if there is an appeal, then the circuit court can decide whether the sentence was reasonable. The reasons have to reflect your assessment of the nature of the crime and the defendant's characteristics. Shortly after I had expressed my frustration to the drug counselor about the drugs coming into our country from Colombia, I had to sentence a courier from her native country. While I was able to speak openly to my fellow passenger, I learned the hard way that you cannot always do that during a sentencing proceeding. You have to be politically correct.

In sentencing this particular courier—who was a woman— I said that the court "believes that it's necessary to continue to send a message, especially to those who have Colombian roots that they'll be dealt with harshly by the laws of this country." I got reversed. Although the Court of Appeals noted that from reading everything I had said it was clear that I was not motivated by any improper sentencing consideration, it nonetheless held that the defendant had to be resentenced—and by a different judge—to protect the

221

"appearance of justice" because a reasonable person might think that my reference to "Colombian roots" meant that the defendant's national origin played a role in the sentence.

Although I like to have an honest and open sentencing proceeding and have a full discussion about what is on my mind so that the lawyers—and particularly the defendants—have a full opportunity to address my concerns, I must pay close attention, ever since I got reversed for referring to "Colombian roots," to the thoughts that come into my head. While it is impossible not to have thoughts about what bothers you, I know that I must sometimes disregard them. For example, when I had to sentence a defendant who never had worked but had seven kids—three born in the same year—with five different women before his 25th birthday, I could not help thinking that the longer I put him away, the fewer additional children he could father. I had to put that idea out of my mind because simply having children is not relevant to the goals of sentencing—punishment for a crime, prevention of future crimes, and the like. However, his irresponsible lifestyle said something about the character of the person before me, an appropriate factor for my consideration. I sentenced him to the top of the guidelines range, and told him that he could have as many kids as he wanted, but his unwillingness to support those he had was part of the reason for my high sentence.

Judges have different thoughts about similar situations. As shown by Judge Kennedy's study, they bring their unique personalities and sensibilities to the bench which influence, consciously or not, their sentences. In addition to how I feel about young people who irresponsibly bring lots of kids into the world, my nature and view of the human condition undoubtedly impact the way I sentence defendants. This is not to suggest that I do not follow the law. To the contrary, I carefully evaluate the nature of the crime and the defendant's characteristics—as the law requires—and mete out punishment that squares with the goals of sentencing. My colleagues do the same, but different people will not necessarily see things the same way. It is simply the nature of the human animal.

Some judges, therefore, get a reputation for being tough sentencers; others for being lenient. Here's how it has shaken out for me in the major sentencing categories I deal with.

First and foremost are the drug couriers. While I will hand out high sentences if—like in the case of the Colombian woman—I believe that I am dealing with someone who is a real bad apple. I am more forgiving of desperate people—especially swallowers—who have no jobs or money and come from impoverished places. If it is their first offense, I will usually sentence them to between 18–24 months, although the *Guidelines* range is much higher. Most of them are undocumented, but some are permanent resident aliens. Because they are not citizens, they will all be deported after they serve their sentence. The resident aliens are shocked to learn this. Many have family in the United States. I am also mindful that it costs $28,000 a year to keep a criminal in jail. I'm not sure that this is a factor that I can legally take into account, so I don't. Instead, I try to arrive at a sentence that balances the need to punish and deter drug crimes against the reality that the defendant before me will eventually be deported.

Many of my sentences involve resident aliens who have been found in the country after having been deported because they committed a felony in the United States. They will be deported again once they serve their time. Their circumstances vary greatly, and these affect my sentence. If they have no roots here and have committed another crime after having snuck back into the country, I'll give them a high *Guidelines* sentence to protect the public. They will know that they will pay a stiff price if they try to come back again. If, however, the prior crime was not one of violence and the motive for return was to visit the family they left behind, I will give them a below *Guidelines* sentence and explain that they just can't live here anymore.

When it comes to guns, I tend to sentence within the *Guidelines* range. Most of these cases involve "felons in possession." It is a federal crime for someone who has committed a felony to have a gun. I'm tough on ex-felons who are caught carrying them. They are dangerous.

* * *

I believe in giving realistic sentences. For example, Congress has required that the judge impose a period of supervised release after a defendant serves his jail time. It usually runs from one to five years. If a death is involved, it could be 10 years. Supervised release is a good idea. The Probation Department is charged with checking on how the recently incarcerated defendant is adjusting to freedom. The judge many times orders special conditions that must be complied with. For example, a person with a drug problem can be required to get treatment either as an outpatient or in a residential drug facility. If a condition of supervised release is violated, the judge can put the violator back in jail for up to two years.

Curiously, Congress did not carve out an exception for those who had to be sentenced to life without parole. It probably just slipped through the cracks. In my first such sentence, I blindly followed the strictures of the law and sentenced the defendant to 10 years of supervised release. Later I thought how silly this was, and I did not do it the next time. I was willing to run the risk of being reversed by the appellate court for not requiring the defendant to be supervised after he died. If I were to do it, I imagine that I would have to provide that the devil would be the deceased's supervisor. I remembered Dickens' lamentation about the law being an ass, and could not bring myself to be a donkey.

Because I do not believe in artificial sentencing, I would not have sentenced Bernie Madoff to 150 years. However, Judge Chin calculated that this was what the strict application of the *Guidelines* called for and that, in any event, it was an appropriate symbolic thing to do. I know Denny Chin. He now sits as a highly regarded Second Circuit judge. Like Sonia Sotomayor, he also has a compelling life story—raised by hardworking immigrant parents in Chinatown—and has outstanding legal skills and academic credentials. If I were the President, I would nominate him as the

224

first Asian-American Supreme Court Justice. He would be a lock for confirmation even though he is a Democrat. After all, what Republican Senator would vote against a judge who wanted to keep Bernie in jail for decades after his death.

There are times when I have been highly critical of the *Guidelines* for making absolutely no sense. For example, when a defendant is convicted of securities fraud, the *Guidelines* usually call for a life sentence. This is because Congress has throughout the last several years politically reacted to the public's outcry against Wall Street's greed by sending the guidelines for white-collar criminals literally through the roof.

Thus, I sentenced two brothers who had been convicted of engaging in what is commonly referred to as a "pump and dump" stock scheme to 60 months although the *Guidelines* range was 360 to life. It was absurd. If not for the Supreme Court's decision in *Booker* making the *Guidelines* advisory, I would have had to put them in jail for at least 30 years.

While it was true that the defendants had pumped up the value of their stock in their publicly traded small business by making material misrepresentations about their business operations and then dumped the stock at a profit, they were hardly in the same category as murderers or the major corporate predators who had bilked the public out of billions. They made a relatively small profit by their misdeeds, and there were not a lot of people who lost much money. They deserved to be put in jail, but not for life. In a written opinion—*United States v. Parris*—I stated that the case "represents another example where the guidelines in a securities fraud prosecution 'have so run amok that they are patently absurd on their face.'" I drew support from language which I quoted from a circuit court decision in a different case—*United States v. Ebbers*—where the appellate court noted that "[u]nder the Guidelines, it may well be that all but the most trivial frauds in publicly traded companies may trigger sentences amounting to life imprisonment." While I acknowledged that the *Guidelines* "reflect Congress' judgment as to the appropriate national policy for such crimes," this did not mean that the sentencing guidelines for white-collar crimes "should be a black stain on common sense."

There have been times, however, when I have been so shocked at the nature of a crime that I imposed a sentence way above the bottom of the advisory *Guidelines* range. Gerardo Flores Carreto had pleaded guilty to white slavery. He brought young women into the country from Mexico under false pretenses and forced them into prostitution. The sentencing range was 360 to life. Although I have a sense of what the punishment should probably be in a case before I walk into the courtroom to render my sentence from reading the PSRs and the letters I get, I pride myself on keeping an open mind until I have listened to everyone during the sentencing proceeding. In addition to the lawyers and the defendants, the victims are also entitled to speak. In Carreto's case, I was thinking that the minimum recommended sentence would be appropriate. Thirty years is a long sentence when no one has been killed. However, when I listened to victim after victim tell how they were kept as prisoners, threatened with their lives, and treated like animals if they would not turn tricks every day and hand over all of their hard-earned monies to their captor, I became visibly upset. When the defendant showed no remorse, I sentenced him to 50 years.

On the more charitable side of the ledger, I am sympathetically disposed to give a lenient sentence to someone who is possessed of enormous untapped creative abilities. Aaron Myvett was a case in point. He had pled guilty to a number of serious crimes which exposed him to more than 20 years of jail time. However, he had entered into a cooperation agreement, which meant that I could give him a below-guidelines sentence.

The law allows the government to enter into cooperation deals with criminals. Only the government decides who gets one. The prosecutors size up a case and decide what they need to button down a conviction. About 20% of the time, they will offer a cooperation agreement to a witness who is willing to testify against a codefendant. It is the number one prosecutorial tool. The concept is simple. The cooperator is in the best position to testify about his fellow criminal's misdeeds. The idea is to send out a little fish to catch a big one. To induce the cooperator to turn, the government must dangle a bait. The cooperation agreement, therefore, provides that if the cooperator pleads guilty and testifies honestly against his criminal buddies or otherwise renders "substantial assistance," then the government will let the court know. The court can then give the cooperator a break when it sentences him. While the judge is required to assess the nature and effectiveness of the cooperator's handiwork, as a practical matter the judge has total discretion in fixing the punishment.

The national figures assembled by the United States Sentencing Commission show that the average sentence for a cooperator is 50% of what he would otherwise get if not for his cooperation. Without cooperators there often would not be enough evidence to convict, and many hardened criminals would go free. While the court is free to sentence the cooperator harshly—and disregard his cooperation—if it were to do that, word would get out, and the pool of cooperators would dry up. To that extent, the sentencing judge is in league with the government and becomes an important agent in enticing criminals to cooperate.

The cooperator, however, runs a big risk. The government has enormous discretion. If it believes that the turncoat has not fully and honestly cooperated, it will tear up the cooperation agreement. Unless the court determines that the government did so in bad faith, it must then sentence the defendant in accordance with his plea.

In Myvett's case, because the government was totally satisfied with his cooperation he was entitled to a big break. At the time of his sentence, he had been in jail for about two years. Because of the serious nature of his crimes, I was inclined to keep him in jail for a few more years. However, when he came to court to be sentenced, he gave me a sketch that he had done of Mother Teresa which looked just like her. He also gave me a number of sketches that he had done of fellow inmates. Everyone did a double take. He obviously had enormous talent, but he had an all-too-common impoverished upbringing: no known father; a mother hooked on drugs; and cast to the winds on the streets of a dangerous neighborhood where dealing drugs was viewed as the only means of survival. What a shame that he took a wrong turn in the road and never capitalized on his creative gift.

I was intrigued. I adjourned the sentence to explore with the Probation Department whether there might be some way to give Myvett an opportunity to exploit his talent during the term of supervised release that I would impose once he was out of prison. In the meantime, he asked me whether he could sketch me. I gave him a photo.

On the adjourned sentencing date, Myvett proudly presented me with the sketch. It was perfect. In the meantime, the Probation Department had found a Catholic school that was willing to let Myvett decorate its kindergarten with Disney cartoons. I asked him whether he would have any problems doing Mickey Mouse and Donald Duck. He assured me that it would be a piece of cake.

I let Myvett out of jail that day, but imposed five years of supervised release with the special condition that he render 75 hours of community service at the school. The school is now the proud beneficiary of his artwork. When anyone walks into my office, they can see the sketch hanging by my desk. I wonder how many more Myvetts are in jail?

* * *

There was one high profile cooperation deal that went awry, which required me to sentence Anthony Casso—who went by the charming nickname of "Gaspipe"—to life.

The government was willing to enter into a cooperation deal with Gaspipe—an underboss in the Luchese crime family—because it thought that he might be needed as a backup to Salvatore Gravano—Sammy the Bull—in the John Gotti trial. Gaspipe also was considered a valuable potential witnesses in other pending prosecutions against the Mafia. Pursuant to his cooperation agreement,

Gaspipe had pled before Judge Nickerson and admitted to orchestrating 15 murders. If the government was not satisfied with his cooperation—provided that it acted in good faith—he would have to be sentenced to life.

Judge Nickerson, however, dropped out of the case after the F.B.I. told him that Gaspipe and members of the Colombo crime family had conspired to kill him. He thought that it was best that another judge sentence him to avoid the appearance that he might not be objective. I drew the black bead.

In August 1997 the government pulled the plug on Gaspipe and advised me that he had breached his cooperation agreement. It would not, therefore, be consenting to a lower sentence than the life sentence that the law required for his many murders. I listened to Gaspipe's lawyer's argument that the government was acting in bad faith, but decided that it had properly exercised its discretion. I had no choice but to give Gaspipe life. My decision was upheld on appeal. The circuit court agreed with my finding that Gaspipe had written a letter to the government in which he had falsely disputed the trial testimony of Sammy the Bull during the Gotti trial. The letter contained a number of lies, including that the Bull had admitted to ordering the stabbing of the Reverend Al Sharpton.

Gaspipe did not take kindly to my sentence. He could not understand why he was being put away for life when the Bull got five years and other cooperators got lenient sentences. Judge Glasser had sentenced the Bull to only five years even though he had confessed to killing a lot of people. The judge rewarded him for testifying against Gotti—who was finally convicted after two prior failed attempts. The Bull was one of the highest-ranking mafiosi to break the code of *omertà*. Because he testified to save his own neck—and got such a big break—many others came forward, and the Mafia was decimated in the trials that followed.

Gaspipe complained to the press that his crimes "weren't any worse than theirs" and that he was "being singled out." He later wrote a book. In it he said that his "biggest problem" was Judge Block. He thought that I was "made prejudiced against [him] by the prosecutors telling [me] that I was going to kill his colleague Judge Nickerson, which was a bold-faced lie." He said that it "was the Colombo crew that told me they wanted to do in Nickerson."

Nonetheless, Gaspipe was not kindly disposed to judges. A few months after I put him away for life, the F.B.I. told me that it had learned that he wanted to kill me.

Chapter
6

The Risks

The United States Marshals Service (U.S.M.S.) has primary responsibility for ensuring safety and security for federal judicial proceedings and protecting the federal judges, federal prosecutors, and all other federal court officials. It works in concert with other agencies, including the F.B.I., which is responsible for conducting criminal investigations of threats against the judges, U.S. Attorneys, and AUSAs. These threats have increased dramatically during the last decade, growing from 592 in 2003 to approximately 1,400 in 2010. During this six-year period, there were 5,744 threats directed at federal judges and prosecutors.

Each of the 94 federal districts has a marshal's office with a chief marshal and deputy marshals. The number of deputies varies depending on the size of the district. In the EDNY there are over 60. Their main function is to monitor the court's proceedings and bring the inmates from the local jail into the courtroom whenever they have to appear. Two or three of the deputy marshals will stand watch when the inmates are before the judge.

Each marshal's district office must have one or more judicial security inspectors, who are senior-level deputy marshals. Their job is to oversee investigations and implement protective measures, such as conducting residential security surveys and security briefings for those who have been threatened. As of February 2009, 113 judicial security investigators were assigned to the USMS's 94 districts. The USMS budget for judicial security was $344 million in 2008. It is undoubtedly much more today.

I was told about Gaspipe's threat to kill me by an F.B.I. special agent who looked like he came right out of central casting—tall and handsome, with short-cropped hair. He went right to the point. He told me that the F.B.I. and the Marshal's Service annually investigate over 300 threats against Article III federal judges. This meant that about one-third of the circuit and district court judges were yearly at risk of bodily harm and death. I told him that when I took the job I had no idea that the risk level would be so high. He explained that it was the policy and practice of the F.B.I. and Marshal's Service to tell the judges at once about any threats and that they would be seriously and promptly investigated. After the investigation was completed, a threat-level assessment would be made. It would be either a low threat level, a potential danger level, or a serious threat level. The judge would, of course, be kept abreast of everything that was happening.

I thanked the special agent for giving me the good news. He reassured me by telling me that the threat was picked up through the jailhouse rumor mill and probably would not amount to much. Nonetheless, it would be seriously checked out. He would be in touch with me as the investigation unfolded. I asked him if there was anything that I should do in the meantime. He just told me to be careful. He also asked whether I would like to carry a gun. I told him that I had never shot one in my life and would probably shoot myself by mistake.

* * *

After the agent left, I was curious to learn whether I would be the first federal judge assassinated. I found out that if Gaspipe had his way, I would be the fourth during the last two decades.

John H. Wood was a district court judge for the Western District of Texas. He was assassinated on May 29, 1979, by Charles Harrelson—the father of the actor Woody Harrelson. It was a contract killing orchestrated by the Texas drug lord Jamiel Chagra, who was waiting to be tried before Judge Wood. As a reminder of the dangers that judges face, the San Antonio federal courthouse now bears his name.

Richard J. Daronco was a district court judge closer to home. He sat on the Southern District bench in Manhattan. Judge Daronco was assassinated on May 21, 1988, by the father of a civil plaintiff whose case was dismissed by the judge. He was shot while doing yard work in front of his home.

Robert Smith Vance was a judge for the Eleventh Circuit Court of Appeals. He was assassinated on December 16, 1989, when he opened a package containing a bomb, which immediately exploded. The package was the handiwork of Walter Leroy Moody, Jr., who had lost his appeal before that appellate court from his criminal conviction for possessing another bomb. Ironically, Judge Vance had nothing to do with the case; he was neither the trial judge nor on the appellate panel that affirmed Moody's conviction.

A few months later, the F.B.I. special agent returned and told me that Gaspipe's death threat had been classified as low risk. There was no tangible evidence that any contract had been placed on my life, and since Gaspipe was in a maximum security prison for the rest of his life, there was no risk that he could kill me—as long as he did not escape.

Since then I have had two other death threats by other less-than-model citizens. They, too, were classified as low risks, but the message was clear—being a judge was no bed of roses. You were truly in the service of your country, and—just like in combat—you could lose your life.

Moreover, like the tragedy that recently struck my district court colleague from Chicago—Judge Joan Lefkow—your family was also at risk. On February 28, 2005, Judge Lefkow returned home late in the evening after a long day on the bench. Unbeknownst to her, Bart Ross, a disgruntled plaintiff in a medical malpractice case that the judge had tossed out of court, had learned where she lived and had come there earlier in the night to kill her. Judge Lefkow's mother and husband were at home waiting for her. When the judge finally arrived, Ross was nowhere in sight, but she found her mother and husband in the basement. They had been murdered.

Judge Lefkow had also been the target of threats five years earlier from Matthew Hale, a white supremacist. The judge had enjoined him from using the name that he had chosen for his organization. Hale was subsequently sentenced to a 40-year prison term for soliciting an undercover F.B.I. informant to kill her.

These incidents led Congress to focus on providing better protection for the judiciary. In 2006, it approved spending more than $12 million for the installation of alarm systems in the homes of the federal judges. I installed one in my home, but it hardly put me at ease. In a report issued in December 2009, addressing "threats against judges," the U.S. Department of Justice concluded that the Marshals Service "does not consistently provide an appropriate response for the risk level posed by the threats, does not effectively coordinate with other law enforcement agencies to respond to these threats, and personnel are not trained adequately to respond to these threats."

The state judiciaries also have hardly been immune from violent attacks from disgruntled litigants. In the same year that Judge Lefkow's mother and husband were killed, shootings outside of the local courthouse in Tyler, Texas left two people dead and four others wounded. A judge, a court reporter, and a deputy sheriff were also murdered in the Fulton County courthouse in Atlanta, Georgia.

Jerry Markon, a respected reporter for the *Washington Post*, noting that threats to federal judges and prosecutors were on the rise, recently attributed the trend to "disgruntled defendants whose anger is fueled by the Internet; terrorism and gang cases that bring more violent offenders into federal court; frustration at the economic crisis; and the rise of the 'sovereign citizen' movement—a loose collection of tax protesters, white supremacists and others who don't respect federal authority." There are, in short, a lot of loose screws out there. Harold Turner was one of them.

Since 2001 Turner had been broadcasting an incendiary Internet radio show from his home studio in North Bergen, New Jersey, gaining notoriety because of his anti-immigrant and anti-Semitic remarks. He was arrested in 2010 for making death threats against three federal circuit court judges from Chicago. He took exception to a decision that they had rendered upholding a handgun ban and posted a message on his Web site expressing his outrage. He called the judges "cunning, ruthless, untrustworthy, disloyal, unpatriotic, deceitful scum." The Free Speech Clause of the First Amendment of the Constitution gave him the right to make these obnoxious comments, but he did not stop there. He went on to write that, "These judges deserve to be killed," and later wrote, "If they are allowed to get away with this by surviving, other judges will act the same way." To make matters worse, he posted their home addresses and photos.

Harold Turner was convicted for his frightening conduct. A jury in my courthouse—where the case was tried—determined that he had crossed the line that the First Amendment draws; you can't yell "fire" in a crowded theater. Turner was sentenced to three years in jail, but the three judges that he wanted dead have to wonder if some kook out there might be hiding in wait for them or their families. The Turner case punctuated how vulnerable judges are to losing their lives in the service of their country.

* * *

The Justice Department's report in 2009 followed on the heels of a frightening incident that happened in my courtroom on March 11, 2008. Victor Wright was brought into the court to be sentenced by me to life after being convicted for serious drug crimes. He seemed to accept his impending fate because he had not shown any signs of hostility at any other time when he had been in court—but not on this occasion. As he walked into my court—followed closely by two marshals—he bolted past his attorney, razor in hand, and lunged at the prosecutor, Carolyn Pokorny, a 38-year-old AUSA, and started to choke her. All mayhem broke loose. Within seconds, Ron Tolkin, the court reporter (who was right there) and the marshals

235

jumped on Wright. The razor fell to the ground, and the marshals were on the verge of inflicting a deadly choke hold on the defendant when he took his hands off the AUSA's throat.

I sat frozen and startled. I did not leave the bench and join in because the judges had been told during periodic security briefings not to do that because they would only be interfering with the trained marshals and could make matters worse. However, I took it on the chin in the Internet chat rooms the next day for being a wuss and not whacking the defendant with my gavel. Instead, I had followed instructions and pressed the security button under the judge's bench. Within 30 seconds, marshals were swarming all over the place, and the frightening potential disaster had been averted. Carolyn Pokorny had barely escaped with her life, but the imprint of Victor Wright's fingers on her neck—which did not disappear for two weeks—made her realize how close she had come to dying.

The incident was captured on tape by the monitors that are in every courtroom and was shown on national TV that night. It has become a training video for the Marshals Service. It also raised a debate as to how to best guard against future violent courtroom episodes, and all hell was raised as to how the defendant was able to bring a razor into the courtroom.

In some courts throughout the country, every defendant brought into a courtroom who is in custody is cuffed; some are also shackled. I handled a few sentences last year in the New Orleans federal courthouse. One of the defendants had been incarcerated for just a few months. I sentenced him to time served for possessing a small quantity of drugs. His family was in the courtroom, including his uncle, who was a local sheriff. The defendant was hardly a threat, yet he stood before me in handcuffs. I was told that the judges had no say in the matter. It was simply the policy that had been put in place by the district's chief marshal.

We do not do this in the EDNY. While security has been tightened as a result of the Victor Wright incident, there is no one-cuff-fits-all policy. With rare exceptions, I do not allow defendants to be handcuffed while I sentence them. I think that it is demeaning and dehumanizes the individual. If, however, the defendant is being sentenced for a violent crime, I make sure that the marshal's office knows this and will require the defendant to sit at the counsel table—with the marshals right behind him—so that he is not close to me and the AUSA.

* * *

Court security is also of concern in a number of other respects. Everyone entering the EDNY's courthouses has to be screened by a metal detector—even the lawyers and the court personnel. In addition, the general public is not allowed to bring cell phones into the buildings. They have to be checked at the marshal's desk at the entrances. There is no uniformity throughout the country. Each district adopts its own cell phone policy.

The no cell phone policy in the EDNY used to also apply to the lawyers but was changed a few years ago at the insistence of the judges. We did not deem it to be a security threat. We thought that lawyers' cell phones were an essential tool of the lawyers' trade and that they should have ready access to them. One restriction was imposed, however. They had to be shut off while the lawyer was in the courtroom. Some of the judges were concerned that lawyers would forget to do this and that ringing cell phones would become a distraction. Their fears turned out to be unfounded. On only one occasion has a cell phone gone off in my courtroom. It was mine.

Of greater concern than cell phones is the absence of adequate security around the perimeter of the Brooklyn courthouse. While the Manhattan courthouse is protected by the closure of all of the streets near the building to vehicular traffic with metal fences and by concrete barriers everywhere, the Brooklyn courthouse only has a few marshals sitting in cars parked around the perimeter. On April 11, 2005, I was quoted in *New York* magazine as commenting that "the Eastern District gets treated ludicrously." Comparing the difference in security between Brooklyn and Manhattan, I said, "It's like we're in Fallujah and they're in the Green Zone."

I made these comments during a criminal hearing when a single marshal brought out a group of prisoners for sentencing and lined them up against a wall three feet away from me and the AUSA. Believing that this was inadequate security, I refused to go ahead and walked off the bench. I was incensed when the Chief Marshal later told me that the EDNY was short of marshals because 15 deputies had recently been transferred to the Southern District. While extra protection for Manhattan may be justified because of the many high profile terrorists prosecuted there, Brooklyn is hardly small potatoes. At the time when I made my comments, Sheik Mohammed Ali Hasan al-Moayad, accused of funneling money to al-Qaeda, was awaiting sentencing here. Indeed, at the present time, the terrorists who tried to blow up New York City—and others—are being prosecuted in the EDNY. Still, there are no protective barriers, and only a handful of patrol cars remain parked around the perimeter. Moreover, they are gone by 5 p.m., leaving the outside of the courthouse totally exposed. The rationale is that no one, other than the judges and their clerks—who regularly work well into the evening—are there after hours. The same *New York* magazine that quoted my comment about Fallujah and the Green Zone also reported that I said—given the absence of security after everyone, other than the judges and their clerks, have gone home—that the marshals "must think we're expendable. Or that the terrorists keep bankers' hours."

Happily, although it has taken too many years, Congress has provided funds this year to create proper perimeter security for the Brooklyn courthouse. The cost of protecting the country's federal courthouses and its judicial personnel continues to skyrocket. It is a sad testament of the times.

* * *

The risks that come with the job of being a federal trial judge have not affected my ability to handle my cases. While I had no idea what was in store for me—and my colleagues—when I took the oath of office 17 years ago, I somehow have—without fear—taken it all with a fatalistic grain of salt. I wondered, though, as I thought about the representative high profile cases that I would

write about in the last part of this book, what dangers might lurk
in the future.

The Baby Judge with his older brothers Leonard and Sheldon
(in the middle).

This widely distributed cartoon really hit the nail on the head and hurt
the Governor. Hy Rosen, Times Union (Albany). Used with permission.

On the campaign trail with Robert F. Kennedy in 1964.

Sitting with Governor Carey and our *ad hoc* court reform team around his
conference table shortly after he tried to condemn his Shelter Island neighbor's
property. From left to right: Richard Bartlet, myself, Michael Cardozo, Judge
Charles Breitel, Governor Carey, Cyrus Vance, Alexander Forger, Judah Gribetz
and Haliburton Fales.

241

My dad's replica of the Utrillo painting that he completed only seven
months before he died.

Is Judge Judy discussing what should be the title of
her next book? © REUTERS/Fred Prouser

The poster got better reviews than the show.

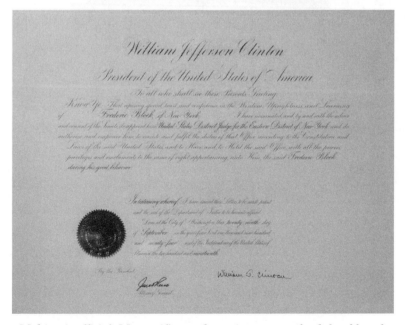

Making it official: My certificate of appointment to the federal bench.

Robert Heineman, Clerk of the Court, administering the oath
of office with Nancy holding the bible and Cooky looking on.

Kitty Genovese's killer (in the middle) 30 years before I met him. © New York Daily News
Archives/Getty Images. Used with permission.

Justice: Death penalty bid for drug kingpin 'absurd'

JUDGE
BLOCKHEAD

SEE PAGE 5 & EDITORIAL, PAGE 28

The Daily News headline with picture making me look like a mobster. © Daily News, L.P. (New York). Used with permission.

Does Gaspipe look like he would threaten to kill me?

Lemrick Nelson pondering his fate
while the jury was deliberating during
his first federal trial before Judge
Trager. © REUTERS/Peter Morgan

Yankel Rosenbaum's funeral procession. © New York Daily News Archives/Getty
Images. Used with permission.

Aaron Myvett's portrait of me before I let
him out of jail. Created by Aaron Myvett.
Used with permission.

Iman Ahmad Wais Afzali just before he
was deported. © REUTERS/Cary
Horowitz

Betsy (in middle), Tina (left) and Debbie (right) riding camels in Egypt by the Pyramids while I was in the Court of Cassation in Cairo.

Justice Sotomayor brought tears of joy to Carlos. © REUTERS/Larry Downing

Peter Gotti on the day of his arrest. ©
New York Daily News Archives/Getty
Images. Used with permission.

The Lump walking behind two of his co-
defendants. © Daily News, L.P. (New
York). Photograph by Ronald Antonelli.
Used with permission.

Peter Gatien walks to court wearing sunglasses
instead of his signature eye patch. © New York
Daily News Archives/Getty Images. Used with
permission.

My Greek school diploma. I had to look up some of the words.

PART
III
THE BIG CASES THERE

Chapter
1

Death

It was bound to happen sooner or later—my first death penalty case. Kenneth McGriff, known as "Supreme," had been indicted with several others for being part of a criminal organization whose members and associates engaged in murder, narcotics trafficking, and money laundering. McGriff was aptly nicknamed because he was the kingpin of this gang of criminals. The government sought to put him to death because of his involvement in the murders of Eric Smith and Troy Singleton, neither of whom were choirboys themselves: Smith had killed Supreme's best friend, and Singleton, who was Smith's buddy, was rumored to be arranging to kill McGriff before Supreme could get revenge on Smith.

Rather than dirty his hands by doing the actual killings, Supreme hired four others to do them for the princely collective sum of $25,000. However, the government did not seek the death penalty against them; instead, it allowed these killers to enter into cooperation agreements and had three of them testify against McGriff at his trial.

It took me almost three weeks to select the jury. As is the general practice in death penalty cases, the process started with the distribution of a lengthy questionnaire to hundreds of prospective jurors—randomly called for jury duty—which they completed while in the courthouse. The questions were prepared collaboratively by the prosecution and defense lawyers, but were subjected to my review and approval. Each questionnaire was numbered; the prospective jurors' names were known only to me and my staff. It had 107 questions designed to give the lawyers an opportunity to learn about the prospective jurors' work, family circumstances, hobbies, and attitudes about the death penalty. They were asked to rate their opinion as to whether they favored the death penalty on a scale of 1–10.

The lawyers reviewed the questionnaires and agreed which prospective jurors should be disqualified for cause. For example, they would not qualify if they wrote that under no circumstances could they vote for or against the death penalty. I then called those who had survived the cut, one by one, in the order of their questionnaire number to separately question each to assure myself that he or she would be qualified to sit. This meant that the juror would consider all of the circumstances of the case and have an open mind on whether to vote for death. I carefully explained that the alternative to the death penalty was life in prison without parole. The process was tedious, complicated by the fact that each side could, and did, excuse 20 prospective jurors for any reason, provided that it would not be based on race, color, religion or national origin.

Although the questioning of each potential juror was exhausting, it did indeed result in smoking out a number who had slipped through the cracks and had to be disqualified. For example, one of the potential jurors, although stating in the questionnaire that she could keep an open mind, responded to my questions in court as follows:

Q: [I]f you found the defendant guilty of committing murder . . . it would be lights out, that you would automatically vote for the death penalty, that's all you have to know. Is that your belief?

A: Yes.

Q: Are there any circumstances under which you would not vote for the death penalty for somebody who was found guilty of murder?

A: If the person is found guilty. I'll vote for the death penalty.

Q: Without any exception?

A: Yes.

Q: So, for you, the issue is, if someone does take another life, their life should be forfeited and that's the end of the process.

A: Yes.

Ultimately, 12 jurors were selected, but I wondered how many death penalty jurors were selected by judges who did not exercise the necessary care to make sure that this type of closed-minded person would not sit on a death penalty case. In addition, I chose eight alternates in case jurors got sick or were otherwise unable to sit throughout the entire trial. Although I usually have two alternates in the normal criminal case, I decided on this number because death cases usually take a long time to try.

Not surprisingly, the jury found McGriff guilty of murder for hiring the killers to murder Smith and Singleton. It then had to decide whether Supreme should be put to death.

* * *

Because of the unique balance struck by the Founding Fathers between federal and states' rights, each state may decide for itself whether to invoke the death penalty for crimes committed in its state. In addition, Congress can determine which federal crimes should carry the death penalty.

At the time when the Constitution came into being, each of the 13 states had the death penalty. In addition, the first Congress made treason, murder, piracy, and, surprisingly, forgery capital crimes. Over the years, it has provided for the death penalty for an assortment of federal crimes.

The Eighth Amendment, however, proscribes punishments, be

253

they prescribed by the state or federal governments, that are "cruel and unusual." It had been generally assumed by the Supreme Court that "[p]unishments [were] cruel when they involve[d] torture or a lingering death; but the punishment of death [was] not cruel within the meaning of that word as used in the constitution;" rather, it implied "something unhuman and barbarous," not just "the mere extinguishment of life." However, it was not until 1972, in the case of *Furman v. Georgia*, that the high court squarely addressed the issue of whether death was cruel and unusual, and hence beyond the power of the states, as well as the federal government, to inflict. Two of the justices said that it *was* under all circumstances; four said that it was not; the other three, which constituted the plurality, limited their decisions to striking down the imposition of the death sentence in the three Georgia cases before the court because they believed that Georgia's statutory scheme gave unguided and unchecked discretion to jurors in deciding who should live or die.

While the *Furman* case wended its way to the Supreme Court, there had been a national death penalty moratorium in effect since 1967. The high court's decision in *Furman* had the effect of continuing this moratorium until 1976 when, in *Gregg v. Georgia,* a majority of the justices gave their approval to Georgia's new statutory scheme. Under that scheme, the punishment and guilt portions of the trial would be bifurcated. If the jury returned a guilty verdict, it would then hear additional evidence and arguments, based upon certain specific aggravating and mitigating factors, before determining whether to impose the death penalty.

Each of the nine justices wrote separate opinions in *Furman,* and five of them chose to separately write in *Gregg,* befitting of the reality that perhaps nothing has animated the passions of Americans throughout our country's history more than the death penalty. In recognition that society's attitudes about the death penalty have fluctuated throughout the years, the Supreme Court has recognized that the proscription of cruel and unusual punishments "is not fastened to the obsolete, but may acquire meaning as public opinion becomes enlightened by a humane justice," and that the clause "must draw its meaning from the evolving standards of decency that mark the progress of a maturing society."

* * *

After *Gregg*, each state, as well as the federal government, was free to decide whether it wished to adopt the substance of the process approved by the Supreme Court in that case and embrace the death penalty. To date, 35 states, plus the federal government (but not the District of Columbia), have opted to do so. While we accept the fact that each state may decide whether to invoke the death penalty, the notion that whether a person can be put to death for committing a crime depends upon the place where the crime is committed within our country is unique to us. I know of no other civilized country that does not have one universal law that governs such a fundamental issue as whether one should live or die.

Presently, 93 countries have the death penalty; 139 do not. Our neighbors, Canada and Mexico, do not put people to death, nor does Russia, Israel, or any Western European country. No country can become a member of the European Union if it subscribes to the death penalty. On the other side of the ledger, in 2007 we ranked fifth—behind China, Iran, Saudi Arabia, and Pakistan—in executions. Rounding out the top 10 of the company we kept were Iraq, Vietnam, Yemen, Afghanistan, and Libya. We executed 42 people that year, all by just 10 of our states. Leading the pack was Texas with 26, followed by three each in Alabama and Oklahoma, two each in Indiana, Ohio, and Tennessee, and one each in South Dakota, Georgia, South Carolina, and Arizona. All were men; 28 were white; 14 were black.

The last pre-*Furman* federal execution took place in 1963. Federal death penalty prosecutions then lay dormant until 1988, when Congress enacted constitutional death penalty procedures patterned after those approved in *Gregg*. In 1994 Congress passed the Federal Death Penalty Act, which vastly increased the array of crimes eligible for death penalty consideration. There are now some 40 death-eligible federal crimes. The overwhelming majority involve murder or, at least, an act such as hijacking that results in death; however, three—treason, espionage, and large-scale narcotics trafficking—do not.

The reluctance of Congress to sanction the death penalty for crimes that do not result in death may be due, in part, to the Supreme Court's admonition that capital punishment should not be applied to a defendant "who does not himself kill, attempt to kill, or intend that a killing take place or that lethal force will be employed." In 1977, for example, in *Coker v. Georgia*, the high court held that the crime of raping an adult woman could not be punished by death. In 2008, it extended that holding to child rape in *Kennedy v. Louisiana* by a 5-4 vote. Writing for the majority, Justice Kennedy noted that "as it relates to crimes against individuals . . ., the death penalty should not be expanded to instances where the victim's life was not taken." He carved out an exception, however, for "treason, espionage, terrorism, and drug kingpin activity."

* * *

Who should decide when the death penalty should be sought? At the federal level, this critical task has been given to the Attorney General. Under present protocols, an internal Attorney General's Review Committee on Capital Cases makes a recommendation to the Attorney General—after receiving the local U.S. Attorney's recommendation and submissions from defense counsel—who then makes the final decision.

Since the reappearance of federal death penalty prosecutions in 1988, the Attorneys General have authorized, beginning in 1990, 416 prosecutions nationwide: 180 were authorized during the 1990s, for an average of 18 per year; since 2000, 236 have been authorized, jumping the yearly average to almost 40. In New York State, 12 were authorized during the 1990s; since then, there have been 30 more. Given the length of time necessary to prepare and defend against a death penalty prosecution, many of the 236 cases authorized since 2000 have yet to be tried.

Nationwide, there have been 50 federal death penalty verdicts since 1990, but because of the lengthy judicial review process before someone is put to death, there have only been three executions, the most notable being that of the Oklahoma City bomber, Timothy McVeigh.

In New York, 17 of the authorized death penalty cases had been tried through 2007, but only one death penalty verdict had been returned, against the murderer of two police officers, and it was reversed on appeal. In my district there were only three death penalty trials between 1990 and 2005. That number was matched in 2007 alone, and six more were on the boards, representing a significant surge in death penalty prosecutions ordered by Attorney General Alberto Gonzales during his tenure.

Statistics to the end of 2006 reveal that the federal and state prison systems collectively held 3,228 prisoners under a death sentence; there are undoubtedly a good number more now. This means that we would have to execute just about one per day for the next 10 years to execute all of the people on death row.

* * *

Not only have the courts had to deal with the proliferation of death penalty prosecutions, they have also had to decide how the convicted should be put to death without inflicting cruel and unusual punishment. Until the late 19th century, hanging was the overwhelmingly predominant method of execution used by both the state and federal governments. Since that time, federal and state authorities have made use of gas chambers and the electric chair; a small number of states have also used firing squads.

The Supreme Court has upheld electrocutions, the firing squad, and, most recently, in *Baze v. Rees,* lethal injection—the current preferred method for execution in 33 states plus the federal government, and the method used in 41 of the 42 executions in 2007. However, it was not until the *Baze* case that the high court established the standard to be employed in determining whether a particular means of death would constitute cruel and unusual punishment: It must present a "substantial" or "objectively intoler-

257

able" risk of serious harm. Applying that standard, a majority of the Justices upheld Kentucky's so-called "three-drug cocktail" lethal injection protocol.

Befitting the controversy that continues to swirl around the death penalty, two of the justices in *Baze* dissented, and five separate opinions were issued. Although concurring in the judgment, Justice Thomas was of the belief that a method of execution would violate the constitutional proscription against cruel and unusual punishment only if it were deliberately designed to inflict pain. He drew examples from those methods used throughout history which were abhorrent to the Founders—those designed to intensify a death sentence by producing a punishment worse than death. Justice Thomas gave as an example the death sentence pronounced in England against seven men convicted of high treason at about the time of the American Revolution:

> That you and each of you, be taken to the place from whence you came, and from thence be drawn on a hurdle to the place of execution, where you shall be hanged by the necks, not till you are dead; that you be severally taken down, while yet alive, and your bowels be taken out and burnt before your faces—that your heads be then cut off, and your bodies cut in four quarters, to be at the King's disposal. And God Almighty have mercy on your souls.

The Founders must have realized that this might have been the fate that awaited them if their revolution failed. Imagine seeing George Washington disemboweled, decapitated, and quartered.

* * *

Justice Stevens also wrote an opinion in *Baze*. At the time of his recent retirement, he was the longest serving Supreme Court Justice, having been appointed in 1975. Jeffrey Toobin commented in his best-selling book about the Supreme Court, *The Nine*, that Justice Stevens was the most respected and admired by his fellow Justices. While Justice Stevens concurred in the judgment in *Baze*, believing that he was bound by precedent to do so, he chose the moment to condemn the death penalty. He referred to it as "the product of habit and inattention rather than an acceptable deliberative process that weighs the costs and risks of administering that penalty against its identifiable benefits." He then examined the three rationales for keeping the death penalty—incapacitation, deterrence, and retribution—and concluded that "[t]he time for a dispassionate, impartial comparison of the enormous costs that death penalty litigation imposes on society with the benefits that it produces has surely arrived."

In respect to incapacitation, Justice Stevens argued that given the rise in statutes providing for life imprisonment without the possibility of parole, it is "neither a necessary nor a sufficient justification for the death penalty." As for deterrence, he noted that "[d]espite 30 years of empirical research in the area, there remains no reliable statistical evidence that capital punishment in fact deters potential offenders." He might have cited for support a 2000 *New York Times* survey that found that during the prior 20 years the homicide rate in states with the death penalty was 48 to 101% higher than in states without the death penalty, and F.B.I. data showing that 11 of the 12 states without capital punishment in 2006 had homicide rates below the national average.

As for retribution, which Justice Stevens acknowledged "animates much of the remaining enthusiasm for the death penalty," he reasoned that "by requiring that an execution be relatively painless, we necessarily protect the inmate from enduring any punishment that is comparable to the suffering inflicted on his victim." He reasoned, therefore, that while this is required by the Constitution's proscription against cruel and unusual punishment, it "actually undermines the very premise on which public approval of the retribution rationale is based."

Justice Stevens also addressed other concerns, including the risk of error—given the number of those who have been exonerated— and the discriminatory application of the death penalty. Even though he had supported the death penalty in the past, he now came to the conclusion, based upon his extensive exposure over the years to countless cases for which the death penalty was authorized, "that the imposition of the death penalty represents 'the pointless and needless extinction of life with only marginal contributions to any discernible social or public purposes.' " He reasoned, therefore, that "[a] penalty with such negligible returns to the State [is] patently excessive and cruel and unusual punishment violative of the [Constitution]."

In retort, Justice Scalia, true to his reputation as a believer in adhering to the original intent of the Framers, took issue with Justice Stevens' view because "the very text of the [Constitution] recognizes that the death penalty is a permissible legislative choice," and the Constitution "generally leaves it to democratically elected legislatures rather than the courts to decide what makes significant contribution to social or public purpose."

* * *

During the course of the guilty phase of McGriff's trial, it became clear to me that there was no realistic chance that a unanimous jury would impose the death penalty. The victim was a drug dealer who had killed McGriff's best friend. Moreover, McGriff did not do the killing, and those who did—although at his behest—testified against him in exchange for cooperation deals to save their own necks. They were an unscrupulous lot, led by a wanton killer nicknamed "Manny Dog," who made his living by killing people for money. Unlike McGriff, they had no apparent redeeming virtues. They were arguably better candidates for the death penalty.

Since it was apparent to me and, I suspect, the government as well, that the prosecutors would simply be going through the motions and wasting everybody's time and valuable judicial resources, as well as the taxpayers' money, I suggested to the government's lawyers at the conclusion of the trial phase—before the jury was to begin its deliberations—that they should ask Attorney General Gonzales to consider whether he still wished to seek the death penalty if the jury returned a guilty verdict. The jurors were not present.

The prosecutors had previously told me that the Attorney General kept an open mind and was amenable to reevaluating his initial death penalty decision based upon how a trial unfolded. My exact words: "Will you kindly advise Washington that in this judge's opinion, there is not a chance in the world there would be a death penalty verdict in this case?" I did add, however, that the government's effort to seek McGriff's execution was "absurd," that it would be a "total misappropriation" of taxpayer funds, and that "[i]f I'm wrong, I will have egg on my face, but I will not be incorrect."

No one, other than those involved in the case, was in the courtroom when I made these remarks, but word got out, and the press picked it up. The next day, all of the papers accurately reported what I had said, without fanfare, except the *Daily News*. The *New York Times*, for example, simply described my remarks as "unusually blunt for a judge to deliver from the bench." The *Daily News*, however, made it a *cause célèbre*. It did a hatchet job on me. On the front page, in large, bold print, it called me "Judge Blockhead."

The Attorney General refused to reconsider his decision. The jury would have to decide whether to put McGriff to death. In retrospect, I should have at once placed my comments under seal—which I had intended to do—to guard against any possibility that they would be made public. It was not what I had said that troubled me; rather, that it could be prejudicial to the government if the jurors learned of my comments during the death penalty phase. Fortunately, they each assured me that they had followed my instructions at the beginning of the trial not to read anything about the case and that they did not know about any newspaper coverage.

It took the jurors less than an hour—over lunch—to do what everyone following the case believed would happen. They rejected the death penalty in favor of life imprisonment without parole. On the verdict sheet the jurors had to report how many found that there were specific mitigating factors that contributed to their decision. The results reinforced my belief that it was a complete waste of time and valuable judicial resources to seek the death penalty against Supreme. For example, five jurors believed that the favorable plea agreements offered to the cooperating witnesses weighed against the imposition of the death sentence; seven thought that the murders were motivated, in part, by McGriff's sincere belief that the victims were out to kill him; 11 considered that the victims contributed to their own deaths by voluntarily choosing to engage in violent criminal conduct; five believed that McGriff had proven himself capable of acts of generosity and kindness; four thought that he was otherwise attempting to move his life in a positive direction; and nine were of the opinion that his life had value.

To its credit, the *Daily News* reported the next day that Judge Block's prediction was right.

* * *

I had never been vilified by the press before the *Daily News* did its number on me. It was shocking, and I got a wake-up call as to how vulnerable judges are. Papers like the *Daily News* do not care about destroying a judge's reputation; selling papers is all that counts. Realizing this, I asked my friends and colleagues who wanted to take on the *Daily News* in my defense not to do so since it would only feed the flames, much to the delight of its editors. I chose, instead, to try to put it out of my mind and continue to try to be the best possible judge.

I do owe the *Daily News* a debt of gratitude. It animated me to write a featured op-ed article for the *New York Times* explaining to the public the need for responsible and intelligent decisions as to which cases should be selected for the death penalty. I pointed out that, given the enormous costs and burdens to the judicial system, it was being unduly burdened with death penalty prosecutions.

I succeeded in drawing attention to the issue. The *New York Law Journal*, commenting on the article, reported that the surge of death penalty cases in New York had rankled lawyers because of "the lack of death sentences, and the high cost of those trials." It also reported that Senator Feingold had cited the article during a Senate Judiciary Committee hearing when questioning a district court nominee on her views about the death penalty. Moreover, Justice Stevens cited it with approval in his opinion in *Baze*.

I had pointed out in my op-ed piece that the taxpayers had to foot the bill for both the costs of prosecution as well as the costs of defense. Because this was a death penalty case, McGriff was being represented by two assigned counsel at taxpayers' expense. Like almost all death penalty defendants, he could not afford a lawyer. I pointed out that the vouchers submitted by the defense alone exceeded $500,000, and assuming the costs of prosecution to be at least equal—efforts to obtain the prosecutors' costs from the Department of Justice were unavailing—$1 million would appear to be a fair estimate of the costs for the trial alone. If there had been a death verdict, the costs of appeal would have added many more dollars.

I concluded, therefore, that we probably had spent upwards of $17 million on the 17 federal death penalty trials in New York State through 2007, with only one death verdict to show for it (which was later reversed on appeal). Thus, the taxpayers would be footing the $9 million bill for the prosecutions of McGriff and the eight other death penalty cases that were scheduled to be tried in my courthouse.

I also explained that all this came at a time when the federal judicial system was struggling with unprecedented budgetary cuts, but that costs were not the only concern. It takes about three weeks just to select a death penalty-qualified jury and months to try a case. This would mean that the eight judges of my court—approximately one-third of the bench—handling all of the other death penalty cases would be hard-pressed to do the rest of their judicial work. The same problem would confront the prosecutor's office. The enormous amount of time consumed by death penalty prosecutions would deplete the office's resources and its ability to attend to its backlog of non-death penalty cases.

In writing my article I was influenced by the thinking of the current Chief Judge of the Ninth Circuit Court of Appeals, Alex Kozinski, who is highly regarded by the conservative Federalist Society. He is not opposed to the death penalty, but in a speech that he gave some years ago, he noted that "the number of executions compared to the number of people who have been sentenced to death is minuscule," and concluded that "whatever purposes the death penalty is said to serve—deterrence, retribution, assuaging the pain suffered by victims' families—those purposes are not served by the system as it now operates."

I agreed with Judge Kozinski's conclusion that instead of overwhelming the courts with death penalty cases, the Attorney General, in the discharge of his awesome responsibility, should only seek the death penalty for the most depraved killers "lest the judicial system be overwhelmed, the community's will ignored and taxpayer dollars improvidently spent."

* * *

In retrospect, I can appreciate the temptation of the headline writers for the *Daily News* in not passing up the opportunity of trading off my name. After all, "Judge Scaliahead" could never work, nor "Judge Ginsburghead," nor, perhaps, anyone else but me. What headline writer worth his or her salt could realistically pass up the opportunity to tack "head" onto "Block?" I laugh at it now. It's really funny. I feel badly about only one thing. My innocent grandchildren, Jordan, Kyra, Kelsey, Brandon, and Ryan, have to go through school being called Little Blockheads.

Chapter
2

Racketeering

In 1970, Congress passed the Racketeer Influenced and Corrupt Organizations Act, better known as "RICO." Coming on the heels of *The Godfather*, its avowed goal was to put the mob out of business. Congress pulled no punches. It was blunt in declaring that the purpose of the Act was "to seek the eradication of organized crime in the United States."

The principle way in which RICO sought to do this was by focusing on patterns of criminal behavior rather than on individual crimes. It did this by creating the concept of a criminal "enterprise." Once you were found to be a member of a criminal enterprise, you could be convicted of racketeering under RICO if twice within a decade you engaged in any of a broad range of criminal activities—including murder, robbery, extortion, bribery, and mail and wire fraud—that were part of the common goal of generating money for the enterprise. These were traditionally state crimes, but with RICO Congress provided the hook to make these federal racketeering crimes so long as the affairs of the enterprise had any affect upon interstate commerce—which, like taking someone's money or simply using the telephone, was easy to establish.

RICO authorized heavy prison sentences. It also carried a deadly economic punch. Convicted defendants would have to forfeit all of their ill-gotten gains, including all proceeds from the enterprise's activities. They would also be subject to treble damages for any monies that they took from their victims.

Membership in a Mafia family would be the textbook example of being part of a criminal enterprise. Before the passage of RICO, the government's efforts against the mobs were piecemeal. It attacked isolated segments of the criminal organization as its members engaged in single criminal acts. The leaders, when caught, were only penalized for what seemed to be unimportant crimes. The larger meaning of these crimes was lost because the big picture would not be presented in a single criminal prosecution. With the passage of the Act, the entire picture of the organization's criminal behavior and the involvement of all of those associated with the enterprise could be captured.

Thus, RICO could be employed to wipe out an entire criminal organization by rounding up and prosecuting its members in a handful of criminal prosecutions. It was designed, therefore, not merely to put mobsters behind bars—even for long periods—but to attack the underbelly of a criminal enterprise by taking both its leaders and their "family" off of the streets in one fell swoop. The typical Mafia racketeering prosecution, therefore, would have multiple defendants. Once they were linked to a Mafia family, it was relatively easy to convict them of racketeering. For example, if threats were made by a mobster over the telephone on just two occasions over a 10-year period to collect a debt for his criminal enterprise, he would not simply be guilty of making the threats, but also of the more serious crime of racketeering.

* * *

The impact of the federal government's use of RICO on the mob has been devastating. At its height, the Mafia had about 2,000 "made" members nationwide. However, its largest concentration was in New York and its metropolitan suburbs, where the Genovese, Luchese, Bonomo, Gambino, and Colombo families coexisted for half a century. By 1990 numerous RICO convictions against the families were having their intended effect. The head of the F.B.I.'s organized-crime branch in New York reported that although the Gambino and Genovese families were still functioning, "their power

[was] dwindling." As for the other three New York families, he viewed them as "shattered and pretty well beaten."

A number of these convictions happened in my courthouse. The EDNY had long been viewed as an appropriate venue to try the leaders and members of New York's five Mafia crime families since they invariably lived within the EDNY—in either Queens, Brooklyn, or Staten Island—and did a lot of their dirty work there.

The most notorious Mafia chief—John J. Gotti—was tried twice in the EDNY courthouse. He was the boss of the Gambino crime family from 1985–1992. In 1986 the F.B.I. identified the Gambino family as the largest and most powerful Mafia family in the country, with 400 to 500 members. In 1984, just before he became the boss, Gotti had been acquitted in a state court trial. A refrigerator repairman, Ronald Piecyk, accused him of slapping him and taking $325 from him during a parking dispute in Queens. When he initially identified Gotti, Piecyk was unaware of his reputation as a mobster. However, he knew who he was at the time of the trial. On the witness stand, a tense Mr. Piecyk had a sudden lapse of memory and could no longer recognize Gotti. The judge had no choice but to dismiss the case.

In 1987 a jury acquitted Gotti of federal RICO charges in the first case against him in the EDNY. Judge Nickerson was the judge. The foreman of the jury was later convicted of accepting a $60,000 bribe arranged by Sammy the Bull—Gotti's underboss—to vote to acquit. It was the most stinging courtroom defeat suffered by the government in its campaign against the Mafia. Law enforcement officials grudgingly conceded that John Gotti's back-to-back acquittals had wrapped him in a perceived cloak of invincibility.

In 1990 Gotti was brought to trial in state court in Manhattan on an indictment charging him with ordering the shooting of a carpenters' union president after a labor dispute. Again he was acquitted, despite secretly recorded tapes in which he was heard discussing preparations for the shooting and despite damning testimony from a participant in the plot. Later, a New York City police officer assigned to the investigation was convicted on charges that he was employed by the Gambino family and had given it the names and addresses of the jurors. John Gotti was now a celebrity criminal and became known as the "Teflon Don."

The Teflon Don's luck finally ran out that year. The F.B.I. had secretly bugged an apartment above his hangout, the Ravenite Social Club. For several months, the bugs recorded conversations that implicated him and others in a host of crimes, including murder. He was arrested in December 1990 and charged under RICO for murder, conspiracy, gambling, obstruction of justice, and tax fraud. The case was his second trial in the EDNY. This time Judge Glasser was the judge. In April 1992 the Teflon Don was convicted on all counts and sentenced to life in prison. His conviction was sealed by the testimony of his right-hand man, the turncoat cooperator Sammy the Bull.

John Gotti died in jail in 2002 of cancer at the age of 61. After he had been imprisoned, he had been succeeded as the Gambino family boss by his son, who was known as "Junior." However, the apple did not fall far from the criminal tree, and in 1999 Junior pled guilty to racketeering and extortion charges. He was sentenced that year to 77 months in prison. According to the government, Peter Gotti— the Teflon Don's older brother—then became the acting boss of the Gambino crime family. His buddies affectionately called him Uncle Peter.

It took the government three years to get the goods on Uncle Peter. It believed that he clung to power in the Gambino crime family as a way to keep the Gotti clan in control of millions of dollars of criminal proceeds. Fed up with the Gambinos' continued criminal misdeeds—especially its corrupt control of the main longshoreman's union that ran the New York waterfront—the government swept broadly to try to deliver a fatal blow to the family. In 2002, it indicted Peter Gotti and 16 others in a 68-count indictment. In essence, the government charged the defendants under RICO with being Gambino family members engaged in racketeering schemes involving labor unions and businesses operating at piers and terminals in Brooklyn and Staten Island by extortion, illegal gambling, wire fraud, and money laundering. Nine pled guilty to various crimes. The remaining seven—including Peter Gotti—opted to go to trial.

The only one of these crimes that Uncle Peter was charged with was money laundering, meaning that monies from the enterprise's criminal misdeeds were funneled to him. Nevertheless, the government also charged him with racketeering and racketeering conspiracy under RICO because it believed that the monies were given to him because he was either the acting or actual boss of the Gambino crime family. As such—under RICO—he was deemed to have condoned all of the crimes committed by the codefendants, including the extortions. One of the extortion charges was that a Gambino captain and his underling threatened to kill the Kung Fu actor Steven Seagal if he did not pay them $3 million.

Since Judge Glasser had handled the trial which resulted in the conviction of the Teflon Don, the government had the case assigned to him. At that time, it could pick the judge if it believed that the new case was somehow related to a prior case that the judge had presided over. The prosecutor's office was obviously happy to have Judge Glasser. The government had also steered a number of other successful Mafia racketeering prosecutions his way. Judge Glasser, however, had had his fill of Mafia trials and thought that a single judge should not preside over all of the Mafia cases. He insisted that the case be put in the criminal wheel for random assignment. I got it.

* * *

Peter Gotti was arrested and jailed on June 4, 2002. On August 10, I denied his application to be released on bail pending his trial, which would not take place for several months. Six days later, the prison warden took him out of the general prison population and placed him in administrative detention. This meant that Peter would be confined to a tiny cell with only a metal bed; there was no TV or any other amenity. He would be let out just one hour a day during the week—but not on the weekend—to walk around a little.

The warden thought that Peter should be locked down after he had been informed by the F.B.I. of a threat by the Gotti family to kill the warden of the jail where John Gotti had been housed for allegedly mistreating his younger brother before he died.

On September 2, Peter's lawyer, Gerald Shargel, asked me to order that his client be placed back into the general population. He argued that there was no basis to the threat and that it was illegal to punish Peter while he was in jail waiting for his trial. The issue was a serious one. As a pretrial detainee, Peter was entitled to the presumption of innocence. Under the Constitution he could not be punished by being locked down in the absence of a credible reason. I thought that the right thing to do was to have a factual hearing so that the government could tell me why he should remain in isolation.

To guard against any confidential information getting out, I held the hearing "in camera"—in my private chambers—and ordered that the transcript be placed under seal. Based upon information ascertained during the in camera hearing, I gave the government until September 10 to "report back as to whether Gotti would be released from administrative detention, and in the event Gotti was not released, to provide the Court with information that would justify continued administrative detention." When I did not get a response, on September 10th I ordered that Peter's lock-down had to end. He had now been kept in deep freeze for just about one month.

The government took issue with my decision and got a stay from the circuit court of appeals pending a full argument before the appellate court. This did not happen until October 7. In the meantime, Peter Gotti remained locked down in his tiny cell. At the argument, his lawyer repeatedly told a three-judge panel that it was unconstitutionally punitive to keep "a presumably innocent man in a box, 23 hours a day and 24 hours on weekend"—with no relief in sight—based upon unconfirmed rumors. One of the panel members was Judge Sonia Sotomayor. She had no idea that years later she would be appointed to the Supreme Court. When the government's lawyer,

Andrew Genser, rose to speak, Judge Sotomayor immediately said that Gotti's lawyer was "absolutely right" and asked rhetorically, "Why isn't it punitive?" Genser never gave her a satisfactory answer. He argued instead that the Prison Litigation Reform Act prevented judicial review of the conditions of confinement for a pre-trial detainee.

The appellate court was not impressed. Although it reserved decision, it was pretty apparent to courtroom observers that it would come down hard on the government. The *New York Law Journal* reported the next day that the judges "aggressively challenged Assistant U.S. Attorney Andrew Genser to justify the isolation of Mr. Gotti from other inmates" and "made the prosecutor work hard to back up his contention that the Prison Litigation Reform Act prevents judicial review." Seeing the handwriting on the wall, the warden put Gotti back into the general population on November 10—before the court came down with its decision. By doing so, he was able to dodge the judicial bullet since the court then held that the issue was now moot.

I thought that Judge Sotomayor and her colleagues should nonetheless have addressed the merits and taken the government to the woodshed. Regardless of what people may have thought about the Gottis, it was unconscionable for the government to keep him locked up like an animal for one-third of a year for no supportable, legitimate reason.

* * *

The trial started on January 14, 2003. Nobody, except me and my staff, knew the names or addresses of the jurors. Knowing of the Mafia's history of jury tampering, I decided that the jurors should be anonymous. This is not normally the case, but I could do that if I concluded, as I did, that there was strong evidence to believe that the jury needed protection. The prospective jurors would each be referred to by number. The 12 jurors and alternates were selected from a group of 501 who were required to answer a 47-page questionnaire. While every effort was undertaken to protect their anonymity, they had to reveal some personal information, such as their marital status, income, and hobbies, to give the lawyers a fair shot at exercising their peremptory challenges. From this group the lawyers for both sides agreed that 200 should be excused for cause. The main reasons were that they were either biased against the Mafia or were too frightened to sit, given the mob's well-earned reputation for violence. Those who were not excused were called into the courtroom in the order of their number and questioned by me to determine whether they could give both sides a fair shake and base their verdicts solely on the evidence. Ultimately, the requisite 12 jurors—and a number of alternates—were selected.

I tried my best to assure them that every effort had been made to ensure their safety. They would not be locked up overnight, but if they wished, they could be picked up and taken home by court marshals. They had to promise me, however, that they would not let any biases or fears prevent them from being fair and objective. I also told them that they were not to read anything about the case in the newspapers or watch TV reports. If they saw or heard anything, they were to report it at once to the court's clerk. I tried to impress upon them that the case was to be tried in the court-room—not in the press—and that only the evidence presented during the trial could be considered by them.

Picking a jury in a high profile Mafia case is a tall order. No matter how hard I tried, there was no escaping the reality that the jurors knew what they were in store for. Any Gotti trial would be a feeding frenzy for the media—especially one where a movie star was in the mix—and the jurors would have a hard time staying focused and fearless. I think that I picked a good jury, and I hoped that the Gambino family would not find out who the jurors were.

* * *

All criminal trials start with the government's opening statement. However, first I welcome the jurors with my usual informal remarks. Thus, I told the Gotti jurors on the first day of the trial that they could not talk to anyone about the case—except to tell their loved ones and friends that the judge looked just like Brad Pitt—and how important it was for them to be in court on time. I gave them an estimate of how long the case might last—about several weeks—and tried to make them feel at ease. As part of my general instructions, I explained that the defendants were entitled to the presumption of innocence; that the government had the burden of proving each defendant's guilt by proof beyond a reasonable doubt; and that the defendants could participate in the trial if they wished. They could, however, just sit back and do nothing. If so, the jury could not hold that against them. If the jury did not find that the government had met its high burden of proof, it would have to return not guilty verdicts.

Finally, I told the jurors that since the government had the burden of proof, it would have to call its witnesses and present its evidence right after the lawyers gave their opening statements. I had told them that the defendants' lawyers had told me that they wished to also make opening statements. I cautioned the jurors that what lawyers say in their opening statements is not evidence; it is just lawyer advocacy. I explained that the purpose of the government's opening is something like a road map. The government will lay out what it hopes to prove. The defendants' lawyers will then have the opportunity to stake out their positions in their openers.

The government's opening remarks were delivered by AUSA Rick Whelan. He and two other AUSAs—Genser and Katya Jestin—would be the prosecutorial team. Whelan had a low-key but forceful style. He told the jury that the government would prove through tapes and videos that Peter became the Gambino family boss after Junior Gotti went to jail and that as the boss he took a cut of the proceeds of the monies his codefendants, Anthony Cicone, Primo Cassarino, Jerome Brancato, and Richard Bondi—appropriately known as "The Lump"—had extorted from innocent victims through shakedowns on the docks in Brooklyn and Staten Island. Whelan said that the other two codefendants, Peter's brother Richard V. Gotti and his nephew Richard G. Gotti, were intermediaries who funneled the cash to Peter. Whelan acknowledged that Peter himself did not participate in any of the extortions—and was only charged with money laundering—but stated that because he was the boss he should also be found guilty of racketeering conspiracy.

Whelan laid out a number of other crimes that Peter's codefendants had committed. The most striking was the government's charge that Cassarino and Cicone tried to shake down Seagal at the behest of the actor's former producer—an alleged Gambino family associate—to pay the family $150,000 for each film that he made. Whelan told the jury that the actor would testify and said, "You'll hear them laugh at how scared Seagal was at one of the meetings" on tapes that had been secretly recorded. I knew right then that this would be a major media event. The jurors would hear the macho martial arts film celeb cowering in fear of his life.

In their opening statements, the defendants' lawyers cautioned the jurors to keep an open mind and told them that while they would hear the defendants use lots of four-letter words on the tapes, they should not be convicted for not speaking the Queen's English. They told the jurors that in the final analysis there would be a reasonable doubt as to their clients' guilt.

Peter's lawyer took particular pains to caution the jury not to punish his client because he was a Gotti. Shargel told them, "The presence of John Gotti in this courtroom will be palpable," and said that Peter was a proxy for the prosecutors trying to milk more mileage out of his late brother's notoriety. His defense was simple. Peter was not the boss of the Gambino family. He was just a retired sanitation worker living off a disability pension and social security. Shargel drew a chuckle from some of the jurors when he said, "When Mario Puzo wrote 'The Godfather' he did not have Peter Gotti in mind." He drove home his point by telling them that, "No actor on 'The Sopranos' plays Peter Gotti."

The battle lines had been drawn. In order to convict Peter Gotti of racketeering, the prosecutors would have to convince the jurors that he was indeed the acting or actual Gambino boss. They would have to do this by proving that he knowingly associated with the

Gambino family and conducted or participated in the affairs of that criminal enterprise.

* * *

The government tried to establish that Peter was the boss right out of the chute with its first witness, F.B.I. "Special" Agent Greg Hagarty. AUSA Genser—who had locked horns with me over my ruling that there was no legitimate basis to keep Gotti in deep freeze—questioned him. Hagarty was called by Genser as an expert on the structure and organization of the Mafia. He had acquired his expertise over a number of years in the course of the many Mafia investigations which he had conducted. This type of testimony was permissible for general background purposes to explain to the jurors the hierarchy of the Mafia's families. Hagarty could educate the jurors, for instance, as to the roles of the bosses, captains, consiglieres, and soldiers, and about the type of criminal activities which the families engaged in. However, Genser had more in mind, and when he asked Hagarty if he knew who the boss of the Gambino family was, Shargel shot to his feet to object before he could answer. Hagarty was obviously going to finger Peter Gotti.

Shargel's objection was well taken. I excused the jury while I asked Hagarty if he had any personal knowledge that Peter Gotti was the boss. He candidly said that he did not, but that it was generally understood that he was. I sustained the objection. Hagarty's answer would be pure hearsay. His testimony had to be limited to his knowledge of the general organization and practices of the Mafia.

Genser was upset and took me on. He told me that Hagarty had testified in John Gotti's case before Judge Glasser and was permitted to tell the jury that the Teflon Don was at that time the Gambino boss. To rub it in, he said that all of the other judges who had tried Mafia cases had allowed Hagarty to name the bosses. I said that I would not allow that to happen in this case because here the issue of whether Peter Gotti was the boss was the central issue of the racketeering charges against him. The government would have to establish that Peter was the boss through the testimony of someone with personal knowledge.

It tried to do this two days later by calling Michael D'Urso to the stand. D'Urso had been a Genovese crime family associate and was a mob informant who had testified in a number of organized crime cases. Nevertheless, D'Urso also told me that he, too, had no direct knowledge that Peter Gotti was the Gambino boss. His only knowledge came from an unidentified Genovese soldier who told him after John Gotti and Junior had been imprisoned that Peter had told him that he had risen from acting boss of the Gambino family. Peter's exact words were—according to the soldier—"I'm not acting. I'm official. I run this family." This, too, was hearsay, but under the rules of evidence, it could nonetheless be admissible if D'Urso and the Genovese soldier were involved in the events which were at the center of the government's case. They were not.

Genser would not give up. He asked me three times to reconsider my ruling barring D'Urso's testimony, as well as Hagarty's. In an effort to appease him, I relented to the extent that I said that I would allow Hagarty to testify about the status of people not on trial. In a prickly exchange I told him, "You've got to have better evidence than that to justify a conviction." He shot back, "Obviously we have, your honor."

Proving the adage that no good deed goes unpunished, the next day the *Daily News* reported that because I had modified my ruling about Hagarty's testimony, the feds were concerned about my "decision-making style." It also reported that, "[a] senior law enforcement official familiar with yesterday's ruling complained that Block apparently failed to grasp parts of D'Urso's testimony." I do not know who these unidentified sources were, but the comments were obviously designed to paint me in a negative light. They were cheap shots. They were also totally unprofessional because these out-of-court statements by the government could prejudice the jurors if they saw them. I hoped that Genser had no part of it, but I braced for a war.

* * *

It did not happen. Things calmed down, and the next several days the government played tons of tapes that it had gotten over the years from cell phone intercepts and the bugs which it had planted in the social club. The intercepted conversations were between most of the defendants and went a long way toward proving the government's case against all of them. Peter Gotti was not in any of them, but there were some conversations that would give the jury the opportunity to infer that he was indeed the boss.

The tapes gave the jurors a poignant taste of how the defendants spoke to each other. For sure, the Queen's English was never spoken. To the contrary, every conversation was laced with profanity. It made for some awkward moments. For example, the courtroom is open to all. I could only bar the public from listening to the trial if there were real safety reasons. Cursing was not one of them. When I came to court on the morning of Friday, February 14, there were six high school students from Bronx Morris High School sitting in the public seats. They were on a school-sanctioned field trip and obviously thought that the Gotti trial would be worth the trip. However, they got an earful when the government played tapes of Casarino spewing obscenities at an alleged loan sharking victim. I squirmed in my chair as they heard him bellow:

> I don't give a fuck if the F.B.I. is listening, you're pushing your motherfucking luck. I don't give a fuck about the law. Ya know what you are? You're a greaseball fuckin' scumbag, that's what you are. You're a greaseball no good motherfucker.

Peter Gotti—concerned that the students would have a bad impression of him—immediately turned to them and said, "That's not me cursing on the tape." Later, outside the courtroom, Shargel was reported as having told the press that, "We haven't heard a tape with Peter Gotti's voice on it." Moreover, Richard Levitt, Casarino's lawyer, was quoted as saying—in the understatement of the year—that the students "heard language in the courtroom that they don't normally hear in the classroom." I invited the students to my chambers during the morning break to give them an opportunity to talk to me. They assured me that it was not the first time that they had heard this type of language. They thanked me for letting them listen in. They told me that they were riveted by this real life courtroom drama. Five of them said that they wanted to become lawyers.

* * *

There were other real life experiences. One day I walked into the public elevator coming back to court after lunch. At that time there was no private judges' elevator because the courthouse was under renovation. I had no choice. It was either take the elevator or walk up four flights of stairs to the courtroom. However, as the elevator door was closing, in walked "The Lump." He was the least culpable defendant. His only alleged crime was that he helped Cassarino collect an extortionate debt that was owed to the family. His role was simply to stand in the doorway of the victim's house—all 400 pounds of him—while Cassarino told the poor guy who opened the door that he "better pay up or else." Obviously "The Lump" was the "else." The debt was paid on the spot.

Because of his limited role, "The Lump" was out on bail. He was free to come and go as he pleased. It was easier for him to take the elevator than to risk a heart attack by walking up the stairs. No one else came into the elevator. In one sense it was a good thing. "The Lump" took up so much space, anyone else would have had to squeeze in. In another sense, I thought of that guy who paid up as soon as he saw him. Sensing my discomfort, "The Lump" tried to put me at ease by telling me, "You'se a good judge. We all like you and have a lot of fuckin' respect for you. Otherwise, I would squash you like an ant." I wondered what he would have said if I had let Agent Hagarty testify the way Genser wanted him to.

Then there was the day when Betsy came to court.

* * *

There was not a day during the trial when the defendants' wives did not come. The lawyers had pointed them out to the jurors during the course of the trial. It was their way of showing that they supported their husbands. They sat together in the second row on the right side of the aisle. However, the lawyers never mentioned who the women were who were sitting in the third row on the other side of the aisle. They also came to court each day. They were considerably younger than the wives and generally more attractive. They had a certain sexy look—long blond hair, tight skirts, high heels. Many of them wore sunglasses. I remember from *The Godfather* movies how family-oriented the mafiosi were. They would never divorce their wives and were admirably protective of their families. However, this did not prevent them from having women on the side. I was told by the marshals that they believed that the sexy gals in the third row were some of the defendants' girlfriends.

Betsy did not know this when she came into the courtroom during the first week of the trial to see what was happening. She unwittingly sat in the third row. In my biased opinion she was better looking than the women who surrounded her, but with her Cartier aviator sunglasses, long blond hair, high heels and mini skirt, she fit right in.

Months after the trial had ended, I ran into Peter Gotti's lawyer at a bar association function. Shargel told me that Betsy had created quite a stir. The boys did not know who she belonged to. They thought that they knew all of the girlfriends and were annoyed that someone was holding out. The ones who had girlfriends each swore that Betsy was not their other woman. No one believed anyone. Cassarino thought she must have been Peter's and accused him of cheating on his regular girlfriend. Shargel finally made peace by telling the gang that the mystery woman was the judge's girlfriend. They were astonished—but they told Shargel that their respect for the judge just went right through the "fuckin'" roof.

Peter did indeed have a girlfriend. I knew who she was because she introduced herself to me one day while I was having lunch at the local Greek diner. She told me that her name was Marjorie Alexander and that she was the woman sitting every day on the far end of the third row. I told her that I could not talk to her, but she insisted on telling me that she and Peter had been together for many years and were madly in love with each other. Although I cut the conversation short, it did not end there. It seemed like every day I would get a letter from Marjorie telling me everything about her life with Peter and how much she was in love with him. I kept them in the court's file. Little did I know then what she would do after the trial was over.

* * *

At the beginning of the fourth week of the trial, Steven Seagal took the witness stand, raised his right hand, and swore to tell the truth. The courtroom was packed. There were reporters all over the place—many from L.A.—who were champing at the bit to write about Seagal's involvement with the Gambino family. The 58th count of the indictment charged Cassarino and Ciccone of conspiring to extort money from the movie star, and the 59th count charged them with actually attempting to do that. They were not the most important charges in the case—and had nothing to do with Peter Gotti or the Gambino family's control of the waterfront—but they certainly brought out the crowd.

Conscious of his public persona, Seagal—with his painted hairline and red bracelets dangling from his neck—was clad in a chocolate-brown silk kimono, jeans, and construction boots. He testified that he was licensed to carry a gun and always carried one when he was in New York. I made sure that he did not have one with him in court. He had just flown back from Thailand—where he was making his latest movie, *Belly of the Beast*—for his court appearance. He described himself as an "actor, producer, director, musician, songwriter." At first he was very combative, befitting a self-proclaimed martial arts expert. However, under aggressive cross-examination his testimony started to get shaky and evasive. I told him that he had to be more responsive: "Listen to me, I don't have any experience in martial arts but I have other powers here. Just listen to the question and answer it." I then took an early lunch break "so people can cool off a little bit." When he came back into the courtroom for continued cross-examination, his tough-guy image was totally shattered. He brought two red shawls with him and asked me if he could place them over his lap to warm his chilly knees. The audience laughed.

In his testimony, Seagal told the jury that he had had a sit-down with Cassarino and Ciccone in a private room at Gage and Toliber, a popular restaurant in downtown Brooklyn. His one-time best friend and former producer, Jules Nasso, was with him. Nasso had ties to the Mafia and enlisted Ciccone to resolve an ongoing dispute that he had with Seagal over money which Nasso claimed that the movie star owed him. Seagal told the jurors that Ciccone began talking to him about "monies that I owed Jules," and "went into the fact that he wanted me to work with Jules." Seagal told Ciccone, "I'm trying," at which point Ciccone ordered him to "look at me when you are talking." Ciccone then said: "Look, we're proud people and work with Jules . . . Jules is going to get a little and the pot will be split up . . . . We'll take a little." The meeting ended with Seagal stating that "he would try to work with Jules." Seagal testified that as he walked out of the restaurant, Jules started walking with him and said, "You know, it's a good thing you said this and didn't say that because if you would have said the wrong thing, they were going to kill you." Seagal told the jurors that he had broken up his relationship with Nasso because Nasso was using mood-elevating drugs and "going into psychotic rages." Nonetheless, he testified that he paid Nasso between $500,000 and $700,000—he was not too good with numbers—after he had escaped with his life.

As Seagal recounted his real life adventure, he seemed to regain his composure and warm to the audience. He began making dramatic faces—complete with his famous furrowed brow—in response to questions. He grinned at a juror. When he finished his testimony and I told him that he could step down, he bowed twice to the crowd and said, "Thank you all." The media event was over. It was time to get back to the rest of the trial.

* * *

The trial lasted for about another month. On March 5, I charged the jury. Because there were so many counts and defendants, my written instructions were 119 pages. I had to explain to the jurors the law that applied to each of the 68 counts and tell them which defendants were charged in each count. Although they were all charged in the two racketeering counts, they were not all implicated in the other 66 counts. Moreover, there were 33 racketeering acts that were the underlying predicates for the racketeering charges. Not all of the defendants were alleged to have participated in each of these acts. The jury had to sort it all out and decide whether each defendant had committed at least two of these racketeering acts within the last 10 years before they could convict a defendant on the RICO charges. It was complicated stuff.

I gave the jury copies of the charge as a guide, but since the law required me to also deliver it orally, I spent the entire day doing that. We took a brief lunch break and other mini-breaks throughout the day to stretch and use the bathrooms. As was my practice, I stood before the jurors. I did not read the charge verbatim. I varied from the script many times to more fully explain what was on the written page. I tried to make as much eye contact with the jurors as possible to keep them alert. I felt sorry for them. It was a tedious process. At the end of the day everyone was exhausted. I had lost my voice.

The jury deliberated for the better part of the next two weeks before they informed the marshal sitting outside the jury room that it had reached a verdict. Since the jurors had to decide whether each of the racketeering acts had been proven, the verdict sheet was 40 pages long. The jurors unanimously found each of the defendants guilty of the racketeering counts. Nonetheless, they were very responsible. They carefully went through each racketeering act and found that the government had not proven a number of them. It had proven enough of them, however, to warrant the racketeering convictions. The jury also found some of the defendants not guilty on the other counts.

As Peter Gotti was led out of the courtroom to be sent back to jail, he grumbled "Gottis are easy to convict, all you have to have is the name." I thanked the jurors for their extraordinary public service. The marshals escorted them out of the courtroom. The trial for them was over. I, however, was hardly finished. I would have to decide how to sentence each defendant.

* * *

It took the next several months to prepare for the sentencing. The Probation Department had to prepare a lengthy presentence report for each defendant, and the lawyers needed time to submit sentencing memoranda. After that, I would need time to review them, as well as to read the letters which I had received from the defendants' friends and relatives. Almost all were from Marjorie. In them she poured her heart out for Peter and begged me to go easy on him. They were highly personal. She recounted many intimate details about their loving relationship.

I began Peter Gotti's sentencing proceeding on Friday, March 26, of the following year. I started by identifying all of the papers that I had in my sentencing file. I made sure that the lawyers had received the PSR and each other's written submissions. I then told them that I had received a letter from Peter's wife, one from his son, and many letters from Marjorie Alexander. They were sent to me in private and—unlike the other submissions—were not part of the public record. Because they were sent in confidence, I did not disclose their contents—other than to say that they were basically supportive and "really don't deal with sentencing issues." However, I would let the lawyers see them if they wanted to. None of the lawyers took me up on the offer, but Andrew Genser—who was handling the sentencing for the government—said that he would like to make copies of them for the government's file.

I listened to the lawyers' lengthy arguments that day and started to make some of the calculations required by the *Sentencing Guidelines*. I stopped short of delivering the actual sentence and

283

set it down for a date several days later. I wanted some time to reflect on a number of issues.

In a break in the proceedings late that afternoon, my clerk, Mike Innelli, told me that a reporter from the *Daily News* had asked him whether the press could see the letters. Since I considered them confidential, I told him to tell him that they would not be released. On Monday, Mike told me that Genser had asked for copies of the letters. He made the copies and sent them to Genser's office, but he left a voice message to remind him that the letters were not for public consumption; they were only being furnished pursuant to his request.

On Wednesday night I learned that Marjorie Alexander had committed suicide. She had checked into a Red Roof Inn in Nassau County earlier that day, taken a fistful of anti-depressants, and tied a bag around her head. She left a note in the room apologizing to the hotel maid for any trouble that she had caused. She had last been seen on Monday when she had spoken to a *Daily News* reporter about her public declarations of love for Peter Gotti. She had told him that, "I took a chance. Life is all about taking chances. Now, I am destroyed."

The next day Marjorie's suicide was reported in the papers. In addition, the *Post* printed intimate excerpts from her letters that had been given—in confidence—to Genser. They spoke of her personal relationship with Peter over the previous 14 years, about her broken spirit and her need for anti-depressant medication. I was shocked. I immediately called Genser's office. He was not there, but his assistant, who had been in court during the sentencing proceeding, answered. He told me that Genser had told him on Monday that he should copy the letters once he received them from the court and give them to the *Post* reporter. I wondered whether Marjorie knew that the *Post* had those letters before she decided to end her life.

In fairness to Genser, I gave him an opportunity to explain what had happened. He apologized. He told me that he honestly had "some misunderstandings about the status of these letters" and that he had put "some naive trust in the promise of the reporter" not to publish them unless he first received the court's express approval.

Genser was a very zealous and accomplished lawyer for the government, but he was too cozy with the press. I concluded, however, that he had not acted maliciously and was satisfied that he was truly contrite. I used the occasion to write an opinion about when, if at all, judges should make sentencing letters public. My research disclosed that there was very little law on the subject. Balancing the competing interests of the public's general common-law right to have access to court documents with the private rights of confidential letter writers, I set down a series of guidelines that I would abide by in the future. Basically, the lawyers could still look at the letters—in confidence—and I would only make specific references to them during the sentencing proceeding if I believed that they would have a significant bearing on the sentence. The one exception was that I would disclose any letters received from public officials seeking to use their office to influence the sentence.

All of the sentences were handed out before the Supreme Court made the *Guidelines* advisory. They varied, based upon the nature of the crimes which the defendants committed and their racketeering activities. In Peter's case it was all for his money laundering—receiving thousands of dollars as the fruits of the family's crimes. Nonetheless, the jury—having found him guilty of racketeering—must have determined that he was the Gambino boss. I gave him 112 months. The sentences that I handed out to the others varied based upon their particular criminal misdeeds. I gave Ciccone and Cassarino the most time—150 and 135 months, respectively. "The Lump" got 57 months; Brancato got 36; Peter's brother, Richard G. Gotti, was sentenced to 33 months; and his nephew, Richard V. Gotti, got 12 months and a day.

All of the guilty verdicts were upheld on appeal. It marked the end of one of the most difficult and lengthy trials which I had ever had. It was not, however, the end for Peter. He was subsequently indicted and convicted in the Southern District of New York for plotting to kill Sammy the Bull for ratting out his brother. In a secretly recorded conversation in May 1997, while John Gotti was rotting in prison, he told Peter that not a day went by when he did not dream of chopping Salvatore Gravano and other turncoats "in little pieces." At Peter's second trial, a Gambino associate testified that in 1999 he learned that Gravano was living in Phoenix and went there on orders from Peter to kill him. The Bull, however, was not there. Nonetheless, Judge Casey sentenced Peter to 25 more years for his efforts. Like the Teflon Don—and Gaspipe Casso—he, too, will die in jail. Sammy the Bull, however, lives on.

It was all within the cards, befitting the fate of those who joined the Mafia. Cassarino had summed it up during one of the intercepted tapes: "That's life. That's the life we chose."

Chapter
3

Guns

Felon-in-possession cases are perhaps the simplest cases coming before a federal district court. Certainly, they require the simplest charge: all that is needed is for the jury to determine whether the defendant was previously convicted of a crime punishable by imprisonment for more than one year, whether the defendant knowingly and intentionally possessed the firearm, and whether the firearm was shipped or transported in interstate or foreign commerce. Defense counsel invariably stipulate that the defendant is a prior felon so that the jury will not know the nature of the felony, and the interstate commerce element is often stipulated to as well, since the government can easily establish that a component part of the gun was manufactured outside of the state, which is sufficient to support that element. Thus it all comes down to whether the defendant possessed the gun, and the jury is succinctly instructed, in a direct possession case, that: " 'Possession' simply means having physical custody or control of an item; that is, a person who has direct physical control over an object at a given time has possession of that object. Proof of ownership is not required to show possession."

These trials are short and simple, lasting just a day or two. In the typical case, one or two police officers testify that while patrolling in a high crime area late at night, there was a legitimate basis to stop and search someone and that, during the search, the gun was found in his possession. However, the defendant can get two bites of the apple. First, he can make a motion to preclude the government from introducing the gun at the trial. The judge would then have to conduct a hearing—without the jury being present—to determine if the Fourth Amendment protection against unlawful searches and seizures has been violated. If so, then the case would have to be dismissed. If not, then the gun could be introduced into evidence, and the trial would go forward. Under Fourth Amendment jurisprudence, a person could be stopped for a simple traffic violation, like failing to signal for a turn, and the police officer could seize a gun in plain view. If someone was walking down the street, he could be stopped and searched if he was observed simply smoking a joint or acting in a covert manner.

* * *

In two recent jury trials before me, the juries acquitted the defendants even though I had denied the motions to suppress the guns. While these cases, given their simplicity, could hardly be called "big cases," like the death penalty case against Supreme or the racketeering trial against Peter Gotti and his fellow mobsters, they reflected the schizoid nature of our country's gun laws and the deadly consequences that flow from our nation's infatuation with guns.

In denying the suppression motions, I found the police officers' testimony totally credible—finding that there was a clear justification for the seizures and searches of the defendants. In the first case, the officer testified that he saw the defendant pull the gun out from his waistband while he was running up the stairs of his apartment building with the police officer in hot pursuit, and that he then saw the defendant toss the gun into the garbage in his apartment's kitchen, where it was retrieved. In the second case, after the police stopped the defendant for failing to signal a left-hand turn, the officer testified that he saw the butt of the gun sticking out of the defendant's waistband, and the police officer actually pulled it out of the waistband. The cases, therefore, were not tossed out by me, and the government was allowed to introduce the guns into evidence before the jury at the trial. The jury would not be told of my decision.

The testimony at the trials tracked the testimony at the suppression hearings. How, then, could the juries acquit in the face of such direct, compelling testimony?

While at first blush it may well have been that the jurors simply did not believe the officers' testimony, I suspected that there was something different about these types of gun possession prosecutions that troubled jurors. Thus my curiosity led me to inquire whether my two acquittals were aberrational.

They were not. A bureau chief from the prosecutor's office candidly told me that the acquittal rate in simple felon-in-possession cases was the highest in the office. Moreover, when I recently had lunch with a former law clerk who, after her clerkship, was hired by the office and became a star prosecutor, she bemoaned the fact that the only case that she lost was a "lay-me-down" felon-in-possession case—the easiest case that she ever had to try.

This confirmed my suspicion that jury nullification might be afoot—a suspicion which had actually first surfaced when I spoke to the jurors after the first acquittal. One of the jurors blurted out that it was difficult for him to convict a young man just for carrying a gun. As best I can recall, he said: "If I lived in that neighborhood, I would carry a gun also; most Americans have guns; the NRA opposes any restrictions on any type of gun; they are legal in most states; kids can buy them in places like Texas and Florida; and the Supreme Court has recently said it's OK to carry a gun to protect yourself."

While his understanding of the law was not precise, his comments are understandable considering the complex, confusing nature of our gun laws and the harsh statistics pertaining to gun violence.

* * *

Much of the public's confusion about our gun laws is the by-product of the compromise by the Founding Fathers—reflected by the 10th Amendment—permitting each state to determine the nature and scope of criminal conduct within its borders, subject to overarching proscriptions by the federal government under the Supremacy Clause if, via the Commerce Clause, interstate commerce is affected. Thus, in the absence of permissible federal interdiction, each state may decide for itself how, if at all, it will regulate the sale or possession of firearms.

To get an overview of why confusion abounds when it comes to guns, let's begin by first getting a grasp of the overarching federal laws. Because Congress has declared that "the gun, its component parts, ammunition, and the raw materials from which they are made have considerably moved in interstate commerce," Congress' power to regulate the sale and possession of guns could conceptually empower it to cover the entire field. It has not, however, acted in this preemptive fashion, instead allowing state laws to govern in those areas not proscribed by federal law.

What has Congress done? It has criminalized the possession of *certain* weapons by anyone, and has criminalized the possession of *any* weapon by certain prohibited persons; through the broad application of the Commerce Clause, these proscriptions apply in all the states. The universally proscribed weapons are stolen firearms; firearms with obliterated serial numbers; machine guns; and firearms undetectable by metal detectors or x-ray machines. Those persons who are prohibited from possessing any type of firearm are convicted felons, fugitives, unlawful users of controlled substances, "mental defectives," illegal aliens, those dishonorably discharged from the Armed Forces, anyone who has renounced his or her United States citizenship, those subject to restraining orders, anyone previously convicted of a misdemeanor domestic violence offense, and anyone who possesses a firearm in furtherance of a crime of violence or drug trafficking. In addition, juveniles (i.e., those under age 18) are federally prohibited from possessing handguns, but may possess other guns which are not on the list of universally banned firearms—even, ironically, military-style assault weapons.

What else has Congress done? In 1968 it enacted the Gun Control

Act, requiring gun dealers to be licensed; however, those "not engaged in the business" of selling firearms, or who make only "occasional" sales, are exempt. Thus, as a practical matter, under what has commonly become known as the "gun-show loophole," federal law does not preclude unlicensed sellers from selling privately owned firearms at gun shows or other temporary locations. In 1993 Congress passed the Brady Act, requiring those covered by the Gun Control Act to secure a background check on the putative purchaser to ensure that he or she was not a prohibited person in one of the categories mentioned previously; however, those within the so-called "gun-show loophole," who were *not* covered by the Gun Control Act, could still sell firearms without a background check. Notably, although the states were free to plug the loophole, 32 have not done so; hence, in those states, there are no licensing or background check requirements regarding the private or occasional seller of firearms.

Other than the handful of firearms proscribed and the persons prohibited from possessing a firearm under the provisions mentioned above, and the limited licensing requirements and background checks under the Gun Control and Brady Acts, the states are free to do as they please. With 50 states weighing in on what is otherwise legal or illegal, it is no wonder that the public may be confused. For example, in 43 states citizens can legally buy assault weapons, although among the seven states where some assault weapons are banned, the definition of such weapons varies. In 46 states there is no limit on the number of guns that can be bought at any one time, while four states impose a limit of one handgun per month. In addition, remarkably, because federal law only bars juveniles from possessing handguns, rather than all firearms, juvenile possession of long guns is legal in many states; counterintuitively, a 12-year-old in North Carolina, although needing parental permission to play Little League Baseball, does not need permission to possess any type of shotgun or rifle (which would include semiautomatic assault rifles). Moreover, in 18 states there is no minimum age requirement to possess a rifle or shotgun.

There are, of course, many states that do require licenses for the possession of firearms which are not illegal under federal law. For example, since I am not a prohibited person under federal law, and the possession of handguns is not federally proscribed, I can legally buy a handgun without a license in a number of states, but I cannot possess one in New York without a New York license; moreover, in New York City, I would also need a license for the possession of a rifle or shotgun.

The maze of state gun laws, ranging from states, such as Maine, which has virtually no gun control law, to Massachusetts and Hawaii, which have highly restrictive laws, and the multiple variations in between from state to state, makes it impossible for the average citizen to know when or where in the United States the possession of a firearm is legal—let alone which type of firearm—without consulting a lawyer or the NRA. Thus, the gun-carrying citizen traveling across state lines may be lawfully in possession of the firearm in one state but not in the other, unwittingly exposing himself to criminal prosecution; for example, even if Plaxico Burress had been lawfully licensed to possess a handgun in his home in New Jersey, this would be no defense to the gun possession charges which he faced under New York law—which landed him in prison for two years. To guard against this, the NRA has published a *Guide to the Interstate Transportation of Firearms* explaining the caveats gun carriers face in their interstate travels.

Congress has also addressed the problem by providing that a firearm may be transported from one state in which that firearm may be lawfully possessed to another such state, thereby insulating the transporter from the laws of states in between where the possession of the firearm may be illegal. Nonetheless, the interstate traveler may not be aware that the statute contains a number of qualifications: the firearm must be unloaded; neither the firearm nor any ammunition can be "readily accessible or . . . directly accessible from the passenger compartment of [the] transporting vehicle"; and if the vehicle does not have a compartment separate from the driver's compartment, the firearm or ammunition "shall be contained in a locked container other than the glove compartment or console."

292

In sum, between the federal and state gun laws, we have a patchwork of laws with many permutations which governs the legality of possessing a particular firearm, leaving the general public bedeviled to understand which guns may be legally possessed and where. It was not surprising, therefore, that the juror who spoke to me after he had voted to acquit the defendant in my first felon-in-possession case had the impression that "most Americans have guns" and that guns were "legal in most states."

The juror's perceptions are borne out by some chilling statistics. First, neither the federal government nor any state totally proscribes nor regulates the possession of all firearms, and many states permit the possession of a large range of firearms with few, or negligible, restrictions; accordingly, it has been estimated that 40% of United States households contain guns. Moreover, our appetite for guns is on the rise: F.B.I. statistics show that there have been 1.2 million more requests for background checks of potential gun buyers throughout the nation during the four-month period from February 2009 to November 2009 (for a total of 5.5 million) than during the comparable period a year before.

Our love affair with guns, bolstered by the effective lobbying efforts of the NRA to keep Congress at bay, has resulted in our country having the highest rate of gun deaths in the developed world; moreover, the relative numbers are truly startling. For example, statistics garnered in 2004 for gun-related homicides show New Zealand having 5; Sweden 37; Australia 56; England and Wales 73; Canada 184; and the United States 11,344. Even if adjusted for population disparities, the differentials are palpable: U.S. per capita homicide rates are two to 10 times those of all other developed countries. *New York Times* columnist Bob Herbert recently pointed out that there are 283 million privately owned firearms in America; that someone is killed by a gun in this country every 17 minutes; that eight American children are shot to death every day; and that since September 11, 2001, "nearly 120,000 Americans have been killed in non-terror homicides, most of them committed with guns," which is "nearly 25 times the number of

Americans killed in Iraq and Afghanistan." Herbert further noted that nearly 70,000 Americans are shot nonfatally each year, leading to "well more than $2 billion annually" in medical costs.

*　*　*

The perceptions of that juror, who candidly expressed his unwillingness to convict someone for merely possessing a gun, led me to believe that the degree of difficulty that the government has experienced in obtaining felon-in-possession convictions in the EDNY may well be the product of jury nullification due to the public's confusion about our gun laws—such as they are, or are not—and the public's strongly held feelings toward guns.

Perhaps the textbook example of jury nullification in a gun possession case is the recent acquittal of Cpl. Melroy H. Cort. As reported in the *Washington Post,* the defendant, a United States Marine whose legs had been amputated above the knees when he was wounded by a makeshift bomb during his third tour of duty in Iraq, was traveling from his home in Ohio to Walter Reed Army Medical Center in D.C. for treatment. While traveling in Washington, he got a flat tire, forcing him to pull over at a car repair shop; a witness noticed that he had a gun in his jacket pocket and called the police, who arrested him as he was sitting in his wheelchair. He offered no resistance and readily admitted that he was traveling with the gun.

Since the defendant was not licensed to possess the gun in Washington, as required by D.C. law, his court-assigned attorney advised him that he had no defense to the charge and encouraged him to plead guilty. Cort refused, fired his lawyer, and represented himself at trial. He testified about the loss of his legs and explained that he had a permit to carry the gun in Ohio and had brought it with him because he had moved out of his house in anticipation of an extended stay at Walter Reed. He told the jury that his commanding officer had advised him to take the gun to the armory on Walter Reed's base as soon as he arrived. Given that the defendant

294

admitted that he possessed the gun in violation of D.C. law, his acquittal clearly amounted to jury nullification.

The province of a jury to disregard the law and engage in nullification has spawned debate and controversy throughout the years and can certainly be, and has been, the subject of extensive commentary.

The origin of jury nullification traces back to the mother country in the 1670 decision in *Bushell's Case*, which arose out of the underlying prosecution of Quakers William Penn and William Mead for unlawful assembly. At trial, the evidence of the defendants' guilt under the applicable statutes was "full and manifest," but the jury "acquitted [the defendants] against the direction of the court in matter of law, openly given and declared to them in court." After juror Bushell was imprisoned for disobeying the judge's instructions, he sought habeas relief in the Court of Common Pleas, where Chief Justice Vaughan ruled that the detentions were unlawful, stating that "how manifest soever the evidence was, if it were not manifest to [the jury], and that they believed it such, it was not a finable fault, nor deserving imprisonment . . ." *Bushell's Case* is widely cited as the first precedent for the independence of the jury.

Closer to home, the John Peter Zenger trial in 1735 is the foremost historic example of jury nullification in the United States. Zenger was charged with publishing seditious libels against the Governor of New York; it was clear that he had published the writings. Although the court instructed the jury that it could only consider whether Zenger had printed the material and could not consider the truth or falsity of the writing, the jury nonetheless acquitted him, believing that he should not be convicted for printing the truth.

As exemplified by the Zenger trial, the independence of the jury emerged as a central value of liberty in the new American republic. As one commentator has noted: "The proponents of the jury's power and *right* to nullify the law suggest that juries have traditionally had that power and right. The nullification power was explicit in the American courts until the 1850s." Even as late as 1910, Harvard

Law School's eminent Dean Roscoe Pound wrote: "Jury lawlessness is the greatest corrective of law in its actual administration. The will of the state at large imposed on a reluctant community, the will of a majority imposed on a vigorous and determined minority, find the same obstacle in the local jury that formerly confronted kings and ministers."

* * *

There subsequently arose a more formalistic, anti-nullification view, as articulated by the Supreme Court in *Sparf v. United States*. In that case, which arose from a murder trial, the trial court had refused to comply with the jury's request for instructions on the "lesser" charge of manslaughter because, while the evidence supported a murder conviction, it did not support a manslaughter conviction. While the jury apparently did not believe that it could acquit entirely, its request for instructions as to manslaughter showed that it was considering exercising leniency by convicting of the lesser offense, notwithstanding its legal inapplicability to the scenario at issue. The Supreme Court held that the trial judge had not erred in refusing the jury's request. The *Sparf* court read *Bushell's Case* narrowly—not as explicitly permitting jurors to nullify based on their personal view of the law, but merely as holding that Bushell could not be punished because "it could never be proved" that his refusal to convict was based upon his disregard of the law (which would have been impermissible), rather than his personal view of the evidence (which would have been permissible, however questionable). The *Sparf* court's holding followed from its fear that "[p]ublic and private safety alike would be in peril if the principle [were] established that juries in criminal cases may, of right, disregard the law as expounded to them by the court, and become a law unto themselves."

This anti-nullification view was expressed once again in *Horning v. District of Columbia*, where the Supreme Court gave its approbation, over Justice Brandeis's dissent, to the trial judge's jury instruction that "a failure by you to bring in a [guilty] verdict in this case can arise only from a willful and flagrant disregard of the evidence and the law." Hewing to its formalistic approach, the majority opinion in *Horning* stated: "In [a case where the facts are not in dispute,] obviously the function of the jury if they do their duty is little more than formal." While the Supreme Court recognized that the trial judge had "[p]erhaps [displayed] a regrettable peremptoriness of tone" in his comments on potential jury nullification, it concluded that "[i]f the defendant suffered any wrong it was purely formal since . . . on the facts admitted there was no doubt of his guilt." In disagreeing with this view of the role of the jury, Brandeis retorted that "[w]hether a defendant is found guilty by a jury or is declared to be so by a judge is not, under the Federal Constitution, a mere formality," and opined that "the presiding judge [had] usurped the province of the jury." The holding from *Horning*—that a trial judge may effectively order the jury to convict a defendant—has since been repudiated.

The debate over the efficacy and acceptance of jury nullification has animated the circuit courts. In *United States v. Dougherty*, Judge Leventhal, writing for the D.C. Circuit, traced the evolving attitude toward jury nullification reflected in American jurisprudence. He noted that "in colonial days and the early days of our Republic [there were a] variety of expressions . . . from respected sources—John Adams; Alexander Hamilton; prominent judges—that jurors had a duty to find a verdict according to their own conscience, though in opposition to the direction of the court; that their power signified a right; that they were judges both of law and of fact in a criminal case, and not bound by the opinion of the court." However, he continued, "[a]s the distrust of judges appointed and removable by the king receded, there came increasing acceptance that under a republic the protection of citizens lay not in recognizing the right of each jury to make its own law, but in following democratic processes for changing the law."

Sparf was the natural end point of this evolution—Leventhal wrote—establishing that "[t]he jury's role was respected as significant and wholesome, but it was not to be given instructions that articulated a right to do whatever it willed." Judge Leventhal

297

concluded that juries ought not be advised of their power of nullification, as "its explicit avowal risks the ultimate logic of anarchy"; as for the occasional exceptional case where nullification was indeed appropriate, he believed that "[t]he totality of input [from literature, media, word of mouth, history and tradition] generally convey[s] adequately enough the idea of . . . freedom in an occasional case to depart from what the judge says," such that instructions to that end were not necessary. Judge Bazelon, in dissent, criticized as "sleight-of-hand" the practice of intentionally hiding the right of nullification—the existence of which the majority had acknowledged—from the jury.

The Second Circuit, whose precedents I am bound to follow, has perhaps taken the hardest line against jury nullification. In sanctioning the removal of a juror during deliberations for wishing to acquit despite believing that the defendant was guilty, Judge Cabranes, writing for a unanimous court in *United States v. Thomas*, explicitly held that trial courts "have the duty to forestall or prevent" nullification by dismissing jurors who are reported during deliberations to be determined to acquit despite the evidence. Departing from the D.C. Circuit's view in *Dougherty*, the Second Circuit "categorically reject[ed] the idea that, in a society committed to the rule of law, jury nullification is [ever] desirable or that courts may permit it to occur when it is within their authority to prevent." The court explained that while nullification was a "de facto *power*" of the jury, it was not a "right," and in fact was "a violation of a juror's sworn duty to 'apply the law as interpreted by the court.'" Accordingly, the Second Circuit held that "it would be a dereliction of duty for a judge to remain indifferent to reports that a juror is intent on violating his oath," and that "a presiding judge possesses both the responsibility and the authority to dismiss a juror whose refusal or unwillingness to follow the applicable law becomes known to the judge" either during the trial or during deliberations.

In my district, Judge Weinstein articulated his view on the issue:

In spite of the recent trend towards discharging jurors who may nullify—a particular problem with the selection of jurors in capital cases—I am hesitant to dismiss intelligent prospective jurors . . . . Concerns about jury nullification are largely unwarranted. Differences about evaluation of the facts based on differing life experiences ought not to be mistaken for nullification. There is some tendency to nullify based on conscience or individual circumstances in the face of laws a juror believes to be unjust. In my courtroom, I do not instruct juries on the power to nullify or not to nullify. Such an instruction is like telling children not to put beans in their noses. Most of them would not have thought of it had it not been suggested. I do believe, however, that judges can and should exercise their discretion to allow nullification by flexibly applying the concepts of relevancy and prejudice and by admitting evidence bearing on moral values. Judge Bazelon was correct when he wrote:

> I do not see any reason to assume that jurors will make rampantly abusive use of their power. Trust in the jury is, after all, one of the cornerstones of our entire criminal jurisprudence, and if that trust is without foundation we must reexamine a great deal more than just the nullification doctrine.

Unlike Judge Weinstein, I have reflexively incorporated into my jury instructions what can only be viewed as an anti-nullification charge: "You should not be concerned about the wisdom of any rule I state. Regardless of any opinion that you may have as to what the law may be or ought to be, it would violate your sworn duty to base a verdict on any view of the law other than that which I give you." Obviously this instruction did not deter the juries from acquitting in my gun possession cases, but nonetheless, Judges Weinstein's and Bazelon's insightful rationales—and the story of that Marine amputee—have given me pause to wonder whether I should refrain from giving this charge in the future and simply tell the jury—as I always do—that "You must accept my instructions of law and apply them to the facts as you determine them."

Chapter
4

Drugs

Little did I realize when I was getting drunk at the Limelight on the opening night of *Professionally Speaking* that 12 years later—in 1998—I would be presiding over the trial of its owner, Peter Gatien, for allegedly running an illicit drug emporium there. The club was housed in a deconsecrated church in downtown Manhattan which Gatien bought in 1982. He thought that the building was better suited for parties than for prayers. After being renovated by him, it soon became a hot disco/rock club.

Shirley Herz, our top-notch P.R. gal, thought it was the ideal place for the show's opening night party. It was the "in" place for the paparazzi and the rich and famous. I had never seen anything quite like it before. The pulsating music and strobe lights flashing through the dimly lit rooms made it difficult for me to see or hear those who sought me out to tell me how much they liked the show.

It was not, however, until the early 1990s that the Limelight became the crown jewel of the drug-infested, club-scene culture that captivated the bridge and tunnel crowd from the burbs and the cool city kids who thought that growing up meant getting high on coke, heroin, ecstasy, and meth, and being part of where the action was. Gatien had transformed the Limelight into a hot new mecca for clown-faced, baby-costumed "club kids" and shaven-headed, shirtless ravers. Major D.J.s, like Junior Vasquez and Funkmaster Flex, spun there. The club featured go-go dancers writhing in cages suspended over crowds awash in high-tech lighting.

Capitalizing on this juvenile behavior, Gatien opened up more clubs. By the mid-'90s he had added Club U.S.A., the Palladium, and the Tunnel to his empire. Peter Gatien was now known as the King of Clubs. He was now raking in half a million dollars a week—but it would not last.

In 1995, as part of Mayor Giuliani's campaign to get the squeegee men, hookers, and druggies off the streets and clean up New York City, the police started to seriously check out what was going on at Gatien's clubs. Agents from the Federal Drug Enforcement Agency also got into the act, disguising themselves in club-kid attire to gain access to the clubs. Their undercover work culminated in Gatien being indicted by the feds a year later for racketeering and conspiracy to distribute vast amounts of ecstasy, cocaine, and other drugs at the Limelight and Tunnel. The indictment alleged that Gatien was at the top of an "employment hierarchy" that included: (1) directors, who were responsible for scheduling theme parties and seeing to it that drugs would be available for sale at these parties; (2) party promoters, who were responsible for recruiting club kids to attend the parties to buy the drugs; (3) "house dealers," who distributed the drugs at the parties; and (4) bouncers, who failed to eject the house dealers and their patrons for selling and buying drugs. Forty-three of these directors, house dealers, or party planners were also indicted.

The trial promised to be a wild ride through the drug-infested, after-midnight club scene of the '90s. The indictment painted a sordid picture of how drugs had taken root in "clubland" and often destroyed the lives of the kids who thought that it was cool to be part of that world. Many became addicts. Some even OD'd. One committed suicide. One was murdered.

Gatien's trial, which began on January 14, 1998, lived up to its advance billing. The press jumped all over it. It was intrigued by the notion that Gatien, who cut a swarthy image with an eye patch over his left eye—the result of losing the eye in a hockey game when he was a kid—was not the legitimate businessman that he claimed to be, but rather a drug impresario who turned his nightclubs into "virtual ecstasy supermarkets" staffed by house dealers where peddling drugs was the order of the day.

The advent of ecstasy, a so-called designer drug, also whetted the press' appetite. It was a new hallucinogenic that had only recently been outlawed by the federal government; New York would not get around to prohibiting it until a year later. Because of its heralded "love inducing" effect, it became the mainstay of the drugs distributed at Gatien's clubs.

It is no wonder, therefore, that books have been written about the Gatien trial. Even now—13 years later—a documentary movie of the trial has made its way into the movie houses. Appropriately named *Limelight*, it ironically opened at the Sunshine movie theater in the East Village of Manhattan while I was writing this chapter of the book. Naturally I went to see it. It brought me back into the case and refreshed my recollection of many things that I had forgotten. What really got my attention was how widespread the attraction to drugs was amongst so many young people, and in particular the affluent kids who were doling out their parents' money—while they were attending college—to buy cocaine and ecstasy. I thought again about my conversation with the Colombian drug counselor on my plane ride to visit my brother and wondered whether the so-called "war on drugs" which the federal government had been mounting during the past few decades was succeeding.

* * *

The history of drug use in our country and Congress' reactions trace their beginnings to the racism and xenophobia that motivated early drug laws. Many different kinds of intoxicants were available in the mid to late 19th century and the early part of the 20th century; nevertheless, only those drugs that were associated with nonwhite racial groups were targeted.

The first anti-drug law in our country was a local law in San Francisco passed in 1875. It outlawed the smoking of opium and was directed at the Chinese because opium smoking was a peculiarly Chinese habit. It was believed that Chinese men were luring white women to have sex in opium dens. In 1909 Congress made opium smoking a federal offense by enacting the Anti-Opium Act. It reinforced Chinese racism by carving out an exception for drinking and injecting tinctures of opiates that were popular among whites.

Cocaine regulations also were triggered by racial prejudice. Cocaine use was associated with blacks just as opium use was associated with the Chinese. Newspaper articles bore racially charged headlines linking cocaine with violent, anti-social behavior by blacks. A 1914 *New York Times* article proclaimed: "Negro Cocaine 'Fiends' Are a New Southern Menace: Murder and Insanity Increasing Among Lower Class Blacks Because They Have Taken to 'Sniffing.'" A *Literary Digest* article from the same year claimed that "most of the attacks upon women in the South are the direct result of the cocaine-crazed Negro brain." It comes as no surprise that 1914 was also the year Congress passed the Harrison Tax Act, effectively outlawing opium and cocaine.

Marijuana prohibition also had racist underpinnings. This time it was the Mexicans. Just as cocaine was associated with black violence and irrational behavior, in the southwest border towns marijuana was viewed—beginning in the early 1920s—as a cause of Mexican lawlessness. A Texas police captain suggested that marijuana gave Mexicans superhuman strength to commit acts of violence:

> Under marijuana Mexicans [become] very violent, especially when they become angry and will attack an officer even if a gun is drawn on him. They seem to have no fear. I have also noted that under the influence of this weed they have enormous strength and it will take several men to handle one man while, under ordinary circumstances, one man could handle him with ease.

The American Coalition—an anti-immigrant group—claimed as recently as 1980: "Marihuana, perhaps now the most insidious of narcotics, is a direct by-product of unrestricted Mexican immigration."

The racial fallout from our drug laws has persevered. In her article, *The Discrimination Inherent in America's Drug War*, Kathleen R. Sandy reported in 2003 that black Americans then constituted approximately 12% of our country's population and 13% of drug users. Nevertheless, they accounted for 33% of all drug-related arrests, 62% of drug-related convictions, and 70% of drug-related incarcerations.

The country's concerted crackdown on drugs—and the imposition of increasingly harsh punishment for illicit usage, importation, and distribution—probably owes its genesis to the appointment in 1930 of Harry Anslinger as the commissioner of the newly created United States Narcotics Bureau. He started a media campaign to classify marijuana as a dangerous drug. For example, he wrote a major article titled "Marihuana, the Assassin of Youth." It was rife with accusations that marijuana was responsible for encouraging murder, suicide, and insanity. Anslinger's campaign was wildly successful. Before he took office only four states had enacted prohibitions against nonmedical usage of marijuana—California (1915), Texas (1919), Louisiana (1924), and New York (1927)—but by 1937 46 of the nation's then 48 states had banned marijuana.

Since then Congress has enacted a spate of comprehensive anti-drug laws with strict penalties. For example, today one can be sentenced to life for distributing one kilogram of heroin; 40 years for distributing 100 grams, and 20 years for distributing any quantity at all. Nevertheless, this has not stemmed the country's appetite for illicit drugs in spite of every administration's continued "war on drugs" since President Nixon established the Drug Enforcement Agency in 1972, which has grown through the years to a staff of almost 10,000 employees and a budget of $2 billion.

According to data from the 2010 National Household Survey on Drug Use and Health, almost 120 million Americans 12 or older— roughly 47% of that population—reported illicit drug use at least once in their lifetime; 15.3% admitted to using an illegal drug in the prior year; and 8.9%—roughly 23 million people—did it within the prior month. The *New York Times* recently reported that one out of every 15 high school students smokes marijuana on a near daily basis. It is no wonder that the sale of drugs was booming at Peter Gatien's clubs.

* * *

Although 44 defendants were indicted, almost everyone eventually pled guilty. In addition to Gatien, amongst the few who did not plead were the manager of the Limelight and Tunnel—Steve Lewis—and two of the Tunnel's bouncers—Ray Montgomery and Jose Otero. All those who pled would be sentenced by me after the trial. They were mostly young kids who were the house dealers, party planners, and bartenders. Many were college kids—both men and women—from NYU. They apparently thought that getting stoned at night and pushing drugs reduced the pressures and tedium of school. In addition to forking out lots of money to send their children to this prestigious school, their parents now had to pay big bucks for lawyers to try to keep them out of jail.

As for Lewis, Montgomery, and Otero, they did not want to be tried with Gatien. Accordingly, they brought severance motions claiming that it would be highly prejudicial to be lumped together in one trial with him. The first motion was brought collectively by Montogomery and Otero. In a written decision I first explained the law governing severance. I wrote that while there was "a strong policy favoring joinder of trials, especially when the underlying crime involves a common plan or scheme and defendants have been jointly indicted," a severance should be granted if a joint trial would be so prejudicial that it would amount to "a miscarriage of justice." Basically, this came down to whether the two bouncers would be denied a fair trial if forced to be tried with Gatien and Lewis.

I ruled that they would be. I wrote that I was "immediately struck by the disparity in the nature of Montgomery and Otero's involvement in the alleged conspiracy on the one hand and the involvement of Gatien and Lewis on the other." I pointed out that the government did not contend that the two bouncers had attended any of the elaborate parties allegedly staged at the nightclubs or that they played any role in planning or promoting them. They were each part-time bouncers at the Tunnel, and the government acknowledged that their role was simply that they took some money from the house dealers "to look the other way" when narcotics were sold at that club.

By contrast, Gatien was alleged to be the mastermind of a RICO enterprise engaged in the promotion of elaborate parties at which the sale of controlled substances took center stage, and Lewis was alleged to be one of the directors of the enterprise. I noted that the government had set forth sensational and sordid details about the types of parties held at the clubs. For example, it said that a "Disco 2000" party took place at the Limelight where "men dressed as nurses wrote fake prescriptions for controlled substances and escorted patrons to a private 'Emergency Room' where free drugs were placed in the patrons' mouths." The government also was planning to introduce sensational evidence of Gatien's lifestyle, including pictures of him snorting coke at private orgies in expensive hotel rooms. It was clear to me that the introduction of all of this evidence would substantially prejudice Montgomery and Otero and that they would be deprived of a fair trial if they were tried together with Gatien and Lewis.

Soon after I granted the bouncers' severance motion, Lewis also moved to be severed. His lawyer, Douglas Grover, forcefully argued that he, too, would be prejudiced if tried with Gatien. I agreed. Lewis would be tried together with Montgomery and Otero at a separate trial after Gatien's trial. Thus, Gatien would be tried alone.

* * *

After a five-week trial, Gatien was acquitted. The jury, consisting of seven women and five men, had deliberated for just a few hours. When the verdict was announced, the courtroom—which was packed with club kids—erupted into a wild celebration. I wondered whether they were high on drugs. Afterwards, Gatien denounced the government for prosecuting him: "They went out for me any way they could," he said. "This was an evil, meanspirited prosecution. Right now, I'm just grateful to God. I want to go to church." It was not clear which church he was referring to, but he vowed to reopen the Limelight—which had been shut down.

Some of the jurors spoke to the press after the verdict. One of them, a 62-year-old tractor-trailer driver, said that the jurors were split when deliberations began but soon decided that they could not trust the testimony of the government's witnesses. It was no wonder. They were all drug dealers, many of whom admitted to a laundry list of crimes and lies of their own. As the juror explained: "These witnesses have been in so much trouble, how could I say I believed them."

He had a point. The government's main witness, Michael Caruso, had testified that in 1991 Gatien agreed to put drugs in the budget for Caruso's Friday night parties. The ecstasy punches which were dished out by him at the parties became a rave; hordes of kids lined up to gobble them down. As Caruso crowed: "The punches created a buzz." He also testified that the first time that he met Gatien, he asked Caruso for 20 hits of ecstasy. While Caruso's testimony supported the government's theory that Gatien was indeed running a drug supermarket at his clubs, the problem was that Caruso—who went by the club name Lord Michael—admitted that he ran a violent crew of drug dealers and had participated in a series of armed robberies of rival dealers.

The government's case also apparently was not helped by several of its other witnesses. For example, one of them, Jenny Dembrow—whose charming club-kid name was "Genitalia"—had testified that she attended lavish private parties that Gatien threw at posh Manhattan hotels like the Mayfair and Four Seasons, which featured piles of cocaine and prostitutes playing charades. However, when questioned under cross-examination about the sordid details, she told the jurors: "I don't remember. I was on drugs at the time."

Although the government used a visual representation of its case picturing Gatien at the top of a family tree of more than 50 known drug dealers, they sported monikers like Junkie Jonathan, Mr.

Purple, Goldilocks, Flyin' Brian, the It Twins, Baby Joe, and Sir Paulie—hardly likely to endear them to the jurors as credible druggies.

Perhaps more troubling to the government's case were the potential witnesses which the prosecutors had lined up but who—for an assortment of reasons—were never called to the witness stand. The government had intended to call Michael Alig as its star witness. Alig had invented the "club kid" culture. He had pled guilty to multiple drug charges, but to save his neck, he agreed to be a cooperator and rat on Gatien. His testimony would have been devastating. The prosecutors had said in a hearing before me a few months before the trial opened that he had told them that Gatien had paid him for drugs and had decided which drug dealers would be allowed to work at the Limelight.

However, there was one slight problem. Alig had since pled guilty in state court to manslaughter and would be sentenced to up to 20 years. In a handwritten statement given to the police by his roommate, Robert (Freeze) Riggs, Freeze admitted that he had hit a fellow drug dealer, Angel Melendez, three times with a hammer to stop him from assaulting Alig in their apartment in a dispute over money. He then recounted the gory details of what followed: After the third blow felled Melendez, Alig strangled him and poured "some cleaner or chemical into Angel's mouth." Alig and Freeze then covered Melendez' mouth with duct tape. He was asphyxiated. They then moved the body to a bathtub, where it sat for five to seven days before they decided "we had to do something about this terrible mess." Freeze then went to Macy's and bought two chef's knives and a meat cleaver. Alig dismembered the body. The smell was so unbearable that Freeze "put baking soda in to absorb some of the odor." He and Alig then threw Angel's legs into the Hudson River in a duffel bag but needed a cab to transport the rest of the body, wrapped in plastic bags in a box, to the West Side Highway near 25th Street, where they took the box out of the cab and threw it into the river.

Freeze's account of the killing differed sharply from the version

309

Alig had given to the victim's brother in a telephone conversation secretly recorded by the District Attorney's Office. In this conversation, Alig implicated Melendez and Gatien in drug-dealing ventures at Gatien's clubs. He charged that Freeze killed Melendez for Gatien because "Peter is in trouble right now for drugs" and Melendez—who "knew everything"—was threatening to go to his friend at the Village Voice to "tell him all this stuff."

Gatien's lawyer called Alig's account "absurd." He told the press that his statement was "filled with speculation and sheer lunacy," and he threw the gauntlet down by saying that anyone who proposes using Michael Alig as a witness "is desperate." The government never acknowledged that it was desperate, but it thought better than to rely on the testimony of someone who was implicated in killing and dismembering Angel Melendez. Its star witness had faded. The jury would never hear Alig testify about Gatien's drug dealings with him. At least it would be spared the gory details of Angel's murder.

Nor would the jury hear from Brooke Humphries. Although she had more body piercings than Osama bin Laden's bullet-ridden body, she had a cooperation deal with the government and, as a house dealer, had lots to say about Gatien's knowledge and condonation of the sale of drugs at his clubs. However, two days before she was to testify, she had been quietly arraigned in another courtroom in the courthouse for lying to a federal agent. It seems that shortly after the government had told the jury in its opening statement that Brooke would be an important witness, it found out that she had been picked up for selling cocaine in Dallas. Her value as a government witness had been destroyed.

Another potential government witness, Cynthia Haatja, a.k.a "Gitsie," overdosed on heroin and was found dead in her Queens apartment just a few days before the trial got underway.

To make matters even worse, the government decided that it would not have the two undercover DEA agents testify. They would have been key witnesses since they had infiltrated the clubs and as government law enforcement officials would likely be perceived by the jurors as more credible than the druggies. Nevertheless, they were scratched from the government's witness list at the last minute. The press speculated that the prosecutors may have been aware that Gatien's lawyer was intending to cross-examine them about Alig's allegation—made in a court affidavit—that they had allowed him to snort heroin in the back seat of their car.

I felt sorry for the government's lawyers. Their case was falling apart right in front of their eyes. Gatien's lawyer, Ben Brafman, knew exactly how to capitalize on it. He was brilliant. I had never seen a more skilled criminal defense lawyer. He could do it all. The jurors hung on his every word. He portrayed Gatien as a hardworking, creative nightclub businessman who was being made a victim for the government's crackdown on the City's brazen nightlife. He hammered home on the failure of the government to prove that Gatien had taken any money from any of the so-called house dealers, and claimed that there was no credible evidence linking him to knowing of the widespread sale of drugs at his clubs.

While Brafman never contended that drugs were not sold there, he told the jury that Gatien should not be held accountable—given the massive amount of people frequenting his four clubs—for not keeping them drug-free. He likened the clubs to venues—like Shea Stadium and Madison Square Garden—where hundreds or thousands of young people would be doing drugs while attending rock concerts. He rhetorically asked the jurors why the government had not prosecuted their owners. In sum, Gatien was being made the proverbial scapegoat. Brafman accused the government's lawyers of using him as a trophy. His scalp would be a feather in their caps and would be a career-making win.

In reality, the acquittal was a career-making win for Brafman. While he was well-known among criminal defense lawyers, this was the case that made him a star and earned him a national reputation. He would go on to get Puff Daddy off in 2002 on gun and bribery charges, and would represent Plaxico Burress, Michael Jackson, and most recently, Dominique Strauss-Kahn.

* * *

After licking its wounds, the government tooled up for the trial of Gatien's manager—Steve Lewis—and one of the two bouncers, Ray Montgomery. It had dropped the charges against the other bouncer, Jose Otero. It thought that the evidence against him was too weak. After a two-week trial, Montgomery was acquitted, but the jury nailed Lewis. The key piece of evidence against him was a covert taped conversation where he talked to admitted dope peddler "Baby Joe" Uzzardi about drug-drenched parties at the Limelight while Baby Joe was working there as a promoter. Baby Joe testified as a cooperator and identified his and Lewis' voices on the tape.

The government had told me that it also wanted Baby Joe to testify about other conversations which he had with Gatien—that were not taped—where Gatien told him that he knew that Lewis was allowing drugs to be sold at the Limelight. Under the law, this testimony would be inadmissable because it was a statement made out of court by a third party—Gatien. He would not be called as a witness by the government since he would undoubtedly "take the Fifth." However, there was an exception if I, as the judge, ruled that when Gatien purportedly made this statement he was a coconspirator. This required me to determine if he had knowledge that people at the Limelight had conspired to distribute drugs there and that he joined in that conspiracy in some fashion to further its purposes. Even though Gatien had been acquitted by a jury and could not be retried (it would be double jeopardy), it was incumbent upon me in the Lewis trial to decide whether Gatien knew of—and condoned—the drug scene that was the hallmark of his clubs. I ruled that he did and allowed Baby Joe to tell the jury what Gatien had told him about Lewis.

When it came time to sentence Lewis and all those who had pled guilty, I had 40 sentencing proceedings to conduct. Of the 44 who were indicted, only Gatien, Montgomery, Otero, and one other (whose charges were dropped) would not be sentenced. I sentenced Lewis—who was then 47—to a year and a day plus 300 hours of community service. I gave him credit for testifying against Gatien

312

in a New York State Liquor Authority proceeding which resulted in the cancellation of Gatien's liquor license. The bulk of the other sentences were of the club kids who were party promoters and had cooperation agreements with the government. I placed them on probation for terms ranging from two to five years. I required them to also perform many hours of community service. Perhaps most importantly, I required that they undergo drug counseling. Many of them had become addicts. Some were still in college; others had dropped out. Their parents would sit frozen in their seats as they listened to me tell their children how they had screwed up their lives. I wondered how many other parents did not have a clue as to whether their college kids were druggies.

* * *

The documentary film was produced by Gatien's daughter, Jen. Not surprisingly, it portrayed her father in a sympathetic way and was obviously calculated to restore his reputation. I am sure that when those who saw it left the theater after the final credits had flashed across the screen they believed that Gatien was wrongly put through hell by being unfairly prosecuted. I knew, however, that Gatien was lucky that he was not convicted. The trial was hardly a slam dunk for the defense. If not for the fact that the government's case unexpectedly imploded—and the skills of Ben Brafman—Peter Gatien might very well be behind bars today.

Nonetheless, I enjoyed the movie. It had lots of footage of the club scene during the halcyon days of the club-kid drug culture of the later part of the 20th century and beginning of the current one, and I was amused by the cast of characters that it used to portray Gatien's plight with the law. There—as big as life on the screen— was Lord Michael Caruso, Steve Lewis, and even Michael Alig, all speaking well of Gatien. You would not know that Alig—who was now 45—was talking from jail, where he is still serving time for his role in killing Angel Melendez. You also would not know that Lord Michael had opened a club in Miami and for a short time had man- aged the rap group Wu-Tang Clan. As for Lewis, the film did not mention that he is currently a nightlife blogger and an interior designer for nightclubs and restaurants. However, it portrayed Gatien—now 59—as currently living a quiet, uneventful life in Canada, where he was deported—having never sought citizenship—after pleading guilty a year after his acquittal to failing to report more than $1 million in income.

The highlight of the film for me, however, was watching the principal narrator, Frank Owen. He was a colorful guy who did a great job bringing the whole club scene to life. He had covered the case for the Village Voice and also had written a book in 2003, appropriately titled *Clubland, The Fabulous Rise and Murderous Fall of Club Culture.* In it he wrote about the trial and had this to say about the judge:

> The judge, Frederic Block, presided over the proceedings with a kind face and an easy wit. The affable Block sparked laughter in the courtroom when, following testimony about how to make an ecstasy punch (mix vodka and orange juice with crushed ecstasy), a juror began to cough and was given a cup of water, after which the judge quipped, "I'm sure you'll find it's only water." Block believed there was a wealth of evidence implicating the accused ("I think Peter Gatien knew darn well what was happening," he would say later) but took care not to signal that to the jury. He thought the prosecution was stupid not to call Michael Alig to the stand. Even with the manslaughter conviction. Alig, like no other, could have provided intimate and compelling testimony about the depth of corruption at the Gatien-run Limelight.

I don't remember ever commenting about the government's decision not to have Alig testify, but I was happy that after being taken to the woodshed by the *Daily News* for speaking out about the government's ill-advised decision to seek the death penalty against Supreme, a member of the press actually had something nice to say about me.

Chapter
5

Discrimination

On the civil ledger, discrimination cases dominate the court's docket. Typically, disgruntled employees who have been fired claim that it was because of their race, sex, or age. They come to the federal court claiming that their rights have been violated under the 14th Amendment or any one of a host of civil rights statutes that Congress has passed throughout the years.

In our nation's history there are two decades that stand out when Congress turned its attention to putting meat to the bones of the principle that "all people are created equal." They were just about 100 years apart. It all began right after the Civil War when the 13th Amendment was adopted in 1865 abolishing slavery. This ushered in what has commonly been referred to as the First Reconstruction Era. A year later, Congress passed its first Civil Rights Act over the veto of President Lincoln's successor, Andrew Johnson. It provided that people in the United States were citizens regardless of race, color, or previous condition of servitude, and that everyone had the same rights as white citizens with respect to making and enforcing contracts, suing and being sued, giving evidence in court, and an assortment of property rights. Lincoln obviously would never have tried to scuttle this legislation.

The first Civil Rights Act became part of the Constitution two years later when the 14th Amendment was ratified in 1868. The Amendment's overarching purpose was to make it a constitutional principle that no state would treat its citizens differently because of their color. However, it was also broader in scope than the Civil Rights Act. Its precise language resonates to this day:

All persons born or naturalized in the United States, and subject to the jurisdiction thereof, are citizens of the United States and of the state wherein they reside. No state shall make or enforce any law which shall abridge the privileges or immunities of citizens of the United States; nor shall any state deprive any person of life, liberty, or property, without due process of law; nor deny to any person within its jurisdiction the equal protection of the laws.

The 14th Amendment also provided that "Congress shall have power to enforce, by appropriate legislation, the provisions of this article." Congress wasted little time in doing that. In 1871 it passed the second Civil Rights Act. Andrew Johnson was no longer President, and his successor, Ulysses Grant, signed it into law. This legislation became known as the Ku Klux Klan Act. It was enacted because of the widespread violence perpetrated by white supremacists in the aftermath of the Civil War. It survives to this day, codified in the statutory codes as 42 U.S.C. § 1983. This federal statute gives individuals the right to sue state actors for violations of federal law. Section 1983 lawsuits are today the principal means by which one who believes that a state or local government official or agency has violated his or her federal constitutional or federal statutory rights can sue for injunctive and monetary relief in the federal courts.

In 1875, Congress passed its third Civil Rights Act. It guaranteed equal treatment in public accommodations regardless of race or color. However, the Supreme Court struck it down in 1883. It held that although the 14th Amendment prohibited discrimination by the states, it did not give Congress the power to regulate discriminatory practices by private parties.

It would take a century before the goals of equal rights for minority citizens were achieved. During the 1960s, Congress ushered in the Second Reconstruction Era with far-reaching civil rights legislation. It was brought about by the zeal and passion of a different President Johnson. Lyndon B. Johnson—unlike Andrew Johnson—has gone down in history as the architect and engineer of the statutes which took great leaps—and largely succeeded—in ridding our country of discriminatory treatment of any of its citizens, be it by the government or by private parties.

* * *

Discrimination laws during the Second Reconstruction Era moved way beyond offensive conduct by the states based upon race and color. They addressed injustices on the basis of gender, age, disability, pregnancy, religion, and national origin—and their reach was not limited to state action. It all began in 1963 when Congress passed the Equal Pay Act ("EPA") prohibiting wage disparities based on gender. However, the major legislation happened a year later, in 1964, when Congress enacted the fourth Civil Rights Act—89 years after the last one. It was triggered by events such as *Brown v. Board of Education* in 1954—striking down school segregation—the Montgomery bus boycott of 1955, and the success of the Civil Rights Movement during the '50s and early '60s spearheaded by Martin Luther King.

The Civil Rights Act of 1964 contained 11 parts, called Titles. Collectively, they prohibited discriminatory practices on the basis of race, color, religion, national origin, and sex in the context of voter registration, public accommodations, public facilities, public schools, and—under Title VII—public and private employment if at least 15 people were employed.

Mindful of the Supreme Court's 1883 precedent holding that Congress did not have the power to enact legislation under the 14th Amendment striking down discrimination in public accommodations, Congress relied upon the Constitution's Commerce Clause in enacting the 1964 Act—as well as the EPA the year before. The Clause allows Congress to regulate any activity, however slight, that could have any affect upon interstate commerce. Thus, the Commerce Clause—rather than the 14th Amendment—was invoked to get around the Supreme Court's decision of the prior century precluding Congress from outlawing discrimination in public accommodations. Embracing the Civil Rights Movement of the mid-20th century, an enlightened Supreme Court thereafter accepted this distinction and opened the door to the use of the Commerce Clause to authorize Congress to eradicate discrimination by private parties who dealt with the general public. Thus, both Title VII and the EPA define covered employers in a manner that provides a Commerce Clause hook. The Title VII requirement that employers have at least 15 employees was intended to be a rational measure of whether that employer's business impacts interstate commerce. Additionally, the EPA's constitutionality was deemed to be satisfied under the Commerce Clause by requiring that the employer has at least two employees and does at least $500,000 in annual business.

Congress did not stop its onslaught against discrimination during the '60s with the 1964 Civil Rights Act. In 1967 it passed the Age Discrimination in Employment Act ("ADEA"). It prohibits discrimination by employers of 20 or more employees against employees over 40 years old—once again satisfying the Commerce Clause hook. A year later Congress enacted the Fair Housing Act, prohibiting discrimination on the basis of race, color, religion, or national origin with respect to the renting, selling, and advertising of public and private dwellings. There was more to come.

In 1972, Congress amended Title VII to add coverage of state and local government employers to its power to enforce the 14th Amendment. While Section 1983 already provided redress against state and local government actors who violated federally guaranteed rights, this amendment made such state actors additionally accountable for violations of the complementary discrimination protections articulated in Title VII.

In 1973, Congress passed the Rehabilitation Act, prohibiting discrimination against individuals with disabilities who work in the federal government. 1978 saw the advent of the Pregnancy Discrimination Act—protecting pregnant women against employment discrimination—and the Civil Service Reform Act, designed to promote overall fairness in federal personnel actions; it also protected whistle-blowers from reprisals. In 1990, Congress passed the Americans with Disabilities Act (ADA), extending the reach of the Rehabilitation Act to state and local governments, education institutions, and private employers employing 15 or more people.

In 1991, Congress put more teeth into Title VII of the 1964 Civil Rights Act by codifying the Supreme Court's language that the high court had articulated in 1971 in *Griggs v. Duke Power Company*, that Congress directed the thrust of Title VII "to the *consequences* of employment practices, not simply the motivation." The 1991 Act, therefore, expressly outlawed employment practices which, although not intentionally discriminatory, were in operation disproportionately harmful to minority employees. It also authorized jury trials, and in intentional discrimination cases it allowed for compensatory damages for pain and suffering—including emotional distress. It also permitted punitive damages in such cases to be awarded for willful discrimination (other than against the government or government officials). Previously, victims of discrimination were only entitled to back pay, reinstatement, and injunctive relief.

In keeping with the times, Congress more recently has enacted the Genetic Information Nondiscrimination Act of 2008 (GINA), prohibiting employment discrimination based on genetic information about an applicant, employee, or former employee.

The states have also been active. New York, for example, has passed its own anti-discrimination laws, as has New York City. While they largely track the federal laws, they are in a few situations more liberal, and they ensure that no one engaging in purely intrastate commerce can escape the reach of fundamental anti-discrimination laws.

There is a wide swath of discriminatory practices that come under the umbrella of all of these federal and state statutes. They include, in addition to illicit discrimination, harassment on the basis of race, color, religion, sex, national origin, disability, genetic information or age, and retaliation against an individual for filing a charge of discrimination, participating in an investigation, or opposing discriminatory practices.

* * *

While the federal courts are kept busy dealing with Congress' far-ranging spate of anti-discrimination laws, the greatest number of the discrimination cases that wind up in federal court are Title VII employment cases. Many are frivolous. Time and again I have had to explain to disgruntled employees and their lawyers that they cannot use the federal courts to complain about being fired or to air their grievances against their employers unless they were the victims of impermissible discrimination. However, I have had some memorable trials where the employee rang the bell and the employer was made to pay big time for its unlawful discriminatory behavior. Three stand out. They were each textbook examples of what Congress must have had in mind when it sought throughout the years to protect employees from being discriminated against in their jobs because of their race, color, national origin, religion, sex, age, or disability.

* * *

Since 1996 Patricia Luca has been a correction officer at the Nassau County jail. In 2000 she filed a sexual harassment complaint with the County. She claimed that her male coworkers at the Nassau County Correction Department had made her the butt of lewd comments. There was merit to her claim. The County settled it out of court in 2003 for $90,000. Luca then sought to become a Nassau County police officer. It was a civil service position. Candidates had to pass a comprehensive test and qualify for placement on a civil service list.

Luca passed the exam with flying colors, was highly qualified because of her experience as a correction officer, and was high up on the civil service list. By law she was entitled to be considered for an opening in 2004, but was passed over without explanation. Not surprisingly, she sued the County, claiming that its police department had retaliated against her because she had held the County accountable for the inappropriate behavior of its male correction

320

officers. It was a classic retaliation lawsuit against the municipality under Section 1983 and Title VII.

I thought that the parties should have tried to settle the case, and I encouraged them to do so. If memory serves me correctly, Luca would have taken in the neighborhood of $150,000 and remained a correction officer—but the County decided to dig in its heels. It did not want Luca to become a police officer, and it did not want to seriously consider a monetary settlement. Luca was entitled to a jury trial. I told the County's lawyers that I thought that a jury might be sympathetic to her plight and that they were running a big risk by going to trial.

Settlement negotiations are tricky. The judge runs the risk of being perceived by one of the parties as being heavy-handed. However, I believe that a judge should take an active role in trying to get the parties to settle their differences if the case is to be tried by a jury. I will not engage in settlement discussions if the trial will be a bench trial. I would then be deciding the facts, and I do not want to know what they are prior to the trial. Nevertheless, when there is a jury, it will be deciding the facts, and there is no risk that the parties will be prejudiced by open settlement negotiations before the judge. I will not press for a settlement, however, if I believe that there is a good reason for a party to draw a line in the sand and insist on its day in court. In this litigation the jury would be deciding the basic retaliation factual issue. If it found liability it would then have to decide whether to award Luca compensatory monetary damages for her emotional distress and pain and suffering. Under the law, I would then have to decide whether the police department would have to hire her or whether, instead, she should receive additional compensation for any future lost wages; she had not made any claim for back wages.

The trial was a disaster for the County. Over several days its witnesses offered a host of reasons for not allowing Luca to become a police officer. From watching the jurors' reactions, it was clear that they were not buying any of them, and the trial got testy. The County's lawyers thought that I had it in for them. Be that as it may, I thought that I had bent over backwards to give both parties a fair trial.

The jury did not take long to hold that the Nassau County Police Department's decision not to hire Luca was motivated by retaliatory animus and to award her compensatory damages of $150,000. I then decided—in a written opinion—that it would be improvident to put Luca on the force since I concluded that "the Police Department and its employees continue[d] to bear such hostility toward Luca" that forcing her on the department "would not be a viable remedy." I then had to calculate her future lost wages because police officers made more money than correction officers. Therefore, I had to determine the difference between what Luca would have earned as a police officer through the date when she would be eligible to retire and what she would be earning as a correction officer during the same time period. It turned out to be a considerable sum—$604,589. The County was also required by law to pay attorney's fees and court costs. When everything was added up—together with the jury's award—the total monetary judgment that was entered against the County was $949,973.86.

The County appealed. In a summary order, the circuit court held that I had conducted a fair trial and had properly calculated the postverdict monetary damages. However, in light of an intervening decision which it had rendered in another case, it remanded the case to me for reconsideration of the attorney's fee award. In another written opinion, I adhered to my original award. I also awarded additional attorney's fees that were incurred for the appeal, and I summed up the practical consequences of the County's decision to retaliate against Patricia Luca because she had filed a sexual harassment complaint against its correction department:

> The County, of course, had the absolute right to pursue an appeal. The stark reality, however, is that the Court of Appeals, by summary order, made short shrift of the County's appeal and that the County has now incurred an additional $127,060.45 in attorney's fees for the plaintiff. When added to the judgment appealed from, the total monetary judgment which the County must now pay the plaintiff for

the privilege of keeping a highly qualified woman from becoming a Nassau County police officer (with interest running until the judgment is paid) is $1,077,034.31.

The County paid the million dollar judgment.

* * *

Airborne Freight is a major private mail service. It has lots of delivery drivers in New York City—and elsewhere—who have daily delivery routes. Most are white; some are black. Kevin Hill and four of his fellow New York City African American coemployees— Breck Harrison, Duval Tyson, Mark McCord, and Damian Alvarez— sued Airborne for intentionally discriminating against them because of their color by subjecting them to harsher discipline than their white counterparts for comparable, minor, work-related infractions. Specifically, they claimed that they were each terminated and had to resort to arbitration under their union's collective bargaining agreement to seek reinstatement; by contrast, the white employees were merely suspended for a few days or not disciplined at all.

After several days of trial, a jury agreed. It determined that during the period of time when the plaintiffs were terminated at least five white employees were either suspended or not subject to any discipline at all for committing the same types of infractions. The jury also found that Airborne had retaliated against Hill by causing him all sorts of grief after an arbitration panel found that he was wrongly terminated and reinstated him. At a later arbitration, the arbitration panel found in favor of Airborne, and Hill was fully terminated.

In determining whether Airborne had engaged in intentional discrimination against the plaintiffs, the jury was entitled to consider numerous instances where managers made disparaging remarks about African Americans and evidence that Airborne assigned delivery routes to drivers on the basis of their race. As for disparaging remarks, they consisted of a manager telling an African American employee who was singing a gospel song that, "he didn't want to hear none of those slave songs," another manager stating that he did not like the fact that a "fucking black guy" was in a white neighborhood because he didn't believe in "mixing" between the races, and the plaintiffs' supervisor calling a black employee "boy." The jury awarded the five plaintiffs varying amounts for compensatory damages, totaling $685,000. They also socked Airborne for $1,800,000 in punitive damages; each of the plaintiffs were awarded $300,000 for the intentional discrimination, and Hill was given an extra $300,000 because of the retaliation. Airborne obviously was not happy. It was on the hook for almost $2.5 million dollars. It was now also stigmatized as a major corporation that discriminated against African Americans. This was a bitter pill to swallow. Not surprisingly it sought to overturn the jury's verdict. Instead of appealing right away, it first asked me to do it. It was allowed to have two bites of the apple; it could make a motion to set aside the verdicts before me and then appeal if I denied it.

I am often asked whether a judge can overturn a jury's verdict. It can, but only in limited circumstances. In a criminal case, if there is an acquittal, that's it. The defendant goes free. If he is convicted, I can do one of two things. I can set it aside and acquit the defendant if I determine that there was no evidence that could rationally justify a conviction. Because double jeopardy would attach, the defendant could not be tried again for the same crime. If there is some evidence that could support the jury's verdict I can nonetheless order a new trial if I believe that the verdict was seriously erroneous or a "miscarriage of justice." However, this should only be done in "exceptional circumstances."

The same principles broadly apply to civil trials as well. However, when it comes to damages I can determine whether they are either too much or too little. If so, I can either order a completely new trial, a new trial just limited to damages, or I can reduce the damages if I determine that they are excessive. In that latter regard, I must give the affected party a choice. The plaintiff or defendant—as the case may be—can accept my damage award or insist on a totally new trial. Whenever I countermand a jury's verdict, whether in a criminal or civil case, the party on the short end of the stick can always ask the circuit court of appeals whether my decision was correct.

I refused to set aside the jury's liability verdicts for four of the five plaintiffs. I decided, in a written opinion, that there was ample evidence to sustain the jury's findings and that there was no basis for a retrial. However, I tossed out the jury's verdict for McCord since there was no evidence that he was treated differently than his white counterparts. He would not be entitled, therefore, to the compensatory damages which the jury had awarded him—$85,000 and the $300,000 punitive damage award.

I also reduced the damage awards for each of the four successful plaintiffs. The law required me to compare their awards to damage awards in comparable cases. Since none of the four suffered physical injuries, they were relegated to recovering compensatory damages only for their emotional distress. They did not have a lot. I reduced the residual total jury awards of $600,000—after subtracting the $85,000 for McCord—to a total of $185,000; each of the four plaintiffs got varying amounts based on their individual circumstances.

I also held that punitive damages were justified. They are warranted if an employer's managers have acted "with malice or with reckless disregard to the federally protected rights of an aggrieved individual." In addition to serving as punishment, punitive damages are designed to deter others from misbehaving. I ruled that "it was reasonable for the jury to infer that Airborne's managers knew that their actions were in violation of federal law simply by virtue of the well-established Supreme Court case law on discrimination and retaliation, the long standing statutory schemes proscribing such conduct, the size of Airborne, and the common knowledge in today's society that employment discrimination is impermissible." Using other punitive damage cases for comparisons, I cut each punitive award for the four successful plaintiffs by a third. The residual total of $1 million was still a pretty significant number.

I gave the plaintiffs 20 days to decide if they would take the lower compensatory and punitive damage sums or whether they wanted a retrial. They decided to take the money.

There were two other issues that had to be resolved. While in the Luca case I had to decide whether she should be hired, here I had to decide whether any of the successful plaintiffs who had been terminated should be reinstated. Hill, Tyson, and Harrison wanted their jobs back—Alvarez was not terminated. The lawyers had also agreed that I, rather than the jury, would determine whether any of them were entitled to lost back wages or front pay. I had to hold a postverdict hearing.

After listening to testimony from both sides, I concluded, once again in a written opinion, that reinstatement would not be a wise thing. There was just too much ongoing acrimony between these plaintiffs and their supervisors to allow for peaceful coexistence. For example, I learned that Hill, Tyson, and Harrison had called their supervisor "pussy," "faggot," "Uncle Tom," and "slave to the master." They were also hostile to other members of Airborne's management; Hill had called one of them a racist and a member of the Ku Klux Klan. While all this did not permit Airborne to discriminate against them, it was clear to me that it should not be required to rehire them.

I did not give them any front pay since they were each now working for other employers. They were entitled, however, to lost wages until they got their new employment. I calculated Hill's back pay to be $110,527; Tyson's to be $15,405, and Harrison's to be $157,758. When these amounts were added to the compensatory and punitive damages awards, Airborne was facing a total monetary judgment— even after I had tossed McCord's case out of court and reduced the compensatory and punitive damage awards—in the neighborhood of $1.5 million dollars. In addition, the successful plaintiffs were entitled to attorney's fees. I would have to fix them if the parties could not agree to the amount—which they later did.

Not surprisingly, Airborne appealed to the circuit court of appeals; so did McCord, who argued, of course, that I should not have dismissed his case. Hill, Harrison, and Tyson also appealed, claiming that they were entitled to be reinstated. With the many decisions that I had had to make, I was concerned that the appellate court might not agree with all of them. That was, happily, not the case. In a summary order it rejected Airborne's appeal "substantially for the reasons articulated by the district court," and agreed with my dismissal of McCord's case because, as I had written, "[u]nlike his fellow plaintiffs, McCord was not disciplined more harshly" than similarly situated white employees. It also upheld my decision that Airborne did not have to reinstate Hill, Harrison, and Tyson as "not an abuse of discretion," and my determination that they should not be awarded any front pay as "not clearly erroneous."

Looking back on the case years later, I wonder whether this bitter litigation did more to resolve the racial disharmony at Airborne Freight than to foment it. Hopefully, it was the former.

* * *

Molly Perdue was the coach of the Brooklyn College women's basketball team for the 1991 and 1992 seasons. She was also the women's sports administrator. Brooklyn College is a public university, being part of the City University of New York State. In 1991 Molly was paid a total salary of $42,881 for the two jobs she was doing. By contrast, the coach of the men's basketball team, Mark Reiner, was paid $69,477 just for coaching the men's team. In the following year, Molly's salary was increased to $44,077, but Reiner's was increased to $70,110. To make matters worse, the men's sports administrator, Ron Kestenbaum, was paid almost the same salary as Perdue even though this was his only job. In 1991, Perdue's salary was $66,596 less than Kestenbaum's and Reiner's combined salaries; in 1992 it was $68,233 less.

Molly thought that she was worth at least as much as Reiner, especially since she turned the Brooklyn College Lady Knights basketball team into a winner, while Reiner's men's squad was a disaster. In 1992, the Lady Knights posted a winning 17-11 record; Reiner's team was an abysmal 5-21. Molly also believed that since she was doing the same jobs as Kestenbaum and Reiner—albeit as athletic director and basketball coach for the women—she merited the same pay as their combined salaries.

Molly sued the college under the Equal Pay Act. She also sued for intentional gender discrimination under Title VII. She scored on both counts. The day after the jury's verdict the *Daily News* reported that it was "the first award of its kind in New York City's college sports scene."

On her Title VII claim, the jury awarded Perdue $85,000 for emotional distress. As for her EPA claim, it determined that she was entitled to the same combined pay as Reiner and Kestenbaum. It also decided that the college's violation of the EPA was willful. Under the Act, a violation is willful if "the employer either knew or showed reckless disregard" for its wrongful conduct. Upon a finding of willfulness, the EPA required that the damages be doubled.

The parties agreed that I, rather than the jury, should make the disparate wage calculations. Since there was no dispute as to the salaries, it was easy to do. The differential in wages for the two-year period was $134,829. When doubled, Perdue was entitled to $269,658. I decided that she was also entitled to an additional $5,262 in unpaid retirement benefits.

As in the Airborne Freight case, the employer asked me to set aside the jury's verdicts or, alternatively, to order a new trial. I held, however, that there was ample evidence to support the verdicts and explained why in a written opinion.

As for the jury's verdict that there was a willful violation of the EPA, I explained that under the statute an EPA violation occurs "when an employee pays lower wages to an employee of one gender than to substantially equivalent employees of the opposite gender in similar circumstances." To show a violation, "a plaintiff need not prove that an intention to discriminate on the basis of gender motivated the pay disparity." During the trial Perdue provided extensive testimony regarding her responsibilities and duties as women's basketball coach and women's sports administrator.

As for her coaching duties, she did everything that Kestenbaum did. They coached the same number of games, had the same number of players, and had the same number of practices. They both managed their team's budgets, scholarships, assistant coaches, scouting of opponents, game preparation, and ordering of equipment. They both were responsible for the supervision, guidance, and counseling of their players, and they were both accountable to the same person.

As for her administrative job, she and Reiner had the same 11 duties. They were both responsible for the daily operations of sports, game scheduling, organizing team budgets and student orientation, and administering their respective athletic programs. They also reported to the same individual. In addition, Perdue had the extra duty of "being available for guidance of all female athletes."

The jury was clearly entitled to conclude, therefore, that Molly Perdue performed equal work on jobs requiring equal skill, effort, and responsibility as those performed by both Kestenbaum and Reiner under similar working conditions for far less pay.

It was also justified in finding that the college's misconduct was willful. Perdue had constantly complained to her supervisors—to no avail—about conflicts of practice time between the men's and women's basketball teams, that she had to clean the gym before the Lady Knights' basketball games, and that she had to do her team's laundry. She testified that when her complaints were presented in a report at a meeting of the presidential advisory committee, the college's athletic director stated, "Let the woman sue."

There was also plenty of evidence to support the jury's verdict of intentional gender discrimination under Title VII. The jury was entitled to consider the same evidence that supported Perdue's EPA claim to determine if there was a gender-based motive to discriminate against her. In addition, there was testimony that her office was "in what was the equivalent of a broom closet" and that, contrary to the men's locker room—which was carpeted and had individual lockers and chairs—the women had to use the general women's locker room which had no privacy and was "just a mass group of lockers and benches." As a clincher, Perdue testified that

Reiner told her—after he had watched her run in a race—that he had never realized how large her breasts were. Moreover, a vote was taken by the guys as to their size.

In addition to her compensatory damage award and her double back pay, Perdue was also entitled to attorney's fees, court costs, and prejudgment interest. When it was all added up, the total judgment came to just slightly under $800,000. Just like the Luca and Airborne Freight cases, the defendant paid a heavy price for violating the nation's anti-discrimination laws.

The significance of the case was captured in comments made to the press. Perdue was quoted in the *New York Times* as "hop[ing] that this will help reduce discrimination against women athletes at all levels." Debbie Banks, a former senior counsel to the National Women's Law Center, told the *Times*: "This case is very important for the cause of equality for women in sports and everywhere else. It demonstrates the increased ability individuals now have to fight large public institutions because of changes in the civil rights laws in the early 1990's." Linda Carpenter, a phys ed teacher at the college, told the *Daily News* that she was pleased that the case was not settled out of court: "The more court decisions are publicized as opposed to being subject to confidential settlements, the more they become educational tools for the public. The more we see of this the better."

* * *

Perhaps nothing has animated debate over the reach of Title VII as much as the Supreme Court's interpretation of the statute in *Griggs*—as subsequently codified in the Civil Rights Act of 1991—opening the door to lawsuits by minorities claiming that an employment practice, although not the product of intentional, direct discrimination, had in practice a disparate impact upon them. When in 2004 the city of New Haven's civil service board threw out promotional exams for firefighters because the black firefighters scored poorly, the debate really heated up. Eighteen of the high-scoring white firefighters sued, including the lead plaintiff, Frank

330

Ricci, claiming reverse discrimination. Ricci added an emotional kicker to the lawsuit because he was dyslexic and had to study for eight to 13 hours a day to pass the exam.

New Haven argued in the Connecticut federal district court that it had acted in good faith in tossing out the exams, fearing a disparate-impact suit from the minority firefighters. My district court Connecticut colleague, Judge Janet Arterton, agreed. In a lengthy decision—rendered September 28, 2006—she carefully analyzed the nature and extent of the test's disparate impact under established Second Circuit Court of Appeals precedent. New exams would have to be devised that would hopefully result in better scores by the minority test takers.

The white firefighters appealed. Adhering to its precedent, the circuit court, on February 15, 2008, succinctly unanimously affirmed in a short summary order "for the reasons stated in the thorough, thoughtful, and well-reasoned opinion of the court below." As the three-judge panel explained:

> In this case, the Civil Service Board found itself in the unfortunate position of having no good alternatives. We are not unsympathetic to the plaintiffs' expression of frustration. Mr. Ricci, for example, who is dyslexic, made intensive efforts that appear to have resulted in his scoring on one of the exams, only to have it invalidated. But it simply does not follow that he has a viable Title VII claim. To the contrary, because the Board, in refusing to validate the exams, was simply trying to fulfill its obligations under Title VII when confronted with test results that had a disproportionate racial impact, its actions were protected.

One of the judges on the panel was then Circuit Court Judge Sonia Sotomayor.

Applying the circuit court's precedent, as I was obliged to do, I handed down a lengthy decision three months later on May 28, 2008, granting permanent appointments and retroactive seniority to dozens of black, Hispanic, Asian, and/or female New York City school custodians and custodial engineers. The case came to be commonly known as the *Brennan* case. It was launched by the federal government under Title VII in 1996 at a time when 99% of the custodians or custodial engineers—who supervised school handymen and cleaners in 1,200 city schools—were men and 92% were white. The government claimed, and I agreed, that three exams administered to the custodians and custodial engineers had a disparate impact on blacks and Hispanics.

Three white custodians had intervened as affected parties, and they appealed. I was confident that just like the *Ricci* Connecticut firefighters case, the circuit court would summarily affirm. I thought that because—like Judge Arberton—I had written such a comprehensive decision that the appeals court would also write that I, too, had rendered a "thoughtful, and well-reasoned opinion." However, a year later, on June 29, 2009, while the appeal was pending in the circuit court, the Supreme Court overruled the appeals court's decision in *Ricci,* by the barest 5-4 vote. Writing for the majority, Justice Kennedy reasoned that the possibility of a lawsuit from minority firefighters was not a lawful justification for rejecting the test results because the higher scoring candidates were white. "Fear of litigation," Justice Kennedy wrote, "cannot justify an employer's reliance on race to the detriment of individuals who passed the examinations and qualified for promotions."

Nevertheless, the majority did not rule out consideration of disparate impact altogether. It recognized that in "certain, narrow circumstances," employers may disregard test results if they can demonstrate "a strong basis in evidence" that using the results would cause them to lose a disparate-impact suit. As Justice Kennedy explained, this new, heightened standard would require employers to show that the tests were not relevant to the jobs at issue or that other "equally valid and less discriminatory tests were available."

The new standards articulated by the majority were viewed as making it much harder for employers to discard the results of hiring and promotion tests even if they had a disproportionately negative impact on members of a given racial group. For the dissenters, Justice Ginsburg criticized the majority's decision as undermining a crucial aspect of Title VII. She wrote that "Congress endeavored to promote equal opportunity in fact, and not simply in form," and that "[t]he damage today's decision does to that objective is untold."

When I read the Supreme Court's *Ricci* decision, I knew right away that my decision in the *Brennan* case would have to be reversed by the circuit court, but I had to wait for almost two years before the axe would fall. I could not understand why it was taking the circuit judges so long. I found out when, on May 6, 2011, the Court finally handed down its decision. It was 122 pages long. The case would be remanded to me to apply the new heightened standard. However, Judge Calabresi, who authored this magnum opus, used the occasion to write a treatise on the subject. He tried to limit the reach of the impact of the Supreme Court's holding and took pains to give me detailed instructions on how I should now handle the case. I suspect that it will take years before the litigation ends.

After the Supreme Court came down with its decision in *Ricci*, my heart went out to Sonia Sotomayor. She had just been nominated to the high court by the President and was scheduled to soon appear before the Senate Judiciary Committee. Those opposed to her confirmation used the occasion to unjustly criticize her because she was one of the three judges who affirmed Judge Arterton's decision. Senator Jeff Sessions, the ranking Republican on the Judiciary Committee, commented that "[e]very citizen has a right to have his or her case heard by a judge who will rule on the laws, the facts, and the Constitution—and not play favorites." That is exactly what Judge Sotomayor did. She was bound by her court's precedent and—together with the other judges on the panel—applied it. No one had a crystal ball that a 5-4 Supreme Court would adopt a new standard for assessing disparate-impact cases. Fortunately more rational voices prevailed, and Senator Sessions found himself in the minority when the Senate voted to confirm Judge Sotomayor's nomination.

Chapter
6

Race Riots

At 8:30 in the evening of August 19, 1991, a station wagon driven by a Hasidic Jew, Joseph Lifsch, collided with another vehicle at the intersection of President Street and Utica Avenue in the Crown Heights section of Brooklyn, veered out of control, and struck two black children—seven-year-old Gaven Cato and his nine-year-old cousin, Angela. The station wagon was part of a police-led motorcade accompanying Rabbi Menachem Mendel Schneerson, the spiritual leader of the Hasidic community.

Within minutes, an ambulance from a private Jewish organization arrived; soon, a New York City ambulance came. A group of African Americans had gathered at the site of the accident; several physically assaulted Lifsch and his two passengers. A police officer directed the Jewish ambulance to take Lifsch and his passengers to the hospital, while the City ambulance took the two black children to the hospital, where Gavin Cato was pronounced dead.

The accident sparked an immediate and violent reaction among members of the African American community, which escalated into what has become known as the Crown Heights riots, considered to this day to be amongst the most gripping racial riots in the City's history. Angry crowds of African Americans beat up over 100 Jews, broke the windows of their homes, shouted "Heil Hitler," and burnt the Israeli flag—shocking the country. The riots were fueled by the perception of African Americans that the Hasidic community received preferential treatment from the City because of police escorts routinely given to the Rabbi and the unjustified rumor that the Jewish ambulance had failed to render aid to the seriously injured black children, favoring the less injured Hasidic driver and passengers.

The most violent aspect of the riots occurred just hours after the accident when a group of African-American men accosted a rabbinical student, Yankel Rosenbaum, who was stabbed to death. The next day, Lemrick Nelson was arrested and charged with Rosenbaum's murder.

Nelson was tried in a Brooklyn state court a year later before a jury consisting of six blacks, four Hispanics, and two whites. He was charged with murder. The jury was given the option of finding him guilty of manslaughter if it thought that he killed Rosenbaum in the heat of passion. Surprisingly, he was found not guilty on both counts, sending shockwaves throughout the City. The verdict seemed to defy common sense since Nelson admitted to the police that he was the one who stabbed Rosenbaum; police found in Nelson's possession a bloody knife; blotches of blood with the same type as Rosenbaum's were on Nelson's pants; and before Rosenbaum died, he identified Nelson as the one who had stabbed him. Ultimately, however, an official investigation concluded that the jury had little choice but to acquit in view of the incompetence of the police and the bungling of the case by the Brooklyn D.A.'s Office.

Nonetheless, the jury's decision was attributed by many to the perception that black and Hispanic jurors were reluctant to convict a black for murdering a white and to the pervasive anti-police sentiment within the City's black and Hispanic population. That the jury had celebrated at a victory party hosted by Nelson's attorney did not help to resolve the racial discord which the acquittal fomented; the jury's verdict kept the riots on center stage and caused unprecedented divisiveness between Jews and blacks which took years to heal.

An outraged public, of all racial persuasions, would not let the matter rest with Nelson's acquittal, and pressure was placed upon the federal government to act. The groundswell for federal intervention culminated in a unanimous Senate resolution calling for the Justice Department to launch a full-scale investigation into whether civil rights violations occurred during the riots and Yankel Rosenbaum's murder. This led to the impaneling of a federal grand jury in Brooklyn, which indicted Nelson for violating Rosenbaum's civil rights. In 1997 Nelson was tried in the Brooklyn federal courthouse, convicted, and sentenced by District Court Judge David Trager to 19 1/2 years—the high end of the sentencing guidelines range. The jury consisted of five whites, two of whom were Jewish; three blacks; and four Hispanics.

Although this seemingly marked the end of law enforcement's efforts to put Nelson behind bars, the circuit court of appeals overturned the verdict because it disapproved of the manner by which Judge Trager selected the jury; instead of providing for random selection, as the law required, the judge, in order to select a jury with "moral validity," tried to balance the jury's racial composition, which the appellate court struck down as impermissible "jurymandering." The case would have to be retried before a new judge.

I was the judge assigned to preside over Nelson's third trial.

* * *

Although in enacting the 1964 Civil Rights Act Congress had provided in Title VII that civil law suits could be brought to remedy discrimination in public accommodations, the Act did not provide for any criminal culpability. This changed a few years later, against the backdrop of severe race riots in several major cities, when Congress in 1968 made it a crime to willfully injure or interfere with "any person because of his race, color, religion or national origin and because he is or has been participating in or enjoying any benefit, service, privilege, program, facility or activity provided or administered by any State or subdivision thereof."

Congress put real teeth into the statute by providing that "if death results from the acts committed in violation of this section" the perpetrator may be "imprisoned for any term of years or for life," and even "may be sentenced to death."

This was the criminal civil rights statute that the government invoked to try Lemrick Nelson in federal court after he had been acquitted of murder in the state court.

While the circuit court of appeals sent the case back after Nelson's first federal conviction because it disapproved of Judge Trager's "jurymandering," it also addressed Nelson's appellate lawyers' challenge to the constitutionality of the statute. To get around the thorny issue of whether Congress had the power to reach private action through the 14th Amendment, the appellate court upheld the statute under the 13th Amendment's prohibition of slavery and involuntary servitude.

To do so, the circuit court had to decide whether Jews were considered a race within the meaning of the 13th Amendment. It held that they were. Next, the appellate court had to consider whether the sidewalk on which Rosenbaum was killed was a "facility" within the meaning of the statute. The court adopted Webster's definition that a facility was something built to "promote[] the ease of any action" and "perform some particular function or facilitate some particular end," and held that a street qualified by easing and facilitating travel. Nelson could be tried for violating the federal statute even though he had been acquitted of murder and manslaughter in the state prosecution.

* * *

The onset of federal criminal civil rights statutes dates back to the decades immediately following the Civil War. State governments in the Jim Crow South were unable or unwilling to protect the civil rights of black citizens. The Ku Klux Klan came into existence in 1866. It perpetrated waves of murders and assaults against the blacks.

Congress faced mounting pressure to take some action and passed statutes that would allow the federal government to prosecute the Klan. The Enforcement Act of 1870 prohibited the use of violence to prevent blacks from voting. They had been given the right to vote by the 15th Amendment, which was passed earlier in that year. The Enforcement Act specifically targeted the KKK practice of terrorizing the nation's new black citizens so that they would stay away from the ballot box. The Act is still on the books. It was used as recently as 1964, after three civil rights activists—who were working to register blacks to vote in Mississippi—were murdered by members of the KKK and the state refused to try the killers. The federal government stepped in and prosecuted 18 Klansmen under the Enforcement Act for conspiring to deprive the victims of their civil rights. Seven were found guilty and sentenced to prison.

The Civil Rights Act of 1871, in addition to prohibiting "anyone acting under color of state law from depriving a person of their constitutional rights," also made it a federal crime to intimidate witnesses or parties to a legal action, use threat or force to influence jurors, or "go in disguise upon the public highway, or upon the premises of another, with intent to violate" the Constitution or federal laws. In broadening the bases for federal prosecutions of racially motivated crimes, Congress once again had the KKK in mind. The Act also permitted the President to suspend habeas corpus in the event of violent conspiracies against the federal government. President Grant did so in that year in response to uncontrolled KKK activities in South Carolina, and hundreds of KKK members were arrested.

Despite the efforts of Congress, failures of the states to successfully prosecute crimes motivated by racial biases continued well into the 20th century. For example, in 1955 a 14-year-old African American boy was murdered by two white men after he reportedly flirted with a white woman. In state court, an all-white jury acquitted the murderers after only an hour of deliberation. Protected by double jeopardy, they later publicly bragged about their crime. In 1965, a white civil rights volunteer was murdered by four KKK members in Alabama. The state prosecution resulted in an acquittal.

339

Such racial violence, and the frequent failures of state legal systems to bring the perpetrators to justice, once again spurred the federal government to respond. Right after Martin Luther King, Jr. was assassinated in April 1968, it enacted the statute that the federal government used to prosecute Lemrick Nelson.

* * *

I have often been asked why if Nelson was prosecuted in federal court, O.J. was not after he had been acquitted in his California state trial of murdering his wife. The answer is simply that O.J.'s heinous crime was not racially motivated. He only hated his wife. Moreover, he killed her in their home—not on the streets. In other words, there was no federal criminal statute that could be used to give the feds a second bite of the apple. I have invariably then been asked the logical follow-up question. What about double jeopardy? It's a real good question. Regardless of the differences between the state murder statutes and the federal statute used as the hook to retry Nelson, the underlying facts were still the same.

A part of the Fifth Amendment provides that "[n]o person shall be . . . subject for the same offense to be twice put in jeopardy of life or limb." This bar on double jeopardy has ancient roots in both common and civil law reaching back past the Dark Ages to the Greeks and Romans. The double jeopardy clause is meant to ensure that "the State does not make repeated attempts to convict an individual, thereby exposing him to continued embarrassment, anxiety and expense, while increasing the risk of an erroneous conviction."

I applied the Fifth Amendment's double jeopardy clause in a case in my court where the government tried to prosecute a defendant a second time after a jury had acquitted him of murder. Even though I personally thought that the jury got it wrong and the defendant should have been convicted, I had no choice but to dismiss a subsequent indictment and let him go free. An acquittal is sacrosanct since I am not allowed to overturn it, and the government's effort to reprosecute the defendant was a classic example of double jeopardy.

At the trial the government had, in my opinion, provided ample evidence that the defendant, Quasim Duffy, went into the basement of the home of two brothers who ran a legitimate landscaping business to rob them of their hard-earned money. When they resisted, he shot them. One was killed. Duffy was identified by a witness as he fled, but that witness did not see the shooting. The surviving brother could not unequivocally identify him. However, the casings of the bullets were retrieved in the basement and matched a gun that the government had found in the defendant's apartment.

The government was understandably not happy, nor was I, that a murderer would be roaming the streets and no one would be held accountable for the victim's death. It quickly reindicted Duffy. In the new indictment the government charged him with possessing the ammunition. I had to dismiss it. I wrote an opinion explaining the reach of the double jeopardy clause and its application to this regrettable case. I concluded that the new charge "arose out of the same robbery and shooting that gave rise to the original charges, and that the ammunition Duffy is charged with possessing are the shell casings that were recovered at the scene of the attempted robbery." It would, therefore, violate the Fifth Amendment's double jeopardy clause to retry Duffy.

The government appealed. I kept Duffy in jail while the circuit court decided whether I was right. I would not let him be free pending the appeal since I held that he was a danger to the community because I believed that he was the murderer. Six months later, the appellate court upheld my decision that double jeopardy attached "[f]or the reasons set forth in the district court's opinion." Quasim Duffy went home that day a free man. I can only imagine how he must have celebrated having dodged the bullet—unlike his victim—that would have undoubtedly put him in jail for the rest of his life.

There is only one exception to the double jeopardy clause—but it's a big one. It is called the dual sovereignty doctrine. Under this doctrine, the states and the federal government are viewed as separate entities, each with the power to enact its own laws, provided that they do not violate the Constitution. Thus, while New York State could prosecute someone for a murder committed in the state, it could not prosecute him for a murder committed outside the state since that would be prohibited by the Constitution. However, the federal government could also prosecute that person if the murder also violated a constitutional federal statute; it could not prosecute him simply for murder unless there was that federal hook. Thus, a mafiosa who killed someone in Brooklyn could be prosecuted by the state for murder. However, he could also be prosecuted by the feds for the same murder if it was in aid of racketeering—the federal hook. Another example: If someone kills a person while holding up a bank in Brooklyn, he can be prosecuted by the state for murder. However, if the bank was federally insured, he can also be prosecuted for the murder in federal court under the Hobbs Act, which makes it a federal crime to commit robbery that affects interstate commerce—the federal hook. The Justice Department, sensitive that reprosecutions after a state jury has rendered an acquittal has a double jeopardy odor, has adopted an internal policy of reprosecuting only in the exceptional cases. It had determined that the Lemrick Nelson case, with its divisive racial overtones, was one of them.

Thus, the federal government could not have prosecuted O.J. Since he had committed a pure state murder, there was no federal hook. By contrast, under the dual sovereignty doctrine, Lemrick Nelson could be reprosecuted for the same murder in federal court since the federal hook in his case was the alleged violation of Yankel Rosenbaum's civil rights under the statute that Congress had passed in 1968.

* * *

The trial before Judge Trager brought out the crowd. Although it had taken several years before the case reached the federal court, the wounds of the racial tensions that precipitated the Crown Heights riots and Yankel Rosenbaum's death had not healed. Each day the courtroom was packed. The passions and emotions triggered by the crime and its politically charged aftermath could still be felt. They came to a crescendo when Judge Trager sentenced Nelson. Although he stood convicted, he insisted that he was innocent. "Even though I've been found guilty of this crime, I'm like a scapegoat," he said as he turned to the spectator benches and addressed Yankel Rosenbaum's mother—Fay Rosenbaum—sitting with members of her family. "I had no part in it."

Minutes before, Fay Rosenbaum had told Judge Trager that she would "never be able to adequately express the enormity of the loss" of her 29-year-old son. "There have been no apologies from those responsible for Yankel's murder, convicted in this court, no remorse, nothing," she said. His attackers, she continued, had "vented their putrid violent hate, calling for his cold-blooded murder and carrying it out with no regard or respect for Yankel the person, but with a blind baseless bigotry aimed at what Yankel was—a Jew."

Before she had spoken, Nelson's mother, Valerie Evans, had walked across the courtroom to Fay Rosenbaum during a recess, offered her hand, and introduced herself. It was the first time that the two mothers had met. A *New York Times* reporter captured what they said to each other: "I understand your community's pain," Ms. Evans said. "I understand your pain and loss. But I don't believe my son is a killer." Mrs. Rosenbaum responded: "Before my son lost consciousness, he identified your son. He would never have picked him out if it wasn't him. Are you arguing the fact that it wasn't your son who murdered my son?" "Yes," Ms. Evans replied. "I don't think my son is the killer, the way the Government portrays him."

In imposing the maximum guidelines sentence, Judge Trager said that in his view "the defendant represents a danger to the community. He is prone to violence and the use of weapons. I have seen no authentic remorse." As Nelson was led from the courtroom and returned to jail, his father told reporters that "we'll win the appeal." They did, but all they would get would be a retrial before a properly selected jury.

Because of all of the time eaten up by the state prosecution, the trial before Judge Trager, and the circuit court reversal, it was not

343

until 2003—12 years after Yankel Rosenbaum was killed—that I selected the jury for Lemrick Nelson's third trial.

* * *

There was one other aspect of the Crown Heights riots that I had to deal with, well before the retrial took place. In 1996, 43 Hasidic Jews had sued the City of New York for monetary damages under an assortment of civil rights statutes. They claimed that they were injured during the riots and the City should be held responsible for not taking effective action to quell the riots. They also sued Mayor Dinkins and the Commissioner of Police, Raymond Brown, personally. They wanted them to pay out of their pockets for the plaintiffs' injuries.

Under the law, these officials were off the hook if I determined that they were entitled to "qualified immunity." I wrote a lengthy opinion and concluded that they should not be held personally liable for the regrettable consequences that flowed from the race riots. I explained that a governmental official cannot be held personally liable unless the applicable law was "clearly established" at the time and, in addition, that it was not "objectively unreasonable" for the government officer "to believe that his conduct was lawful." As the circuit court had put it: In qualified immunity cases, "we are not concerned about the correctness of the defendants' conduct, but rather the 'objective reasonableness' of their chosen course of action given the circumstances confronting them at the scene."

In my decision I first explained that the City could be found liable if a jury were to determine that the police department emboldened the rioters and increased the danger to the Hasidic community by failing to arrest individuals for unlawful assembly and by ignoring pleas for assistance by both individuals and the community at large. This would be a violation of the plaintiffs' due process rights. The jury, therefore, would determine whether Dinkins, Brown, or any other state actor "had assisted in creating or increasing danger to the plaintiffs and, if so, whether such actions were the proximate

344

cause of any injuries which plaintiff sustained." I held, though, that this "state-created" theory of liability was established by the Supreme Court two years after the riots; hence, it was not "clearly established" law when the riots occurred.

I also held that, in any event, Dinkins' and Brown's actions in dealing with the riots were "objectively reasonable." The plaintiffs claimed that they had inappropriately sanctioned a policy of discouraging police officers from making mass arrests for the violence that was unfolding in front of the Mayor's and Police Commissioner's eyes; moreover, the police were not to engage in aggressive crowd control tactics. Specifically, the plaintiffs contended that the police—acting under this strategy of restraint—refused to make arrests when they observed members of the crowd of African Americans hurl bricks and other items at Hasidic-owned homes. In addition, one of the plaintiffs attested to being seriously injured when she was accosted by a group of African Americans shouting anti-Semitic epithets as she walked home, but police officers stood less than five feet away during the confrontation and turned away in order to be avoid becoming involved. Another plaintiff attested that he and his son were surrounded by a group of African American youths chanting "Jew, Jew, Jew," and that nearby police officers did not intervene as the crowd surrounded them and beat them with fists, bricks, and bottles.

There were many other acts of violence that did not result in arrests. It continued for three days until the Police Commissioner decided that the strategy of restraint was not working. He then implemented a new policy and started to make arrests for unlawful assembly and take a more aggressive approach to combat the ongoing violence. The new policy proved effective. It quickly put an end to the violence, and order was reestablished.

Dinkins and Brown testified at depositions. They thought that restraint was appropriate in the first instance for fear that an overly aggressive approach would cause the unrest to spread outside of Crown Heights to other areas of the City. Dinkins testified that as soon as he was notified of the attack against Rosen-

345

baum, he went to Kings County Hospital and visited with him before he died. He and Brown also met with police officials and community leaders. He also visited Cato's residence the day after he was killed, but was confronted by a belligerent crowd of African Americans that threw projectiles at him. He also appeared on evening news programs and urged calm. He and Brown had met to discuss their common concerns about the continuing violence and the need for devising a new police strategy.

At the end of my opinion, I summed up the reasons why neither the Mayor nor the Police Commissioner should be held personally accountable for the aftermath of the riots:

> It may appear to many that the strategy implemented by the police, at the assumed behest and approbation of Dinkins and Brown, was unwise or imprudent. Dinkins and Brown's presumed misjudgment does not translate to personal liability for violating the Constitution. As a civilized society, we rely upon government officials to act decisively in times of crisis, and we hope that the decisions they make effectively address the crisis. We should not, however, impose upon them the penalty of civil liability every time a critical decision, made under emergent, stressful conditions, does not have the desired effect or results in unanticipated consequences. Dinkins and Brown confronted chaotic conditions in Crown Heights and acted reasonably under the circumstances within the contours of the objective reasonableness standard that drives the qualified immunity inquiry. Both the clear weight of controlling precedent and the common sense policy rationale that underlies the qualified immunity doctrine compel the conclusion that they should be immune from personal liability.

Although Dinkins and Brown were off the hook, the civil case would proceed against the City because it could still be held liable under the civil rights statutes for the actions of its officials if a jury were to find that the police did indeed violate the plaintiffs' due process rights or denied them equal protection under the 14th Amendment. I then met with the parties' lawyers to see whether the case could be settled to avoid what would likely be a contentious trial that would rekindle all of the anger and hostility that

346

had in the interim been laid to rest. Eventually a settlement was hammered out. The City agreed to pay the plaintiffs collectively a little over $1 million.

Years later, former Mayor Dinkins—then a professor at Columbia University—was still nursing the wounds that he suffered from the Hasidic community. He lamented: "Notwithstanding what I think is a superb record of support for Jewish people and the State of Israel, all that was swept aside and I was accused in the most awful fashion."

* * *

The third trial of Lemrick Nelson began—six years later—with the selection of the jury. Emotions were immediately rekindled. Yankel Rosenbaum's younger brother, Norman, who attended every day of the prior two trials and would do so once again, was quoted in the press at the outset as saying that he still seethed with "disdain and hate" for Nelson. Because this was such an emotionally charged high profile case and the media would be all over it, I decided to use an anonymous juror questionnaire to protect the jurors' privacy. Just like the Peter Gotti trial, the names of the jurors would only be known to me and the court's clerk.

As the prospective jurors were randomly called and questioned by me, I told them: "The fact that this case has racial overtones concerns me. I feel like I have to work extra hard to put this out of your mind. You have to be color-blind." A number of the potential jurors candidly told me that they could not be fair, and as I excused them, I thanked them for their honesty. For example, one woman, who identified herself as a Russian Jew, said: "To be Jewish myself and hated by another nationality . . . I think I will not be so objective. I'm not proud of it."

After days of painstaking questioning, I was satisfied that the 12 jurors who were selected—and the six alternates—would try their best to be fair. Realistically, however, I had some concerns that there would be at least some subconscious biases. Eight of the 12 primary jurors were black, two were Guyanese-Americans, the

347

other two were white; none were Jewish. Could they all truly render a color-blind verdict?

After the jury had been chosen, the trial began on April 28, 2003, with the opening statement by one of the government's two lawyers, Lauren Resnick. She set the tone of the government's case by first telling the jury: "One of the essential values of the American way of life is the right to be free from physical harm or discrimination on the basis of your race, ethnic background or religious belief." She then said that on August 19, 1991, "our system of law broke down in the Crown Heights section of Brooklyn and for a few hours violence and hatred took over the streets." The rest of her remarks focused on setting out for the jury what the government anticipated proving during the trial. She told them that she expected that the government's evidence would show that after the car accident that killed Gavin Cato, "a gang of angry thugs decided to take the law into their own hands" because "it believed the police reaction to the incident was symptomatic of a larger complaint at the time, that the New York City Police Department favored the Hasidic residents of Crown Heights over the African-American community."

Turning her focus to Yankel Rosenbaum, Resnick told the jury that he "was readily identifiable as Jewish by his beard and his yamulkah," that he "happened to be walking down the wrong street on this very angry night and he paid for it with his life" when the gang saw him, an Orthodox Jew, "and turned its anger and its prejudice on him" by attacking him. She then told the jury that during the attack "the defendant, Lemrick Nelson, a member of that cowardly gang, took a knife from his pocket and stabbed Yankel Rosenbaum, inflicting the wounds that caused Mr. Rosenbaum's tragic death." She described the case as "very straightforward." She explained that the indictment contained only one count: "The defendant, Lemrick Nelson, is charged with attacking Yankel Rosenbaum because of his religion and because of his use of public facilities, in this case, the streets of the City of New York." Finally, Resnick told the jurors that the federal government "takes the lead in these types of cases to make sure that justice is done because violence based upon bigotry is wrong no matter who commits it or who is its victim."

The jurors were riveted as one of Nelson's two lawyers, Richard Jasper, then rose to speak to them. He acknowledged that the attack did indeed take place and that "what happened to Yankel Rosenbaum was horrible and terrible." He also acknowledged that his client had stabbed Rosenbaum. However, he told the jurors that they would hear evidence that Nelson told the detectives that night, right after they had arrested him, that he "was high because I was drinking beer" and that "I stabbed somebody, but not because he was a Jew, 'cause I was drunk, I had been drinking." Jasper explained, therefore, that the case "will not turn upon blood in the pants, or DNA, but on the intent, the why." He concluded his remarks by reminding the jury that the government had the burden of proving that Nelson's conduct was motivated by racial hatred and told the jurors that at the end of the trial "we will be returning to you to ask for a verdict of not guilty of violating Yankel Rosenbaum's civil rights and no intent to prevent him from using the public streets."

The legal beagles weighed in on the defense's strategy. Gerald Shargel—the lawyer who would later represent Peter Gotti—said that in theory admitting to the killing could be a good trial strategy: "If a jury understands that this extra element"—the requirement that the prosecution prove religious animus—"is part of the case, it forces the jury to come to terms with it." Yale Kamisar, a distinguished law professor, commented that the strategy might stop the prosecution from dwelling on evidence that was now uncontested; therefore, it would limit "the powerful evidence that is likely to stir up a jury, that gets them in a surly mood." However, James Orenstein, a former federal prosecutor, questioned the strategy. He thought that it was "always risky to admit the act and contest intent."

The battle lines had been drawn. It remained to see how they would play out during the trial.

349

* * *

The trial was marked by two controversial evidentiary rulings which I had to make. The first required me to decide whether the jury should be permitted to hear evidence that Kings County Hospital, where Rosenbaum was taken after he was stabbed, was ultimately responsible for his death. Rosenbaum had identified Nelson at the scene and was alive when he arrived at the hospital. The doctors were optimistic that he had a good chance to survive. Nelson's lawyers wanted to try to pin the blame for his death on the hospital, contending that it failed to notice and treat a wound in his back. Since the jury would be required to determine if Nelson's attack resulted in Rosenbaum's death, there was some superficial appeal to the defense's position. However, this would require the door to be open to, in effect, trying a medical malpractice case against the hospital. I carefully researched the law and concluded that I would not let that happen. Regardless of what happened at the hospital, the events that led to Rosenbaum's death were triggered by Nelson's stabbing. Under the law, the hospital's alleged negligence was irrelevant to Nelson's criminal culpability. I ruled, therefore, that the government's prosecutors got it right when they argued that medical malpractice would not "relieve an assailant from responsibility for a death resulting from wounds he inflicted during a criminal trial." While the jury knew that Rosenbaum had been taken to the hospital and died there hours later, it would not, therefore, be allowed to hear evidence about the treatment which he received at the hospital.

The second ruling required me to decide whether I should allow the prosecutors to tell the jurors that during the prior federal trial, Nelson's lawyer, Trevor Headley, stated flatly during his opening statement: "The evidence will show, ladies and gentlemen of the jury, that it is not true that Lemrick Nelson stabbed Yankel Rosenbaum." The government contended that the prior denial called into question the credibility of Nelson's claim that he stabbed Rosenbaum because he was drunk and simply got caught up in the excitement. I once again ruled in the government's favor. Headley's

350

statement constituted a judicial admission on behalf of his client. I applied a circuit court of appeals precedent that counseled that it would undermine the function of trials as "truth-seeking proceedings" if defendants were free "to make fundamental changes in the version of facts within their personal knowledge between trials and to conceal these changes from the final trier of fact." The defense was obviously unhappy. It had argued that "[n]either defendant nor his current attorneys should be penalized for misguided or mistaken arguments of his prior counsel."

* * *

The trial only lasted six days, but there were dramatic moments. The government produced witnesses who testified that Nelson attacked Rosenbaum after people had shouted: "There's a Jew. Get the Jew." Others who had witnessed the attack heard Rosenbaum ask Nelson, "Why did you stab me?" The prosecutors also elicited testimony from the detective who spoke to Nelson after he was arrested that although he said "I stabbed him because I was excited and I was drinking a 40-ounce beer," he did not appear drunk.

It seemed to me to be a pretty open and shut case, especially since the defense did not call any witnesses or have Nelson testify. Nonetheless, in his summation, Nelson's other lawyer—Peter Quijano—made the best of it. He did not press the argument that Nelson was drunk when he stabbed Yankel Rosenbaum. Instead, he harped on the law, telling the jury: "The facts of this case simply do not fit the definition of the law. Whatever horrible, senseless, inexcusable thing Lemrick Nelson did to Yankel Rosenbaum, whatever crime he committed that night, it wasn't this crime." Quijano hammered away on the issue of intent. He reminded the jury that the scope of the statute was restricted to acts of force or threat of force that involve two distinct kinds of discriminatory attitudes with respect to the victim: First, a motive or an animus against the victim on account of his race. Second, an intent to act against the victim on account of his using public facilities. Quijano cleverly argued that even if the jury believed that Nelson attacked Rosenbaum because

351

he was a Jew, the government never established that he intended to stab him because he was using the streets.

After the lawyers had summed up, I charged the jury. I carefully explained what the government would have to prove—beyond a reasonable doubt—before the jury could convict Nelson of violating Rosenbaum's civil rights: (1) that the defendant acted by force; (2) that he "injured, intimidated or interfered with Yankel Rosenbaum, or attempted to do so;" (3) that the defendant acted "because Yankel Rosenbaum was a Jewish person and because he was or had been enjoying a facility," namely "the public streets;" (4) that the defendant acted willfully; (5) that "bodily injury to Yankel Rosenbaum resulted."

At the government's request I also told the jury that even if the government did not satisfy its burden of proof with respect to those five elements, it "may nonetheless find the defendant guilty of the crime charged if you find beyond a reasonable doubt that he aided and abetted the commission of the crime." I explained, therefore, that the jury may convict the defendant "if you find beyond a reasonable doubt that the government has proved that another person or persons actually committed the offense with which the defendant is charged, and that the defendant aided or abetted that person or persons in the commission of the offense."

Last, I told the jurors that if they found that Nelson had violated Rosenbaum's civil rights, "either directly or as an aider and abettor," it would then have to answer—as a separate question—whether his actions "resulted in Mr. Rosenbaum's death." In that respect I cautioned the jurors that it "was not necessary for the United States to prove that the defendant intended Mr. Rosenbaum to die as a result of his actions." That was the reason why I would not let the jurors know about the hospital's alleged negligence. I instructed the jurors that they simply had to determine if Rosenbaum's death "was a natural and foreseeable consequence of the defendant's acts."

After deliberating for four days—during which they had sent me a number of notes which indicated to me that they were "muddled and confused"—the jurors sent another note. It gave me a sinking feeling: "We are unable to reach a unanimous verdict." I muttered under my breath: "My God, don't tell me there is going to be yet another trial." There are no limits to the number of times the government can retry a defendant if there is a hung jury. It can keep on trying until it gets a verdict or decides to just give up. The defendant's lawyers asked for a mistrial. I denied it and asked the jurors to tell me "whether there is any profit to continuing your deliberations." They continued deliberating until 4 p.m. and then asked to break for the night. I told them to "have a good night's sleep," avoid talking about the case with friends or loved ones, and not "let personality clashes cloud your assessment of the evidence."

The next day the jury rendered a verdict. It convicted Lemrick Nelson of violating Yankel Rosenbaum's civil rights. However, surprisingly, it found that Nelson's actions did not result in Yankel Rosenbaum's death. Nelson slumped in his chair in apparent relief that the split verdict would spare him from being sentenced for murdering Rosenbaum—and then flashed a broad smile. The outcome—and Nelson's joyful reaction—brought tears to Norman Rosenbaum. He later told the press outside the courtroom: "Him smirking and smiling pains me. He's thumbed his nose at the justice system. We don't see the smile on my brother." Obviously, the mixed verdict did not bring peace to the Rosenbaum family.

* * *

Somehow, shortly after the verdict came down, the *New York Times* found out who the jury forewoman was. She was willing to talk to one of its reporters on condition that her name not be published. He wrote that she told him that the jury cleared Nelson of causing Rosenbaum's death not because of anything that came up at trial, but because jurors knew from old news accounts that Rosenbaum's family had a pending negligence lawsuit against the hospital where he died. "Everybody knew that," she said, and asked rhetorically: "How can you sue Kings County Hospital for negligence and at the same time tell people this guy stabbed him to death." The reporter recounted that I had ruled that the jury could not hear testimony about the hospital's alleged mistreatment of Rosenbaum because under the law it was irrelevant—all that mattered was whether the death was foreseeable—but he commented about the practical realities that face prosecutors in trying a high profile case, especially 12 years after the fact: "Jurors take an oath to try a case solely on the evidence put before them and to disregard anything they have read or heard about it, but some facts are apparently hard to put aside."

The forewoman also told the reporter, however, that the jury did not believe that Nelson was a racist: "He just followed the crowd."

Although I was not happy to learn that the jurors had considered facts that had not been allowed in evidence, I would let the verdict stand. Although juror misconduct could be the basis for setting aside a verdict, it was time to put the Crown Heights riots to rest.

On August 20, 2003, Lemrick Nelson appeared before me to be sentenced. Before rendering the sentence, I listened to Yankel Rosenbaum's mother make another impassioned speech. I choked up. Nelson also spoke. He first apologized to the Rosenbaum family and fessed up—in a way—to his culpability. While he never said that he was the one who had stabbed Rosenbaum, he told them that he was a 16-year-old boy "who made a terrible mistake which eventually led to the unfortunate, untimely and needless death of an innocent, and harmless man." He said, "If there is anything I could do to bring his life back, believe me, I would do it in a heartbeat." He ended his comments by telling me "that there is not a day that goes by that I don't think and I remember that Mr. Rosenbaum lost his life unnecessarily and I realize that is something that I have to carry with me for the rest of my life."

I sentenced Nelson to 10 years. It was the maximum under the law. I could have sentenced him to a lower sentence because the sentencing guidelines range for a civil rights violation not resulting in death was lower. However, under the law, I could upwardly depart to the maximum if I believed that Nelson should be held responsible for Rosenbaum's death. It was an easy call. I determined that Yankel's death "was an actual and foreseeable consequence" of Nelson's acts.

Although I gave Nelson the maximum sentence that I could give under the law, I was vilified by a columnist for the *New York Post*. In his article the next day, Steve Dunleavy wrote that he was "still reeling from the message given by wacky jurors and a judge who sent them up a blind alley." He accused me of opening the door "for the jury to find Nelson not guilty of murder—spitting in the face of a more sensible jurist." I have no idea what he was talking about. The jury was told explicitly that if they found Nelson guilty of violating Rosenbaum's civil rights, which they did, they then had to determine if it was foreseeable that death would result. I had charged the jury correctly on the law. Dunleavy also criticized the fact that I only gave Nelson 10 years. He failed to mention that under the law I had given him the maximum. He concluded his diatribe against me by hoping that I would "sleep well tonight."

There is nothing much a judge can effectively do when he is the target of an irresponsible reporter. He has to simply have a tough exterior and chalk it up to one of the by-products of wearing the robes. However, the danger of this type of news coverage is that the reader is likely to believe it. Because of this, I take pains to tell jurors that they must not always believe what they see in the press. Having Dunleavy's comments in mind, I explain that there are times when the press is just plain wrong, and they must not let what they might happen to read influence their verdict. However, I guess that I should be grateful to Steve Dunleavy. At least he didn't call me Judge Blockhead.

After the sentence, Mayor Bloomberg called Yankel's parents and told them that while he understood their disappointment, his death had led to positive changes because in the aftermath of the riots, the blacks and Jews in the Crown Heights community had made great strides to heal their tensions. I felt the same way.

I also agreed with the sentiments of Alan Vinegrad, who was the U.S. Attorney for the EDNY when Nelson was tried before Judge

Trager. As he wrote in an article published by the *New York Law Journal:*

> Nelson's guilt is clear. But legal scholars and citizens may never agree on whether justice was fully achieved in this case. Viewed one way, Nelson will serve no more than 10 years in jail for a cold-blooded, riotous hate crime perpetrated against an innocent victim and resulting in his death. Viewed more sympathetically, Nelson has spent nearly half of his life on trial and in jail for an offense that he committed just after his 16th birthday in which he never intended to kill his victim and, indeed, would not have killed him, but for inadequate treatment at the hospital. What seems clear, however, is that the criminal justice process has seen far better days than the ones it spent determining the fate of Lemrick Nelson Jr.

* * *

With the passage of time, the events of August 1991 are now history. Soon after Nelson's conviction, Richard E. Green, who then ran the Crown Heights Youth Collective, just as he did that hot summer, aptly noted that for the teenagers in the neighborhood 12 years later, Rosenbaum, Nelson, and Dinkins were all figures from a distant time. "They were babies. They were not cognizant of what happened in 1991. Their concern is their everyday lives."

Happily, there have not been any racial disturbances in New York City since the Crown Heights riots that have been as ferocious or full of such hatred. Moreover, the African American and Hasidic communities have made laudatory efforts to come together as a peaceful community. While the riots may be a distant memory to those who were babies at the time, the trial still looms large in my head. Given its racial overtones and the omnivorous presence of the press, it was the most challenging and difficult trial I have had to manage.

Chapter
7

Terrorism

On March 4, 2010, Imam Ahmad Wais Afzali pled guilty before me for lying to the feds about his relationship with Najibullah Zazi, who had recently pled guilty to participating in an al-Qaeda plot to bomb the New York City subways.

Zazi, a 24-year-old legal immigrant from Afghanistan, had carefully prepared for a terrorist attack. He attended an al-Qaeda training camp in Pakistan, received training in explosives, and stored in his laptop nine pages of instructions for making bombs. Zazi admitted that he drove to New York from Colorado in 2009—a day before the eighth anniversary of 9/11—with explosives from which he would make his bombs. He planned to blow himself up on a crowded subway as soon as the bombs were ready. Attorney General Eric Holder called the case one of the most serious threats to the United States since the 9/11 attacks: "Were it not for the combined efforts of the law enforcement and intelligence communities it could have been devastating," he said. "This attempted attack on our homeland was real, it was in motion, and it would have been deadly."

There had been a number of additional arrests in the case, including Zazi's father, uncle, and two of his classmates at Flushing High School in Queens. As part of his guilty plea, Zazi agreed to cooperate with the government in its ongoing investigation to determine the full extent of the plot and all those who might have been involved.

Zazi was born in 1985 in a small village in Paktia Province in eastern Afghanistan and moved with his parents and siblings to Pakistan when he was seven. In 1999, the family settled in Queens, where he went to high school. He eventually moved to Colorado, where he was employed as a driver for an airport shuttle van.

Zazi told the court during his plea that he had decided to go with friends to Pakistan in August 2008 to join the Taliban in fighting the United States in Afghanistan. While there, after receiving his training in making bombs, he was persuaded by al-Qaeda to return to America to be a suicide bomber. His handlers discussed possible targets, including the New York subway system. Zazi explained that he was willing to blow himself up to bring attention to what the United States military was doing to civilians in Afghanistan "by sacrificing my soul for the sake of saving other souls."

When he came to New York in September 2009, Zazi suspected that he was under surveillance. He decided to abort the operation and flew back to Colorado. He was arrested the following week. Government officials believed that he was tipped off that investigators were asking questions about him. They had been investigating him for some time. However, the feds did not want to arrest him at that time—hoping that he would lead them to many other al-Qaeda operatives in the United States. Since Zazi now knew that the federal government was on his trail, though, the investigation had been compromised, and there was no reason not to arrest him then.

Apparently, it was Imam Afzali who had tipped off Zazi. Standing in front of me in a beige suit and a white skullcap, the imam, who was 39 years old, wiped away tears as he confessed that he had told Zazi that law enforcement officials had inquired about him and that he had lied to the F.B.I. when they asked him whether he did that. He explained that over the past few years he had worked as a liaison between the police department and his community and that the police had asked him for his assistance in providing information about Zazi and two of his friends. He had told them that he had known Zazi and one of the friends—Adis Medunjanin—since they were teenagers. They used to come to his mosque for prayers and volleyball. He told me that "[t]he police interest in these men" led him "to believe that they were involved in some criminal activity," but that he "had no idea of the seriousness."

The imam then laid out the details of his conversation with Zazi:

I had told Najibullah Zazi that law enforcement authorities had been seeing me about him. I told him that I wanted to set up a meeting with the authorities over the next few days. I told him that our phone call was being monitored. I told Zazi do not get involved in Afghanistan garbage, or what's happening in Afghanistan and Iraq garbage, that's my advice to you as an imam.

The imam then said that he believed the F.B.I. "was angry at me for calling Zazi." He then admitted that when he was asked by the government "what I told Zazi about the law enforcement being interested in him, I lied and I said I did not." He said his intention in lying "was not to protect Zazi, but to protect myself." He seemed truly repentant, as he concluded: "I failed to live up to my obligation to this country, to my community, my family, my religion. And I'm truly deeply sorry for what I have done." I believed him and let him stay at liberty pending the sentence—which would not take place for some months.

Never in my wildest imaginings did I ever believe when I first got on the bench—seven years before 9/11—that I would be presiding over a terrorist case.

* * *

Three days after 9/11, President George W. Bush declared a national emergency "by reason of the terrorist attacks at the World Trade Center . . . and the Pentagon, and the continuing and immediate threats of further attacks on the United States." The "war against terrorism" had officially begun. Defense Secretary Donald Rumsfeld explained that it was "a very different kind of war" because "[t]he people we're dealing with have no armies or navies or air force or battle ships or capital cities, even, or high-value targets."

In quick order, Congress enacted a spate of laws to deal with this new, unprecedented threat to our nation's security. Four stand out. Two were enacted within days of 9/11; the third 14 months later, and the fourth in 2008.

On September 18, 2001, only seven days after the twin towers were destroyed, Congress enacted a joint resolution entitled "Authorization for Use of Military Force." It authorized the President "to use all necessary force against those nations, organizations, or persons he determines planned, authorized, committed, or aided the terrorist attacks that occurred on September 11, 2011, or harbored such organization or persons, in order to prevent any future acts of international terrorism against the United States by such nations, organizations or persons."

The most comprehensive of all of the post-September 11 legislative enactments was the USA PATRIOT Act, which President Bush signed into law on October 26, 2001. A *New York Times* article described its passage as "the climax of a remarkable 18-hour period in which both the House and the Senate adopted complex, far-reaching anti-terrorism legislation with little debate in an atmosphere of edgy alarm, as federal law enforcement officials warned that another attack could be imminent."

The declared purpose of the USA PATRIOT Act was "[t]o deter and punish terrorists in the United States and around the world [and] to enhance law enforcement investigatory tools." When signing the bill, the President remarked:

> We're dealing with terrorists who operate by highly sophisticated methods and technologies, some of which were not even available when our existing laws were written. The bill before me takes account of the new realities and dangers posed by modern terrorists. It will help law enforcement to identify, to dismantle, to disrupt and to punish terrorists before they strike.

The Act is complex. It adds 300 pages to the United States Code and amends 15 statutes. Its contents can roughly be categorized as falling into five main areas: (1) provisions creating new terrorism-related crimes; (2) provisions relating to the treatment of foreign terrorist organizations; (3) provisions expanding the government's authority to search for evidence of crime; (4) provisions facilitating interagency sharing of information, and (5) provisions relating to funding. As I sifted through the Act, a few key provisions caught my interest.

As for the terrorism-related crimes, the Act included within its criminal grasp—and provided for severe punishment for—attacks against "mass transportation systems"; bulk cash smuggling; cyberterrorism; and the possession of certain kinds of biological agents. The assets of groups engaged in planning or perpetrating domestic or international terrorism could also be seized.

As for searches, the Act caught up with digital-age technology, permitting officers to obtain search warrants to seize voice and electronic mail and track Internet use. In that respect, the Act expanded the use of "pen registers"—devices that capture outgoing information, such as telephone numbers—by specifying that their use was not limited to telephone lines, but could, for example, be used to monitor e-mail. The Justice Department claims that these devices allowed its investigators to trace communications to terrorist conspirators and to obtain valuable information concerning the kidnaping and murder of *Wall Street Journal* reporter Daniel Pearl.

Prior to September 11, there were only limited mechanisms permitting law enforcement officials to share important information, particularly foreign intelligence information. Many believed that if there had been better coordination amongst the country's many law enforcement agencies of various bits and pieces about the 9/11 terrorists' activities before they struck, then the attacks could have been nipped in the bud. The Act facilitated cooperation and sharing among the government agencies involved in ferreting out terrorist activities. For example, it provided for greater access to the National Crime Information Center, which, according to the Department of Justice, was "the nation's principal law enforcement automated information sharing pool." Since enactment of the Act, the F.B.I. has provided the State Department with millions of records and has furnished the Immigration and Naturalization Service with information regarding military detainees in Afghanistan, Pakistan, and Guantanamo Bay.

The third key piece of legislation that Congress enacted soon after 9/11 was the Homeland Security Act, which President Bush signed into law on November 25, 2001. It created the Department of Homeland Security. Among the primary missions of the new department were to "prevent terrorist attacks within the United States, reduce the vulnerability of the United States to terrorism, minimize the damage, and assist in the recovery, from terrorist attacks that do occur in the United States," and to act "as a focal point regarding natural and manmade crises and emergency planning." To achieve those ends, the Department would assume control over a number of federal agencies—including the Coast Guard, Customs Service, Immigration and Naturalization Service, and Border Patrol—and would consolidate their functions into four "Directorates": Science and Technology; Information Analysis and Infrastructure Protection; Border and Transportation Security; and Emergency Preparedness and Response.

The fourth key piece of legislation that Congress enacted occurred on July 8, 2008. It changed the landscape for wiretap searches. In 1978, Congress had passed the Foreign Intelligence Surveillance Act (FISA) in response to revelations of widespread abuse of government wiretaps. The law governed the surveillance of people in the United States for the purpose of collecting intelligence related to foreign powers. A special secret court, known as the FISA court, was created to hear requests for such warrants. Safeguards were put in place to ensure that investigators pursuing criminal matters did not obtain warrants under FISA that they could not get from an ordinary judge—but that was all before 9/11.

Weeks after the September 11 attacks, President Bush secretly authorized the National Security Agency (NSA) to wiretap international communications of Americans suspected of links to al-Qaeda without first getting approval from even the FISA court. He believed that this eavesdropping fell within his war powers, buttressed by Congress' September 2001 resolution authorizing him to wage war on terrorist organizations. This covert practice was discovered and disclosed by the *New York Times* four years later. Administration officials argued that working under FISA would have been too cumbersome and time consuming. They reasoned that rights of privacy had to give way to warrantless wiretaps whenever there was any risk that delay might result in another terrorist attack on American soil. According to the *Times* article, the NSA was monitoring up to 500 people within the United States and another 5,000 to 7,000 people overseas at any given time—without obtaining any search warrants.

Soon more than 40 lawsuits were "churning through federal courts, charging AT&T, Verizon, and other major carriers with violating customers' privacy by conducting wiretaps at the White House's direction without court orders." The public disclosure of the secret wiretapping program set off a fierce national debate over the balance between protecting the country from another terrorist strike and ensuring civil liberties.

The law that Congress passed in the wake of this debate granted immunity from suit to the phone companies. The bill also gave the executive branch broader latitude in eavesdropping on people abroad and at home—without first obtaining a search warrant—if it believed that they were tied to terrorism. In effect, Congress overhauled the Foreign Intelligence Surveillance Act to bring federal statutes into closer alignment with what the Bush administration had been secretly doing.

In sum, during the 10-year aftermath of 9/11, the United States became legislatively armed to combat the unprecedented new breed of terrorists that were committed to destroying our country. Not the least of which was the USA PATRIOT Act's requirement that the intelligence agencies share information with each other. In 2009, the Assistant Attorney General for National Security, Lisa Monaco, told NPR in a written statement that the ability of F.B.I. and intelligence analysts to work together helped the country move quickly in September of that year to find the man trying to target the New York City subway system. If not for that, I would not be sentencing

Imam Afzali for the role which he played in alerting Najibullah Zazi that the feds were on his tail.

* * *

I sentenced Afzali on April 14, 2010. One of the prosecutors, Jeffrey Knox, told me that the imam was "almost certainly" unaware of the seriousness of his conduct. Knox had contended, however, in a letter that he had written to me, that "Afzali is many things, but naive is not one of them." He wrote that the imam "knew that what he did was wrong, and that is the reason why he hid it from the N.Y.P.D. and later lied about it to the F.B.I." Nevertheless, the government did not view him as a terrorist and did not ask that he be sentenced to jail. It was content to let him "self-deport" to a country of his choosing; although he had lived here since he was a child, he never became a citizen.

Afzali's lawyer was Ron Kuby. For years he had been associated with the renowned civil rights lawyer William Kuntsler, who had represented the notorious Chicago Seven and many radical clients. After Kuntsler died, Kuby continued the controversial work of his late mentor. He won a judgment of $43 million against Bernhard Goetz, won a release for two men imprisoned for 13 years for a murder which they did not commit, got a reversal of a murder conviction for a mentally ill homeless man who had accidentally caused the death of a firefighter, and won close to a million dollars for another wrongfully convicted man who had spent eight years in prison. He was a zealous advocate who did not mince words when he was championing the rights of the underdogs. He had been described as "the last of the in-your-face leftist lawyers." He brought something different to the bar: He lived modestly in a 850-square-foot co-op on the Lower East Side and took on causes for many clients who could not afford to pay him.

While Kuby was often accused of playing to the press and of being abrasive, I always found him polite and professional. He had tried a drug case before me some years ago and did an excellent job representing his client. On this occasion he spoke to me about how the imam had been working together with the police for many years because he loved the United States: It was "the country that took him and his family in when they were refugees from Afghanistan from the Soviet invasion." Kuby concluded his remarks by exhorting me not to put his client in jail because his deportation would be sufficient punishment: He would never be able to return, and "[h]e'll be leaving his elderly parents behind, he'll leave his children behind, and certainly his father he may never see again."

For its part, the government acknowledged at the sentencing that Azali never realized "the full seriousness of his conduct," and although he had lied to the F.B.I., the government was satisfied that deportation would indeed be an appropriate punishment. I agreed. The imam would have 90 days to leave the country. Before I rendered the official sentence, the imam spoke: "I'm standing in front of you as a convicted felon, a lying imam, which is a physical, emotional and spiritual burden far greater than any sentence you could impose." He added: "Honest to God, it was never my intention to help those idiots for what they do in the name of Islam."

Afterwards he told the press outside the courthouse that he wondered which country would have him: "Anywhere I go I'm going to be known as the imam that worked with the American government, guy used, abused and kicked out. What country would take me?"

Saudi Arabia did. Eighty days later Ahmad Wais Afzali, dressed in a flowing white robe with black and beige trim, entered the security line at JFK with his wife, Fatima. In their hands were one-way tickets for a 2 p.m. flight to Riyadh—the capital of that country.

* * *

Zazi has yet to be sentenced. In the meantime, on July 18, 2011, his father, Mohammed Wali Zazi, was convicted in a jury trial before my colleague, Judge Gleeson, for lying to agents, encouraging others to lie, and forming and carrying out a plan to destroy evidence that his son had left behind in a relative's garage in Colorado—including solvents, chemicals, masks, and goggles. Although

Mohammed's son did not testify against his father, other relatives did. His brother-in-law, Najib Jali, said that Zazi's father was among five people who planned to dispose of the bomb-making materials.

Jali had pled guilty to conspiring to obstruct justice and had signed a cooperation agreement. Another cooperating witness, Amanullah Zazi—the defendant's nephew—had also pled guilty to that charge and testified that he destroyed evidence at his uncle's direction.

The successful prosecution of the imam and those who were planning to blow up New York City's subways was yet another example of how the federal courts were relied on by the government as the principal forum for successfully prosecuting terrorists. Although the recent public reaction to holding the trial of the principal planner of the 9/11 attacks, Khalid Shaikh Mohammed, and four cohorts in the Manhattan federal courthouse fueled concerns about whether the courts are capable of handling terrorist trials, statistics compiled by the New York University School of Law's Center on Law and Security since 9/11 in a *Terrorist Trial Report Card* have shown that they are.

As recounted in the report, from September 11, 2001 to September 11, 2011, there were approximately 300 prosecutions in the federal courts related to jihadist terror or national security charges. Almost all resulted in convictions. The most serious ones occurred since 2009. They included, in addition to Zazi; Faisal Shahzad, the "Times Square Bomber"; Umar Farouk Abdulmutallah, the "Christmas Day Bomber" who attempted to blow up a plane over Detroit; David Coleman Headley, an American-born operative with Lashkar-e-Taiba who conspired in the 2008 Mumbai attack and was arrested after also plotting an attack against a Danish newspaper; Major Nidal Hasan, the Fort Hood shooter who killed 13 soldiers; Carlos Bledsoe, a Muslim convert who wounded one soldier and killed another at an Army recruiting station; and, most recently, Ahmad Khalfan Ghailani, who was sentenced to life for his role in the 1998 bombings of two United States Embassies in East Africa. He was, however, the only one who had been imprisoned at Guantanamo Bay.

The report ended with a strong endorsement of the federal judicial system's ability to handle terrorist trials:

> Over time, the strategy of federal terrorism prosecutions has become more confident and focused, buttressed by a strong record of convictions and the fact that no major terrorist attack has followed 9/11. Perhaps, over the next decade, the record of prosecutorial success demonstrated in this Report will lead to an increased political and popular faith in the justice system's ability to protect the public safety as well as individual civil liberties.

Nevertheless, the five planners of the 9/11 attacks—who were also held at Guantanamo Bay—probably will not be tried in the federal courts. Although that was supposed to be, the Obama administration backed off in response to a huge public outcry that their trial would bring traffic to a standstill and cause all sorts of logistical and safety problems. Many of the critics proposed that they be tried by a military commission, and Congress voted to impose strict new limits on transferring detainees out of Guantanamo Bay, dealing a major blow to President Obama's vows to shut down the prison and give federal court trials to many of the detainees—who had been kept there for years in legal limbo. Because of the many reports of abuses and the failure of the government to give the detainees judicial redress, Guantanamo Bay had become a black eye to the American system of justice.

As recently as April 2011, 172 of the more than 700 original detainees were still housed at Guantanamo Bay. They were considered to be the "worst of the worst." The others had been repatriated over the years. One reputable study by a professor from Seton Hall University concluded that 55% of the detainees were not suspected of having committed any hostile acts against the United States and that 60% were only accused of being "associated with" terrorists, the lowest categorization available. The study revealed that 86% were captured either by the Northern Alliance or by Pakistan soon

367

after 9/11 "at a time in which the United States offered large bounties for capture of suspected enemies."

The creation of military commissions was the handiwork of President Bush. In November 2001, he announced his intention to try those captured in the "war on terror" and sent to the Guantanamo Bay prison in these newly created forums. Their protocols bore little resemblance to the procedural protections afforded by federal courts. The judge and the jurors were all military officers; only two-thirds of the jury were needed to convict; hearsay testimony was permissible; evidence obtained without a search warrant was admissible, as well as incriminating statements obtained without *Miranda* warnings. Because of their controversial nature, very few commission prosecutions have actually taken place; according to the military commission's website, as of 2011 only three had been completed.

When, if ever, the Guantanamo Bay prison will be closed and the remaining prisoners will be prosecuted—and where—remains up in the air.

* * *

In addition to the imam, I had another terrorist case to handle—and it was truly up in the air.

On August 22, 2004, weeks away from the third anniversary of 9/11, Tarik Farag and Amro Elmasry, both Arabs, flew from San Diego to JFK on American Airlines Flight 236. When they landed in New York, they had a little surprise waiting for them. They were greeted by 10 armed police officers in SWAT gear with shotguns and police dogs, ordered to raise their hands, frisked, handcuffed, and taken to a police station, where they were placed in jail cells. Farag and Elmasry were, in effect, arrested. Unbeknownst to them, two counterterrorism agents happened to also be on the plane and suspected that they were terrorists.

They were anything but. Farag, 36, was a retired New York City police officer and was then employed by the United States Bureau of Prisons as a corrections offer. Elmasry, 37, held a high position with General Electric. What they had in common was that they were both born in Egypt and were best friends. Farag had come to the United States when he was five and later became an American citizen. Elmasry was an Egyptian citizen, but he had a valid Unites States visa. He was employed in Egypt by General Electric as an area sales manager for its Africa-East Mediterranean region.

Farag and Elmasry were released from prison after they were interrogated for four hours. They then sued the United States and the two agents for monetary damages for false arrest. The government asked me to dismiss the case. The material facts were not in dispute. I had to decide if under the Fourth Amendment's proscription against unreasonable searches and seizures there was probable cause for the agents to cause the plaintiffs to be arrested. Under the law, probable cause would exist if the two agents had "knowledge or reasonably trustworthy information of facts and circumstances that are sufficient to warrant a person of reasonable caution in the belief that the person to be arrested had committed or is committing a crime." The Government contended that there was probable cause to believe that Farag and Elmasry had been conducting terrorist surveillance or probing operations.

There wasn't any. The Government trotted out a number of innocuous things in an effort to convince me otherwise. Its main argument was that Elmasry—who was sitting behind Farag—was talking loudly to Farag across the aisle over the heads of other passengers in a mixture of English and Arabic and otherwise was calling attention to himself by talking to the stewardess to change his seat so that he could sit closer to Farag. The agents also thought that it was suspicious that Elmasry looked at his watch upon take-off, landing, and at various other times during the flight, and that he deleted five or six telephone numbers from his cellular phone while he waited for the plane to reach the gate after it had landed.

In a written decision, I wrote that "the heavy reliance" which the Government placed on Elmasry's conduct was "counterintuitive" because "it simply made no sense that if Elmasry were a terrorist he would speak 'loudly' across the aisle to his companion," and talk to the flight attendant to change his seat. I reasoned that "[w]hat terrorist engaged in surveillance activity would behave so conspicuously? One would expect that such activity would be characterized by secrecy."

As for Elmasry looking at his watch during takeoff and at other times, I wrote that "the proportion of airline passengers who do this is probably higher than the proportion who do not." As for the deletion of the telephone numbers, I concluded that it was "utter speculation" because the Government did not assert "that Elmasry made any telephone calls during or after the flight, and the record gives no indication that Elmasry suspected he was about to be caught sufficient to imbue his acts with a suggestion of guilt."

The Government argued, however, that the plaintiffs' Arab ethnicity and use of the Arabic language were relevant factors in the probable cause calculus because "all of the persons who participated in the 9/11 attacks were Middle Eastern males" and "the United States continues to face a very real threat of domestic terrorism from Islamic terrorists." I rejected the argument. I immersed myself in searching for precedents and concluded that "[a]lthough the question whether race or ethnicity may be used as one factor among others in evaluating reasonable suspicion or probable cause (outside of the identification scenario, and absent any compelling statistical evidence) remains unresolved by either the Supreme Court or the Second Circuit, there is a significant body of pre-9/11 precedent concluding that race is not indicative of criminal propensity." I concluded:

> The Court fully recognizes the gravity of the situation that confronts investigative officials of the United States as a consequence of the 9/11 attack, and that the mind-set of airline travelers has understandably been altered by 9/11. This justifiable apprehension must be assuaged by ensuring that security is strictly enforced, and by the passage of time without, hopefully, other episodic affronts to our country; but fear cannot be a factor to allow for the evisceration of the bedrock principle of our Constitution that no one can be arrested without probable cause that a crime has been committed."

The next day the *New York Times* reported my decision and quoted the associate director of the New York Civil Liberties Union: "This case is important because, for the first time, a federal court has squarely rejected the claim that Arabs can be stopped and detained as suspected terrorists because of their race. Hopefully this will mark a turning point in the ethnic profiling that has pervaded law enforcement in the aftermath of 9/11." I knew, however, that not everyone would be happy with my decision. Sure enough, a blogger—the Angry White Dude—expressed the sentiments which others might share:

> Political correctness has killed common sense. I don't believe in giving my enemy first shot on me. I trust people until they prove they cannot be trusted. Muslims fall into that category. Must we lose even more thousands in the next terrorist attack before common sense again sets in? Or are we too far gone?

He concluded his comments by taking a shot at me and my masculinity: "Judge Block, I hope your next flight is with the Iran Males Choir."

The Angry White Dude would be happy to know that soon after I had sentenced the imam, I was placed on the Terrorist Watch List. I found that out when I went to JFK a week later to fly to San Francisco to sit as a visiting judge on the Ninth Circuit Court of Appeals. When I went to check in, the guy behind the JetBlue ticket counter did a double take after he put my name into the computer. He told me that he could not give me my boarding pass. I was taken to a little office around the corner where a Homeland Security officer was sitting behind a small desk. I showed him my official judge's credentials and asked him "what the heck was going on."

He seemed puzzled and left the room to speak to someone. When he returned, he told me that I was cleared to go and gave me a form to fill out if I wanted to find out why I had been put on the Terrorist Watch List. I didn't have time to do it since I was more concerned about missing my plane—I just made it. From speaking to some law enforcement officers after I returned from California, my best guess is that the folks who compile the Terrorist Watch List check

371

out the newspapers. Apparently when my name was linked to Zazi in an article that the *New York Times* had written when I sentenced the imam, it got me on the list. They never stopped to read that I was the judge—not the terrorist.

* * *

The Government did not appeal my decision granting judgment for Farag and Elmasry. I'm confident that it knew that it was correct. It settled the case for $75,000. However, I realized that the passengers on that airplane were probably happy that the agents did what they did; better safe than sorry. I also recognized that the case reflected the understandable, growing tension between the fears engendered by post 9/11 domestic terrorism and the preservation of our cherished civil liberties. Nonetheless, I would have compromised my oath of office if I had not applied the law. There was simply no legal basis to arrest the two Arabs.

Chapter
8

Foreign Affairs

We are now living in a truly global world. Nowhere is this more evident than in the cases that now come before the federal courts which had their origins in foreign lands. I've had my share.

In the first one—and biggest—I was a bit player. In late 1996 and early 1997, class action lawsuits were brought by victims of the Holocaust against Swiss banks. The plaintiffs, who sued in behalf of all of the victims, alleged that they were subjected to persecution by the Nazis, including genocide, the wholesale and systematic looting of personal and business property, and slave labor. They charged the Swiss banks with knowingly retaining and concealing the assets of Holocaust victims, accepting and laundering illegally obtained Nazi loot, and transacting in the profits of slave labor. The plaintiffs asked for a wide range of relief, including a full accounting by the banks, as well as compensatory and punitive damages. It was heady stuff. Forty years after the end of World War II, the Swiss banks were being accused in my courthouse of being in league with the Nazis; and the plaintiffs wanted a United States federal court to hold them accountable.

The case was randomly assigned to Judge Bartels, who was then 99 years old. He had been appointed to the bench by President Eisenhower in 1959, the same year that I graduated from law school, and was still functioning as a district court judge almost 40 years later. He had been persuaded by his colleagues to stop handling criminal cases when he was 95, but was still in the civil assignment wheel. Judge Bartels was still in control of his faculties but realized that he would not survive the litigation. He thought that Judge Korman would be the ideal judge to take it over, and instructed his clerk, Mike Innelli, to have the case reassigned to him. He was right.

Judge Bartels died shortly afterwards—just months shy of his 100th birthday—soon after the voluminous Holocaust litigation file had been dropped off in Judge Korman's chambers. In May 1997, just three months after Judge Bartels had been laid to rest, the Swiss banks filed a host of motions before Judge Korman trying to deep-six the litigation. They argued that the plaintiffs had failed to state a claim under Swiss and international law, failed to join indispensable parties, lacked personal and subject-matter jurisdiction, and lacked standing. They also argued that Switzerland, not the United States, was the proper forum to adjudicate all of these issues. In other words, they tried to put every conceivable legal roadblock in the path of the plaintiffs' efforts to have a United States district court judge resolve the litigation.

While all of these motions were pending, the Swiss government recognized that the international community was not taking kindly to the Swiss banks' intransigence. The Swiss were being viewed as virtual Nazi collaborators. Typical of the negative press their banks were receiving were the comments of one of the lead lawyers for the plaintiffs, as reported in *The Washington Post* soon after the litigation had been started:

> The accountability of the Swiss banks is tied directly to the history of the immoral origins of the illegal monies they accepted, deposited and disposed of on behalf of and in collaboration with their German partners. Knowing participation in the disposal and concealment of Jewish and other assets systematically looted or the profits of slave labor, both part of a systematic program of extermination, is not the business of banking. It is an offense against humanity.

The Swiss were also aware that the "Volcker Report" was nearing completion and would soon be released. It would mark the completion of an extensive, three-year study by an independent committee chaired by the renowned economist Paul A. Volcker that had been established in May 1996 by the Swiss Bankers Association, the World Jewish Congress, and other Jewish organizations to conduct an audit of the Swiss banks to identify accounts from the World War II era that could possibly belong to victims of Nazi persecution. Rather than wait for the completion of the Volcker committee's report—which would reveal that approximately 54,000 Swiss bank accounts had a "probable" or "possible" connection to a Holocaust victim—the Swiss banks thought that it was provident to try to resolve the litigation.

The settlement stage had also been set when in 1997 New York City threatened to boycott Swiss banks after a Swiss security guard discovered and saved from a shredding machine a trove of documents detailing Nazi and other wartime bank accounts. Scores of cities, states, and other entities vowed to join the boycott.

In August 1998, the Swiss banks reached an informal agreement to settle the case for $1.25 billion.

It was up to Judge Korman to decide whether to approve the proposed settlement agreement. It provided that the monies would be paid to five different classes of victims: (1) Deposited Assets Class; (2) Looted Assets Class; (3) Slave Labor Class I; (4) Slave Labor Class II; (5) Refugee Class. These five classes were to cover, therefore, the victims or targets of Nazi persecution who had assets on deposit with any Swiss bank, had artwork and other assets looted by the Nazis from nonbanking Swiss entities, had performed slave labor for companies that had deposited proceeds in Swiss banks, or were mistreated by the Swiss when they sought refuge from the Nazis. Those eligible victims would be all of the victims of Nazi persecution falling within those classes, including—in addition to Jews—gypsies, Jehovah's Witnesses, and gays and lesbians.

Judge Korman conducted a "fairness hearing," after making extraordinary efforts to reach as many potential claimants as humanly possible. This included notice in over 500 worldwide newspapers and the sending of more than 1.4 million notice packages—explaining the settlement terms and the claims process—

directly to potential class members in at least 48 countries. Thousands responded. Judge Korman considered all of the responses, and amendments to the proposed settlement agreement were made. Finally, on July 26, 2000, in a comprehensive written decision, he gave the final product his blessing. He also appointed Judah Gribetz as special master "to develop a proposed plan of allocation and distribution of the Settlement Fund, employing open and equitable procedures to ensure fair consideration of all proposals for allocation and distribution." Governor Carey's former counsel—and the one person perhaps most responsible for me becoming a federal judge—would have to figure out who would actually get the money.

Judah Gribetz was eminently qualified to take on this daunting task. As Judge Korman pointed out in his decision, he had a "deep understanding of all issues related to the Holocaust," and had "contributed his time and energy to charitable and community organizations too numerous to recite." He has devoted himself over the past decade to processing claims from hundreds of thousands of victims throughout the world. Almost all of the settlement funds have now been distributed. In total, 453,523 claimants have received money. About 60% of the fund (about $710 million) has gone to those who were able to lay claim to monies deposited in the Swiss banks. The remainder went mostly to the looted class claimants ($205 million) and slave labor claimants (about $290 million).

However, as a spokesperson for the Conference on Jewish Material Claims—Alissa Kaplan—aptly put it: "In terms of justice, which is very, very important, no amount of money can ever make good again." As she added: "When you hear about the Swiss bank settlement, it's a lot of money, but no one gets rich off it. There are Holocaust survivors living in extreme poverty and still suffering. It's very, very badly needed."

* * *

Since he took over the case from Judge Bartels 15 years ago, Judge Korman continues to preside over every facet of the case. He has poured over thousands of documents and has written eight opinions. His brilliant handling of the lawsuit has been the singular challenge and achievement of his outstanding judicial career. The circuit court has given him kudos for "the thoughtful analysis and scrupulous fairness" with which he "has approached every step of this litigation." Senator Moynihan obviously made the right choice in picking him for the judgeship back in 1985.

As for my small role, I had to decide two issues which Judge Korman thought that he should not handle. The first was whether the settlement funds should bear simple or compound interest while they were sitting in an escrow account awaiting distribution. The settlement agreement had provided that the funds would be deposited into the escrow account in four stages, and that the banks would pay interest while the claims were being processed and the monies distributed. It was anticipated that this could—and it did—take years. However, while the agreement provided for the percentage of the interest, it was inadvertently silent as to whether it would be compound or simple interest. The parties estimated that the difference would be about $4.8 million. I decided that compound interest was warranted.

The other issue involved the compensation for the lawyer whom Judge Korman engaged to assist him in the resolution of many difficult decisions that he had to make in determining how the monies should be distributed. Judge Korman had favored the poor, most of whom resided in the former Soviet Union, over the wealthier claimants, most of whom lived in the United States. This spawned a great deal of controversy. Judge Korman relied on the skills of his hand-picked lawyer to help him deal with this issue—and many other contentious ones. The lawyer had submitted a significant bill for his services. Judge Korman thought that it was best for another judge to decide his compensation.

The Holocaust litigation was a historic example of the reach of the federal courts into the world beyond our domestic borders. I was happy to be a small part of that history.

* * *

I used to believe that the federal courts handled every type of case except family matters—such as divorces and child custody cases—which were the exclusive province of the state courts. However, when I had my first Hague Convention trial, I realized that there was one exception—child abduction cases.

Iris and Mattiyahu Elyashiv were Israeli citizens and had lived there all of their lives. They had three young children. Mrs. Elyashiv, however, was tired of allegedly being in an abusive relationship and escaped to Brooklyn to live with her sister. She took the kids with her and refused to return them. Mr. Elyashiv didn't care if his wife never came back, but he wanted his kids. He got a lawyer from New York and sued his wife in my court under the Hague Convention for abducting his children.

Child abduction cuts two ways: children are abducted from other nations into the United States and vice versa. As recently as 2009, the State Department received that year 1,135 requests for assistance in the return of 1,621 children to the United States from other countries. On the other side of the ledger, there were 324 applications during 2009 from Hague Convention partners concerning abductions to the United States involving 454 children.

The abduction of children is not a new problem. In 1998 Jesse Helms, then chairman of the Senate Foreign Relations Committee, decried "the failure by the United States to initiate vigorously diplomatic and law enforcement tools seeking the return of these children," and then Senator-Biden branded the act of abducting a child across international borders "a heinous crime." Nonetheless, an increasing number of child abductions are reported every year as binational marriages become more common in an era of globalization. For example, there are a number of cases where Japanese mothers were living in the United States—after having married American servicemen—but returned to Japan with their children and kept their fathers from having contact with them.

The most notorious opposite case, where a child was brought into the United States, is the saga of Elian Gonzalez, which captivated the public back in 1999. Elian was the five-year-old boy whose mother fled Cuba with him in a small, overloaded, 17-foot boat that sunk while the boat people tried to navigate the Florida Straits to escape from Castro's repressive regime. Elian's mother drowned, but he miraculously clung to an inner tube for two days until fishermen found him and brought him to American soil. The case created an emotional stir. Elian's relatives in Florida wanted him to stay with them. The boy's uncle, Lazaro Gonzalez, expressed their sentiments: "His mother was bringing him to freedom, and we don't want him to go back to a Communist system." Nevertheless, Elian's father—who lived in Cárdenas, Cuba—was a loving, caring father and wanted his son back.

The State Department agreed that the boy had to be returned. As Attorney General Reno stated: "The law is very clear. A child who has lost his mother belongs with his sole surviving parent, especially with one who has shared a close and a continuous relationship with his son." The Attorney General was moved by her meeting with Elian's father—who had come to the United States to bring his son home—which had ended with a hug between them. As she described it: "All you had to do was listen to him and look at him and see how much he obviously loves this little boy." Elian, now a teenager, lives today with his father in Cuba.

Although, unlike the United States, Cuba is not a signatory to the Hague Convention, Elian's return to Cuba by the United States was in keeping with the Convention's underlying purpose: to bring about the prompt return of children who have been wrongfully removed from or wrongfully retained outside the country of their "habitual residence" in violation of the left-behind parent's (LBP's) rights of custody.

* * *

The Hague Convention is the product of a treaty currently subscribed to by the United States and 68 other countries. Concluded in 1980, it has proven to be the most effective tool available for LBPs to reunite with their abducted children. It requires each country to provide for a judicial or administrative mechanism for determining whether the child has been wrongfully abducted and should be returned. The United States has placed this responsibility in the laps of the federal judicial system. A district court judge—after a full hearing—makes the decision, subject to appeal to the circuit court of appeals.

The decision in an abduction case is not to be confused with custody cases where the court has to determine what is in the "best interests" of the child. That determination must be made in the country where the child had resided. The law is clear that a custody determination would be "contrary to a primary purpose of the Convention to preserve the status quo and to deter parents from crossing international boundaries in search of a more sympathetic court."

The court's sole role in an abduction case is to determine whether the child was "habitually resident" in the LBP's country and that the LBP had—and was exercising—custodial rights under the law of that country at the time when the child was abducted. If so, the child must be returned unless the abducting parent can establish one of five reasons why that should not be the case: (1) more than a year has elapsed since the child was wrongfully removed, and "the child is now settled in his new environment"; (2) the LBP had acquiesced in the child's removal; (3) "there is a grave risk that [the child's] return would expose the child to physical or psychological harm or otherwise place the child in an intolerable situation"; (4) "the child objects to being returned and has attained an age and degree of maturity at which it is appropriate to take account of its views"; and (5) the return of the child "would not be permitted by the fundamental principles . . . relating to the protection of human rights and fundamental freedoms."

The Elyashiv case was one of three abduction cases that have come before me. Because of the profound effect of my decision on the children and their parents, I agonized over these cases. In one of the cases the mother may never see her child again. I hope I got them right.

* * *

I allowed Iris Elyashiv to let her three kids stay in the U.S. I concluded that although the children had been "habitual residents" of Israel and that their father had not relinquished his custodial rights, they would be at "grave risk" if they were returned to him.

Both parents testified at the hearing I conducted. Mrs. Elyashiv testified in person. Thanks to modern technology, Mr. Elyashiv testified via video hookup from Israel. Mrs. Elyashiv's brother-in-law and a friend also testified, as well as a child psychiatrist retained by her as an expert. The children, who were then 14, 11, and eight, had been living in Brooklyn for over a year, were in school, and were happy to be in our country with their mother.

Mrs. Elyashiv had been a chemistry professor at an Israeli university. Her husband earned his living as a martial arts instructor. Mrs. Elyashiv testified at length to being subjected to severe domestic violence throughout the couple's almost 20-year marriage. She also testified that her husband would beat the two oldest kids. Not surprisingly, Mr. Elyashiv denied all of her accusations and portrayed himself as a loving, caring parent. I had to determine which parent to believe.

Making credibility determinations is one of the most challenging aspects of a judge's job. When you listen to diametrically opposite testimony, there is simply no surefire way of knowing whom to believe. I believed Mrs. Elyashiv, and I am confident that I made the right call. I was aided greatly by the psychiatrist's testimony, which convinced me that Mrs. Elyashiv had all of the classic symptoms of a battered wife. The psychiatrist had also interviewed the children and reported that the two oldest told her that they were hit by their martial arts father.

In the final analysis, however, I found Mr. Elyashiv's wholesale denial of any abuse of his wife "simply not credible," which colored the rest of his testimony. He described his relationship with his wife as "li[ving] in wonderful harmony," but he admitted that he had had a long-standing affair during the marriage.

I also found his denial of abusing the children equally suspect. The psychiatrist, who had spent two hours interviewing Mr. Elyashiv, found his "presentation was entirely consistent with those of parents who are chronically abusive." I concluded that the children would be at "grave risk" if I sent them back to their father.

* * *

I did not let Evans Tayson's infant child stay with him in the United States, however, after he refused to return him to his mother in London. Here the issue was whether the child was "habitually resident" in England at the time that his father brought him here. The child was not at grave risk if she were returned to her mother, and there were no other reasons to allow the father to keep her here. The Hague Convention did not define "habitual residence," but the Second Circuit Court of Appeals—in a different case—had articulated the standard which I was bound to apply:

> First, the court should inquire into the shared intent of those entitled to fix the child's residence (usually the parents) at the latest time that their intent was shared. In making this determination the court should look, as always in determining intent, at actions as well as declarations. Normally the shared intent of the parents should control the habitual residence of the child. Second, the court should inquire whether the evidence unequivocally points to the conclusion that the child has acclimated to [a] new location and thus has acquired a new habitual residence, notwithstanding any conflict with the parents' latest shared intent.

It was not easy to decide where the child was habitually resident. The couple was married in London but within the year relocated to the United States, where their daughter was born seven months later. The child remained in the United States for approximately one year, living with her parents in New Jersey. However, Mr. Tayson allowed his wife to take the baby to live with her maternal grandmother in Ghana. The parents' marriage was apparently on the rocks, and they would get divorced a few years later. In the meantime, Mr. Tayson stayed in the U.S.A., and Mrs. Tayson returned to London. The child was raised in Ghana by her grandmother for several years. Mrs. Tayson visited her daughter once a year. Mr. Tayson did not visit her but occasionally spoke to her via telephone.

Eventually, Mrs. Tayson brought the child to live with her in London. She would not let her ex-husband know where they were living or have any contact with his child. Mr. Tayson eventually found out where they were and went to London to see his daughter. Initially, he accused his ex-wife of kidnaping her, but calmed down when she agreed to let the child visit him in the United States for the Christmas holiday. Once he got her here, he would not let her go back. He contended that his daughter wanted to live with him in the United States. Mrs. Tayson asked me to order him to send their daughter back to London.

I decided that the parties only had a shared intent that the child would be brought up by her grandmother in Ghana. However, she was no longer habitually resident in Ghana, and there was little evidence that the parties had a new shared intent that the child would then be brought up in England. However, I thought that there was enough evidence—although barely—to allow me to draw that conclusion. Moreover, I concluded that even though the child had only been in London for one year before coming to the United States, she "acclimatized" to living there and had acquired a new "habitual residence."

Thus, even if the child wanted to stay in the U.S.A., she had to go back to England. Nonetheless, I was disturbed by the fact that neither parent wanted to raise the child when she was an infant and pawned her off on her grandmother far away from both of them. I wondered who would really be the best parent to raise the child. That, however, was not my call. That decision would have to be made by an English custody court.

* * *

The third abduction case that I had was the most gut-wrenching. Unlike the others, I did not let the child stay with the mother. The boy would be raised by his father in the United States and not be able to live with his mother in Ecuador.

Angela Rosa Bonilla was a native-born Ecuadoran. She had given birth to two sons there out of wedlock but left them with relatives after she met Claudio Sinchi. He had been born in Ecuador and was visiting his native land when he met Angela. They became romantically involved. Claudio was an American citizen. He lived and worked in New York. Angela followed him to New York, and soon their son was born there. He, like his father, was an American citizen. His mother was an illegal immigrant.

Angela and Claudio returned to Equador when their new son was an infant. Their intent was that Angela would live there with their son until Claudio made arrangements for her and her two other children to become U.S. citizens. However, while in Ecuador, Claudio learned that Angela had been cheating on him. He surreptitiously took his son back to New York with him and scrapped the plans to make Angela and her older children United States citizens.

Angela sought to get her son back. Through the efforts of the New York City Bar Association, she was able to get pro bono counsel and bring her Hague Convention petition before me. However, she could not come in person for the hearing. Since she had been in the country illegally, she could not get a visa. However, just like Mr. Elyashiv, she was able to testify on a large video screen. She spoke from her lawyer's office in Ecuador. In order to get to the bottom of things, I asked her lots of questions.

I had to rule in the father's favor. It was clear to me that when the parties left with their baby for Ecuador, both agreed that their son would stay there temporarily for a period of time reasonably necessary for Claudio to pursue the contemplated citizenship applications. Neither party envisioned that their son would stay in

Ecuador permanently. When Claudio changed his mind—after he had taken his son back to the United States—Angela had no choice but to stay in Ecuador. Without her estranged husband's support, she could never become an American citizen because she had been an illegal immigrant. Nevertheless, she wanted all of her children to live with her. That could only happen in Ecuador.

I could not, however, order that her little boy be returned to her. My duty was to determine the place where the parties intended that their son be raised "at the last time that their intent was shared." That place was clearly the United States.

Although I correctly applied the law under the Hague Convention, I agonized over my decision because, as I wrote, I was "keenly aware of the human consequences"; since Angela was barred from entering the United States legally, she might never again see her son if his father would not let him visit her in Ecuador.

There was, however, one recourse that she might have, and I gave her some free advice. She could try to gain custody or visitation rights in a New York State court since the Hague Convention did not preclude her from filing a custody or visitation claim in state court under the state's laws. If she were successful, the state's decree could be enforced under the Convention. Hopefully she would have the means and the wherewithal to do that. However, unlike the state court, I had no authority to award Angela custody or visitation rights. Having determined that the parties' child was "habitually resident" in the United States, I had no choice but to deny Angela's petition to return her son to her.

* * *

The Hague Convention remains the principal way for those countries who have subscribed to it to deal with internationally abducted children. Nevertheless, of the 1,621 children who were taken from the United States in 2009—the last year that statistics were reported—only 324 were ordered to be returned by foreign Convention partners. The largest number were in Mexico, followed by the United Kingdom, Canada, Australia, and El Salvador. For its part, the United States returned 154 children. Once again Mexico led the pack, with 53, followed by Germany, Canada, the UK, and Australia.

Regrettably many countries have not embraced the Hague Convention. For example, India, Japan, and the Phillippines are not partners. Parents whose children are wrongfully abducted to those countries have no recourse under the Convention to get their children back.

Ernie Allen, the past president of the National Center for Missing and Exploited Children, has aptly characterized child abduction as a "global problem." He pointed out the need for all countries to embrace the principles of the Hague Convention and join together in "a system that creates a uniform, constant enforceable process so it doesn't make a difference whether the child is taken to Brazil, or Iceland, or Kuwait or the United States."

From my perspective, I am constantly saddened when I have to deal with international abduction cases. After all, the children—as they are shuttled from one country to another—are innocent victims of their parents' broken marriages. As a result of the inability of their parents to get their act together, research has shown that these kids are particularly "at risk of serious emotional and psychological problems," including "anxiety, eating problems, nightmares, mood swings, sleep disturbances, aggressive behavior, resentment, guilt, and fearfulness." Regardless of the decisions that I hand down under the Hague Convention, there is not much that I can do about that.

* * *

On October 31, 1999, EgyptAir flight 990 en route from New York to Cairo crashed into the Atlantic ocean 60 miles off the coast of the United States, killing all 217 on board. The crash strained relations between the American and Egyptian governments. The *Guardian* reported that "experts at the National Transportation Safety Board are . . . convinced . . . that a suicidal pilot caused the crash." However, the Egyptian government pressed the theory

Content

that the plane, a Boeing 767, developed a mechanical fault in its tail.

The U.S. investigators believed that the words of the reputedly suicidal pilot, Gamil El-Batouti—a 59-year-old Egyptian believed to be the copilot—which were retrieved from the cockpit's voice recorder, were those of a man saying a farewell prayer: "Tawakilt ala Allah"—in English, "I put my faith in God." Egyptians said, however, that the Americans misunderstood El-Batouti's words—a Muslim prayer. "This prayer would never be said in times of crisis," said a spokesman for the Egyptian government. "It's definitely not to be said by someone who is going to commit suicide because suicide is against Islam." Nevertheless, the voice recorder also revealed that the captain, Mahmoud El-Habashy, had been in the lavatory while El-Batouti was in the cockpit. When he returned—as the plane was going into a nose dive—he said: "What's happening, Gamel, what's happening? What is this? Did you shut the engines?" The Captain then ordered, "Pull, pull with me, pull with me."

The investigators believed that there was even more to support suicide as a motive: the flight data recorder did not suggest mechanical failure; during the plane's dive, someone turned off the engine contrary to any emergency routines; and at the end of the dive, the plane's elevators were pointing in opposite directions, as though the pilot and copilot were struggling with each other for control. They informally rejected the Egyptian theory of mechanical failure. Egyptians "don't care about solving it, they want to cover themselves," said one.

Indeed, the crash caused enormous embarrassment to the Egyptian government. The airline was government-owned. It was Egypt's flagship international carrier. It had a staff of 18,000 and 38 aircraft. Although it had recently come under attack by Egyptian dissidents for inferior service and inadequate pilot training, EgyptAir was, nonetheless, the face of Egypt over foreign waters. The idea that an Egyptian pilot would commit suicide and bring down the plane was just too much for Egyptians to swallow. Rather than acknowledge what appeared to be obvious, the Egyptian press was rife with conspiracy theories. It put the blame on the U.S., claiming that in pointing the finger at El-Batouti it was covering up for the malfunctioning of the American-made Boeing airplane.

Soon lawsuits against EgyptAir were filed all over the United States under a multinational treaty subscribed to by the United States—the Warsaw Convention. Many of them were filed in my court. There were 131 Americans on board. Fifty-four were senior citizens who had booked a trip up the Nile. I got the cases. A Brooklyn jury would decide whether the copilot committed suicide.

* * *

The Warsaw Convention applies "to all international transportation of persons, baggage, or cargo performed by aircraft for reward." Its purpose was to create "the uniform regulation of international air carrier liability." Within its broad confines, it calls for the subscribing countries to enact implementing legislation. Instead of enacting new legislation, Congress uses the Death on the High Seas Act (DOHSA). It provides that "whenever the death of a person shall be caused by wrongful act, neglect, or default occurring on the high seas" beyond 12 nautical miles from the shores of any state, the personal representative of the decedent may maintain a suit for damages in the district courts of the United States "for the exclusive benefit of the decedent's wife, husband, parent, child, or dependent relative" against the party at fault. Damages could be awarded—in accordance with U.S. law—for pain and suffering, economic loss, and loss of the "care, comfort and companionship" of the decedent.

The Convention provides, however, that a lawsuit can only be brought in one of four fora: "1) where the carrier is domiciled; 2) where the carrier has its principal place of business; 3) where the contract of transportation was made; or 4) the place where the transportation was to end."

Since EgyptAir was domiciled and had its principal place of business in Egypt, and the plane would be landing in Cairo, the only basis for bringing suit in the United States was if the ticket was bought here. If it was purchased in Long Island—as was the case with many of the senior citizens planning to cruise the Nile—then the case could be properly brought in the EDNY. Tickets had also been bought in California and other states; therefore, lawsuits were also brought in the federal district courts in those states. They were all transferred to my court, however, by a special panel of federal judges who decide where the best forum to handle a multidistrict case is.

Those who did not buy their tickets in the United States could not avail themselves of the American courts. They included the Egyptian crew and many Egyptians who bought their tickets in Egypt. Their only recourse against EgyptAir under the Convention would be to bring suit in Egypt. However, they could—and a number of them did—sue Boeing in the United States, as well as a company that had manufactured parts for the plane, under general principles of tort law for allegedly manufacturing a defective plane. I also got those cases.

* * *

There was no way that the Egyptian government was going to put its fate in the hands of a Brooklyn jury. On January 25, 2001, the lawyers for EgyptAir marched into my courtroom and wisely told me that it would not contest liability. However, one of them said that the airline was not acknowledging any fault on the part of a crew member. "Absolutely not," he said. "This is simply an acceptance of legal liability . . . It's not the same as admitting fault. We certainly are not doing that." In short, given the diplomatic sensibilities, EgyptAir would not fess up but would pay the piper. It would be left to me to resolve how much money the survivors would be entitled to for the loss of their loved ones who had bought their tickets in the United States.

The plaintiffs' lawyers were a small, select group of attorneys who had cornered the market in airline crashes. I do not know how they managed to sign up all of the cases, but they obviously had their ways. They were skilled in negotiating settlements. I would conduct conferences in my chambers and watch them do their thing.

389

Since they did not have to establish liability, their work was simple. They mostly would assemble binders of pictures of the deceased and their loving families at various family events. The damages were composed of basically two components: any economic loss which the families would suffer if they were being supported by the decedent, and compensation for their "loss of care, comfort, and companionship." There were no significant claims for pain and suffering for the crash victims because death was instant.

The settlement negotiations quickly resolved almost all of the claims. Where the deceased was a young, wealthy businessman with lots of dependents, the economic loss—measured by the victim's life expectancy—often would be several millions of dollars. Most of the awards, however, were in the one to three million dollar range. Nonetheless, it was a lot of money, and the lawyers made a killing; many had one-third contingency fee arrangements. There were, however, four cases that I had to decide because EgyptAir thought that the plaintiffs were either not covered by the Warsaw Convention or were asking for too much money.

* * *

In the first one, I ruled that the stepchildren of one of the passengers could not recover under DOSHA because under the case law they had to be "children." They could, however, qualify as "dependent relatives," but they had not established that they were financially dependent on their stepparents.

Next I had to dismiss two claims brought by representatives of the estates of Egyptian passengers who had bought their tickets in Cairo since they could not sue EgyptAir in the United States. I explained that under the Convention they had to bring their lawsuits against the Egyptian airline in Egypt and that any money which they might be entitled to receive would have to be determined in accordance with Egyptian law.

The last two cases required me to conduct trials and fix the damages. In one, I awarded the four adult children of Edith and Larry Kowalsky $1.52 million collectively, and the three adult children of Joan and Norman Shapiro $1.2 million. EgyptAir had offered $600,000 for the Kowalsky children and $450,000 for the Shapiros. The awards were to compensate the children for the loss of the "care, comfort and companionship" of their parents. The two families had been extraordinarily close, and the children's parents were the best of friends. They were elderly but were able to travel on their dream vacation to Egypt to celebrate their long lives and good fortune. It was pretty tough for me to keep my emotions in check as I watched videos of joint family get-togethers throughout the years and heard testimony of the love and affection these two remarkable families had for each other. I was struck in particular by the outpouring of love which the Kowalskys and Shapiros had showered upon their children. "Given the closeness of all the children to their parents and the almost intertwining of the children's lives with their parents"—as I wrote—EgyptAir's offer was too low.

The families were well-off. The children apparently could care less about the money. My sense is that they needed to vent their grief. The money would simply represent some sense of closure, but they knew that it would never get them what they really wanted.

The other damage trial also packed an emotional wallop. Sami Makary was a 28-year-old Egyptian young man. For most of his life he lived in the family home in Alexandria, Egypt, with his parents, his four sisters, his younger brother, and a cousin. In 1997, after he graduated from an Egyptian university, he started his own import/ export business in Egypt, where he employed one of his sisters and his cousin. Sami moved to the United States the following year. At the time of the crash, he was traveling back to Egypt to close his business there. Since he bought his ticket in the United States, his estate's lawsuit properly belonged before me.

Sami was survived by his whole family. He would regularly send his parents in the neighborhood of $2,000 a month and several hundred dollars to his siblings and cousin. He was the pride and joy of his family. His earning capacity at the time of his death was significant.

There were tears in the spectators' rows in the courtroom when

Sami's father testified. He was a proud man, a former member of the Egyptian Parliament and a distinguished Egyptian lawyer. After he had completed his term of office in the Parliament, he had returned to his prior employment as director general of the Egyptian Custom House in Alexandria. He traveled to Brooklyn to honor his son by explaining to me that the eldest son is celebrated in Egyptian culture as "the one who carries his father's name afterwards and completes his father's mission." As such he "has the same responsibilities for the whole family as [the] father," and is expected to care for his parents in their old age.

I gave Sami's parents over $1.3 million for, as I wrote, "the loss of their eldest son, a central figure in the Egyptian family and, certainly, a central figure in the Makary family." I also wrote: "Without marginalizing the impact of the death of a parent on a child, a child expects to survive his or her parent; no parent ever wants to live to bury his or her child." While, once again, no amount of money could ever serve as a substitute for the loss of a loved one, I thought that Sami would want me to make sure that his parents would not want for anything in their old age.

I was pleased to read in the *New York Law Journal* the next day that the attorney who represented the Makary estate told the press that "it was important that the judge recognized a tradition in Egyptian heritage, which dictates that the first-born son is responsible for the well-being of his parents and family." However, looking back, while I try not to let my emotions trump the law, I'm not sure that I did that when I compensated Sami's parents for their son's death.

* * *

Although all of the claims against EgyptAir under DOHSA had now been resolved, I still had to deal with lawsuits filed by 40 Egyptians who could not bring DOHSA claims in the United States but who sued Boeing and the parts manufacturer. The Egyptian government had settled each of the claims which they had brought against EgyptAir in Egypt for the equivalent of about $200,000. It was a lot of money for someone living in Egypt but paled by comparison to the millions that were being handed out to the U.S. claimants. It was not easy for them to understand why the Makarys became Egyptian millionaires just because their son had bought his ticket in the United States.

The lawyers for the insurance company which represented Boeing and the parts manufacturer wanted to resolve the lawsuits that had been brought against the two American companies in the United States even though they thought that they were meritless. The National Safety Board had issued its final report finding that there was no mechanical failure. However, the claimants had hired American lawyers, and even though they knew that it would be difficult to pin liability on the American companies, they were pressing forward with the litigation. It was likely to drag on for years, and the expenses of litigation would be costly. The Egyptian government also wanted closure to avoid the prospect that the litigation would result in a formal decision that its copilot was the culprit.

From my perspective any additional money that the Egyptians could get over what they received in Egypt would be found money because there was no realistic chance that Boeing and the parts manufacturer would ever be found culpable; there was absolutely no evidence pointing the finger at them.

In October 2006, the lawyers for all of the parties presented a unique settlement proposal to me. The claimants would be given a choice. They could take $100,000 each to settle their claims at once or have me decide how much should be given to each family in excess of that amount, up to a cap of $225,000. The proceedings would be in the nature of an informal, but binding, alternative dispute resolution process. The parties would be allowed to present oral testimony at hearings conducted by me in Cairo, "or at such other place or by such other means (e.g., video conference) as agreed by the parties and Judge Block." I would be given the option of having "an informal advisor or officially appointed master" to assist me in conducting the hearings. The damage claims would be governed by Egyptian law, and I would have to determine "the amount of damages customarily awarded by the Courts of Egypt in similar cases."

I was more than happy to do what I could to effectuate the parties' desire to end all of the lawsuits but I would be traveling—literally and figuratively—in foreign waters. It was way off the charts from what judges are usually called upon to do. To make matters more daunting, the lawyers thought that the settlement hearings would have a better chance of success if they would be conducted in Egypt—and I presided.

I asked for guidance from the General Counsel of the Administrative Office of the United States Courts. I was advised that "[t]here is no authority to conduct United States district court business in a foreign country, even at a U.S. embassy." It was suggested that since my personal presence was requested, I may appoint a special master to attend the meetings in Egypt and arrange to be present "through a telephone or video link." The special master could not, however, perform any official judicial duties in Egypt. Moreover, I was told that I should get assurance that whatever arrangements I might make did not violate Egyptian law, and was cautioned that "as with any international travel by federal officials, there are inevitably personal security concerns."

Finally, it was suggested that I contact the State Department Legal Advisors Office, to find out "whether the conduct of American judicial proceedings in the nation in question would raise foreign policy concerns or might be viewed by that nation as a violation of its sovereignty." I did that, and advised the State Department of the settlement proposal.

In short order I was advised that the proposal had been sent on to the Bureau of Consular Affairs, who in turn would be contacting the American Embassy in Cairo. If the embassy approved, it would speak to the Egyptian government, whose permission would be needed before conducting any legal proceedings in its country, including proceedings by a special master. I was cautioned that "[i]f the request doesn't go through the right channels of bureaucracy, some people could get offended and then we'd have big problems."

Days later my State Department contact advised me that the U.S. Embassy spoke to the chief of Egypt's Office of International Cooperation, who told him that generally Egyptian law does not prohibit informal conversations with Egyptian citizens, "but any formal questioning in Egypt must be done through the Egyptian judicial system." I was asked to submit a letter to him—with a request that he "pass it on to the Chief through the normal channels." He suggested that the letter explain that I would not be "taking evidence for introduction in court proceedings, depositions, administering oaths, etc., but rather that you are planning informal discussions at the request of the Egyptian citizens concerned, as a gesture of good will and a convenience to them."

In my letter I laid out the details of the parties' proposal. I also wrote that I was willing to have the "informal fact-gathering process" conducted in Cairo "[f]or the convenience of the Egyptian families involved." I would appoint a special master who "was familiar with Egyptian law and culture to manage the logistics of the process." I also wrote that "I will be present throughout the process so that I can meet informally with the families," but "I will not, however, engage in any official judicial conduct during my stay in Egypt." I ended the letter with these comments:

> I believe that this proposal is a creative solution to a difficult legal problem, and I applaud the parties' efforts in reaching it. More important, though, is the promise of much-needed resolution to the litigation that will afford additional compensation for those Egyptian families that have already settled with EgyptAir. I hope that my involvement in the process will not only encourage greater participation among the plaintiffs' families, but will also foster goodwill between our two nations."

Many of my Brooklyn colleagues told me that I was nuts for agreeing to go to Cairo. It would be dangerous and way beyond my judicial obligations. If the Egyptians did not want to come to Brooklyn, so be it. Nevertheless, I was ultimately persuaded by all of the lawyers—and encouraged by Ambassador Sherif El-Kholi— the Egyptian Consul General in New York City—to do it. The lawyers representing the Egyptian families pleaded with me to go. The families could not all afford to come to Brooklyn; moreover, it would be difficult to get special visas for all those who wanted to be heard. The lawyers also thought that having the American judge at the hearings would add great credibility. As they wrote: "We recognize that this is an unusual request, and is not one that we make lightly. However, we believe that your involvement will greatly increase our chances of maximizing the family participation in the process and resolving all of the remaining passenger and crew claims in this litigation." I thought about it long and hard before I made my decision, but I thought about the Makary family and was willing to do what I could to help.

On January 10, 2007, I received the green light from the State Department. My contact there had received a letter from the Egyptian Advocate General of the Office of International Cooperation: "Nothing stands in the way under Egyptian law for Judge Block to meet informally with Egyptian families, with their consent."

* * *

I had to pick the right special master. It was an easy choice. I had met Yassin El-Ayouty a number of years ago. Among his many accomplishments he had served in the United Nations from 1954 to 1986 and was its spokesman during the Algerian war of independence. He had drafted the statute of the UN Institute for Training and Research and was its director of training. He had a Ph.D from NYU in international law, a J.D. from the Benjamin Cardozo School of Law, was a member of the United States Supreme Court bar, the Egyptian bar, and the bar of the Egyptian Court of Cassation—the equivalent of our Supreme Court. He was a member of the Egyptian Council for Foreign Affairs and an adjunct professor of law at the Cairo University School of Law.

Dr. El-Ayouty had founded and was president of SUNSGLOW. It was an organization devoted to transnational judicial and legal training, especially in the developing world, with a corps of volunteers from several countries and 12 regional liaison centers around the world. I was at that time an advisory member of its board of directors. In 2005, Dr. El-Ayouty had invited me to be part of a symposium at the Cairo Law School for judges from Egypt, Iraq, the Palestinian Authority, and Afghanistan. I spoke about the need for an independent judiciary and commitment to the rule of law. It was an extraordinary experience. Six Iraqi judges got there. A seventh was supposed to come but was assassinated two days before. Saddam Hussein had yet to be caught, and Iraq was struggling to get its judicial house in order. Judge Medhat Al-Mahmoud was there. He was the President of the Supreme Iraqi Judicial Council—the equivalent of the Chief Judge of our Supreme Court. Judge Al-Mahmoud was a gentle and courtly presence. He told me to have faith in the Iraqi judiciary. It had a long and distinguished history. He described its current plight as being like under a preliminary injunction and assured me that his country would once again have a stable and functioning judiciary.

I was also struck by my conversations with the other judges, especially the four from the Palestinian Authority. They knew that I was Jewish, but the ice was broken at dinner, and they were warm and friendly. The leader, who was from Gaza, shared with me, through an interpreter, how much had to be done to get its legal system up to snuff. He thanked me for my speech. One judge was from Ramallah. He spoke English and was very proud of the progress the judiciary in the West Bank was making, although he, too, told me that there was much to do. At the end of dinner he asked me if I could give his brother in America a call when I got back home and tell him about our meeting. He owned a deli in Minnesota. I told him that I would—and I did.

My Egyptian trip was climaxed by a speech that I delivered to the Egyptian Council for Foreign Affairs. I had just written an article for the New York University *Review of Law & Social Change* on civil liberties during our country's national emergencies, and Dr. El-Ayouty thought that it would make a good topic for a speech. The members of the council were a distinguished group of current and former Egyptian ambassadors. Its president at that time was Abdel Raouf Elreedy, who had been Egypt's ambassador to Washington. It was a heady experience.

* * *

After I appointed Dr. El Ayouty as the special master, he took over. Soon he arranged that the family members would be invited to attend a series of informal hearings in Cairo at the Court of Cassation. I would be there to welcome them and then turn the proceedings over to him. He told me that I would be sitting at the bench with him and Counselor Nabil Omran—the Deputy Chief Justice of the Court of Cassation. Judge Omran told me that he had been designated by Chief Justice Mokbel Shaker "to supervise the process and all of its details, and to exert all necessary efforts for the success of the mission." He arranged that the proceedings would be held in the Court of Cassation's largest and historic Abdel Aziz Pacha Fahmy courtroom. I would be the first American jurist to preside over a proceeding, albeit "informal," in Egypt's high court.

On the first day of the hearing, May 28, 2007, I was ushered into the Court of Cassation under heavy guard. The courtroom was packed. It looked like hundreds. It was standing room only. I was shaking like a leaf, but managed to get to my feet and speak:

Salem Alechem:

You are here to have your claims adjudicated pursuant to a settlement agreement which many of you have already signed. I have reviewed it and believe it to be fair and reasonable. It will also provide peace and closure.

I cannot adjudicate these claims for you personally in Egypt since the law does not permit me to preside over proceedings away from my court. Therefore, pursuant to the agreement I have appointed Dr. Yassin El-Ayouty to do so and he has my every confidence. I have known him for many years. We have been together in Egypt before. I have come personally to extend my sympathies for the losses suffered by you and to share in your grief.

I also come in the spirit of international judicial cooperation and

398

thank, in particular, Counselor Omran for making this possible. Welcome to court. I now turn the proceedings over to Dr. El-Ayouty who will explain how they will proceed. I thank you all for the privilege and honor of granting me this opportunity to be with you and wish you all the very best.

Enshallah and peace.

All did not go smoothly. After Dr. El-Ayouty spoke, we decided to take a little break and the lawyers, Judge Omran, Dr. El-Ayouty, and I were taken to a conference room. Soon we heard lots of commotion coming from the courtroom. A fight had broken out instigated by dissidents who were opposed to the settlements. They were led by El-Batouti's nephew—Waleed El-Batouti. They thought that it was all part of an American conspiracy and an affront to their dignity. As Judge Omran later explained to me:

> Many families of the victims preferred to seek damages from an American court in the hope of receiving millions of dollars in damages. The issue took another dimension that related to 'dignity' and Egyptian's sense of pride. Those who refused the judicial settlement in Cairo thought it was degrading to accept what they believed were lower sums and propagated in Egyptian media outlets the view that Egyptian blood wasn't any less valuable than any other passenger, particularly Americans, who they said received larger sums in damages.

When things calmed down, I was escorted by the security guards back to the hotel where I was staying.

The hearings continued for the rest of the week. I decided to get out of Cairo while Dr. El-Ayouty took over. Betsy and her two children—Tina and Debbie—had come to Egypt with me and had been having lots of fun riding camels by the Pyramids while I was shaking in the courtroom. I spent the next several days cruising up the Nile with them. Although I was later assured that I was not in danger, I was happy that I was still alive. When we got back to Cairo, I was invited once again to be the guest of the Egyptian Council for Foreign Affairs. They were anxious to hear about how the settlement proceedings had gone.

399

The next morning, Betsy, Tina, Debbie, and I were driven by a security agent to the Cairo International Airport to catch the Delta plane back to New York. As we drove the five-mile route to the airport, I was impressed by the soldiers who were lined up on both sides of the highway. I thought it was over-the-top protection for us, but was quickly dissuaded from thinking that they were there to assure our safe exit from their country. President Mubarek was also going to the airport at that time.

* * *

All of the families did not agree to participate in the settlement hearings, but 10 did. The awards Dr. El-Ayouty recommended—and I approved—ranged from $100,000-$225,000. Most were on the high side. They were promptly paid. I was happy for the recipients. It was the sensible thing to do. Soon thereafter, 20 more agreed to settle. The handful who held out—thinking that there was gold in the hills—got nothing.

I returned to the cozy confines of Brooklyn and caught up with my more mundane cases. I wondered again, though, whether judges should be doing these types of things. The answer came when I received a letter from Ambassador El-Kholi in behalf of the Egyptian government expressing its "sincere gratitude for the work you have undertaken in Egypt to resolve the issue of compensation to the families of the victims of the Egypt Air crash of 1999." He added that "[w]e know it was a difficult assignment, but your creation of a mechanism for Alternative Dispute Resolution was a unique exercise that have dissipated a good portion of that important issue."

It was, understandably, not the Queen's English, but I thought that if ever I would write a book about the life and work of a federal trial judge, it would be a fitting end.

Epilogue

The big cases that I have written about are amongst the most memorable and go a long way in giving context to my work as a federal trial judge, but there were others that deserve some mention to round out the broad range of most of the types of cases that come before the federal trial courts. Foremost are the securities-fraud cases. This is an area of the law that—thanks to the likes of Bernie Madoff, Enron, WorldCom, and a host of others—has dominated the news during the recent economic downturn.

In 2011, I presided over the criminal trial of the two Bear Stearns hedge fund managers—Ralph Cioffi and Matthew Tannin—who many blamed for the collapse of that Wall Street pillar which precipitated the collapse of the financial markets. Clearly this would have qualified as one of the big cases and would have given me the opportunity to explain the securities laws and the dramatic aspects of that trial, which ended in their acquittals. Nevertheless, I decided not to do this since the Securities and Exchange Commission (SEC) had brought a related civil lawsuit against Cioffi and Tannin which at the time I wrote the book was scheduled to be tried before me in the near future. Under those circumstances, I thought that it would be ethically inappropriate to write about them. I don't mind commenting, however, about the title of an article appearing in the *Wall Street Journal* when the criminal trial broke: *A Look at Judge in Bear Case: He's Fair, Funny and Frank*. It was a lot better than Judge Blockhead.

Then there are the official-corruption cases. They are regrettably all too common, and it always troubles me to see someone who has been given the public's trust become a criminal—especially law-enforcement officers. I vividly remember Jamil Jordan and Anthony

401

Trotman. They had two jobs. They were police officers and also members of a band of robbers who regularly held up people. Jordan pled guilty; Trotman went to trial and was convicted. When I sentenced Jordan, I gave him the max—13 years—and told him that "other police officers have to know if they violate the law, they will be punished by as much as the law allows." Trotman originally faced a 10-year sentence but was let out of prison after five years because he became a cooperator and turned against his fellow gang members.

Other areas of the law that frequently dot the federal court landscape are cases involving the environment, social security disability benefits, immigration, and intellectual property. Two of the environmental cases stick with me. In one, a leading importer of caviar was convicted for violating the country's endangered-species laws. Little did those dining at fancy restaurants realize that the caviar which they were eating at $100 a pop was being smuggled into the country in the laundry bags of Lot Polish airline stewardesses.

The other environmental case was a civil trial. A band of working-class homeowners took on the Town of Brookhaven for allowing what was once a pristine, beautiful pond in their community to be polluted and turned to mud because of leachates that seeped into the pond when the town closed one of its landfills. The Town mounted all of its resources against its citizens when they brought the Town to court to make it clean up the mess which it had created. I took the Town to task and praised the residents for persisting and using a provision of federal law that allows citizen lawsuits when municipalities fail to act to protect the environment. I appointed an expert to educate me about how the pond could be restored to its prior condition and made the Town do it.

As for social security cases, if someone is turned down by the Social Security Administration for disability benefits, then an appeal can be brought to the federal district courts. We get lots of these cases. They are frequently reversed. I try to give them priority since the claimants are often suffering from severe disabilities and really need the money to make ends meet.

Immigration cases present special problems. Congress has decided that if the immigration authorities order someone's removal from the United States, the only recourse is to bypass the district courts and take an appeal directly to the circuit courts of appeals. Because of the high number of these appeals, the circuit courts covering—in the main—New York, Florida, and California have been overwhelmed with them. Nonetheless, they have devised processes to effectively and fully deal with each appeal. Most of the appeals are denied, but there are a few where the courts have determined that the immigrant had qualified for citizenship or should not be removed for a limited number of reasons, such as a well-grounded fear of persecution if returned to his or her native country.

Because of the advent of the Internet, the number of intellectual property cases is on the rise, and the judges have to deal with the complexities of the new-age technology. Trademark disputes also are common sources of litigation. Sometimes they take on curious aspects. For example, after Rabbi Schneerson died—a few years after the Crown Heights riots—a bitter dispute broke out amongst his followers over the ownership of his letters. I presided over the trial that resolved the dispute. In doing so, I had to explain that the secular laws governing intellectual property litigation had to trump religious-based notions of who should be the beneficiaries of the Rabbi's writings; thus, I had to discount testimony that the Rabbi had resolved the issue by speaking to his flock from the grave.

* * *

In 2005 I took senior status. The vacancy I created was filled by Brian Cogan. I am so happy that Judge Cogan is my successor. We are of different political persuasions, but I admire his intellect and moral compass. He is highly regarded by his colleagues and the legal community. Above all, I am grateful for his friendship.

Although I could now cut back on my judicial work, I chose to keep a full caseload. Nevertheless, becoming a senior judge also made me think about what else I might do with my life. The idea of this book started to take shape. My daughter, Nancy—an engaging, creative young woman—encouraged me to do it; however, I was not then motivated to make the effort.

In the summer of 2009, after I had finished a busy year trying cases in my court as well as in the district courts of Chicago, New Orleans, and Lafayette, Louisiana—as a visiting judge—and sitting as a designated judge for the Ninth Circuit Court of Appeals in San Francisco, I decided to go to Greece and think about what I would do come September—and whether I should take a shot at writing the book. I did, however, have another motive for going. Betsy was born there, and she and her daughters speak Greek. I thought that it was time for me to make an effort to learn how to speak to them in their native tongue.

When I told my brother Leonard that I was thinking of enrolling in summer school in Greece, he threw down the gauntlet by telling me: "Nobody your age is ever going to learn how to speak Greek." The next day I signed up for an intensive, month-long, five-day-a-week, four-hour-a-day Greek language course at the Greek Language School in Chania, Crete.

I can now read, write, and chit-chat in Greek. I had a wonderful, unique experience and realized how important it was for me, and I surmise for all of my judicial colleagues, to be periodically detached from the routine of our judicial lives and to continue to acquire new life experiences at all ages. I must confess, though, that there were some challenging times. After I finished my second week of classes, I was sitting in a taverna feeling pretty good about what I had learned. Lying next to me was a dog. His apparent master, sitting at the next table, called to him in Greek; the dog got up. The dog responded to a second Greek command and laid down next to the man. The dog then responded to another command and sat up on his hind legs. I was depressed. The dog understood more Greek than I did.

Nonetheless, I happily persevered, but I had one more

comeuppance. I was feeling young and spry one sunny day as I boarded a crowded bus back to town from one of the beautiful beaches of Chania when a woman who seemed to be in her '60s offered me her seat. It was at that moment that I decided that I would write the book.

Endnotes

INTRODUCTION

1. "Judicial lockjaw": Leslie B. Dubeck, *Understanding "Judicial Lockjaw": The Debate Over Extrajudicial Activity*, 82 N.Y.U. L. Rev. 569 (2007).

2. The public needs "reliable and understandable sources of information": Robert F. Copple, *From the Cloister to the Street: Judicial Ethics and Public Expression*, 64 Denv. U. L. Rev. 549 (1987).

3. Rules on extrajudicial conduct: Code of Conduct for United States Judges, available at http://www.uscourts.gov/rulesandpolicies/codesofconduct/codeconductunitedstatesjudges.aspx (last visited December 22, 2011); Committee on Codes of Conduct, *Advisory Opinion No. 55: Extrajudicial Writings and Publications*, http://www.uscourts.gov/uscourts/RulesAndPolicies/conduct/Vol02B-Ch02.pdf.

PART I: GETTING THERE

Chapter 1: Pathways

2. Ed Bloustein: Craig Wolff, *Edward J. Bloustein, 64, is Dead; President of Rutgers Since 1971*, N.Y. Times, Dec. 11, 1989, at B13.

Chapter 2: Practicing, The Sixties

1. Suffolk County demographics: *Bianchi v. Griffing*, 238 F. Supp. 997, 1000 (E.D.N.Y. 1965).

2. *Travels with Charley*: John Steinbeck, *Travels with Charley: In Search of America* (1962).

3. "Suffice it to say that the Board of Supervisors is constituted to serve as the legislative body for the County": *Bianchi v. Griffing*, 238 F. Supp. 997, 1004 (E.D.N.Y. 1965).

4. "In the event that an appropriate governing body": *Bianchi v. Griffing*, 238 F. Supp. 997, 1005 (E.D.N.Y. 1965).

5. The "problem of modernizing antiquated political structures along democratic lines": *Suffolk County's Board*, N.Y. Times, May 5, 1965.

6. Three other cases argued before the Supreme Court that day: *Dusch v. Davis*, 387 U.S. 112 (1967); *Moody v. Flowers*, 387 U.S. 97 (1967); *Sailors v. Board of Ed. of Kent County*, 387 U.S. 105 (1967).

7. Truman Hobbs: Federal Judicial Center, *History of the Federal Judiciary; Biographical Directory of Federal Judges: Hobbs, Truman McGill* [Judge, Middle District of Alabama], http://www.fjc.gov/public/home.nsf/hisj (last visited December 21, 2011).

8. Constitutional Convention, 1967: *See* Judith S. Kaye, *A Double Blessing: Our State and Federal Constitutions*, 30 Pᴀᴄᴇ. L. Rᴇᴠ. 844, 850 (2010); New York State Constitutional Convention, *Directory of Delegates and Staff*, available at http://nysl.nysed.gov/uhtbin/cgisirsi/?ps=pUrnVfh5EK/NYSL/298070074/523/86242 (last visited December 22, 2011).

9. "I'm going to screw you every way I can short of reversible error": *Sarisohn v. Appellate Division of the Supreme Court of the State of N.Y., Second Dept.*, 21 N.Y.2d 26, 47 (1967).

10. Transported "about the countryside at odd hours of the day and night": *People v. Clayton*, 28 A.D. 2d 543, 544 (2d Dep't 1967).

11. The Alabama case only dealt with "one county's governing board": *Moody v. Flowers*, 387 U.S. 97, 102 (1967).

12. The New York State Constitution was amended "to provide for the Court of Appeals judges to be appointed": New York State Archives, *Preliminary Guide to Environmental Sources, Judicial Branch*, http://www.archives.nysed.gov/a/research/res_topics_env_guide_3_jud.shtml (last visited December 21, 2011).

13. The "pronouncement by the Supreme Court during the past week": *Bianchi v. Griffing*, 393 F.2d 457, 460 (2d Cir. 1968).

14. One "of the most blatant exceptions to the one-man, one vote decision": Agis Salpukas, *New Suffolk County Legislature Replaces 287-Year-Old System*, N.Y. Tɪᴍᴇs, Jan. 3, 1970.

15. Justice Earl Warren considered the *Baker v. Carr* line of cases one of his "crowning achievements": Robert C. Post, *Justice William J. Brennan and the Warren Court*, 8 Cᴏɴsᴛɪᴛᴜᴛɪᴏɴᴀʟ Cᴏᴍᴍᴇɴᴛᴀʀʏ 11, 13 (1991).

16. The "most important change in county government": *Republicans and Conservatives Win Entire Suffolk Legislature*, N.Y. Tɪᴍᴇs, Nov. 5, 1969.

Chapter 3: Practicing, The Seventies

1. The Conservative party "claimed that the name 'Conservation' was too similar": *Ottinger v. Lomenzo*, 64 Misc. 2d 103 (N.Y. Sup. 1970).

2. Each "has taken on a special, colloquial meaning": *Ottinger v. Lomenzo*, 64 Misc. 2d 103, 104 (N.Y. Sup. 1970).

3. His decision "would defeat the manifest purpose": *Ottinger v. Lomenzo*, 35 A.D.2d 747, 747 (3rd Dep't 1970).

4. 1970 election, won by James Buckley: Benjamin Sarlin, *America's Least Qualified Senators*, DAILY BEAST, Dec. 18, 2008, http://www.thedailybeast.com/articles/2008/12/18/americas-least-qualified-senators.html.

5. Habeas Corpus as the "stable bulwark of our liberties": William Blackstone, 1 COMMENTARIES ON THE LAWS OF ENGLAND 137 (Clarendon 1765).

6. Facts revealed "a clear pattern of police dominance": *U.S. ex rel. Clayton v. Mancusi*, 326 F. Supp. 1366, 1369 (E.D.N.Y. 1971).

7. Special Meeting of the State Democratic Committee: David Andelman, *State Democrats Barred from Meeting on Burns*, N.Y. TIMES, Dec. 28, 1971, at 20.

8. The special meeting squared with the "intent and purpose of the Rules": *Baranello v. Burns*, 38 A.D.2d 606, 607 (2d Dep't 1971).

9. Judith Hope: The Empire Page, *Judith Hope*, http://www.empirepage.com/iny-biographies/judith-hope (last visited December 21, 2011).

10. Clayton "was under tremendous psychological strain": *Mancusi v. U.S. ex rel. Clayton*, 454 F.2d 454, 455 (2d Cir. 1972).

11. Dismissal in the interests of justice: *People v. Clayton*, 350 N.Y.S. 2d 495 (N.Y. Co. Ct. 1973).

12. Statute used usually to dismiss an indictment for insufficiency of evidence: *People v. Clayton*, 342 N.Y.S. 2d 106, 108 (2d Dep't 1973).

13. *Clayton* case article: Frederic Block, *The Clayton Hearing*, N.Y. STATE BAR J. (Oct. 1973).

14. "Today, *Clayton* hearings are an integral part of the criminal law in New York State": Frederic Block, *Reflections on Guns and Jury Nullification—And Judicial Nullification*, 33 CHAMPION 12, 17 (2009).

15. The Amityville Horror: Jay Anson, *The Amityville Horror* (1977).

16. "Judge Weinstein tossed out the Lutzes' lawsuit": Lynne Kelly, *The Skeptics Guide to the Paranormal*, 78 (2004).

17. Mandatory CLE: 22 N.Y.C.R.R. 1500; The Suffolk Academy of Law, http://www.scba.org/eva/index.php?p=theSuffolkAcademyOfLaw2 (last visited December 22, 2011).

18. The Police Brutality Report: Suffolk County Bar Assoc., *Report of the Civil Rights Committee on Allegations of Police Brutality in Suffolk County.*

Chapter 4: Practicing, The Eighties

1. An "apparent pattern" of police beatings: Abramovitz, *When Suspects Are Abused*, NAT'L L. J. (June 11, 1979).

2. Judge Weinstein, NAACP case: Pranay Gupte, *Court Rejects Brutality Suit Against Suffolk Police*, N.Y. TIMES, July 23, 1976.

3. State Investigation Commission Report: Temporary Commission of Investigation of the State of New York, *An Investigation of the Suffolk County District Attorney's Office and Police Department* (1989).

4. The "natural evolution of the interrogation process": Alfonso A. Castillo and Christine Armario, *Spota: Jurors wanted taping*, NEWSDAY, Feb. 8, 2008, A17.

5. More than 500 police departments throughout the nation: Alfonso A. Castillo and Christine Armario, *Spota: Jurors wanted taping*, NEWSDAY, Feb. 8, 2008, A17.

6. Book review, *Convicting the Innocent*: Jeffrey Rosen, *Criminal Injustice*, N.Y. TIMES, May 29, 2011, at BR16.

7. Creation of the Suffolk County District Court: 10th Judicial District, Suffolk County, http://www.nycourts.gov/courts/10jd/suffolk/dist/history.shtml (last visited December 21, 2011).

8. Governor thought that house would pose a security risk: Bob Wacker, *State Seizes Lot Next to Carey's: Shelter Island home built too close for governor's safety, officials say*, NEWSDAY, Nov. 8, 1980, at 3.

9. It "looks like he misused his office to protect his privacy": Bob Wacker, *Carey Defends House Seizure*, NEWSDAY, Nov. 11, 1980, at 3.

10. Editorials were "just as critical": *Governor's 'Security' Claims Are Weak*, STATEN ISLAND ADVANCE, Nov. 15, 1980, at 8.

11. Jimmy Breslin "vilified him": Jimmy Breslin, *Travels with Carey, the Great Society Governor*, DAILY NEWS, Feb. 10, 1981, at 4; Jimmy Breslin, *Society Carey has his own way to stay high*, March 26, 1981, at 4.

12. Fellow columnists were also all over the story: Barney Fowler, *The Squire of Shelter Island*, TIMES UNION, Feb. 11, 1981, at 11.

13. "Horrific press": Donald Singleton, *Gov's Land Duel to Nick Taxpayer*, DAILY NEWS, Nov. 15, 1980, at 3; Michael Hanrahan and Donald Singleton, *Taxes Paid for Carey Repairs*, DAILY NEWS, Nov. 13, 1980, at 3.

14. "I got the punishment I deserved": Frank Lynn, *Carey Takes Rare Look Back at Administration*, N.Y. TIMES, April 8, 1985, at B3.

15. A "territorial distinction, without any rational basis, cannot withstand constitutional scrutiny": *Weissman v. Evans*, 442 N.Y.S. 2d 80, 82 (2d Dep't 1981).

16. "True unity. . . the jurisdiction, practice and procedures of each of the District Courts": *Weissman v. Evans*, 56 N.Y. 2d 458, 463 (1982).

17. A "delightful new musical review": Leah Frank, *Wry Musical Look at Professionals*, N.Y. TIMES, Feb. 19, 1984.

18. Eastern District of New York established in 1865: *A History of the United States Court for the Eastern District of New York, To Commemorate and to Celebrate a Centennium* (1965), http://www.nyed.uscourts.gov/pub/docs/local/EDNY%20History%201865-1965%20Centennium.pdf.

19. 14 judges in 1985: Israel Leo Glasser, Thomas Collier Platt, Jr., Jack Bertrand Weinstein, Leonard D. Wexler, John Ries Bartels, Henry Bramwell, Mark Constantino, Joseph McLaughlin, Jacob Mishler, Edward Raymond Neaher, Eugene Nickerson, Charles Proctor Sifton, Joseph Carmine Zavatt (died August 1985), and Frank X Altimari (appointed to the Second Circuit in December 1985).

20. One "of the keener entries in the satire stakes": Don Nelson, *Lawyers? I'll tell you about lawyers. . .*, N.Y. DAILY NEWS, May 23, 1986.

21. The "material displays a frisky verbal energy": Stephen Holden, *Stage: A Satirical Revue, "Professionally Speaking,"* N.Y. TIMES, May 25, 1986.

22. A "cocky little review": Edith Oliver, *The Theater, Off Broadway*, THE NEW YORKER, June 2, 1986.

23. The salary disparity "was premised upon precisely the same geographical classifications": *Weissman v. Bellacosa*, 517 N.Y.S.2d 734, 737 (2d Dep't 1987).

24. There were "evident distinctions in caseload": *Weissman v. Bellacosa*, 517 N.Y.S.2d 734, 739 n.5 (2d Dep't 1987).

25. *Cass* "specifically distinguished": *Weissman v. Bellacosa*, 517 N.Y.S.2d 734, 739 n.5 (2d Dep't 1987) (citing *Cass v. State of N.Y.*, 58 N.Y. 2d 460, (1983)).

Chapter 5: Practicing, The Nineties

1. The "material evidence necessary to support the claim at bar": *Deutsch v. Crosson*, 567 N.Y.S.2d, 773, 774 (2d Dep't 1991).

2. $45 million per year: Scott Bowles, *Judge Judy Sets TV Bench Mark*, USA TODAY, July 14, 2010, at 1D.

3. Judge Judy's book: Judy Sheindlin, *Don't Pee on My Leg and Tell Me It's Raining* (1997).

Chapter Six: Payoff

1. His latest book: Daniel Patrick Moynihan, *Pandaemonium: Ethnicity in International Politics* (1994).

2. George W. Bush did not wait for the ABA ratings: Laura E. Little, *The ABA's Role in Prescreening Federal Judicial Candidates: Are We Ready to Give Up on the Lawyers?*, 10 WM. & MARY BILL OF RTS. J. 37 (2001).

3. "Senator Pothole": Michael Starr, *D'Amato Will Be Next TV Judge*, N.Y. POST, June 11, 2008, at 89.

PART II: BEING THERE

Chapter 1: The Start

1. Articles of Confederation: United States Department of State, Office of the Historian, *Milestones*, http://history.state.gov/milestones/1776-1783/Articles (last visited December 20, 2011).

2. Judiciary Act: Library of Congress, *Primary Documents in American History: Judiciary Act of 1789*, http://www.loc.gov/rr/program/bib/ourdocs/judiciary.html (last visited December 20, 2011).

Chapter 2: Breaking In

1. Sentencing Guidelines: U.S. SENTENCING GUIDELINES MANUAL (2010).

2. Darrell Fulton: *U.S. v. Fulton*, No. 93-CR-1049.

3. Patent case: *Russell William, Ltd. v. ABC Display & Supply, Inc.*, No. 88-CV-265, 1996 WL 148486 (E.D.N.Y. 1996).

4. Sparrow gave Mosely "competent and capable counsel": *Mosely v. Scully*, 908 F. Supp. 1120, 1138 (E.D.N.Y. 1995).

Chapter 3: The Judges

1. "About one-third of the district judges are senior judges; about 40% of the circuit judges are senior": James C. Duff, Administrative Office of the U.S. Courts, *Judicial Business of the United States Courts, Annual Report of the Director 2010*, http://www.uscourts.gov/uscourts/Statistics/JudicialBusiness/2010/JudicialBusinesspdfversion.pdf; *Table 1.1: Total Judicial Officers—Courts of Appeals, District Courts and Bankruptcy Courts*, http://www.uscourts.gov/uscourts/Statistics/JudicialFactsAndFigures/2010/Table101.pdf.

2. The Rule of 80: 28 U.S.C. 371(c); United States Courts, *Frequently Asked Questions*, http://www.uscourts.gov/Common/FAQS.aspx (last visited December 20, 2011).

3. Magistrate Judges: Federal Judicial Center, *History of the Federal Judiciary: Magistrate Judgeships*, http://www.fjc.gov/history/home.nsf/page/judges_magistrate.html (last visited December 20, 2011).

4. President Carter judicial appointees: Thomas G. Walker and Deborah J. Barrow, *The Diversification of the Federal Bench: Policy and Process Ramifications*, 47 J. OF POLITICS 596, 597 (1985).

5. Gene Nickerson: Steven Greenhouse, *Eugene Nickerson, Ex-Nassau Politician and Judge in Louima Trials, Dies at 83*, Jan. 3, 2002, at A20.

6. Major League Baseball strike case: *Silverman v. Major League Baseball Player Relations Comm'ee, Inc.*, 880 F. Supp. 246 (S.D.N.Y. 1995).

7. 29 Republican senators voted against Sonia Sotomayor's Second Circuit confirmation: Sheryl Gay Stolberg, *A Trailblazer and a Dreamer*, N.Y. TIMES, May 27, 2009, at A1.

8. Helping judges examine their fact-finding and decision-making styles: John W. Kennedy, Jr. *Personality Type and Judicial Decision Making*, 37 JUDGE'S J. 50 (2002).

9. "The average life expectancy has more than doubled": Centers for Disease Control and Prevention, *Fast Facts, Life Expectancy*, http://www.cdc.gov/nchs/fastats/lifexpec.htm (last visited December 20, 2011).

10. "Rules have. . . been enacted to govern the manner by which the circuit courts are to handle the complaints": Judicial Conference of the United States, *Rules for Judicial Conduct and Judicial Disability Proceedings* (March 11, 2008) http://www.ca2.uscourts.gov/Docs/CE/rules-for-judicial-conduct-and-judicial-disability-proceedings.pdf.

Chapter 4: The Courtroom

1. Dean Prosser did not believe that the bench was an appropriate place for humor: William L. Prosser, *The Judicial Humorist: A Collection of Judicial Opinions and Other Frivolities* (1952).

2. Justice Cardozo, judicial opinion "lightened by a smile": Benjamin Cardozo, *Law and Literature*, 52 HARV. L. REV. 472, 484 (1939).

3. A judge must "without weakening the fabric of seriousness, weave it into a thread of playfulness": George Rose Smith, *A Critique of Judicial Humor*, 43 ARK. L. REV. 1, 4 (1990).

4. Brooklyn lawyers who "deserved to drive in limousines": *Simmons v. N.Y. City Transit Authority*, 575 F.3d 170 (2d Cir. 2009); *Luca v. County of Nassau*, 698 F. Supp. 2d 296 (E.D.N.Y. 2010).

5. Criminal Justice Act plan for the EDNY: United States District Court for the Eastern District of New York, *Revised Plan of the United States District Court for the Eastern District of New York Pursuant to the Criminal Justice Act*, http://www.nyed.uscourts.gov/pub/docs/local/cjaplan.pdf.

6. Executive of public works construction company: John Marzulli and Brian Kates, *Construction exec commits suicide two days before sentencing for $19 million federal highway fraud*, DAILY NEWS, March 14, 2011.

Chapter 5: Sentencing

1. "7.3 million people are presently either in prison or on parole or probation": Solomon Moore, *Study Shows High Cost of Criminal Corrections*, N.Y. TIMES, March 3, 2009, at A13.

2. The United States, "with 5% of the world's population, now accounts for 25%of the world's inmates": Editorial, *Falling Crime, Teeming Prisons*, N.Y. TIMES, Oct. 30, 2011, at SR10.

3. Federal Bureau of Prisons: Kevin Johnson, *Budget Would Give Federal Prisons $528M Boost; Top priorities: Closing Gitmo, hiring guards*, USA TODAY, Feb. 4, 2010, at 2A; Carrie Johnson, *Report Notes Sexual Misconduct by Prison Workers*, WASH. POST, Sept. 11, 2009, at A03.

4. "Probation and parole is at the bottom of the pole": Solomon Moore, *Study Shows High Cost of Criminal Corrections*, N.Y. TIMES, March 3, 2009, at A13.

5. Recidivism: Bureau of Justice Statistics, *Reentry Trends in the U.S.*, http://bjs.ojp.usdoj.gov/content/reentry/recidivism.cfm (last visited December 19, 2011).

6. "We cannot say we are doing everything we can to keep our communities and our families safe": Jarvis DeBarry, *Keeping our brothers out of jail*, TIMES PICAYUNE, July 26, 2011, at B05.

7. Eastern District of New York, sentencing statistics: United States Sentencing Commission, *2010 Sourcebook of Federal Sentencing Statistics, Appendix B: Selected Sentencing Statistics by District* (2010), http://www.ussc.gov/Data_and_Statistics/Annual_Reports_and_Sourcebooks/2010/Stats_NYE.pdf.

8. Mandatory minimums: United States Sentencing Commission, *Report to Congress: Mandatory Minimum Penalties in the Federal Criminal Justice System, Chapter 7* (October 2011), http://www.ussc.gov/

Legislative_and_Public_Affairs/Congressional_Testimony_and_Reports/
Mandatory_Minimum_Penalties/20111031_RtC_PDF/Chapter_07.pdf.

9. "What has caused concern in courts across the nation. . .": A.G. Sulzberger, *Defiant Judge Takes on Child Pornography Law*, N.Y. TIMES, May 22, 2010, at A1.

10. "Real children are harmed in the production of these images": A.G. Sulzberger, *Defiant Judge Takes on Child Pornography Law*, N.Y. TIMES, May 22, 2010, at A1.

11. "Drugs accounted for 43% of the sentences in the EDNY last year": United States Sentencing Commission, *Statistical Information Packet Fiscal Year 2010 Eastern District of New York* (2010), http://www.ussc.gov/Data_and_Statistics/ Federal_Sentencing_Statistics/State_District_Circuit/2010/nye10.pdf.

12. "Colombian roots": *U.S. v. Rosero*, 80 Fed. Appx. 710 (2d Cir. 2003).

13. Supervised release: 18 U.S.C. 3583.

14. Gerardo Flores Carreto: Jennifer 8. Lee, *Metro Briefing New York: Brooklyn: Sentences in Sex-Trafficking Case*, N.Y. TIMES, April 28, 2006, at B5.

15. Cooperation agreements: Linda Drazga Maxfield and John H. Kramer, *Substantial Assistance: An Empirical Yardstick Gauging Equity in Current Federal Policy and Practice*, 11 FED. SENT'G REP. 6 (1998).

16. Average sentence for a cooperator "is 50% of what he would otherwise get": U.S. Sentencing Commission, *2010 Sourcebook of Federal Sentencing Statistics, Table 30, § 5K1.1 Substantial Assistance Departure Cases: Degree of Decrease for Offenders in Each Primary Offence Category* (2010), http://www.ussc.gov/ Data_and_Statistics/Annual_Reports_and_Sourcebooks/2010/Table30.pdf.

17. Gaspipe: Philip Carlo, *Gaspipe: Confessions of a Mafia Boss* (2009).

Chapter 6: The Risks

1. United States Marshals Service: U.S. Marshals Service, *Judicial Security* (2011), http://www.usmarshals.gov/duties/factsheets/jsd-2011.pdf; U.S. Marshals Service, *Facts and Figures* (2011), http://www.usmarshals.gov/duties/factsheets/ facts-2011.pdf.

2. Judge John H. Wood: *Trial Opens for 3 in Judge's Killing*, N.Y. TIMES, Oct. 8, 1982, at A19.

3. Judge Richard J. Daronco: Robert D. McFadden, *Federal Judge Slain by a Gunman in Westchester*, N.Y. TIMES, May 22, 1988, at 32.

4. Judge Robert Smith Vance: Michael Tackett, *Security Tightened after Judge's Death*, Chicago Tribune, Dec. 18, 1989, at 3.

5: Judge Joan Lefkow: *Federal Judges Hail Lefkow's Slain Kin*, Chicago Tribune, March 1, 2006, at 1.

6. Incidents "led Congress to focus on providing better protection": Jeff Coen, *Judges get home security; Lefkow slayings spur expansion of measures to safeguard jurists*, Chicago Tribune, June 25, 2006, at 1; U.S. Department of Justice, *Review of the Protection of the Judiciary and the United States Attorneys* (2009), http://www.justice.gov/oig/reports/plus/e1002r.pdf.

7. State judiciaries: Jennifer Dlouhy, *Bill aims to curb attacks on judges; Rash of violence prompts Tyler lawmaker to seek stiffer sentences and other changes*, Houston Chronicle, May 1, 2005, at A21; Beth Warren, *Judges focus on safety; Security training targets courthouse*, Atlanta Journal-Constitution, Sept. 29, 2005, at 8JN.

8. "Disgruntled defendants": Jerry Markon, *Threats to Judges, Prosecutors Soaring; Worried Court Personnel Resort to Guards, Identity Shields, Weapons*, Wash. Post, May 25, 2009, at A01.

9. Harold Turner: John Eligon, *Two Views of a Radio Host on Trial Over Threats to Judges*, N.Y. Times, Dec. 3, 2009, at A34.

10. Victor Wright: Corey Kilgannon, *Drug Defendant Attacks Prosecutor in Court*, N.Y. Times, March 12, 2008, at B6.

11. "It's like we're in Fallujah and they're in the Green Zone": Eric Wolff, *Furor in the Court: "It's like we're in Fallujah." Brooklyn Judges say they're not as safe as their Manhattan counterparts*, N.Y. Magazine, April 18, 2005.

PART III: THE BIG CASES THERE

Chapter 1: Death

1. Cruel and unusual punishment "is not fastened to the obsolete": *Weems v. U.S.*, 217 U.S. 349, 377 (1910).

2. States that have adopted the death penalty: Death Penalty Information Center, *Facts About the Death Penalty*, http://www.deathpenaltyinfo.org/documents/FactSheet.pdf.

3. Countries that have adopted the death penalty: Amnesty International, http://www.amnesty.org/en/death-penalty/abolitionist-and-retentionist-countries (last visited December 20, 2011).

4. The death penalty "should not be expanded to instances where the victim's life was not taken": *Kennedy v. Louisiana*, 554 U.S. 407, 437 (2008).

5. Federal death penalty prosecutions: Frederic Block, *A Slow Death*, N.Y. TIMES, March 15, 2007, at A27.

6. New York death penalty cases: Frederic Block, *A Slow Death*, N.Y. TIMES, March 15, 2007, at A27.

7. Methods of execution: Death Penalty Information Center, *Facts About the Death Penalty*, http://www.deathpenaltyinfo.org/documents/FactSheet.pdf.

8. Justice Stevens concurrence: *Baze v. Rees*, 553 U.S. 35, 78 (2008).

9. The "homicide rates in states with the death penalty was 48 to 101% higher than in states without the death penalty": Ford Fessenden, *Deadly Statistics: A Survey of Crime and Punishment*, N.Y. TIMES, Sept. 22, 2000, at A23.

10. Justice Scalia concurrence: *Baze v. Rees*, 553 U.S. 35, 87 (2008).

11. Judge Blockhead: *Bow Out, Judge Blockhead*, DAILY NEWS, Jan. 26, 2007, at 28; John Marzulli, *Judge Gives Wiseguy a Weigh Out of Jail*, DAILY NEWS, March 5, 2007, at 12.

12. *New York Times* op-ed: Frederic Block, *A Slow Death*, N.Y. TIMES, March 15, 2007, at A27.

13. The "lack of death sentences, and the high cost of those trials": Tom Perrotta, *Death Penalty Query Delays Court Nominee*, NEW YORK LAW JOURNAL, May 10, 2007.

Chapter 2: Racketeering

1. "The impact of the federal government's use of RICO on the mob has been devastating": Selwyn Raab, *The Mob in Decline—A Special Report; A Battered and Ailing Mafia Is Losing Its Grip on America*, N.Y. TIMES, Oct. 22, 1990, at A1.

2. The Gambino family was "the largest and most powerful Mafia family . . . with about 400 to 500 members": Selwyn Raab, *The Mob in Decline—A Special Report; A Battered and Ailing Mafia Is Losing Its Grip on America*, N.Y. TIMES, Oct. 22, 1990, at A1.

3. "Based upon information ascertained during the 'in camera' hearing": United States v. Gotti, 2002 WL 31015623, at *1 (E.D.N.Y. 2002).

3. Ronald Piecyk: Selwyn Raab, *John Gotti Running the Mob*, N.Y. TIMES, April 2, 1989, at 30.

4. 1987 acquittal of John Gotti: Robert D. McFadden, *Jury Foreman in 1987 Gotti Trial Is Indicted in Plot to Sell His Vote*, N.Y. TIMES, Feb. 25, 1992, at A1.

5. *New York Law Journal* report, Second Circuit oral argument: Mark Hamblett, *Panel Questions Government on Gotti's Solo Confinement*, NEW YORK LAW JOURNAL, Oct. 7, 2002, at 22.

6. *Daily News* report, "Block failed to grasp parts of D'Urso's testimony": John Marzulli, *Judge Boots Key Witness Vs. Gotti*, DAILY NEWS, Jan. 17, 2003, at 6.

7. The *Post* printed intimate excerpts from Marjorie's letters: Kati Cornell Smith, Kieran Crowley and William J. Gorta, *Mob Mistress Checks Out—Body Found in L.I. Motel Room*, N.Y. POST, April 1, 2004, at 3.

8. "I used the occasion to write an opinion about when, if at all, judges should make sentencing letters public": *U.S. v. Gotti*, 322 F. Supp. 2d 230 (E.D.N.Y. 2004).

Chapter 3: Guns

1. "the gun, its component parts, ammunition, and the raw materials from which they are made have considerably moved in interstate commerce": 18 U.S.C. § 922.

2. "What has Congress done?": Bureau of Alcohol, Tobacco, Firearms and Explosives, *Federal Firearms Regulatory Reference Guide* (2005), http://www.atf.gov/publications/download/p/atf-p-5300-4.pdf.

3. "Guide to the Interstate Transportation of Firearms": National Rifle Association, *Guide to the Interstate Transportation of Firearms*, http://www.nraila.org/GunLaws/Federal/Read.aspx?id=59 (last visited December 19, 2011).

4. "Congress has also addressed the problem by providing that a firearm may be transported": 18 U.S.C. § 926A.

5. "40% of United States households contain guns": *Loaded and Lethal—and Unlocked*, WASH. POST, July 11, 1999, at B08.

6. The U.S. has "the highest rate of gun deaths in the developed world": *U.S. leads world in gun deaths*, THE STAR-LEDGER, April 17, 1998, at 7.

7. "There are 283 million privately-owned firearms in America": Bob Herbert, *A Culture Soaked in Blood*, N.Y. TIMES, April 25, 2009, at A19.

8. Corporal Melroy H. Cort: Keith L. Alexander, *Marine Amputee Acquitted on Gun Possession Charges*, WASH. POST, Jan. 14, 2009, at B01.

9. "The proponents of the jury's power and *right* to nullify the law": Irwin A. Horowitz, *Jury Nullification: The Impact of Judicial Instructions, Arguments, and Challenges on Jury Decision-Making*, 14 L. & HUM. BEHAV. 440 (1988).

ENDNOTES

10. "Jury lawlessness is the greatest corrective of law": Roscoe Pound, *Law in Books and Law in Action*, 44 Am. L. Rev. 12, 18 (1910).

11. "Public and private safety alike": *Sparf v. U.S.*, 156 U.S. 51, 101 (1895).

12. A "willful and flagrant disregard of the evidence and the law": *Horning v. District of Columbia*, 254 U.S. 135, 140 (1920).

13. The holding of *Horning* has since been repudiated: *U.S. v. Gaudin*, 515 U.S. 506, 520 (1995).

14. Noting that "in colonial days and the early days of our Republic": *U.S. v. Dougherty*, 473 F.2d 1113 (D.C. Cir. 1972).

15. The "the duty to forestall or prevent such conduct": *U.S. v. Thomas*, 116 F.3d 606, 615 (2d Cir. 1997).

16. "Jack Weinstein articulated his view on the issue": Jack B. Weinstein, *The Role of Judges in a Government of, by, and for the People: Notes for the Fifty-Eighth Cardozo Lecture*, 30 Cardozo L. Rev. 1, 121 (2008).

Chapter 4: Drugs

1. Limelight "was housed in a deconsecrated Church in downtown Manhattan which Gatien bought in 1982": *BRIEFLY Cornwall whiz kid plans to expand*, The Globe and Mail, Feb. 19, 1985.

2. Ecstacy as a "love inducing" drug: Bill Brownstein, *Limelight takes a hard look at Canadian king of (night)clubs*, The Gazette, Sept. 23, 2011, at C2.

3. *Limelight* the documentary: Tim Murphy, *Peter Gatien, Club King Without a Club*, N.Y. Times, Sept. 21, 2011, at E1.

4. The first anti-drug laws: Morris B. Hoffman, *The Drug Court Scandal*, 78 N. C. L. Rev. 1437, 1454 (2000).

5. "Negro Cocaine 'Fiends' are a New Southern Menace": Edward Huntington Williams, *Negro Cocaine "Fiends" Are a New Southern Menace: Murder and Insanity Increasing Among Lower Class Blacks Because They Have Taken to "Sniffing" Since Deprived of Whisky by Prohibition*, Feb. 8, 1914.

6. "A Texas police captain suggested that marijuana gave Mexicans superhuman strength to commit acts of violence": The History of the Drug Laws, http://druglibrary.org/schaffer/library/histdrug.htm (last visited Dec. 19, 2011).

7. "The Discrimination Inherent in America's Drug War": Kathleen R. Sandy, *The Discrimination Inherent in America's Drug War: Hidden Racism Revealed by Examining the Hysteria over Crack*, 54 Ala. L. Rev. 665 (2003).

419

8. Harry Anslinger: The History of the Drug Laws, http://druglibrary.org/
schaffer/library/histdrug.htm (last visited Dec. 19, 2011).

9. 2010 National Household Survey on Drug Use and Health: U.S. Department of Health and Human Services, *Results from the 2010 National Survey on
Drug Use and Health: Summary of National Findings* (2010), http://
oas.samhsa.gov/NSDUH/2k10NSDUH/2k10Results.pdf.

10. "One out of every 15 high school students": Anahad O'Connor, *Marijuana
Use Growing Among Teenagers*, N.Y. Times Well Blog (Dec. 14, 2011).

11. "Some of the jurors spoke to the press after the verdict": Devlin Barrett,
Jury Decides Club King Is No Drug Knave, N.Y. Post, Feb. 12, 1998, at 7.

12. Murder of Angel Melendez as described by "Freeze": Barbara Ross and
Stephen McFarland, *Grisly Disco-Drug Slay Tale Papers: Body Kept in Tub, Cut
Up*, Daily News, Jan. 23, 1997, at 20.

13. Michael Alig "implicated Melendez and Gatien in drug-dealing ventures":
Barbara Ross and Stephen McFarland, *Grisly Disco-Drug Slay Tale Papers: Body
Kept in Tub, Cut Up*, Daily News, Jan. 23, 1997, at 20.

14. Death of "Gitsie": Frank Owen, *Nightclubs, Downtown and Dirty; In New
York, a Drug Trial Exposes After-Dark Secrets*, Wash. Post, Feb. 14, 1998, at B1.

15. Press speculation about undercover DEA agents: Frank Owen, *Nightclubs,
Downtown and Dirty; In New York, a Drug Trial Exposes After-Dark Secrets*,
Wash. Post, Feb. 14, 1998, at B1.

16. Ben Brafman: Patricia Hurtado, *Strauss-Kahn Lawyer Brafman Defended
Rappers, Mobsters, Michael Jackson*, Bloomberg, May 26, 2011.

17. *Clubland*: Frank Owen, *Clubland: The Fabulous Rise and Murderous Fall
of Club Culture* (2004).

Chapter 5: Discrimination

1. Reconstruction and the history of civil rights laws: Jack M. Beermann, *The
Unhappy History of Civil Rights Legislation, Fifty Years Later*, 34 Conn. L. Rev.
981 (2002).

2. The Police Department would "bear such hostility": *Luca v. County of Nassau*, No. 04-CV-4898, 2008 WL 2435569, at *2 (E.D. N.Y. 2008).

3. McCord was "not disciplined more harshly": *Hill v. Airborne Freight Corp.*,
212 F. Supp. 2d 59, 67 (E.D.N.Y. 2002).

4. The decision was not an "abuse of discretion": *Hill v. Airborne Freight Corp.*,
93 Fed. Appx. 260 (2d Cir. 2004).

5. *Daily News* report, "the first award of its kind in New York City's college sports scene": Tara Sullivan, *Precedent Grows in Brooklyn, Verdict Levels Women's Court*, DAILY NEWS, Sept. 15, 1997, at 57.

6. Molly Perdue and Debbie Banks quoted in the *New York Times*: Frank Litsky, *College Basketball; Former Brooklyn Coach Wins Damages in Sex Bias Suit*, N.Y. TIMES, July 10, 1990, at C5.

7. Linda Carpenter quoted in the *Daily News*: Tara Sullivan, *Precedent Grows in Brooklyn, Verdict Levels Women's Court*, DAILY NEWS, Sept. 15, 1997, at 57.

8. Ricci was dyslexic and had to study for eight to 13 hours per day to pass the exam: Adam Liptak, *Supreme Court Finds Bias Against White Firefighters*, N.Y. TIMES, June 30, 2009, at A1.

9. "In this case, the Civil Service Board found itself in the unfortunate position of having no good alternatives": *Ricci v. De Stefano*, 530 F. 3d 87 (2d Cir. 2009).

10. Thoughtful and well-reasoned opinion: *Ricci v. De Stefano*, 530 F. 3d 87 (2d Cir. 2009).

11. Fear of litigation "cannot justify the City's reliance on race": *Ricci v. DeStefano*, 129 S. Ct. 2658, 2663 (2009).

12. Senator Jeff Sessions: Jerry Markon and Paul Kane, *No Peril Seen for Sotomayor*, WASHINGTON POST, June 30, 2009, at A03.

Chapter 6: Race Riots

1. Car accident in Crown Heights and state court trial, background: Alan Vinegrad, *Prosecutions of Lemrick Nelson Jr.*, NEW YORK LAW JOURNAL, May 23, 2003, at 5.

2. The "jury's decision was attributed by many to the perception that black and Hispanic jurors. . .": Robert F. Worth, *Juror in Crown Hts. Trial Remains Bitter About Ordeal*, N.Y. TIMES, May 1, 2003, at B6.

3. "The Circuit Court of appeals sent the case back": *U.S. v. Nelson*, 277 F.3d 164, 201 (2d Cir. 2002).

4. The Ku Klux Klan came into existence in 1866: *From Lincoln to Obama: Important dates in the civil rights movement*, THE GAZETTE, Nov. 8, 2008, at A4.

5. Three civil rights activists murdered, 1964: Shaila Dewan, *Widow Recalls Ghosts of '64 at Rights Trial*, N.Y. TIMES, June 17, 2005, at A1.

6. 14-year-old boy murdered, 1955: Richard Rubin, *The Ghosts of Emmett Till*, N.Y. TIMES MAGAZINE, July 31, 2005, at 30.

7. Civil rights volunteer murdered by KKK members, 1965: *Civil Rights Slaying*, WASH. POST, March 26, 1999, at C12.

8. "This bar on double jeopardy has ancient roots in both common and civil law": *Bartkus v. Illinois*, 359 U.S. 121,151–55 (1959).

9. "I'm like a scapegoat . . . I had no part in it": Jerry Capeci and Helen Peterson, *19 1/2 Years in '91 Riot Slay; Defiant Killer Says He Didn't Stab Student*, DAILY NEWS, April 1, 1998, at 5.

10. Would "never be able to adequately express the enormity of the loss": Joseph P. Fried, *19 1/2 Year Term Set in Fatal Stabbing in Crown Heights*, N.Y. TIMES, April 1, 1998, at A1.

11. "I understand your community's pain": Joseph P. Fried, *19 1/2 Year Term Set in Fatal Stabbing in Crown Heights*, N.Y. TIMES, April 1, 1998, at A1.

12. "As the circuit court put it": *Lennon v. Miller*, 66 F. 3d 416, 421 (2d Cir. 1995).

13. Dinkins and Brown: James C. McKinley, *Dinkins, in TV Speech, Defends Handling of Crown Hts. Tension*, N.Y. TIMES, Nov. 26, 1992, at A1.

14. "It may appear to many that the strategy implemented by the police": *Estate of Rosenbaum by Plotkin v. City of N.Y.*, 975 F. Supp. 206, 222 (E.D.N.Y. 1997).

15. "At the end of my opinion I summed up the reasons why": *Estate of Rosenbaum by Plotkin v. City of N.Y.*, 975 F. Supp. 206, 222 (E.D.N.Y. 1997).

16. The City agreed to pay plaintiffs "a little over $1 million": Joseph P. Fried, *Settlement Reported in Suit over Crown Heights Unrest*, N.Y. TIMES, April 2, 1998, at B3.

17. "Notwithstanding what I think is a superb record of support for Jewish people": William Glaberson, *The Crown Heights Verdict: The Legal System; Jury Finds What Many Already Knew*, N.Y. TIMES, May 15, 2003, at B8.

18. "Disdain and hate": John Marzulli, *Crown Hts. Judge: Be Fair*, DAILY NEWS, April 16, 2003, at 22.

19. "If a jury understands that this extra element . . .": Adam Liptak, *Crown Heights Redux: The Best Defense Is an Offense*, N.Y. TIMES, May 4, 2003, at Week in Review, 6.

20. It would limit "the powerful evidence that is likely to stir up a jury": Adam Liptak, *Crown Heights Redux: The Best Defense Is an Offense*, N.Y. TIMES, May 4, 2003, at Week in Review, 6.

21. "Him smirking and smiling pains me": Steve Dunleavy, *Smirk Stabs at Hearts of Loved Ones*, N.Y. Post, May 15, 2003, at 005.

22. The *New York Times* found out who the jury forewoman was: Andy Newman, *Juror Explains Mixed Verdict on Crown Hts.*, N.Y. Times, May 17, 2003, at B1.

23. "I was vilified by a columnist for the *New York Post*": Steve Dunleavy, *Justice Denied to Tragic Rosenbaum Family*, N.Y. Post, Aug. 21, 2003, at 019.

24. "Nelson's guilt is clear": Alan Vinegrad, *Prosecutions of Lemrick Nelson Jr.*, New York Law Journal, May 23, 2003, at 5.

25. "They were babies. They were not cognizant of what happened": William Glaberson, *The Crown Heights Verdict: The Legal System; Jury Finds What Many Already Knew*, N.Y. Times, May 15, 2003, at B8.

Chapter 7: Terrorism

1. Zazi drove to New York from Colorado: Warren Richey, *Al-Qaeda suspect who targeted New York subway system pleads guilty*, Christian Science Monitor, April 23, 2010.

2. "Were it not for the combined efforts of the law enforcement and intelligence communities": A.G. Sulzburger and William K. Rashbaum, *Guilty Plea Made in Plot to Bomb New York Subway*, N.Y. Times, February 23, 2010, at A1.

3. Zazi background: Al Baker, *Reasons Unclear for Terrorist Fears*, N.Y. Times, Sept. 18, 2009, at A25; A.G. Sulzberger, *Imam and Informant Tells Why He Lied*, N.Y. Times, April 16, 2010, at A20.

4. "What I told Zazi about the law enforcement being interested in him": Janon Fisher, *Qns. Imam Blubbers: I Blabbed!—Liar Admits He Did Tip Off Zazi & Pal*, N.Y. Post, March 5, 2010, at 8.

5. "Three days after 9/11, President George W. Bush declared a national emergency": President George W. Bush, Proclamation 7463—Declaration of National Emergency by Reason of Certain Terrorists Attacks, 66 Fed. Reg. 48199 (Sept. 14, 2001).

6. The war against terrorism was "a very different kind of war": Kenneth R. Bazinet, *A Fight vs. Evil, Bush and Cabinet Tell U.S.*, Daily News, Sept. 17, 2001, at 8.

7. Congress enacted the Authorization for Use of Military Force: Authorization for Use of Military Force, Pub. L. 107-40, 115 Stat. 224.

8. The passage of the PATRIOT Act as "the climax of a remarkable 18-hour period": Robin Toner and Neil A. Lewis, *A Nation Challenged: Congress; House Passes Terrorism Bill Much Like Senate's, but with a 5-Year Limit*, N.Y. TIMES, October 13, 2001, at B6.

9. President's remarks when signing the PATRIOT act: Frederic Block, *Civil Liberties During National Emergencies: The Interactions Between the Three Branches of Government in Coping with Past and Current Threats to the Nation's Security*, 29 N.Y.U. REV. L. & SOC. CHANGE 459, 473 (2005).

10. The PATRIOT Act changes: Frederic Block, *Civil Liberties During National Emergencies: The Interactions Between the Three Branches of Government in Coping with Past and Current Threats to the Nation's Security*, 29 N.Y.U. REV. L. & SOC. CHANGE 459, 475 (2005); Alice Fisher, Deputy Assistant Attorney Gen., Prepared Statement to the Subcomm. on Tech., Terrorism, and Gov't Info of the Senate Comm. on the Judiciary of the 107th Congress (2001), http://judiciary.senate.gov/testimony.cfm?id=495&WIT_ID=1249.

11. George W. Bush authorized the NSA to wiretap: James Risen and Eric Lichtblau, *Early Test for Obama on Domestic Spying Views*, N.Y. TIMES, Nov. 18, 2008, at A17.

12. The NSA "was monitoring up to 500 people within the United States": James Risen and Eric Lichtblau, *Bush Lets U.S. Spy on Callers Without Courts*, N.Y. TIMES, Dec. 16, 2005, at A1.

13. Lawsuits against phone carriers: Eric Lichtblau, *Senate Approves Bill to Broaden Wiretap Powers*, N.Y. TIMES, July 10, 2008, at A1.

14. Broader latitude in eavesdropping: Eric Lichtblau, *Senate Approves Bill to Broaden Wiretap Powers*, N.Y. TIMES, July 10, 2008, at A1.

15. Lisa Monaco statement to NPR: Carrie Johnson, *As It Turns 10, Patriot Act Remains Controversial,* NPR NEWS, Oct. 26, 2011, http://minnesota.publicradio.org/features/npr.php?id=141699537.

16. Ron Kuby: Joyce Wadler, *Public Lives; Leftist Lawyer Reaches Right for Audience*, N.Y. TIMES, Jan. 15, 1998.

17. "Anywhere I go I'm going to be known as the imam that worked with the American government": A.G. Sulzberger, *Imam and Informant Tells Why He Lied*, N.Y. TIMES, April 16, 2010, at A20.

18. The Terrorist Trial Report Card: Center on Law and Security, New York University School of Law, *Terrorist Trial Report Card: September 11, 2001-September 11, 2010*, http://www.lawandsecurity.org/Portals/0/Documents/01_TTRC2010Final1.pdf.

19. Criticism of trying terrorists in federal courts: Jack Goldsmith, *Don't Try*

Terrorists, Lock Them Up, N.Y. TIMES, Oct. 8, 2010; Sam Stein, *Terrorist Trials: Lieberman Criticizes Obama Admin for Prosecuting Terrorists in Civilian Courts*, April 4, 2010, www.huffingtonpost.com.

20. "55% of the detainees were not suspected of having committed any hostile acts": Mark Denbeaux, *Report on Guantanamo Detainees, A Profile of 517 Detainees Through Analysis of Department of Defense Data*, http://www.pbs.org/now/shows/230/guantanamo-report.pdf.

21. Military commissions: Jennifer K. Elsea, Congressional Research Service *Comparison of Rights in Military Commission Trials and Trials in Federal Criminal Courts* (November 19, 2009), http://fpc.state.gov/documents/organization/133509.pdf.

22. The "heavy reliance" placed on Elmasry's conduct was "counterintuitive": *Farag v. U.S.*, 587 F. Supp. 2d 436, 459 (E.D.N.Y. 2008).

23. "The Court fully recognizes the gravity of the situation": *Farag v. U.S.*, 587 F. Supp. 2d 436, 468 (E.D.N.Y. 2008) (quoting *Iqbal v. Hasty*, 490 F. 3d 143, 159 (2d Cir. 2007)).

24. "This case is important because. . . a federal court has squarely rejected": Liz Robbins, *Judge Rules That Suspects Cannot Be Detained Because of Ethnicity*, N.Y. TIMES, November 25, 2008, at A26.

25. The Angry White Dude: http://angrywhitedude.com/tag/judge-frederic-block/ (last viewed December 19, 2011).

Chapter 8: Foreign Affairs

1. "The accountability of the Swiss Banks": Michael D. Hausfeld, *Crimes Against Humanity*, WASH. POST, Aug. 5, 1997, at A14.

2. Volcker Report: Independent Committee of Eminent Persons, *Report on Dormant Accounts of Victims of Nazi Persecution in Swiss Banks* (1999), http://www.crt-ii.org/ICEP/ICEP_Report_english.pdf.

3. "New York City threatened to boycott Swiss banks": David Usborne, *Swiss Banks Furious at U.S. Boycott Threats*, THE INDEPENDENT, July 3, 1998, at 17.

4. Judge Korman's decision to approve the proposed settlement agreement: *In re Holocaust Victim Assets Litig.*, 105 F. Supp. 2d 139 (E.D.N.Y. 2000).

5. Judah Gribetz: *In re Holocaust Victim Assets Litig.*, 105 F. Supp. 2d 139 (E.D.N.Y. 2000).

6. "In terms of justice, which is very, very important": Liz Halloran, *Holocaust Survivors Face Evil Memories in Swiss Atonement; Victims of Banks' Nazi Appeasement Sought*, HARTFORD COURANT, July 18, 1999, at A13.

7. "The circuit court has given him kudos": *In re Holocaust Victim Assets Litig.*, 424 F.3d 132, 149 (2d Cir. 2005).

8. The settlement agreement was silent as to compound versus simple interest: *In re Holocaust Victim Assets Litig.*, 256 F. Supp. 2d 150, 152 (E.D.N.Y. 2003).

9. 2009 child abduction statistics: United States Department of State, *Report on Compliance with the Hague Convention on the Civil Aspects of International Child Abduction* (April 2010), http://travel.state.gov/pdf/2010ComplianceReport.pdf.

10. The "failure of the United States to initiate vigorously diplomatic and law enforcement tools": Bernard Aronson, *To get a child back; The U.S. is failing children abducted to other countries*, WASH. POST, Feb. 19, 2010, at A17.

11. Binational marriage: David Crary, *Countries urged to curb child abduction; U.S. parents decry lack of recourse*, BOSTON GLOBE, Dec. 7, 2010, at 13.

12. "His mother was bringing him to freedom, and we don't want him to go back to a Communist system": Editorial, *The Future of Elian Gonzalez*, N.Y. TIMES, Nov. 30, 1999, at A22.

13. "The law is very clear. A child who has lost his mother belongs with his sole surviving parent": David Johnson, *U.S. Set to Order a Speedy Return of Boy to Father*, N.Y. TIMES, April 8, 2000, at A1.

14. "Simply not credible": *Elyashiv v. Elyashiv*, 353 F. Supp. 2d 394, 398 (E.D.N.Y. 2005).

15. The Second Circuit articulated the standard: *Gitter v. Gitter*, 396 F. 3d 124 (2d Cir. 2005).

16. She had "acclimatized": *In re E.D.T. ex rel. Adamah v. Tayson*, No. 09-CV-5477, 2010 WL 2265308, at *5 (E.D.N.Y. 2010).

17. "Keenly aware of the human consequences": *Ordonez v. Tacuri*, No. 09-CV-1571, 2009 WL 2928903, at *7 (E.D.N.Y. 2009).

18. Hague Convention 2009 statistics: United States Department of State, *Report on Compliance with the Hague Convention on the Civil Aspects of International Child Abduction* (April 2010), http://travel.state.gov/pdf/2010ComplianceReport.pdf.

19. Child abduction as a "global problem": Kristina Herrndobler, *Child abduction bill targets foreign cases; Hyde pushes plan for cross-border custody disputes*, CHICAGO TRIBUNE, May 15, 2004, at C14.

20. Kids are "at risk of serious emotional and psychological problems": United States Department of State, *Report on Compliance with the Hague Convention*

on the Civil Aspects of International Child Abduction (April 2010), http://
travel.state.gov/pdf/2010ComplianceReport.pdf.

21. Convinced that "a suicidal pilot caused the crash": Michael Ellison, *U.S.
and Egypt split on fatal plane crash; Suicidal Pilot Brought Down Flight 990
Killing 217 People, Insist NTSB Sources, Not a Mechanical Failure in the Plane*,
THE GUARDIAN, June 9, 2000, at 15.

22. "This prayer would never be said in times of crisis": Michael Ellison, *U.S.
and Egypt split on fatal plane crash; Suicidal Pilot Brought Down Flight 990
Killing 217 People, Insist NTSB Sources, Not a Mechanical Failure in the Plane*,
THE GUARDIAN, June 9, 2000, at 15.

23. "What's happening, Gameel, what's happening?": Sylvia Adcock, *Airline:
We're Liable; But EgyptAir insists crew not at fault in '99 crash*, NEWSDAY, Jan.
26, 2001, at A07.

24. EgyptAir was Egypt's flagship international carrier: Nadia Abou El-Magd,
Rough Ride for Egypt Air, AL-AHRAM WEEKLY ONLINE, Feb. 2000.

25. "There were 131 Americans on board": Corky Siemaszko, *Jet Dives Into
Sea—217 Dead, Airline Heading for Cairo Crashes After Leaving JFK*, DAILY
NEWS, Nov. 1, 1999, at 2.

26. The Warsaw Convention: *Convention for the Unification of Certain Rules
Relating to International Carriage by Air, Signed at Warsaw on 12 October 1929*,
http://www.dot.gov/ost/ogc/Warsaw1929.pdf.

27. "This is simply an acceptance of legal liability": Sylvia Adcock, *Airline:
We're Liable; But EgyptAir insists crew not at fault in '99 crash*, NEWSDAY, Jan.
26, 2001, at A07.

28. Stepchildren could not recover: *In re Air Crash Near Nantucket Island,
Mass.*, No. 02-CV-00101, 2003 WL 21913235 (E.D.N.Y. 2003).

29. Edith and Larry Kowalsky: *In re Air Crash Near Nantucket Island, Mass.*,
307 F. Supp. 2d 465 (E.D.N.Y. 2004).

30. Sami Makary: *In re Air Crash Near Nantucket Island, Mass.*, 462 F. Supp.
2d 360 (E.D.N.Y. 2006).

31. The "judge recognized a tradition in Egyptian heritage": Tom Perrotta,
Relatives of Air Crash Victim Win Nonpecuniary Damages, NEW YORK LAW JOUR-
NAL, Dec. 8, 2006, at 23.

32. Guidance from the General Counsel of the Administrative Office of the
United States Courts: Letter from William R. Burchill, Jr., Associate Director

and General Counsel, Administrative Office of the U.S. Courts, to Honorable Frederic Block (Oct. 2, 2006) (on file with author).

33. Yassin El-Ayouty: SUNSGLOW: Global Training in the Rule of Law, http://www.sunsglow.com/members-yelayouty.shtml (last visited December 19, 2011).

34. Article for the NYU *Review of Law & Social Change*: Frederic Block, *Civil Liberties During National Emergencies: The Interactions Between the Three Branches of Government in Coping with Past and Current Threats to the Nation's Security*, 29 N.Y.U. Rev. L. & Soc. Change 459 (2005).

EPILOGUE

1. "It was a lot better than Judge Blockhead": Amir Efrati, *A Look at the Judge in Bear Case: He's Fair, Funny and Frank*, Wall Street Journal, July 3, 2008, at C1.

2. Environmental case: *Aiello v. Town of Brookhaven*, 136 F. Supp. 2d 81 (E.D.N.Y. 2001).

Acknowledgments

This book never would have happened if not for a special set of circumstances. I thought of writing a book like this a few years ago and pitched the idea to the conventional trade book publishing world. No one bit. That world was then reeling from the onset of the economic downturn—which hit the traditional book publishers particularly hard. They were not taking any risks by publishing unknown and unpublished authors, and they did not think that a law-related book by a judge would make it unless it was a memoir by a newly minted Supreme Court Justice like Sonia Sotomayor. Hopefully, they were wrong.

I had pretty much given up on the idea when, last year, Norman Reimer asked me whether he could talk to Thomson-Reuters (TR) about it. Norman had been president of the New York County Lawyers' Association and was now the executive director of the National Association of Criminal Defense Lawyers (NACDL)—the country's preeminent, and highly regarded, criminal bar association. I had spoken at a number of its conferences and educational seminars and was always impressed with the professional quality of its programs. Norman told me that he had been speaking to the folks at TR about entering into a copublishing arrangement with it so that lawyers would be encouraged to write a wide range of worthwhile books about the law that would get published.

Eventually a deal was struck, and Norman asked me whether I would be willing to be the first batter up. I was reluctant at first because TR's publishing expertise is in the textbook and academic world, and I was planning to write a book that would be of value and appeal to the general public in addition to the legal community.

I had doubts that TR was geared to commercially market it, and I did not want to embark on a fool's errand. I still have some doubts, but after many discussions with a supportive and wonderful group of TR personnel, I decided to give it a go and hope for the best. I was satisfied that TR respected and liked what I was doing and would try its best to make the book a professional and commercial success. That Norm Reimer, his talented staff including Jim Bergmann, Ivan Dominguez and Jack King, and NACDL's dedicated leadership were solidly behind the book and wanted it to succeed as its first joint venture with TR gave me added incentive to do it.

Norman was supportive in so many ways. He would read the manuscript as it was unfolding and offered essential feedback. There were others who also took their valuable time to carefully read and critique it—and who picked up on a number of mistakes that I had made. I now have the opportunity to thank them in print: my colleagues Brian Cogan and Tucker Melancon, and my lawyer friends Gerald Shargel, Nick Robfogel, Marshall Cohen, Frank Velie, Sol Wachtler, John Horan and Alan Smith.

I also appreciate the encouragement of my artist friend Bernard Aptekar, whose unique and compelling body of work has yet to be discovered by the mainstream art world.

My staff was wonderful. Without compromising their official responsibilities, they were a constant source of encouragement and constructive feedback and helped me enormously with the research. Jennifer Dixon rowed the main oar, but other law clerks, Mollie Kornreich, Ty Cone and Alex Zolan, pitched right in, as did my court clerk, Michael Innelli.

During the summer of 2011, I had three volunteer law student researchers who were just outstanding: Carey Alexander, Elyse Schindel, and Rebecca Hutcheon. Before the summer of 2011, there were also several other law students who periodically chipped in: Josh Gajer, Ari Friedman, Tyler McGuire, Mark Son, and Elan Mendel.

I wanted to get feedback from someone who was not in my inner circle, so I let Carlos—my wonderful doorman—read parts of the book after I had given him Justice Sotomayor's autographed picture. His layperson insights were very helpful. And Betsy, Tina and Debbie were always there for me; there was hardly a day that passed when they didn't ask how the book was going and tell me how much they loved me.

I want to thank Doug Palmer for helping with the pictures and the cover, and Harvey Aurbach for giving me the opportunity to write chunks of the book during the summer of 2011 at his beautiful home on the beach in Bridgehampton.

I also want to thank my editor, Darcie Bahr, for believing in the book and encouraging me to make it as good as I could. It was a joy to work with her. I also appreciate the support of Darcie's Thomson Reuters colleagues, including Jessica Brennan, TR's terrific PR gal. Finally, special thanks to Judge Jack Weinstein for writing the Preface and to my entire EDNY judicial family for the warmth and comradery they have extended to me since I took that oath of office 17 years ago.

Index of Names

Owen, Frank	314, 420
Pastore, Alan	180–181, 185
Patterson, Basil	137
Pearl, Daniel	361
Penn, William	295
Perdue, Molly	327–330, 421
Philips, Lee	16
Piecyk, Ronald	267, 417
Pike, Otis	42
Pokorny, Carolyn	235–236
Polen, Ray	2
Porteous, Thomas	192
Poulos, Nick	32
Pound, Roscoe	296, 419
Pratt, George	162
Prestwood, Hugh	134
Priftakis, Betsy	187, 248, 278–279, 399–400, 404, 430
Priftakis, Debbie	248, 399–400, 404, 430
Priftakis, Tina	248, 399–400, 404, 430
Prosser, William	205, 413
Pumilia, Caroline	124
Quijano, Peter	351–352
Raggi, Reena	153
Reagan, Ronald	118
Reiner, Mark	327–330
Reno, Janet	379
Resnick, Lauren	348–349
Ribando, Salvatore	44–45
Richman, Harry	9, 207
Riggs, Robert "Freeze"	309–310, 420
Ritch, Wells	38–39, 45
Robfogel, Nick	136, 430
Rosen, Jeffrey	100–101, 410
Rosenbaum, Fay	343, 423
Rosenbaum, Norman	353, 423